INSIDE CP/M

A Guide for Users and Programmers

with CP/M-86 and MP/M 2

David E. Cortesi

INSIDE CP/M

A Guide for Users and Programmers with CP/M-86 and MP/M2

HOLT, RINEHART AND WINSTON
New York Chicago San Francisco Philadelphia Montreal
Toronto London Sydney Tokyo Mexico City Rio de Janeiro Madrid

To Marian

These terms are trademarks of Digital Research, Incorporated: CP/M, CP/M-80, CP/M-86, MP/M, MAC, and RMAC.

The term Z80 is a trademark of the Zilog Corporation.

Address correspondence to:
383 Madison Avenue, New York, NY 10017

Library of Congress Cataloging in Publication Data

Cortesi, David E.
Inside CP/M: a guide for users and programmers with CP/M-86 and MP/M-2.

Includes index.
1. CP/M (Computer program) I. Title.
QA76.6.C665 001.64 82-2953
ISBN 0-03-059558-4 AACR2

Printed in the United States of America
Published simultaneously in Canada
2 3 4 144 9 8 7 6 5 4 3 2 1

CBS COLLEGE PUBLISHING
Holt, Rinehart and Winston
The Dryden Press
Saunders College Publishing

Preface

This book is both a guide and a reference manual for CP/M, an operating system for small computers. The book has two sections. The Tutorial presents the basics of the management, use, and programming of a small computer and CP/M. In the Reference, CP/M information is organized for quick access by programmers and users.

The Reference Section

The Reference section contains the information that CP/M users and programmers need every day. The commands are displayed in alphabetical order, each with its syntax, its operation, and suggestions for its best use. The BDOS service requests and BIOS entries are presented in numerical order, each with a concise explanation of its function and suggestions for its use. The operation and syntax rules for the two CP/M assemblers are shown, and all of the assembler directives are laid out in alphabetical order with descriptions and examples. A number of summaries and tables are included.

The Reference section is large, but a lot of thought has gone into its organization. The reader should find that, with only a little practice, the answer to any question about the day-to-day use of CP/M can be found in a few seconds.

The Tutorial Section

Choosing an Audience. In the Tutorial I've attempted to teach the use and programming of CP/M. Before I could do so I had to imagine what my readers would be like and what they would want to know. I made the comfortable assumption that the readers would be adults who are already committed to using a computer and motivated to learn about CP/M. Under that assumption I could dispense with gee-whiz rhapsodies on the computer age and could be free to treat the problems of computer use equally with the advantages.

I could safely make no other assumptions. The success of CP/M and the strong public interest in small computers ensure that among the readers there will be people having every degree of computer experience, from complete novices to experienced programmers. I had to design the Tutorial so that it would say something useful to most readers, and I had to resign myself to the fact that no one reader would be interested in all of it.

Chapters 1-4: Addressing the Novices. That a reader is a novice to computers does not imply that he or she is a novice in all things. On the contrary, I picture my novices as bright, agressive business and professional people, uncomfortable at being cast in the role of greenhorn and eager to get on top of this new subject. Chapters 1 through 4 are addressed to these readers. There I introduce terms and buzzwords and describe the parts of a computer system. My aim is to arm the novice to deal with salespeople, consultants, and other jargonauts, and to prepare him or her to make rational purchasing decisions.

Chapters 5-8: Addressing the Users. Chapters 5 through 8 introduce the CP/M commands that nonprogrammers need. Here I assume that the reader is interested in putting the system to use and wants no more explanation of how it works than is absolutely necessary to make sense of its responses. I present the commands as a series of exercises that the reader is expected to carry out at the keyboard, with a running discussion of what is being done and when it is useful.

Chapters 9-12: Addressing New Programmers. The day is long past when the owner of a small computer was of necessity a programmer as well. Thus I expect that when the subject turns to programming, a good part of the audience will head for the door. Those who stay will have to learn the fundamentals of programming from other books. However, Chapters 9 through 12 cover the things that a new programmer needs to know about CP/M, things that aren't likely to appear in books devoted to BASIC, Pascal, or assembly language.

Chapters 13-15: For Programmers. In Chapter 13 the Tutorial finally reaches the point from which the official CP/M documentation departs: programming I/O operations in assembly language. Those who want to write systems programs will find in Chapters 14 and 15 discussions of the directory, space management, and system generation.

Scope of the Book

CP/M is available in several versions, and in variant forms for different hardware. Fortunately, the differences between one CP/M variant and another are very small, so most of this book applies correctly to most systems. However, the book was developed on, and for, CP/M 2.2. The reader should know which versions are covered and to what degree.

CP/M 1.4. I omitted specific coverage of CP/M prior to release 2. Its inclusion would have muddled the Tutorial with many exceptions and special cases. Although CP/M 1.4 can still be ordered, most systems are two years old at this writing; presumably its users have developed their own information sources by now.

CP/M-86. The BDOS and BIOS entries unique to CP/M-86 are included in the Reference. Digital Research's wise decision to make CP/M-86 compatible with CP/M-80 ensures that the first eight Tutorial chapters, and most of Chapters 13 and 14, apply correctly to it. It wasn't possible to include any programming examples for CP/M-86.

MP/M. Several subjects had to be omitted, or an already bulky book would have been completely out of hand. MP/M is included only as notes at the points where a CP/M operation works differently, or is not supported, in MP/M. Tutorial Chapters 1 to 13 apply to MP/M, but there is more to that system than could be said here. The unique MP/M commands and the MP/M XDOS services could not be included.

MP/M 2. The latest version of MP/M includes a number of new services for the programmer. All of these new file-system features have been included in the Reference section, so that a CP/M programmer can prepare compatible programs. When the long-awaited CP/M 3 appears, it will probably support these services as well.

VARIANT HARDWARE. CP/M has been adapted to computers it wasn't originally meant for, notably the TRS-80 line and the Apple. The examples in this book were developed on an S-100 bus system with 64 KB of storage. All the command examples should work as shown on any hardware variant. The example programs may need to be assembled at a different origin. This can be accomplished with a one-line change in the CPMEQU.LIB introduced in Chapter 12.

Acknowledgments

I am indebted to a number of people for their help on the book. The publisher's reviewers made several productive suggestions. Scott Gamble, Paul Brest, and Steve Fields submitted graciously to my fumbling attempts to interview them. I am especially grateful to Ben Mason of California Computer Systems for a thorough technical review. His input made Chapters 14 and 15 much better and deeper. My wife assisted the book in ways too numerous to mention.

My own CP/M system, which acted both as word processor and as guinea pig for my experiments, performed flawlessly through ten months of heavy use. For that I feel some gratitude toward the manufacturers of its components: CCS, Diablo, Godbout, Heath and Morrow.

David E. Cortesi

Contents

Part One

A Tutorial for Users and Programmers

Chapter 1

Computer Fundamentals

This chapter is intended for people who are about to work closely with a computer for the first time. You might own a small business and be shopping for a solution to your bookkeeping problems. You might be a writer exploring the much-touted advantages of the computer as a word processor. You might be an employee whose boss has given you the dubious distinction of becoming a computer operator for the machine she is about to purchase.

Are you anxious about it? New things make everyone anxious. Anxiety about meeting a computer will stem from two things: you don't know what the machine may demand from you. And worse, you don't know what questions to ask or what words to use in asking them. People who know computers use unfamiliar terms and seem to become tongue-tied when you ask for explanations. They prefer to clatter out a cryptic line on a keyboard, point to the screen, and say, "There, see?"—as if they'd clarified something.

The aim of this chapter is to give you a set of concepts that are common to all small computers and the words that are used to name those concepts. Our space is too limited for a complete course in computers, but we'll perform the introductions. There are suggestions for further reading at the end of the chapter, there is the remainder of this book, and there are people to whom you can talk. Once you've added to your vocabulary the terms we'll define here, you'll be able to read, and to ask, and to understand the answers.

THE COMPUTER: AN ORGANIZER

Our first definition is necessarily that of the word *computer*. The word is misleading if you haven't been associated with these machines, for it focuses your attention on computation, and that is not the main use of a computer. The French word is a better description of the functions of the machine. It is *ordinateur*, meaning *that which puts things in order*, a sequencer, arranger, or categorizer. Most computers spend most of their time sifting, sorting, selecting, and finally displaying things. A computer is a machine that arranges things according to some pattern, then either displays the arrangement or saves it.

THE FIRST LEVEL: HARDWARE

At its most fundamental level a computer arranges patterns of electric pulses. The form of this arranging is defined by the machine's wiring, which these days is usually embodied in tiny lines etched on a small piece of silicon: the famous *chip*.

The Chip

The fact that the integrated circuits, or chips, that make up a modern computer are so very tiny should not be important to you. After all, why should you care what size a computer is, so long as it does the job? It is marvellous that such complex patterns can be written so small, but the practical benefit of this achievement is not in the size of the machine but in its price. Because they are so small, and because they are made by automatic equipment, modern computers have become inexpensive. Because computers cost so little, people who would have passed their lives without seeing a computer now have one as a component of a microwave oven or as a toy for their children. When surrounded by more expensive auxiliary devices, the computer becomes an office assistant or an aide to the professional person.

Input and Output

The flake of silicon is helpless and useless without some connection to the rest of the world. Before a computer can move from being an arranger of pulses on a chip to being an assistant (or an oven controller), it must be linked to its environment.

In the jargon of the trade, the links are called *input-output devices*. This is usually abbreviated to *I/O devices*.

Almost any physical effect can be encoded as an electric signal. Think of a tape recorder, which converts sound waves to electrical patterns and records those patterns in the coating of the tape. A computer manipulates patterns of electric pulses. If some physical effect can be coded as pulses of a compatible sort, then the computer can receive and manipulate them. These operations are always spoken of from the viewpoint of the computer, and so the receipt of a signal from outside the chip is called an *input* (of data to the machine).

A tape recorder can go both ways. It can play its tape back, thus converting the stored patterns to sound again. And if there is some device attached to the computer that will convert its patterns into a physical effect, the computer can make something happen outside itself. This act is called an *output* (of data from the computer).

Since almost anything can be coded electrically, and almost anything can be arranged for electrical control, with the right set of I/O devices a computer can be inserted into almost any process. One could imagine a Rube Goldberg contraption of motors and levers that would allow a computer to paddle a canoe. It might not be useful, and it would be too expensive as a joke, but it could be done.

The computers that use CP/M, the subject of this book, never do anything as dramatic as paddling a canoe or as domestic as timing a roast. They are equipped with I/O devices whose purpose is the storage or display of letters and numbers. These computers spend their time receiving input that represents letters and numbers and sending output that also represents letters and numbers, differently arranged.

Instructions

The ways in which a computer can arrange pulses are strictly limited by the circuits engraved on its chip, and they are few and simple. No computer can do very much, but what it does, it does very quickly. Some of the sequences defined for a computer are of this form: Take a train of pulses from here on the chip, combine them with pulses from there, and put the result over there. By specifying the particular ways in which the pulses are combined, the computer's designer can create sequences that perform simple arithmetic. Other sequences just copy data from place to place on the chip, still others compare pulses and produce a signal that says, in effect, "This pattern of pulses, considered as a number, is greater or less than that one."

Each simple operation designed into the computer is called an *instruction*; all together they constitute an *instruction set*. Each instruction can be called into play by an *operation code*, which is simply a number. Thirteen, when received by the computer, might cause it to multiply two numbers, whereas 36 might mean "receive input from that device." A machine's instruction set is sometimes called its *machine language*. This is the first level at which we can view the computer: as a chip, pulses, and instructions.

THE SECOND LEVEL: A PROGRAM

The second-level view of the computer becomes apparent when we provide it with a list of operation codes and watch it run through the list, doing one after another very rapidly. The usefulness of such a list arises from the fact that the computer can jump around in the list on the basis of the outcome of some instruction. The list can say, in effect, "If the sum of two numbers is zero, do these instructions; if not, do those." Or it can say, "Repeat this series of instructions until a certain condition is true." Such a list is called a *program*. The power of the computer, and all its effects on society, come about because it can carry out a program, and because the program can *branch* (make a choice) and *loop* (repeat some number of times). Without a program the machine has no meaning except at the first level and is useless. With a program it can be made to drive its I/O devices in any way the author of the program chooses. Given a different program it can do something else.

Both the power and the weakness of the machine are revealed at this second level—power, in its ability to perform any list of instructions very rapidly, and weakness, because it is quite impossible for the machine to do anything else than its current program, and because the program can only be composed of the very primitive instructions engraved into the machine by its designer. Balky children play the game of doing exactly what they are told to do and no more; the game is meant to be infuriating and is quite successful. A computer is always playing that game. It does precisely what you told it (provided you said it in the machine's tiny, rigid vocabulary). If that is what you meant, fine; if not, too bad. There are no circuits in the machine for judgment or for common sense. It is not possible to engrave values or a sense of ethics on a silicon chip.

Whatever there is of judgment or of ethics in a computer system has been coded there by the person who wrote the program. The machine sees nothing ridiculous in the quantity $0.00. If the author of the program failed to include a test for zero, the machine will rapidly and precisely print a bill for that amount. Most of the computer errors headlined by the media arise from just such oversights. Many a so-called computer crime has been perpetrated by someone who discovered and exploited a programmer's mistake. As computers become more central to the world's systems, the burden of responsibility on the world's programmers becomes heavier.

HARDWARE VERSUS SOFTWARE

Now we have enough background to define two very important terms: *hardware* and *software*. A computer system is composed of the computer chip itself and its many supporting chips, and some mechanical and electrical units that provide its input and output. All these units are known collectively as the *hardware*. The whole purpose of the hardware, its only reason for existence, is to make it possible for you to run programs. The programs used with a computer are called, collectively, the *software*.

It is very important that you grasp the distinction between hardware and software. Here is a metaphor that may help: A program is to the computer as a record is to a phonograph. Software is to a computer system as your record collection is to your hi-fi system. A phonograph is useless without a record to play. Just so, a computer has no value without a program to run.

A phonograph record is a copy of some original performance. Once the master disk is cut, the record company can make copies easily, and anyone who wants to hear that performance can do so at low cost—provided they have the right kind of phonograph on which to play it. A program is a record of one programmer's solution to some problem. Once written, it can be copied and published for the use of anyone who has the right kind of computer on which to run it. There are many companies that publish software, and as the owner of a computer system, you will become as careful in your purchase of programs as the most discriminating audiophile is in searching out and choosing records.

Programs, as we'll see, are written in much the same way that music is written by a composer. In this sense a program resembles a musical score or the script of a play. A program is a copy of the instructions for a performance, rather than a reproduction of the performance itself. We could say that a program is to a computer as a script is to the cast of a play, or as a score is to the orchestra that will perform it. One flaw in that metaphor is that, unlike an actor or a musician, a computer is utterly incapable of improvising. It always follows its script in an exact, mechanical way.

THE THIRD LEVEL: AN OPERATING SYSTEM

On the first level at which we can view the computer we see it as an arranger of electric signals. At the second level we see it performing a program composed of elementary steps. This book is concerned mostly with third-level and fourth-level views of the computer. Creating a program at the second level is a tedious and error-prone business. Exactly the right digits, hundreds of them, have to be entered into the machine. The first programs written for a new type of machine have to be made this way. They are the programs that comprise the third level: an *operating system*.

An operating system is a set of programs that apply the power of the computer to the task of managing the computer. An operating system will contain several kinds of programs. Some of the programs are concerned with managing the operations of the computer's I/O devices. Others use these to keep track of named collections of information, called *files*. Still others are concerned with the job of loading yet other programs on command from a user.

Once we reach this third level, the machine itself becomes unimportant to us except as it runs the operating system programs. Our attention shifts to the programs. They define the relationship between the machine and its users; they give the machine its personality. From this level on, we don't care what kind of hardware we use, for all we see is the software (the whole collection of programs available). To most users a computer is nothing but a means of running programs. Except for its price and its reliability the hardware is irrelevant.

File System and File Storage

Of all the software available the operating system is the most important. And of its parts the most important are those programs that support the *file system*, a means to let the user create a collection of data, give it a name, and store it on a *diskette* or a *tape* for later use. Such a named collection of data is called a *file*. All permanently stored data are kept in files. The file system includes programs that allow you to create files, erase them, and rename them. Utility programs allow you to copy files from device to device (for example, from diskette to a printer for examination). Diskettes and tapes are the computer's permanent storage. Files saved on a diskette are permanent in the way a tape recording is permanent: they remain until they are erased or written over.

Working Storage

Working storage differs from file storage in several ways. Working storage is a rapid-access scratch pad from which the machine reads the operation code numbers of a program, and in which the machine will save the working values needed by the program as it runs. It is closely coupled to the computer chip and can be accessed by it in less than a microsecond. It is made up of integrated circuits, and its contents vanish the instant that power is turned off. All the instructions and data that stream through the computer chip come from working storage. It is a *buffer* or temporary holding location between the computer and file storage.

There are several conventional terms for working storage. The word "memory" is often used. Engineers speak of RAM, short for Random Access Memory. Neither is a good term, and we won't use them in this book. What you and I know as memory bears absolutely no resemblance to any kind of computer storage; it is dangerous to speak of computers in human terms, for then we come to expect too much of them. However, you're likely to meet the terms "memory" and "RAM" elsewhere.

Programs are stored in files, and *loaded* (that is, copied) into working storage before they can be *executed*, or *run*. Both terms mean applying the computer to the list of instructions. One small part of the operating system is resident in working storage; it is loaded there when the machine is started up and remains until it is shut down. This *Monitor* contains the program that will load another program from a file at the user's request, and then *call* the loaded program (turn the computer's attention to that program's instructions).

Programs and Programming

The word "program" appears often in the foregoing paragraphs. Let's draw a breath and think about what a program is and how it is created. A dictionary definition of the word is "an outline of work to be done; a prearranged plan of procedure." Earlier we said that a list of operation codes is a program. That was a "plan of procedure" expressed in *machine language*, so called because the operation codes defined for the machine are its vocabulary, in a sense. When the list has been loaded into working storage the machine can cycle through it, and thus the plan will be carried out.

Programs are composed by people, using the tools provided by the operating system. The act of composing a plan for machine execution is called *programming*, and the person who does it is acting as a *programmer*. The plan expresses the steps of the solution to a problem. Such a step-by-step solution is called an *algorithm*; it is the business of a programmer to design algorithms and express them in programs.

Programming Languages

Thanks to the operating system, the programmer need not write the operation codes but can express the problem in a *programming language*. There are many of these. A programming language really is a language, with parts of speech, a vocabulary, and rules of grammar. Each of these elements is more restricted than the same element of a natural language such as English. It wouldn't be possible to have a conversation in a programming language because its rules would not be flexible enough or its vocabulary general enough to support ordinary speech. A programming language is an artificial language designed for easy expression of the solutions to some class of problem. Each one represents someone's idea of the best way to state those problems for machine solution. None are completely successful; there are always problems that are awkward to solve in one language but easy to solve in another. Programmers, because of their experiences of ease or difficulty, and because they invest a lot of effort in learning a language, become very partial to their languages. There are fads and fashions in programming languages, and one or another will temporarily become the "in thing" to use.

Interpreters and Compilers

A program is composed in the chosen language and entered into the machine as words, numbers, and punctuation. The text of the program is usually stored in a file. Then an operating system program, a language *translator*, is loaded. This program will read the program's text and translate it into a sequence of machine instructions. These can then be executed by the machine, and execution will result in the actions the programmer intended—provided that the programmer wrote what was meant.

There are two types of language translators: *interpreters* and *compilers*. An interpreter program examines each unit (word, number, phrase) of the program text in turn and carries out the machine instructions it signifies. Both the interpreter and the program text remain in working storage during execution, and so the space available for text and for the program's data is limited. Because the translation is carried out each time the program is run, the overhead of machine instructions needed to translate the program is added to the program's execution time. The advantage of an interpreter is that it allows easy testing and *debugging* (locating and fixing errors). When an error occurs, the interpreter can report on the problem in the terms of the programming language that was used. A correction can be made at once and execution continued.

Some language translators are *compilers*. These are programs that perform the translation to machine language just once. The list of machine instructions that results is stored in a file. This translated version of the program text is called an *object program*; it can be loaded and run exactly like an operating system program. A compiled program usually runs faster than an interpreted program, and has more working storage available to it. However, it takes longer, and requires a better knowledge of the operating system, to test and debug a compiled program.

The Lure of Programming

For those who take to it, programming is one of the most fascinating games ever devised. Easier than chess and more varied than bridge, programming is both an intellectual challenge and an act of personal domination over the machine. As programmers gain experience, they try to get the right output in the most efficient way, while expressing the algorithm in the most elegant, concise terms. Because of this challenge, recreational programming can be more absorbing than reading or games. However, programmers, like bureaucrats, are always subject to the temptation to confuse means with ends. In their fascination with the intricate puzzle of machine and language, they are apt to forget the people who will actually use the program.

Program Efficiency

Programmers are often concerned with making a program run as fast as possible. A program's speed depends mostly on the algorithm—there are always faster and slower solutions—and on the speed of the I/O devices that the program uses.

Programs in the operating system must run as quickly as possible in order to reduce the overhead cost of running them. Such programs are usually written in machine instructions rather than in one of the easier programming languages. A language translator called an *assembler* is used for this. An assembler gives names to the operation codes and to locations in working storage. This allows the program to be composed in symbols people can read, thus relieving the programmer of much of the tedium of using the machine at its second level. Writing machine language programs using an assembler is called *assembly language* programming. The terms *machine language* and *assembly language* are often used interchangeably, although the second refers to a symbolic encoding of the numeric codes of the first.

THE FOURTH LEVEL: APPLICATIONS

The collection of operating-system software—file system, language translators, and various utility programs—makes it possible for programmers to build *applications*. An application is any program whose output is dedicated to use by people, rather than to managing the affairs of the computer system. The term covers just about anything you can do with a machine other than programming it: games, simulations, teaching programs, text formatting programs, and commercial accounting all are applications. The programs may be purchased, or written under contract by a professional programmer, or you may write them yourself. Except when it is being used for programming, the machine will spend most of its time running applications.

Applications are the fourth level at which we can view a computer system. The microscopic wonders of the circuits, the ingenious printers and disk drives, the elegant complexity of the operating system—all exist so that application programs can be written and run. Only the applications deliver useful work to aid people in their jobs, and so only the applications can justify the cost of the computer.

FURTHER READING

This has been a very brief survey of the ideas surrounding a computer. We've defined a number of terms in a casual way; these terms and others are listed in the glossary at the end of the Tutorial section.

There is much more to be known about computers than could be told here. Many topics that have been hinted at are outside the scope of this book. Computer architecture (the design of the instruction set and I/O devices) is one field of study; the theory and practice of programming is another. There are books about the correct relation between a program and its user (the so-called man-machine interface), about the proper design of accounting software, and about how to manage the computer as part of a business. Not nearly enough work has been done on the effects that computers are having on our lives and society, but some things are known and have been published.

To use computers you must be willing to read. Any system you buy will be accompanied by pounds of printed matter. Moreover, there has recently been an explosion of books and magazines about computers. Even the smallest bookstores have a dozen or more titles in stock; technical bookstores often have hundreds. Here are a few sources that the author has found useful. Any of them will lead you to others. Good luck!

Computer Magazines

The following magazines try to serve the needs of novices as well as those of experienced computists. They are especially useful because they carry advertisements for new software and hardware. It is difficult to keep up with that fast-changing market in any other way.

Creative Computing (P.O. Box 789-M, Morristown, NJ 07960) concentrates on games and educational computing, with occasional tutorials.

Desktop Computing (80 Pine Street, Peterborough, NH 03458) is directed to professionals and owners of small businesses; it claims to have eliminated all jargon.

Interface Age (16704 Marquardt Avenue, Cerritos, CA 90701) attempts to balance coverage of home and business uses of small computers. It often carries product surveys and reviews of software.

Microsystems (P.O. Box 789-M, Morristown, NJ 07960) is a bi-monthly magazine aimed at programmers and experimenters. It has a strong emphasis on using and programming CP/M systems.

Popular Computing (70 Main Street, Peterborough, NH 03458) aims "to demythologize small computers in a direct and entertaining manner."

Computers in Society

Osborne, Adam. *Running Wild—The Next Industrial Revolution*. Osborne/McGraw-Hill, 1980. An enthusiastic view of the possibilities of small machines.

Covvey, H. Dominic, and Neil McAlister. *Computer Conciousness: Surviving the Automated 80s*. Addison-Wesley, 1980. A more sober analysis that takes care to point out the problems and dangers.

Weizenbaum, Joseph. *Computer Power and Human Reason*. W. H. Freeman, 1976. A thoughtful, philosophical study of what computers can be expected to do and what we should let them do.

Managing Computers

Schneider, Ben Ross. *Travels in Computerland*. Addison-Wesley, 1974. An entertaining account of how a professor innocently blundered into the cutting edge of technology.

Brooks, Frederick P. *The Mythical Man-Month*. Addison-Wesley, 1978. A computer professional's reflections on his career in which he points out the ways in which people and their systems can go wrong.

Bardach, E. *The Implementation Game: What Happens After a Bill Becomes Law*. MIT Press, 1977. Not a computer book, but a practical analysis of the ways that organizations oppose or adapt to change. Essential for anyone wanting to introduce a computer into an existing power structure.

Programming

Amsbury, Wayne. *Structured BASIC and Beyond*. Computer Science Press, 1980. A clear, well-written, methodical introduction to the fundamentals of programming. Uses the BASIC programming language, available on every small computer.

Kernighan, Brian, and P. J. Plauger. *The Elements of Programming Style*. McGraw-Hill, 1978. After you've written a few programs, read this to learn what you've been doing wrong without being aware of it.

Weinberg, Gerald M., *The Psychology of Computer Programming*. Van Nostrand Reinhold, 1971. After you've written a lot of programs, or if you have to manage other programmers, read Weinberg to find out what is going on.

Computer Architecture

The best practical introduction to computer design is to learn the architecture of your own. Get an assembly language manual for your machine and experiment. For the theory behind it try Foster, Caxton C., *Computer Architecture*, Van Nostrand Reinhold, 1970.

Chapter 2

Hardware for CP/M

In this chapter we look closely at the hardware parts of a CP/M system. One aim of the chapter is to introduce the names of the components and the jargon used to describe them. Anyone who uses a CP/M system needs these terms to understand the conversation of salespeople and programmers.

When buying hardware there are choices to be made that affect the usefulness of the system. A second aim of the chapter is to alert shoppers to the important choices and to give some guidelines for making them.

If you are new to computers, you should not attempt to absorb all this information in one reading. Skim the chapter now; return to it when questions arise.

COMPUTER PACKAGING

All systems that support CP/M have certain hardware parts in common. There will be a terminal (a video screen and keyboard) and one or more disk drives. There will be the electronics, the collection of hundreds of integrated circuits. These can be grouped into a few components by function: the processor, working storage, and interface circuits. The terminal and disk drives will be visible; the electronic parts will be housed in a case of some kind.

There are many ways of organizing these parts into cabinets. Some makers put all the parts into a single box (Figure 2-1). Others put the electronic components in a cabinet with the disk drives leaving the terminal separate (Figures 2-2 and 2-3). Or you can buy a

FIGURE 2-1
An all-in-one computer, in which processor, terminal, and two 5-inch diskette drives are packaged in a single cabinet. This system happens to use "memory-mapped" terminal circuitry. (*PAWEKPIX*)

FIGURE 2-2
A system that places the processor and two 8-inch drives in a single cabinet, leaving the terminal separate, to be connected via an RS-232 interface. This system's electronics are on a single circuit board. (*PAWEKPIX*)

system with each component in a box of its own, as we used to buy high-fidelity components (Figure 2-4). The larger the number of boxes, the greater the number of choices open to the buyer. An all-in-one system commits you to that manufacturer's design for all parts of the system. Buying a system such as the one in Figure 2-4 allows you to select each part individually. There is more to this than flexibility of choice. An all-in-one system is tidy and compact; a multibox machine takes more space and there is a tangle of interconnecting cables behind the boxes. A mix-and-match system is open-ended and flexible, but to build one successfully you must know a great deal about the requirements and design of the components, as some components won't work with others.

ELECTRONIC PARTS

The Processor

THE CPU. The heart of a computer system is a single integrated circuit, the Central Processing Unit or CPU. This is the computer on a chip that journalists marvel at (and it

FIGURE 2-3
This system, like that in Figure 2-2, puts electronics and drives in a single cabinet. In this case the drives are of 5-inch diameter, and the electronics are organized around the S-100 bus. (*PAWEKPIX*)

FIGURE 2-4
A component system. From left to right: two 8-inch drives, terminal, and S-100 processor cabinet. This book was written on the system shown. (*PAWEKPIX*)

is marvellous), whose instruction set programmers love or hate, and whose abilities and low price have founded an industry. It is worthless alone. The CPU must be surrounded by a number of support circuits that feed it timing signals and connect it to the rest of the machine. This collection of circuits we call the *processor*.

The Intel 8080 CPU is the machine for which CP/M was written and most versions of CP/M are written in the 8080's assembly language. The Zilog Z80 CPU came a little later. Its instruction set contains all of the instructions of the 8080 and adds a few dozen of its own. Although written in 8080 assembly language, the programs composing CP/M will run correctly on a Z80 machine. CP/M makes no use of the Z80's extra instructions but application programs are free to do so; if they do, they can't be run on an 8080. The Intel 8085 is a later, faster circuit that provides an instruction set almost identical to that of the 8080; it too runs the 8080 form of CP/M.

In the fall of 1980 Digital Research announced CP/M rewritten for the Intel 8086, a new circuit with a different instruction set. CP/M-86, as this rewritten system is called, has the same commands and uses the same types of file storage as the original CP/M. Systems containing the 8086 are as yet rare, as are application programs that will run on them. It seems likely that within a year or two the 8086 will be a very common CPU for CP/M systems.

Working Storage. The processor requires a program, and a program requires *variables,* repositories for the values on which it operates. Both the program and its variables reside in working storage, a storage medium that the processor can *access* (read from or write to) in less than a microsecond (one millionth of a second). Like the processor, working storage is built from an array of integrated circuits.

Working storage, like all storage in the system, is measured in *bytes*, a unit of storage that can hold a single character or a part of a decimal number. In scientific notation the prefix *kilo* signifies a multiplier of 1000. Computer people, always more comfortable with powers of two than with powers of ten, use the same prefix to signify a multiplier of 1024 (two to the tenth). When measuring working storage, it is convenient to talk of *kilobytes*, or units of 1024 bytes. The maximum amount of working storage that can be handled by an 8080, Z80, or 8085 machine is 64 kilobytes (written 64 KB), and this is the usual size sold with new systems. CP/M-86 can make use of more working storage; 128 KB is a typical quantity. In general you can't have too much working storage.

Interface Circuits. The processor is connected to the I/O devices of the system through *interface* circuits: circuits that coordinate the transfer of data. An interface circuit mediates between the timing and electrical levels required by the device on one side, and the timing and electrical levels required by the processor on the other. The interface circuitry is also built of integrated circuits.

Busses and Boards

The computer will contain a couple of hundred integrated circuits. They must be connected to each other in groups, and the groups must be connected. The connections are made through metallic traces laminated to a fiberglass board: a *circuit board* (or circuit card). The way the electronic parts are packaged into boards affects the price of the system, the way it is maintained, and the degree to which it can be expanded.

Some designers place all the electronic components on a single board. Others place each major component (processor, working storage, etc.) on a board of its own, and then connect the boards by plugging them into a *bus*, a set of parallel conductors.

Single-Board Packaging. The single-board design is the most economical but the least flexible. The contents of the computer are established once and for all by the designer; it would be difficult and costly to add features not allowed for in the layout of the board. If something fails, there is no hope of swapping a major component; the entire board will go in for repairs.

Bus Packaging. The bus design (Figure 2-5) costs more; each component has a board of its own and the bus itself is a fairly complex circuit board. The extra cost pays off in flexibility of design. Any board designed to work with that bus layout can be inserted into the computer and put to use (always assuming the software is there).

The S-100 Bus. The most common bus layout for CP/M systems is called the *S-100 bus*. There is a wide variety of circuit boards designed for it, and most of them will work

FIGURE 2-5
Close-up of a bus-organized processor. The bus itself is visible on the floor of the cabinet at the right. The CPU card is marked; the disk controller card has been pulled out for display. (*PAWEKPIX*)

with each other properly. However, not all of them will work because the S-100 bus was not completely defined in its early days. Certain conductors were left optional, and different designers made conflicting choices as to which signals to put on the unspecified lines. The Institute of Electrical and Electronics Engineers (IEEE) has defined a standard for the S-100 bus (IEEE-696). Any two components that claim compatibility with the standard probably can be plugged into the same bus without problems, but only "probably," because the standard is new and there are many older, marginally conforming products still on the market. Within a year or so problems of bus incompatibility should be uncommon.

THE TERMINAL

Human Factors of the Terminal

The *terminal*, a keyboard with a screen, is the point at which the computer and its user come together. You will spend thousands of hours looking at the screen of your terminal, and type hundreds of thousands of strokes on its keyboard. No part of the system deserves more careful consideration of its comfort and usability.

Terminal Screens. Terminals look much alike from a distance, but close up they reveal an astonishing variety. Their differences are far wider, for instance, than those between one office typewriter and another. Look closely at Figure 2-6, which shows the character sets of four different terminals, in the order in which the characters appear on the keyboards. Halftone reproduction probably doesn't reveal the differences in contrast and sharpness that were apparent on the screens, but notice the shapes and proportions of the letters. Some character sets are definitely more pleasing than others.

Terminal Keyboards. Think carefully about the keyboard layouts represented in Figure 2-6. Compare them with the keyboard of an office typewriter. If you are not an experienced typist, minor details of keyboard arrangement won't trouble you, but a touch typist at a keyboard such as that in Figure 2-6a will be seen to fumble, strike over, and fume. It is strange that a designer would create a keyboard layout without considering the keyboards already in existence, yet it happens.

Comparing Terminals. When shopping for a system, consider the person who will spend the most time at the keyboard. That person should give the terminal a thorough trial. The keyboard should have a good touch, something only a typist can recognize. Many terminals have acoustic feedback (they beep or click when a key is pressed). Is that a friendly noise or an irritating electronic one? Cast a critical eye on the screen. Check the contrast (relative brightness of letters and background), the sharpness (definition of the dots composing the letters), and the linearity (straightness of rows, consistency of character size) over all parts of the screen. Using a computer requires an alert, concentrated mind. Eyestrain and misread messages complicate matters.

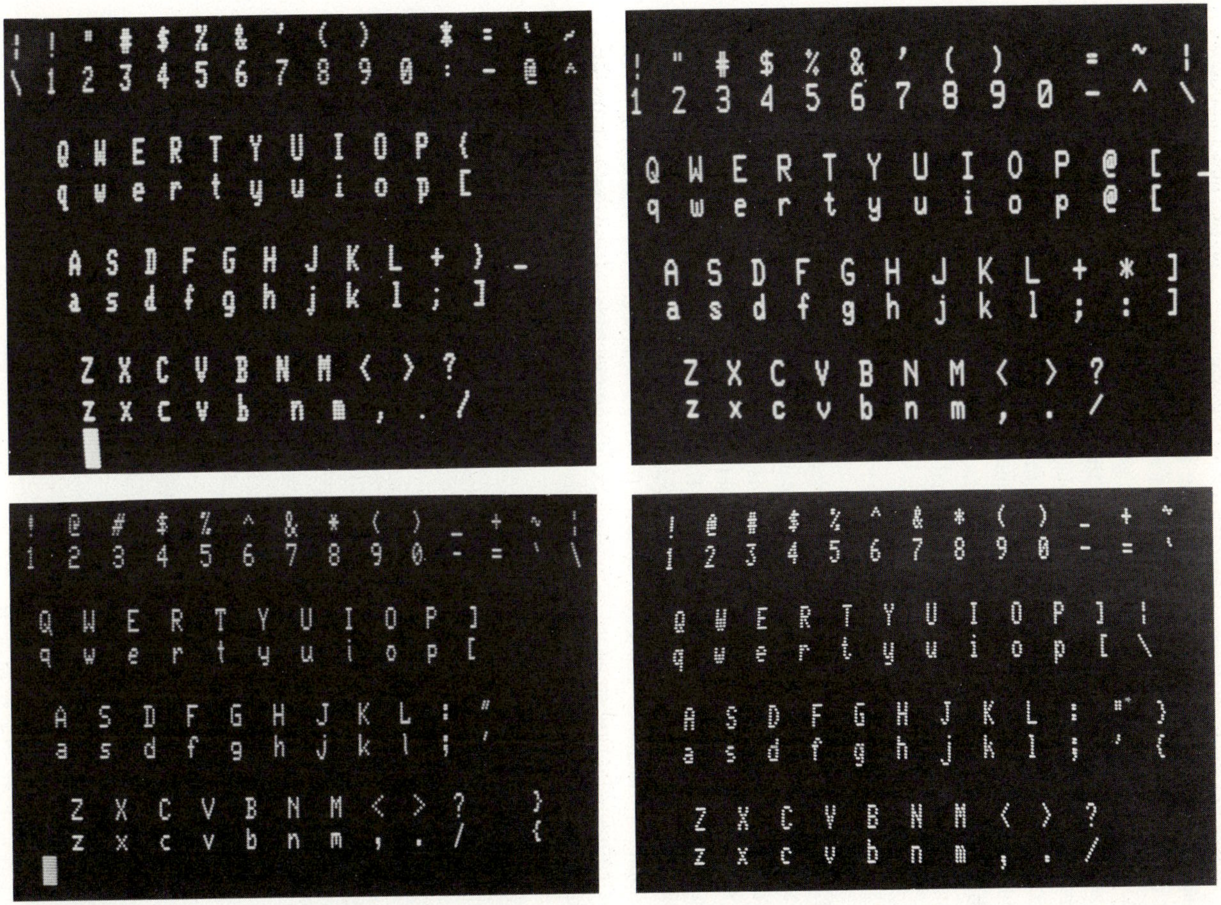

FIGURE 2-6
The character sets of four terminals, ordered as they appear on the keyboards. Note the different arrangements of punctuation, which can upset a touch-typist, and the varying design of the characters.

Hardware Factors of the Terminal

Memory-Mapped Terminals. Terminals can be divided into two categories on the basis of their interface methods. Some terminals are what are called *memory-mapped* terminals; that is, a portion of working storage is shared between the computer and the terminal hardware. What the CPU puts in that area of storage, the terminal displays on its screen. The advantage of this design lies in the great speed with which the display can be updated. The CPU can change the contents of the display storage area in microseconds; only milliseconds will elapse before the display screen reflects the change. Memory-mapped displays give an impression of lively responsiveness. They have the disadvantage that 2 kilobytes (KB) of working storage must be dedicated to the display and are not available to programs. Since the terminal interface hardware must be intimately linked to working storage, a breakdown in the terminal will probably keep the whole system down. There is little chance of plugging in a loaner terminal while repairs are being made.

TTY-Compatible Terminals. The majority of terminals connect to the processor with a standard plug through which pass standard signal lines. These are usually called "TTY-compatible" terminals. The standard is the Electronic Industries Association (EIA) standard RS-232-C, "Interface Between Data Terminal Equipment and Data Communication Equipment Employing Serial Binary Data Interchange." RS-232-C was published in 1969 and has become the nearest thing to a universal interface to be found in the computer world; the 25-pin plug it calls for (Figure 2-7) is seen everywhere. (In 1977 the EIA published a new standard, RS-449, specifying electrical levels better suited to integrated circuits. At this writing RS-449 has had little effect in the marketplace.)

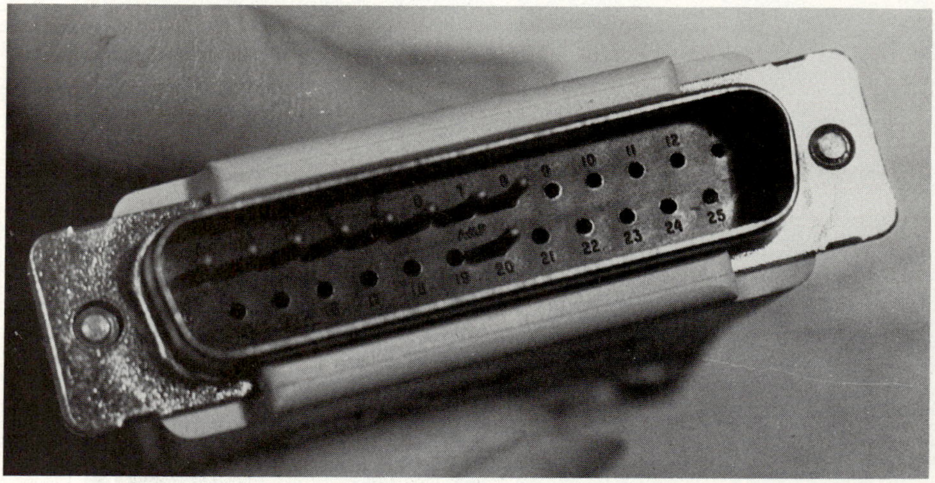

FIGURE 2-7
The business end of a DB-25 plug, the standard connector for the RS-232 interface. It is common for only nine of the pins to be used. (*PAWEKPIX*)

Any terminal equipped with an RS-232 plug can be connected to any computer with an RS-232 socket, but communication isn't guaranteed. The processor (and the software) have to agree with the terminal on several points. The first agreement must be on the signaling speed, or *transmission rate*.

Transmission Rate. As the title of the standard says, the terminal and the computer will exchange serial binary data: they transfer 1 bit at a time. The rate at which bits are sent is the transmission rate; it is given in bits per second (bps). Industry people use the word baud as a synonym for the phrase "bits per second." This is technically incorrect—baud rate and bit rate need not be the same—but has been sanctified by common usage.

Matching Transmission Rate. Clearly, each device must send bits at the rate the other expects them to come. Most terminals are equipped to operate at any of several transmission rates. The standard rates are multiples of 75 bps: 300, 2400, 4800, 9600, and 19,200 bps are the most common. The terminal's rate is usually set from very small switches on an internal circuit board. The I/O interface in most computers will operate at a variety of transmission rates as well. The computer's rate may be set by software or by switches, or even by soldering jumpers on a circuit board. Usually it is best to find out what the processor is set up for and then to set the terminal to agree with it. However the rates are set, the two devices must use the same rate.

Effects of Transmission Rate. The higher the transmission rate is set, the better. The data being exchanged between processor and terminal are sent 1 bit at a time, but the bits represent bytes (each byte containing 8 bits and standing for one character). Each byte sent is framed by start and stop bits. There will always be 1 start bit, but there may be 1, 1½, or 2 stop bits. This is a matter that the two devices must be made to agree on, again by setting switches. One stop bit is normal at rates above 300 bps; that plus a start bit makes a total of 10 bits that must be sent for each character displayed at the terminal. The maximum rate of character transmission is then the bit transmission rate divided by 10. Since the screen contains 1920 characters (24 lines of 80 characters), a transmission rate of 9600 bps will allow the processor to rewrite the entire screen in about 2 seconds. Transmission at 19,200 bps reduces this to 1 second. That is a significant improvement when you are using a full-screen editor or playing a simulation game.

Matching Parity. Terminal and processor must, finally, agree on whether they will use parity-check bits and if so, whether it is to be an odd- or an even-parity check. This again is a matter of finding out what the processor expects and setting switches at the terminal to suit.

Special Features. Provided that its switches have been set correctly, any terminal with an RS-232 plug should work with any processor that has an RS-232 socket, at least for the transmission of normal characters, and that is all that CP/M needs. But modern terminals provide, and some software uses, functions beyond the simple display of letters and numbers. Modern terminals will accept *control sequences*, special character sequences that cause them to clear the screen, move the cursor to a certain location, erase the line the cursor is on, and so forth. Full-screen editors such as the popular *Word Star* and *Magic Wand* programs require these features, and you might want to use them in your own programs.

CONTROL SEQUENCES. Unfortunately, different makes of terminals provide different sets of functions. Where their functions are the same, the control sequences that invoke them may be different. There is no recognized standard for control sequences (the American National Standards Institute has published a suggested standard but it has had little effect, probably because its three- to five-character sequences offend designers whose practice is to use two-character sequences). Therefore, if you write a program that relies on your terminal's features, it will be a *device-dependent* program: one that probably won't work with any other make of terminal. This is no reason not to write such a program, but the program should allow for easy change to suit other devices.

The authors who publish fee software solve the problem with elaborate customizing schemes that tailor their programs to your terminal type. Once tailored by the distributor, the program is just as device dependent as one of your own. Thus if you change terminals permanently or temporarily, some of your most used (and most expensive) software will need modification.

DISK STORAGE

Diskette Storage

The diskette (Figure 2-8) is CP/M's main form of file storage. Unless you are lucky enough to have a hard disk (described in the next section) you will keep all of your software and data as files on diskettes. The reliability, speed, and capacity of your diskettes and their drives will have a lot to do with how reliable, fast, and capacious your system seems.

THE DISKETTE. Figure 2-9 reveals how a diskette is packaged. The plastic jacket is lined with a soft padding. The recording medium is a disk of a tough, flexible plastic, coated with a layer of ferromagnetic material (that is, a highly refined rust); its surface is polished smooth. The thickness of the coating, and the required smoothness of the surface, are measured in units of millionths of an inch.

THE DISKETTE JACKET. The plastic disk is enclosed in a simple jacket lined with soft material. The padding helps keep the disk clean by wiping it as it turns. There are openings in the cover to allow the disk drive to grip the hub of the disk and slide its read-write head over the surface.

At the edge of the diskette jacket is a small notch. This is a write-protect notch, used to prevent the diskette from being written on. Eight-inch diskettes are protected against alteration by exposing the notch. Writing is possible only when the notch is absent or

FIGURE 2-8
The two diskette sizes. Note the write-protect notches, which would be covered with labels like the ones in the photo. Look closely; the large diskette is starting to wilt under the hot lights. (*PAWEKPIX*)

covered with a gummed label. Five-inch diskettes are protected in the opposite way—covering the notch makes it impossible to write on one.

The Diskette Drive. The diskette is inserted into a *drive* for use (each of Figures 2-1 through 2-4 shows a diskette partially inserted into its drive). The drive is a mechanism that holds the diskette, spins it, and reads and writes data on its surface. As the door of the drive closes, an axle centers the disk in its jacket and flanges grip its hub. The edges of the jacket are gently squared in a frame. The axle of the drive rotates the disk within its jacket at 360 rpm (revolutions per minute), or 300 rpm for the smaller 5-inch drives.

The drive contains hinged arms like a pair of tongs that move in and out along a radius of the diskette. At the end of one arm is a *read-write head*, a device that can record data on, and read it from, the magnetic surface passing beneath it. Some *double-sided* disk drives have a read-write head on each arm; they can record data on both sides of the diskette. The more common *single-sided* drives have a pressure pad on the arm opposite the head. The arm can step in and out over the surface of the diskette. Each step defines a *track*, a concentric circle on the surface of the diskette.

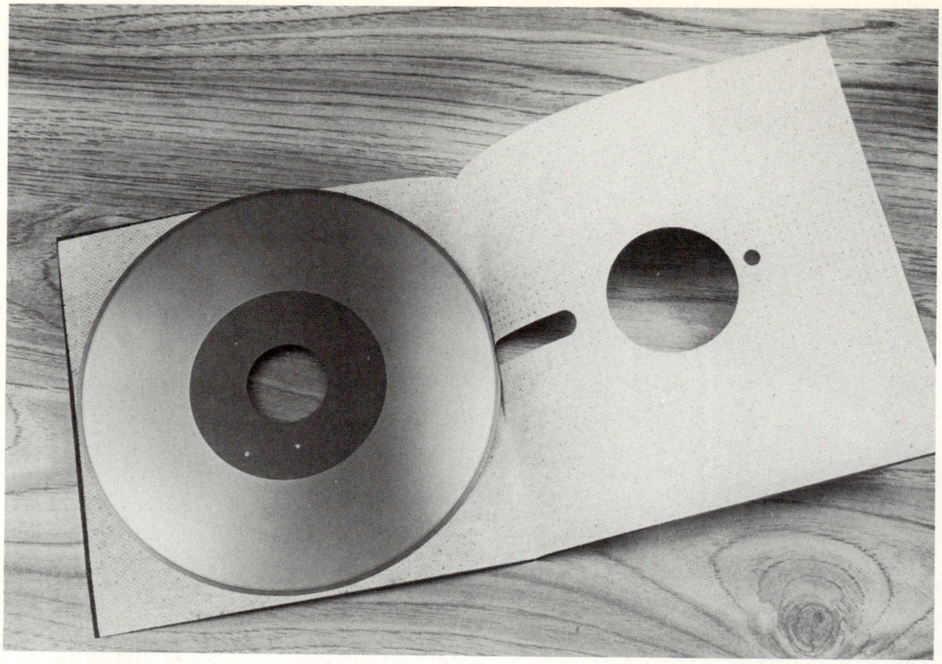

FIGURE 2-9
Secrets of a diskette, revealed: the jacket is lined with padded material, the diskette surface is smooth and reflective. When the index hole in the disk lines up with the one in the jacket it marks the beginning of a track. (*PAWEKPIX*)

Drive Selection. When a program in the processor wants access to the drive, it causes the drive to be *selected*. The arms over the diskette close together, pinching the diskette gently between head and pad (or between two heads). Most drives make an audible click as they "load the head" in this way; some drives have a light that comes on to show that they have been selected.

Seeking. The processor can then command the drive to move its head to a particular track, to wait until a particular part of the track is passing below the head, and then to read or write data. Moving the arm to a particular track is called *seeking*. Most drives make a sound as they seek; some emit a loud buzz, others a soft purr. Once the processor has finished using it, the drive is *deselected*. The access arms open to let the diskette turn without friction.

Tracks and Sectors. Data are stored along the tracks. Nothing is recorded between them; read-write heads contain erase elements that mop up any stray signals that seep out of the line of the track. The diskette is marked by imaginary radial lines into arc-shaped *sectors*. The drive always reads or writes one or more complete sectors. Figure 2-10 shows a diskette surface that was treated to reveal the tracks and sectors. Powdered iron was floated across the surface. Iron particles clung where the read-write head had

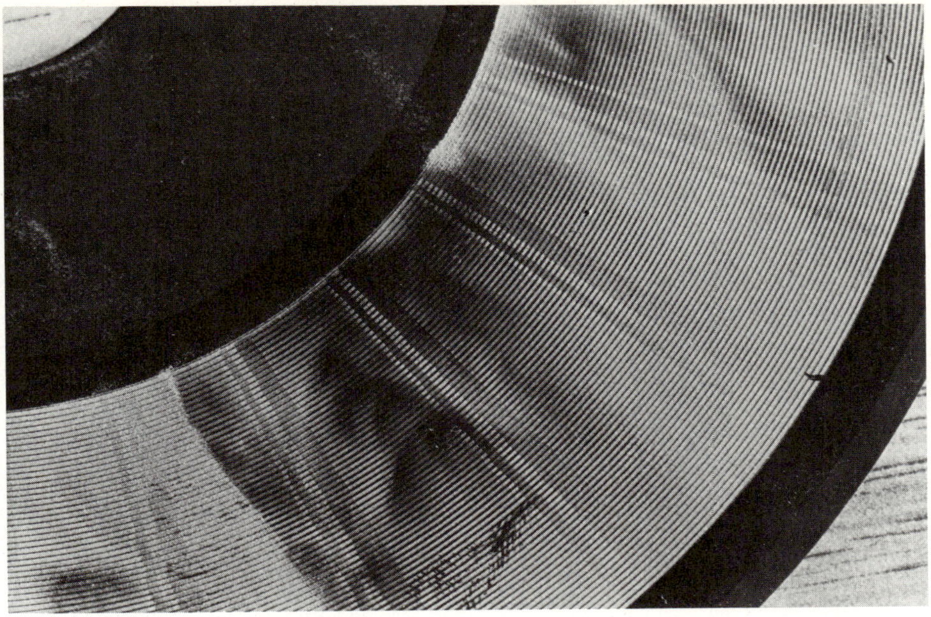

FIGURE 2-10
Powdered iron clings to the magnetized areas of a diskette to reveal the pattern of tracks. The radial marks are formed by the sector boundaries. ***(PAWEKPIX)***

magnetized the surface. This structure of sectors and tracks is the only organization imposed by the hardware.

CP/M's Use of Diskettes

CP/M imposes a higher level of organization on each diskette. It hides the details of track and sector from the user and makes the diskette appear to contain a collection of *files*, each with a name and some quantity of data. The user need not be concerned with the location of a file; a file's data may be scattered in different sectors over the surface of the diskette, but the file can be treated as a single object.

The Directory. CP/M reserves the first (that is, outermost) tracks of a diskette for its own uses. The first two or three tracks are reserved for the bootstrap program, a subject to which we return in Chapter 5. Part of the next track is used for a *directory* of the files on that diskette. The directory lists the files by name, and for each gives the location of the file's data on the diskette. When a file is needed, CP/M can find it by looking it up in the directory.

Storing Files. When a new file is created, CP/M allocates space to it from the available sectors, using those nearest the outside first. When a file is deleted, the space it occupied is made available again. CP/M's main function is to maintain files and keep track of disk space.

Diskette Variations

Everything said so far of diskettes is true for all of them, but there are several characteristics that vary. These have to do with the exact size of the diskettes and their tracks and sectors.

Diskette Diameters. A diskette may have one of two diameters—8 or 5 inches; see Figure 2-8. (These sizes refer to the jackets; the disks inside are slightly smaller.) Diskette drives are designed for one size only. The first diskettes were made in the 8-inch size. The 5-inch size was introduced in an attempt to lower the cost of diskette storage. The attempt was successful; although they hold fewer data, the smaller disks and drives are cheaper. Inexpensive home computers offer 5-inch drives. Most CP/M systems use 8-inch drives because the more serious applications of these systems demand the larger capacity.

Single- and Double-Sided Use. Diskettes may carry data on one or on both sides. The double-sided diskette is a recent innovation; drives with two read-write heads are as yet uncommon. Although all diskettes have magnetic material on both faces, diskettes for double-sided use need to be of higher quality. Double-sided drives have more parts and must be made to tighter standards. Therefore, they are more expensive.

Recording Densities. Diskettes may be recorded at one of two bit *densities*. A *single-density* diskette has bits written along its tracks at a density of 3200 bits per inch; *double-density* recording writes 6400 bits per inch (both as measured along the innermost, or shortest, track). Drives that support double-density recording usually can record at single density as well.

Sector Size. The sectors of a diskette may have one of several lengths. For single-density recording the normal sector size is 128 bytes, although 256-or 512-byte sectors can be used. At double density the sectors may be 128, 256, 512, or 1024 bytes long. The combinations that are possible depend on the drive, its I/O interface circuits, and the software. The sector size determines the number of sectors that will fit along a track. In most cases more data will fit on a track when fewer, larger sectors are used.

Soft and Hard Sectoring. The number and size of the sectors are usually determined by the drive and the software. When this is the case, the diskette is said to be *soft-sectored*, meaning that the sector size can be changed. Some drives require a *hard-sectored* diskette. Such diskettes have a ring of index holes around their hubs; the passage of an index hole marks the end of a sector. *Formatting* is the operation of writing blank tracks and sectors at the size and density that will be used. A soft-sectored diskette can be formatted to any sector size the drive and software will permit; a hard-sectored one cannot.

Choosing Drives. There are five characteristics that must be known about a diskette:

1. the diameter, 8 or 5 inches
2. whether it is hard- or soft-sectored
3. whether it is single- or double-sided
4. whether it is recorded at single or double density
5. the sector size: 128, 256, 512, or 1024 bytes

If all combinations were possible at once, you would be faced with keeping track of diskettes in any of 64 possible formats! Fortunately this is not the case.

Your drives establish the diameter of your diskettes, whether they are hard- or soft-sectored, and whether they can be double sided or not. Thus you have a maximum of eight options when you buy your system. In fact, not all those combinations are possible. Most likely you will be offered a choice only between a less expensive system that uses 5-inch drives (for example, Figure 2-1 or 2-3) and one that uses 8-inch drives (Figures 2-2 and 2-4). If you opt for the larger drives, you will be offered single-sided, soft-sectored, double-density drives as a matter of course; double-sided drives are more expensive, whereas hard-sectored drives are uncommon in general-purpose computers.

Choosing a Format. Having selected a system with 8-inch drives, you must decide on how you will format your diskettes. There are really only two choices. It is customary to distribute software on single-density diskettes with 128-byte sectors. This is the *exchange format*, the only format that every 8-inch drive is sure to handle (there is no agreed exchange format for 5-inch diskettes). As you buy software you will accumulate a collection of such distribution diskettes. If you exchange diskettes with someone else this is the best format to use for the exchange (unless you are positive that their drives are identical to yours). For diskettes that will stay with your own system you will want the maximum storage capacity, and so you will probably use double-density disks at the largest sector size.

Diskette Compatibility

It is common for any diskette drive that handles 8-inch, soft-sectored disks to be advertised as "IBM compatible." Such a claim is both true and false. Compatibility among diskettes has little to do with IBM, and much to do with factors other than the diskette drive.

History of Diskettes. IBM was the first company to introduce diskette storage. IBM used diskettes at first as a convenient way for its service technicians to carry diagnostic programs. The diskette drives were hidden under the covers of the larger components of an IBM computer and were not made available to user programs.

The convenience and low cost of diskette storage attracted the attention of many designers, and the devices were soon built into many kinds of equipment. Dozens of companies placed them in automatic cash registers, word-processing stations, and laboratory data-collection systems—anywhere that data needed to be captured. IBM made diskettes the primary storage medium in some of its smaller machines. When inexpensive personal computers first appeared, the diskette medium was well developed.

IBM Compatibility. Because their machines were first, IBM's diskette formats have remained the de facto standard for the medium. IBM's document GA21-9182, *IBM Diskette General Information Manual*, describes the diskette formats that IBM's different machines will accept (document GA21-9388, *IBM Diskette OEM Manual*, gives detailed engineering specifications). At the most fundamental level, any IBM system is capable of reading a single-density, soft-sectored diskette with a sector size of 128 bytes. There is no formal standard in these matters, but advertisers will use the phrases "IBM compatible" and "industry standard" when describing a diskette drive that is *capable* of handling that format.

A drive may be capable of writing "IBM-compatible" format, but its user may not elect to make it do so. Some of IBM's machines will accept double-density disks; others will not. The same is true of different sector sizes and double-sided diskettes. This can be said of drives from any manufacturer. In the general market, considerations of diameter, hard-sectoring, and fine details of formatting are added as well.

Data Compatibility. In addition to the question of whether or not a drive can read a particular format, there arises the question of how the data are organized. This organization is defined by the operating system—in our case, CP/M—and not by the drive. CP/M organizes the diskette into files in a certain way and that organization is nothing like the scheme used by any IBM system. For example, most IBM software expects a volume label on the first track of the diskette, where CP/M stores a bootstrap program. (You can buy a utility program that runs under CP/M that will read and write diskettes in one format acceptable to a number of IBM's machines, usually called the 3740 format after the most common machine to use it.)

Diskette Exchange Across Operating Systems. Diskettes that are perfectly compatible as far as the drives are concerned will usually be rejected by an operating system other than the one that wrote them. For example, the Radio Shack TRS-80 Model II supports both its manufacterer's operating system, TRSDOS, and a variant of CP/M. Diskettes prepared under one operating system are unacceptable to the other, even though they are written and read on the same drive.

Diskette Exchange Across CP/M Systems. It is easier to exchange diskettes between CP/M systems. There is a standard exchange format for CP/M diskettes: the 8-inch, single-density diskette with 128-byte sectors. Any CP/M system that handles 8-inch diskettes will read that format.

Except for the exchange format there is no agreement whatever between vendors of CP/M systems. There are many technical differences between one system's version of double-density recording and that of another. There is no agreed-upon exchange format for 5-inch diskettes.

Judging Compatibility. If you are preparing to buy a CP/M system, and if part of your plan is to exchange diskettes with another system, you must be wary of all claims of compatibility. It is safest to ignore all statements by manufacturers and salespeople on this subject. The problems of data compatibility are many and subtle; an honest salesperson may still not be fully informed on the needs of a foreign operating system. The only way to ensure that your plan will work is to carry out a trial exchange of data before you are committed to the system.

HARD DISKS

Hard-Disk Technology

Disk technology was pioneered by IBM in the early 1960s. The first disk drives used a stack of rigid platters of aluminum, not a flexible scrap of plastic. The disk drives on large computers today still use this technology, although much refined.

The concepts of the hard disk are much like those of the diskette. There is a rotating disk coated with a recording medium; against the recording surface rides a read-write head on an arm. The differences arise from the hard disk's speed and capacity.

Hard disks are never exposed to the environment in a cardboard jacket; they are enclosed in sealed cases and supplied with filtered air to keep them clean. They usually turn at 3600 rpm, ten times the rate of a diskette. This speed reduces the *latency* of the disk. Latency is the time that elapses between the instant the processor selects the drive until the desired sector rotates under the head. Average latency is simply half the rotation time of the disk: 8.3 ms (milliseconds) for a diskette, 0.83 ms for a hard disk.

Seek time is another area in which hard disks excel. This is the time required to move the access arm from track to track, or across several tracks. The access arms of hard disks are usually driven by more expensive and precise mechanisms that move the arms much faster than a diskette drive's arm will go.

If the read-write head of a hard disk pressed against its surface, the heat of friction would quickly melt the coating and burn the head. The read-write heads of hard disks don't touch the disk's surface; they fly a few millionths of an inch above it, supported on air as a water skier is supported by the flow of water. Once in a very long while, a read-write head might touch down on the disk, probably dragged down by dust or smoke particles. The result is called a head crash and it ruins the disk.

IBM's most-recent-but-one generation of disk drives pioneered a new design of read-write head that was cheaper to make and allowed an even closer flying height of head to disk. A smaller flying height permits data to be written at a higher density; the new head design allowed smaller, cheaper disks that yet held more data than their predecessors. Prior to the announcement of these products, IBM's internal code name for the project was "Winchester." One of the unannounced drives was stolen from the laboratory; in the ensuing trial the code name entered the vocabulary of computer engineers. Other manufacturers have adapted the technology to their own products, and "winchester-technology disk" is the accepted jargon phrase for a collection of design techniques.

The Uses of Hard Disks

Like the minute size of a computer chip, the intricate technology of disk design is not really significant to the buyer or user, except as it delivers more function, more capacity, or a better price.

Disk Capacity. Hard disks far outstrip diskettes in storage capacity. A double-sided, double-density diskette will store about 1000 KB of data (1000 kilobytes or, as it is usually abbreviated, 1 megabyte or 1 MB). A typical hard disk for small computers will contain 20 MB; capacities up to 100 MB are available. For a small system this is an ocean of data space (as a point of scale, the latest generation of drives for large machines offers up to 2500 MB per drive, with strings of four or eight drives not uncommon in large installations).

Estimating Needed Capacity. A quantity of 100 MB of data is not hard to accumulate, but it is not always needed *on-line*, that is, instantly accessible to the computer. A single user over the course of time might accumulate a library of 100 double-density diskettes—data equivalent to that of a 50-MB hard disk. Some of those diskettes would represent history files, and others would be needed only occasionally for use with certain programs. The data capacity needed on-line is determined by the size of the largest single file or group of files needed by one program. It is easy to estimate this need before the system is bought or the program written. Type out the information elements that will be stored in a single record of the file using typical values. Count the characters. Estimate to the nearest thousand the number of records that will be in the file, and multiply. Then add 50 percent for contingencies and for the unwritten law that files always grow and never shrink. If the result is less than 500 KB, the file should fit comfortably on a double-density diskette. If it is between 500 KB and 1 MB, the file is still suitable for diskette storage but more, or double-sided, diskettes will be needed. Files up to 2 MB can be handled on diskette but only sequentially, and both programmer and operator will be put to the trouble of changing diskettes in midrun. If you require files of more than 2 MB, you must consider the purchase of a hard disk. If you acquire a hard disk for your CP/M system, you will enjoy faster response to your commands and faster file access than that of your less affluent peers. You also will be faced with a difficult problem of *backup*, that is, saving copies of your data against the inevitable day when the on-line data are lost. We discuss backup in Chapter 8.

CENTRALIZED DISKS

Recent technological innovations have made the use of hard disks more economical in one special case—when there are to be several CP/M systems close together (in the same building). Then the expensive hard disk can be shared among the systems, holding a set of files for each. When the hard disk's cost is divided in this way, its per-system price can approach that of diskette drives.

CP/NET. One such system is called CP/NET. It is a software solution created by Digital Research, which produces CP/M. Under CP/NET an MP/M system equipped with a hard disk (and perhaps other costly I/O devices) communicates with a number of CP/M systems near it. The central machine makes file space available, transferring data on request from the user systems. The CP/NET software makes the communication between systems invisible to the user, making the remote hard disk act like a local diskette drive.

THE CORVUS "CONSTELLATION." A hardware manufacturer, Corvus Industries, has produced a hard disk packaged with its own processor. The disk-processor combination attaches to one or more nearby CP/M machines in the same way, and uses the same interface electronics, as a diskette drive would be attached. Each CP/M system gets the same responses from the hard disk that it would get from its own diskette drives, but the hard disk plays the role of diskette drive for several systems at once, keeping each system's data in a separate area.

THE USE OF CENTRALIZED DISKS. In both cases the designers have taken pains to make the interface for both programs and users as much like that of a diskette as possible. Users are meant to regard their section of a centralized disk as an invisible diskette that is always loaded. Programs access files on the centralized disk exactly as they do files on a local diskette drive.

FUTURE DEVELOPMENTS. This is a new area for CP/M systems, and one in which the technology is changing rapidly. By the time this book is in print there will surely be more centralization schemes than are presented here. At the same time the corridors of the industry are a-buzz with rumors of smaller, faster, and, above all, cheaper hard-disk drives soon to be announced. It has been the bitter experience of computer buyers since the dawn of the industry that you should never, never make plans on the basis of industry rumor. Equally bitter experience shows that you should never become committed to software or hardware that won't allow you to take advantage of new products when the rumors finally come true. CP/M users are fortunate that their operating system, so far, seems flexible enough to expand as the technology does.

PRINTERS

For all its speed and futuristic flash, the main useful product of a computer is often ordinary words on paper. A printer is a device that writes on paper at a computer's direction. There are several kinds, each with its uses and drawbacks.

Typewriter Printers

The typewriter, in the form of the Teletype, was one of the first I/O devices. For our purposes a typewriter is a printer that prints one character at a time by aligning a raised character image and driving it into ribbon and paper. There are three kinds in common use on CP/M systems: the daisy, the thimble, and the ball (see Figure 2-11). Typewriter printers produce what advertisers like to call "letter-quality output": the fully formed, handsome, highly readable characters that distinguish the best business correspondence.

Daisy, Thimble, Ball. Daisy printers carry the type image on the radial spokes of a wheel. They select a letter by turning the wheel, then bang the chosen spoke tip against the platen. The thimble typewriter is similar, except that the letters are placed at the tips of the slit edges of a cup-shaped wheel (Figure 2-11). The ball typewriter is just the familiar Selectric mechanism, widely, and cheaply, available in reconditioned time-sharing terminals. The venerable Teletype is still to be found, but its slow speed and limited character set make it undesirable as compared with modern typewriter printers.

Typing Speed. Daisy and thimble typewriters operate at speeds up to 55 characters per second; any of them can write one line of a business letter in just over a second, or fill a manuscript page in less than a minute. This is adequate speed for many applications, but not for all. Bulky output such as whole chapters of books or the listings of long programs can tie up the machine for many minutes, even hours. Unfortunately there is no faster way to get high-quality printing from a small computer. Ball typewriters cannot print faster than an ordinary office machine (around 15 characters per second) and should be used where the volume of printing is small.

Special Features. Daisy and thimble printers contain their own processors. When ordered with the right options, most of them can center, underscore, justify, and do proportional spacing on their own. These features, like the special features of terminals, are invoked by sequences of control characters. But unlike the terminal features, the capabilities of the typewriter are usually ignored by the popular text-formatting programs, which handle the same functions from the computer and use the typewriter strictly as an output device. As with terminals, there is no standardization of control sequences.

FIGURE 2-11
Three ways of doing letter-quality printing: the familiar ball, the thimble, and the daisy. (*PAWEKPIX*)

Printer Keyboards. Typewriter printers are available in two models: with a keyboard (KSR, for Keyboard Send Receive) and without (RO for Receive Only). With a keyboard, a typewriter printer can be used like an ordinary office machine, but it doesn't make a very good one because the human factors are all wrong. The touch is not pleasant, and there is sometimes a split-second delay between the keystroke and printing that is maddening to a touch typist.

Sometimes a printer with a keyboard can be useful in a CP/M system. One can be used as substitute for the terminal, or as an input device when testing a program. But generally a printer's keyboard won't be used often enough to justify its cost.

Matrix Printers

The other printer technology in common use on CP/M systems is that of the *matrix printer* (see Figure 2-12). This device has a print head that contains a vertical row of stiff wires pointed at the paper. Each wire can be driven against the ribbon and paper to make a tiny dot. The print head sweeps across the page; as it moves the wires are fired in combinations so that the dots form characters. Each character is printed in a character cell whose height is determined by the number of wires in the print head and whose width encloses some number of steps at which the wires may fire. Each character is formed within a rectangular matrix of possible dots, hence the name "matrix printer."

FIGURE 2-12
A typical small matrix printer. (*PAWEKPIX*)

Matrix Print Quality. The dimensions of the matrix determine the definition of the letters. The coarsest resolution is a five-by-seven matrix (five dots wide, seven dots high). A matrix that size doesn't allow the descenders of characters such as "p" and "g" to fall below the line; when such a printer offers a lowercase character set, its "g" will often resemble its "@." Most printers use a seven-wide by nine-high matrix that allows true descenders and more readable output.

Print Speed and Cost. Matrix printers can be faster than typewriters—the fastest can operate at above 200 characters per second, although 100 characters per second is more usual. Matrix printers are considerably cheaper than typewriters because their mechanical parts are much simpler.

Special Features. The manufacturers of matrix printers are engaged in hot competition. This expresses itself not only in price but in the variety of optional features. Many matrix printers offer a graphics mode in which the application program can control the placement of individual dots on the page. Elaborate pictures, even fairly good halftone images, can be drawn in this way. The programming required to create a picture or a graph is equally elaborate, of course, and such programs will be device dependent.

Character Fonts. Some matrix printers offer variations in the way they form characters. Double-width characters and boldface characters (every dot struck twice for a darker image) are common features (see Figure 2-13). A few printers have ways of

```
ABCDEFGHIJKLMNOPQRSTUVWXYZABCDEFGHIJKLMNOPQRSTUVWXYZ
abcdefghijklmnopqrstuvwxyzabcdefghijklmnopqrstuvwxyz
12345678901234567890!#$%&'()*=+<>?!#$%&'()*=+<>?
EPSON MAKES MORE PRINT MECHANISMS THAN ANYONE ELSE IN THE WORLD.
Epson makes more print mechanisms than anyone else in the world.

ABCDEFGHIJKLMNOPQRSTUVWXYZ
abcdefghijklmnopqrstuvwxyz
1234567890:-!#$%&'()*=+<>?
EPSON MAKES MORE PRINT MECHANISMS
Epson makes more print mechanisms

ABCDEFGHIJKLMNOPQRSTUVWXYZ
abcdefghijklmnopqrstuvwxyz
1234567890:-!#$%&'()*=+<>?
EPSON MAKES MORE PRINT MECHANISMS
Epson makes more print mechanisms

ABCDEFGHIJKLMNOPQRSTUVWXYZABCDEFGHIJKLMNOPQRSTUVWXYZ
abcdefghijklmnopqrstuvwxyzabcdefghijklmnopqrstuvwxyz
12345678901234567890!#$%&'()*=+<>?!#$%&'()*=+<>?
EPSON MAKES MORE PRINT MECHANISMS THAN ANYONE ELSE IN THE WORLD.
Epson makes more print mechanisms than anyone else in the world.
```

FIGURE 2-13
Samples of the various fonts the printer of FIGURE 2-12 can use, provided it is sent the right control sequences. Other printers have similar abilities.

multiplying the effective number of dots in the character matrix. By moving the paper in tiny increments and restriking the letters, they can get the effect of a 14-by-18, or even a 21-by-36, matrix. This produces correspondingly better definition of the characters, but at the cost of slower printing since every letter must be struck two or three times. Some advertisers claim that they can obtain letter-quality printing from their matrix printers by using such techniques. You should verify such claims by inspecting actual output.

Other Printers

Printer technology has been developed to high levels among large computers. Train and band printers place a print hammer behind every character position across the page and spin a strip of type slugs in front of the page at high speed. When the type slug bearing the right character nears a character cell, that cell's hammer fires. In this way these printers can produce an entire line of print in one rotation of the type carrier, printing at a rate of hundreds of lines a minute with good quality.

At this writing no such printer is available at a price consonant with the cost of a CP/M system. However, if CP/NET is used to distribute the use and the cost of a printer among several systems, the fast technology becomes economical. And as small computers proliferate a market is being created that should eventually bring about the development of a band printer, suitably scaled down in price and speed, for small systems.

Printer Interfaces

Serial Interfaces. All printers suitable for CP/M are available with an RS-232 interface (described under "Terminals"). This interface is usually the best choice for a printer; it allows the printer to be swapped, either between systems or during repairs. Like a terminal, a printer has to be set to agree with the processor on the matters of transmission rate, number of stop bits, and parity checking.

Print Buffering. The printer puts characters on paper at a very slow rate, in electronic terms. A typewriter proceeding at the rate of 50 characters per second is consuming data at an effective bit rate of about 500 bps. Not only is this slow, but it does not correspond to one of the standard transmission rates. If the processor sends at 300 bps, the printer will have to idle between letters. If the processor sends at 600 or 1200 bps, the printer will run at full speed but will quickly fall behind the computer. Most printers contain storage for some number of characters until they can be printed; if this *buffer* fills up and the processor continues to send data, characters will be lost or garbled.

Printer Handshaking. The solution to the foregoing problem is to have the printer tell the processor when its buffer is nearly full and to have the processor respect this signal and halt transmission until the printer has caught up. This exchange of signals is called *handshaking*. With handshaking the printer can run at its maximum speed with no danger of losing data. One of the RS-232 signal lines can be used for just this purpose.

Most printers can be set up to signal when they are not ready to accept data because their buffer is full, their paper has run out, or for any other reason. The printer control programming in CP/M must also be set up to recognize the printer's signal (see Chapter 15).

PARALLEL INTERFACES. Some printers provide, instead of the RS-232 serial interface, a parallel interface of some kind. There is no particular standard for signals on a parallel interface, but one arrangement is so common on older machines that it nearly qualifies as such. This is the Centronics interface, named for one of the first inexpensive matrix printers available to hobbyists. The Centronics interface is common, but the RS-232 is the preferred interface because of its interchangeability.

OTHER I/O DEVICES

The basic CP/M system has electronics, a terminal, diskettes, and usually a printer. But the possible choice of I/O devices is far wider than that. Machines that use the S-100 bus can be equipped with an exciting array of special-purpose equipment. Here are a few examples:

1. speech recognition units for voice control of programs
2. voice response units so the program can talk back
3. music synthesizers for computer-generated music
4. color graphics output to a video monitor
5. video image processing for computer recognition of images
6. digitizing tablets for the input of maps and handwriting
7. plotters for drawing graphs and blueprints on paper

There isn't room in this book to discuss these interesting machines. Each provides solutions to problems in a specialized domain. If you have the problem, then you can build a solution based on your CP/M system.

Chapter 3

Software for CP/M

Software for CP/M

This chapter will take you on a brief tour of the software used with a CP/M system. We'll identify and name the important components and sketch their functions. As in the last chapter, we have two aims: to learn the jargon and to give some guidelines for the shopper.

CATEGORIES OF SOFTWARE

The name "CP/M" refers to a package of programs written and published by Digital Research. For most users that package is not sufficient software. You or your dealer will add other programs to make a complete system. It will be easier to talk about this collection of software if we put the programs into categories by their functions.

The Monitor. The *Monitor* is a group of programs that manages the detailed operation of the system. We'll discuss it briefly here; its workings are described for programmers in Chapter 10 and beyond.

The File Commands. The file commands are a group of small, often used programs that we cover in Chapter 5. They make it possible for you to manage the file system and the I/O devices from the terminal.

The Utilities. *Utilities* are programs whose function is to copy and transform files. The most important ones are called PIP and ED, each of which has a later chapter to itself (Chapters 6 and 7). You'll be adding other utilities to the ones that come with CP/M.

Language Translators. Language translators are programs used to convert statements in some programming language into machine language. The CP/M package contains only one, an assembler. Your collection is bound to include others.

Applications. The programs in the first four categories fit the definition of an operating system that we gave in Chapter 1: they are programs that apply the computer to the job of managing the computer's affairs. The remaining category includes all programs whose output is for the benefit of people rather than being directed toward the needs of the system. Such programs are *applications*.

VERSIONS OF CP/M

Digital Research has published several versions of CP/M over the years. Each version has had more capabilities than the last. MP/M is a similar system, but one designed to control larger machines and to support several users at once. This book is written for CP/M, but it applies to MP/M as well.

Each version of the system identifies itself when you call for a *cold start*. We discuss how to cause a cold start in Chapter 5.

CP/M 1.4. The first version of CP/M to achieve wide use was called CP/M 1.4. There are many copies of CP/M 1.4 in use, and it can still be ordered from the publisher. Much of this book is applicable to CP/M 1.4.

CP/M 2. A major revision of CP/M was released in 1979 and called CP/M 2. It has been updated twice since; the version being distributed today is called CP/M 2.2. CP/M 2 contained many improvements on CP/M 1.4. To the user it brought easier typing correction. It gave the programmer the ability to access disk files at random. It gave the system builder much more flexibility in adapting CP/M to different kinds of disk drives. This book is designed for use with CP/M 2.

CP/M-86. CP/M has been rewritten to operate on machines that use the Intel 8086 CPU (notably the IBM Personal Computer). Almost all of this book is applicable to CP/M-86, because its use, and most of its programming conventions, are the same as CP/M 2.

MP/M 1. MP/M was released at the same time as CP/M 2. MP/M is designed to manage the resources of a machine larger than the usual desk-top computer, and to deliver those resources to several users at once. Almost all of this book is applicable to MP/M because Digital Research took pains to make the use and programming of MP/M compatible with the use and programming of CP/M. MP/M has a number of commands and programming features that are not covered here.

MP/M 2 AND MP/M-86. These advanced operating systems have a number of additional features, but their use and programming is still compatible with CP/M 2. Many of their new features are covered in the Reference section.

CP/M 3. Sometime in 1982, a new version of CP/M will probably appear. If Digital Research continues its tradition of compatibility, the commands and programming conventions of CP/M 3 will be substantially identical to those described in this book.

THE MONITOR

One component of CP/M remains continuously in working storage while the system is running. It consists of three programs. Two of these work together to provide services to other programs; the third provides services to the user.

PARTS OF THE MONITOR. The CP/M documentation refers to the first two as the BDOS (Basic Disk Operating System) and the BIOS (Basic I/O System). They are described in Chapters 10 and 15. The third program, whose purpose is to serve the system's user, is called the Console Command Processor, or CCP. The distinctions between these programs will be made clear later. We'll refer to them collectively as the *Monitor*, meaning that part of CP/M that is always present in working storage, monitoring the activity in the system.

Size of the Monitor. The Monitor takes up space in working storage. Its total size is about 12K bytes. If the size of working storage is 64K bytes, then the amount available to application programs is 64K less 12K, or 52K bytes. The CCP is not needed while an application program is running; if its 4K of space is used, the amount available becomes 56K. Application programs have the option of using all of working storage, but if they do so they lose all the services that the Monitor provides, so this is rarely done. Advertisements for fee software sometimes specify the minimum amount of storage required; the number may or may not be exclusive of the Monitor. A program that requires a "54K CP/M system" may require that the machine have 64K of working storage.

Control of I/O. The Monitor justifies the space it takes by performing several essential functions. Its first duty is to control the operation of all the I/O devices of the system. It is the Monitor that contains the machine instructions that read and write characters on the terminal, that cause the disk drives to select, seek, and transfer data, and that send data at the correct rate to the printer. Since these instructions are in the Monitor, they need not be included in any application program. That makes applications easier to write (I/O control code is the trickiest programming of all) and makes them smaller.

Service Requests. The Monitor makes the devices accessible to programs by providing for *service requests*. There are standard machine instruction sequences that allow one program to call upon the services of another. An application program can call upon the Monitor for a number of services. Services are defined for reading and writing at the terminal, at the printer, and at other devices. There are a number of services relating to access to files. By way of these service requests, a program can access all parts of the system without itself containing any device-control logic.

Control of the File System. Besides controlling the operation of the disk drives, the Monitor contains the central logic of the CP/M file system. It is the Monitor that reads and writes the file directory on a diskette, decides where a file's data shall be placed, and finds the data again when needed. The Monitor contains services by which a program can read and write the data in a file without concerning itself with either the details of disk operation or the location of the data on the disk. Other services allow a program to create a file, to rename it, and to delete it.

Advantages of the Monitor. Great economy is achieved by centralizing all the logic of device and file control in the Monitor. If this logic had to be repeated in every program in the system, disk space would be wasted in storing repetitive copies of that code, but this is the least of the savings. If the Monitor's functions had to be repeated in every program, surely some of them would get it wrong, or do it differently than others. Consistency would vanish, and errors would be introduced. Further, the instructions used to control one kind of terminal, printer, or disk drive differ from the instructions needed to drive one of another kind. The number of possible combinations of CP/M hardware is astronomical. If the functions carried out by the Monitor had to be done by the programs, then every program would depend on the particular combination of hardware for which it was written. But the service request interface provided by the Monitor is uniform across all CP/M systems. The service to read a file is the same in any system, regardless of the kind of disk drive that system may have. By containing and hiding the device-dependent logic, the Monitor makes it possible for software to be exchanged between systems. That in turn makes it possible for a profitable software publishing industry to exist, and that has led to the huge number of application programs that you can buy.

The Console Command Processor

When the system is idling between programs, the Console Command Processor (CCP) is in charge. This part of the Monitor exists to be the interface between the user (you) and the operating system. Its job is to accept a line from the terminal and then see that the work the line calls for is carried out.

Commands. The line that you type and that the CCP acts on is called a *command*. Every operating system provides a *command language*, although in this context the word language is used rather loosely. Few operating systems (and CP/M is not among them) provide a true language of commands in the way that a programming language is a self-consistent artificial language. The phrase refers to the set of all commands that the operating system can accept, and the rules for forming them.

Form of Commands. CP/M's command language rules are defined by the CCP, and they are very simple. To the CCP a command is a line of characters broken into groups by *delimiters* (one or more spaces). The first group, or word if you like, is the command's *verb*: it specifies what is to be done. The rest of the line contains the command's *operands*. They specify what is to be acted upon. The verb is always the name of a program. Programs *are* the verbs of the system. The operands give the program any information it needs about what it is to work on, and optional things it should do.

Command Execution. The CCP's method of carrying out a command is simple. When you signal with the return key that the command has been completely typed, the CCP takes the first word of the command and calls on the Monitor to locate that word as the name of a file that contains a program. The Monitor locates the file on disk. The CCP reads the file—which contains an object program—into working storage and then calls the program that has been loaded. The CCP leaves the rest of the command behind in a known location in working storage for the program to reference. When the program is finished, the CCP regains control and waits for the next command.

FILE COMMANDS

Other than the Monitor and the CCP, the operating system consists of command verbs, that is, of programs that can be loaded by the CCP. These commands enable you to construct and then use the application programs.

The file commands are the ones that are used most often. Chapter 5 describes them in detail. They make the services of the Monitor directly available to the user. There are commands that let you list the contents of a directory to see what files exist or to learn the size of a file, to erase a file, or to rename it. Some of these commands are used so frequently that the programs that implement them have been included in the body of the CCP. These can be carried out without having to load them from disk. As far as the user is concerned, the only difference between these resident commands and any other is that they execute a bit more quickly.

UTILITIES

A utility is a command that moves or changes a file's contents in some standard way. The simplest utility is the TYPE command. It displays the contents of a file on the screen of the terminal. TYPE is called so often that it too has been embedded in the CCP. SAVE and LOAD are special-purpose utilities used to build programs; they are described in Chapter 12.

PIP. The most important utility is PIP (for Peripheral Interchange Program, named after similar programs in other operating systems). PIP is used for moving files between one device and another: from one diskette to another, from diskette to printer, or from any device to diskette. It is examined at length in Chapter 6.

Editors. An editor is a program that lets you build and modify a file from the terminal. The file may be a business letter, a list of names and addresses, the statements of a program, or anything else that can be expressed in characters. An editor presents the contents of the file at the screen and takes changes from the keyboard. When the file has been built, extended, or changed as you desire, the editor writes it back onto diskette.

ED. One editor is provided with CP/M; its name is ED. ED descends from a long line of similar editors going back into the dawn of computing. Its functions are organized for easy use from a typewriter terminal and might seem awkward to someone new to computing (or friendly and familiar to one who is new only to CP/M but experienced with computers). The concepts and uses of ED are described in Chapter 7.

Other Editors. ED is far from being the best possible editor. There are a number of editor programs available for CP/M from other software publishers. A good full-screen editor should be one of your first software purchases. See the discussion of word-processing packages later in this chapter.

LANGUAGE TRANSLATORS

Only one language translator is provided with CP/M, an assembler program named ASM. Your system will undoubtedly have others, which will be bought from other software vendors. In Chapter 11 we discuss the differences between translators and how to select the one(s) you need. All language translators can be thought of as parts of the operating system, as they are used to create other programs rather than as an end in themselves. Translators are called as commands, like all other programs under CP/M.

INTERPRETERS. Interpreters accept program statements from the terminal (calling upon the Monitor to read them), and contain some of the functions of an editor in that they allow the programmer to look around the program and make changes in it. At the programmer's option they may read program text in from a file, or save the finished program in a new file.

COMPILERS. Compilers always use the file system. They read a file of program text, translate it into machine language, and write the translation as another file. A compiler or assembler (an assembler is a special case of a compiler) will usually produce another file containing a listing of the program.

APPLICATIONS

As we said in Chapter 1, applications—programs that arrange and display data for the benefit of people—are the true purpose of a computer system. Specific applications may be written, possibly by you, for your own purposes. Several types of application programs are so useful, and so difficult to write, that they are usually purchased as program packages.

Word-Processing Programs

A *word processor* is a program or a package of programs that allows you to create documents of all kinds with the computer. Word-processing packages are reliable and easy to apply. A good one can justify the whole cost of a computer installation. Word processing has two parts: creating the document and printing it.

FULL-SCREEN EDITORS. Every word processor package contains a *full-screen* editor, a more sophisticated version of ED. A full-screen editor uses the screen of the terminal as a window onto the file. The file's contents can be moved under the window like a scroll sliding under glass, up and down at will. The cursor may be placed anywhere in the window and new or changed data typed into the file. The process is simple and natural; just point to the place where a change is to be made and type the correction. The change is recorded in working storage as it is made. The ease and speed of typing with a good full-screen editor are truly remarkable.

Print Formatting. The second part of word processing is the display of the document on the printer. The formatting abilities of word processors go far beyond simple printing. All of them provide for automatic pagination and page numbering. Most can justify the output so that all lines are the same length. When used with a daisy or thimble printer, most can provide for automatic underscoring, bold printing, superscripts and subscripts, and so forth. Given the right hardware (and with considerable practice on the part of the operator), a word processor's output can approach the quality of typesetting.

Spelling Correctors. Several publishers have produced programs that will read a document file and compare it with the words in a spelling dictionary file. When a word in the document can't be found in the dictionary file, the program displays it at the terminal. If the word is truly misspelled, the user can correct it. If it is a correct word, the program will add it to the dictionary so that it will be found next time.

Electronic Worksheets

A few years ago a genuinely new concept in computer applications was invented: the electronic worksheet. The first such program was called Visi-Calc™; it is available for a number of personal computers (but not for CP/M systems). The concept has since been copied by other publishers, and similar programs are available for CP/M systems. Like word processors, worksheet programs are easy to use and can enable the machine to justify its expense quickly. A worksheet program creates in working storage a large array of cells, similar to the columns and rows of an accountant's worksheet. The user can move the screen of the terminal over the worksheet and view the contents of the cells. A number or a descriptive title can be placed in any cell.

The power of the worksheet idea arises from the fact that the user can also put a formula instead of a number into a cell. The formula can specify that the cell's contents are to be some arithmetic combination of other cells. A cell at the bottom of a column can be defined to hold the sum of all the numbers above it, or a percentage of two other cells, and so on. Whenever one cell is changed, the program passes over the whole sheet, recalculating every formula. Thus a change in a detail amount causes an instant, automatic change in the total amount as well. A change of a markup percentage in one corner of the sheet is instantly reflected as a change of gross and net profits elsewhere on the sheet.

Other Application Packages

There are other packages that you might want to have, depending on the use to which your system will be put.

Accounting Packages. Business accounting packages contain programs that keep the standard accounting information and prepare the usual accounting reports: general ledger, accounts receivable and payable, etc. It is hard to write a generalized accounting package that will suit the requirements of every user. Such packages must be studied very carefully to make sure that they meet your needs.

Mailing List Programs. There are programs that will maintain a file of names and addresses. The list can be sorted in various ways, and names can be selected on the basis of zip code or other criteria. All names, or just selected ones, can be printed onto mailing labels ready for attachment.

Sorts and Report Generators. A good general sort program is an important tool in most computer systems. A sort is a program that will read a file and write a copy of it, with the records of the file arranged in sequence according to their contents. An amazing amount of processing can be done with only an editor and a sort. The editor (or any other program) is used to create a file of records in a regular format, with the same kind of information at the same position in each record. Then the sort program can be used to put the records in order by any combination of record fields. To understand the use of this idea, think of a catalog of any collection of similar things, phonograph records, for instance. Imagine the usefulness of being able to sort the catalog on any of its characteristics—catalog number, performer, title—and to print the resulting sorted list.

Report generator programs take the next step beyond simple printing. They read a sorted list of records and, at your direction, produce a formatted report of what they find. A report generator can be used to exclude or include records on the basis of their content. It can count records and keep running totals and subtotals of numeric fields, as well as decorating the report with titles and page numbers.

Database Systems. The word "database" has been badly abused in recent years. Often a simple report generator will lay claim to the word. A genuine database system does a great deal more than select records and print reports.

A database system maintains a file of information in such a way that it keeps not only the records, but the relationships between the records as well. For example, a library might have separate files of books, of authors, and of subjects; a report generator would allow records of one file to be selected and displayed. A library database would manage all the records, linking information about authors to records of the books they've written and linking those in turn to their subjects. A true database system will also be able to present another program with only the information the program wants, in the format the program needs without regard to the format used to store the data.

SUMMARY

With this chapter we've finished naming the parts of a CP/M system. If you have a system, you're ready to turn to Chapter 5 and begin learning how to use it. If you are still shopping, you have enough of the jargon to understand a salesperson's talk.

Chapter 4

Management Problems

This chapter addresses some topics related to managing a small computer installation. We'll talk about the problems of owning a system, especially when it is part of a business organization. Unlike the other chapters, this one doesn't aim at preparing you to operate or program a CP/M system. If that is your immediate interest, skip ahead to Chapter 5 or Chapter 9.

We'll look at four problems: first, the difficulty of buying a computer system, especially computer software; second, setting up a good workplace for the machine and its users; third, planning for breakdowns and disasters; and fourth, keeping data secure against loss, theft, and fraud.

BUYING HARDWARE AND SOFTWARE

In the preceding chapters we've covered most of the jargon of the small-computer marketplace. Having learned that, you're ready to talk to a computer salesperson, or to read computer ads, with some degree of comprehension. However, as soon as you begin to do so you will be struck by how disorganized the computer marketplace is. The longer you shop, the more it will come to resemble an Arab bazaar crossed with a political convention.

Shopping for Hardware

Computers carry prices similar to those of a large office copier or a compact car, but buying a computer is nothing at all like buying one of those products. There are several good reasons for this.

The Computer's Complexity. The first reason is that a computer system is many times more complicated than any other piece of equipment. Think of all the hardware options we covered in Chapter 2. Ponder the different kinds of application packages we sketched so briefly in Chapter 3. The computer shopper is faced with an endless series of choices.

The Market's Complexity. Second, the small-computer industry is dominated by very small, very young companies. These companies must deal with constant technological changes and with a chronic shortage of trained staff. There are several hundred companies, almost all small, making CP/M-compatible systems or hardware bits to plug into them. There are several hundred more firms publishing software for CP/M systems. The growth of the industry since its birth in 1976 has been breathtaking; it has been a striking demonstration of the power of a free-market economy. However, few of these firms are large enough to support mass-market advertising or a large marketing staff. There'll be no tailored salesperson coming around to court you; you'll have to seek out the products you want.

The Need for Task Definition. Many people who go shopping for a computer have no clear idea of what they want the system to do for them. Without that, neither shopper nor dealer can evaluate hardware or software. There are many ways in which a computer can make itself useful. You must isolate one task for it to do—a task that when automated will return the computer's cost over the period during which you'll depreciate it. Having picked that task, define it as clearly as you possibly can.

Use the task definition as the benchmark against which you measure the products you see. The task definition will limit the eligible systems and let you talk specifics with vendors. Your shopping will be greatly simplified. Keep in mind, however, that a computer is a general-purpose tool. Once it's installed, you will constantly find new uses for it. Provided it meets your task requirements, the system that can be extended or upgraded most easily is to be preferred.

The Importance of Advice

There's a huge number of products available and more appear every day. Many are incompatible with each other; not a few are unreliable or are poorly supported by their makers. You haven't a prayer of sorting them out on your own without months of study, which is a waste of the time you need for running your own business. You must make use of someone else to winnow the market for you and propose a comprehensible choice of products that meet your task definition.

Using a Consultant. One way to get advice is to hire a consultant. A consultant is simply a person who knows more than you do and who will share that knowledge for a price. A considerable number of people have hung out their shingles as small-computer consultants in recent years. There isn't any objective standard for consultancy, no licensing board or examinations to pass. Therefore, you must be extremely careful about hiring a consultant. The one you want is the one who knows as much about your business as about computers. There isn't much point in hiring computer knowledge when the possessor of that knowledge doesn't have the background to relate it to your requirements.

Relying on a Retailer. Most cities of middle size and larger contain retail computer stores. There are national franchise groups such as the Computerland chain, and many independent dealers. Retail computer dealers are in a position to know the market, or at least their own product line. Dealers have a strong motivation to select and stock only solid, reliable products. Dealers are usually pressed for time and short of staff, and so are unlikely to be patient with vague questions. However, if you present a clear definition of the job you want a computer to do, the dealer should be able to propose a complete system tailored to that job.

Purchasing Software

CP/M alone is not sufficient software for anyone but the hobbyist. You'll need to buy software from other sources. Except for a simple assembler, CP/M contains no language translators; you'll buy one or more. You will almost certainly want to supplement ED with one of the word-processing packages that contain both a full-screen editor and a print-formatting program. A worksheet program is always useful, as is a report generator. If you plan to apply your system to commercial accounting, you'll buy software for that.

Importance of Software Quality. The quality and usability of an important software package can decide the success or failure of your system. A package that is poorly documented, or full of errors, or simply unsuited to your needs, can cause you to waste the price of your hardware several times over in lost time and duplicated effort. On the other hand, a good package that matches your needs may enable the system to pay for itself in weeks.

The Software Market. A broad and vigorous market in software has sprung up in recent years. Thousands of people and hundreds of small companies are competing for your software purchases. Yet it is difficult to shop for software in the present market. Advertisements appear only in computer magazines and are superficial at best—long on color and dramatic claims, and short on the detailed functional information that would let you decide whether or not the advertised package will do what you need. A reliable computer retail dealer can be a great help in choosing software.

Lack of Consumer Information. A software package is at least as complex as an automobile and the differences between, for example, two word processors are much greater than the differences between two passenger cars. As yet no publication has appeared to do for the software industry what the *Times Literary Supplement* does for the publishing industry or *Road and Track* and others do for the automobile industry.

Evaluating Software

There are four points on which to evaluate a software package: function, documentation, support, and price.

Function. The first point is the most important: Does the package promise to do everything that you require of it? In order to answer the question you must know what you want done, and know it in detail. Then you must find out what each package promises. At present the only reliable way to do that is to read carefully through the documentation for the package, which is usually available at a price.

Documentation. Poor documentation can make an excellent program unusable. The quality of software documentation generally is very low indeed, but there are packages whose documentation is clear and readable. The presence of cryptic, poorly written, or incomplete documentation does not necessarily mean that the program is bad, but it does mean that you will pay an extra, hidden price in time and effort in mastering the program. You should mentally adjust the price accordingly.

Support. The term "support" describes all the human assistance included in the purchase price of a package. Your vendor may offer to train you in the use of the package, or to tailor it to your needs. The publisher will have some method of reporting and fixing errors, and may offer a hot-line phone number that you can call for assistance. All types of support are valuable and increase the worth of a package.

Price. Price is the last, and should be the least, consideration when you evaluate software. A good package with good documentation and support is worth its price. A poor package has negative value regardless of its dollar cost.

SETTING UP THE COMPUTER WORKPLACE

There was a time when a business computer required a special room with raised floors and special air conditioning. Your CP/M system sits on a corner of your desk and emits a faint purr. Its environmental requirements are easy to meet. That allows you to concentrate on making the machine's environment good for the humans who use it. Giving thought to the human factors of the workplace can make the total system—the machine and its operators—run better. Some of the advice we'll give here would seem trivial and obvious, were it not for the many times the author has seen these simple principles ignored.

The Terminal

The terminal is the toughest piece of hardware in the system. As long as it doesn't stand for hours in direct sunlight, and as long as nobody spills coffee or paper clips into its keyboard, it will continue to work. But the terminal is CP/M's primary human interface; no other piece of the system offers more opportunities for optimizing the human factor.

Siting the Terminal. A terminal is used for typing; the typing is done from copy that must be read, or is related to books and listings that must be referred to. The terminal can be located to maximize the comfort of the operator in both reading and typing. The terminal should sit close to a flat work surface where papers and books can be spread convenient to the screen. Its keyboard should fall at the right height for a typist's fingers (this is true whether or not the main user is a touch typist). Study the layout of a secretary's desk in a commercial office. There's a well where the typewriter rests with its keyboard several inches lower than the desktop. That design isn't an accident; it's the result of experience. A high keyboard can lead to backache and subliminal tension, things one can well do without when using a computer.

Lighting the Terminal. The lighting around the terminal is very important. Under the best of circumstances the contrast and resolution of a screen are poorer than that of print on paper. Glare from beyond the terminal or reflections from above it make the screen hard to read. If the lighting is bad, the user will suffer from fatigue, and may even get headaches, and will make more errors. It is important to have even, glare-free lighting at the lowest level consistent with good reading of print.

Improving the Image. There are usually things that can be done to improve the image on the screen. The simplest thing, and one that is often overlooked, is to clean the screen. The author has several times watched people unconsciously strain to read a terminal whose only problem was a grimy screen; a wipe with a sponge made a drastic improvement in the brightness of the display.

Most terminals have a brightness control in some obscure location. A careful adjustment of the brightness of the image sometimes will make an amazing difference in the clarity of the display.

The linearity (straightness, squareness) of the display and the display's dimensions can be adjusted by a service technician. One terminal, the Heath/Zenith H19, stands out because its owner's manual contains instructions for adjusting linearity, focus, display height and width, and contrast.

Diskettes and Drives

Diskette drives need to be within arm's reach of the operator. They also need to be kept as clean and dust-free as possible. The drives ought to be well above the floor and located where there is no chance of spilling or dropping anything on them. If you don't dust anything else in your office, dust around the disk drives. A tiny bit of lint between the read-write head and the diskette can cause a read error, or worse, a badly written record. Be fanatical about smoking around the drives; tobacco smoke condenses in a film on everything. If you smoke, keep the ashtray as far down wind from the drives as you can reach.

The Processor

The box containing the processor and other electronic parts has no special requirements other than that it should not be overheated. Any location that lets you reach the reset signal and allows a free flow of air around the machine is fine. If the electronic components are in a separate cabinet, site the cabinet to allow the most work surface and the least clutter of cables—not an easy pair of requirements to meet.

The Printer

The printer is the only noisy part of a CP/M system. In following chapters we'll assume you can see and hear the printer from the terminal, but that isn't really necessary. The cable between printer and processor may be several yards long. Consider getting a long cable so you can move the printer into a closet or behind a couch, anywhere that will reduce the noise level. Acoustic hoods are available for typewriter printers, and they work very well. A cardboard box lined with old blankets will do a pretty good job as well; paint it a tasteful IBM blue and nobody will ever guess.

PLANNING FOR DISASTER

A computer that is doing its job soon becomes essential to the business that employs it. Such a business, whether in the home of a lone entrepreneur or one department of a large company, must take steps to protect against the loss of the machine or its data.

File Backup

Backup is the term for making extra copies of important files. File storage media are fragile. Files can be made unreadable by very simple, common accidents; they can be erased by careless operation. You should know what the important files are and be aware of the impact that their loss would have. If the diskette containing Accounts Receivable was stepped on today, how long would it take to recreate it?

It's a good idea to keep two levels of backup for really important files. The most recent copy can be kept near the computer, ready for a quick recovery. The generation before that ought to be moved right out of the building. Then if a fire wipes out the office, the older backup copy will still be safe.

It's easy to make backup copies of files with CP/M; we'll go over the techniques in Chapter 8. Your concern as the manager of the system is to set a reasonable backup schedule for the important files and see that it is followed.

Insurance

The subject of insurance is a complicated one. The options open to you depend on your situation and your locality. They should be discussed with your insurance broker. This section sketches some of the possibilities.

Insuring the Hardware. Most small businesses carry a business insurance package covering them for both liability and for the loss of office equipment. When a CP/M system is installed, it probably increases the value of the equipment in the office severalfold, thus making the present policy's coverage inadequate. Once the computer becomes a part of your business, it will be the very first thing you would want to replace after a fire or a flood (or, in California, an earthquake, for which a special endorsement is needed). A computer-using business ought to insure its hardware for full replacement value.

Most business policies do not cover losses that occur off the premises. Photographers and others who carry valuable equipment out to a job can buy an off-premises rider for their business policies. A computer might need the same type of coverage. Without it, a computer that is taken home for the weekend, or one on its way to a business show, might be completely unprotected.

Insurance at Home. Many CP/M systems are used in private homes. If you are self-employed, the business equipment you keep at home is probably not covered by the usual "unscheduled personal property" clause of your home insurance policy. Most home insurance policies do not cover equipment used for business at all! A special endorsement must be purchased to cover the equipment in your home office. You may find that your insurance company has a limit on such endorsements that was designed to cover typewriters and file cabinets, not multithousand-dollar computers.

Insuring the Data. You can purchase a valuable papers rider for your business policy. Such a rider is intended to cover the cost of recreating important records, and it can be written to cover records kept in computer storage as well as ordinary documents. Valuable papers insurance can be expensive, because it is written on the assumption that only one copy of the insured documents exists. However, such insurance can be purchased for any amount you desire. If you make weekly backup copies of critical files, you may want to carry valuable papers coverage only in the amount needed to cover the cost of recreating one week's data. With these data covered, and with second-level backup copies stored off the premises, you can feel quite secure.

DATA SECURITY

Data security is the term used to describe all the techniques used to keep the content of files secure from theft, fraudulent alteration, or unauthorized access. In one sense there is no such thing as a computer crime; all the crimes so reported are just cases of fraud or theft or embezzlement, no different from the same crimes committed in any other way. Computers don't allow new crimes to be invented, but they do permit the old crimes to be carried out in new, and sometimes easier, ways.

Planning for Security

Creative Paranoia. Look at your CP/M machine and, for a moment, try to think like a crook. Given unlimited access to the machine—and it's the nature and greatest blessing of small systems that one may have unlimited access to them—what could you steal without detection? Could you generate a phony purchase order, disburse the amount, and hide the transaction? Are there project disks that would be worth a price to one of your competitors? Given the ease of duplicating files, how hard would it be to keep two sets of books?

CP/M Lacks Security. After that exercise in creative paranoia, it won't reassure you to learn that CP/M offers you no software help in securing your files. In CP/M 1, CP/M 2, and MP/M 1 any user can look at, copy, alter, or destroy any file. Data security in a CP/M 2 system is entirely a matter of procedures and policies that are applied by people.

Security in MP/M 2. Among the improvements in MP/M 2 are some provisions for data security. Its new file system allows you to give a *password* to any file. A password is a word that must be specified before the system will allow the file to be accessed. A file can be set so that its password will be checked when the file is to be read, or when it is to be written, or only when it is to be erased. You can add a measure of security by giving read passwords to sensitive files and erase passwords to valuable ones.

Even if you have MP/M 2 and use passwords, you should not assume that your files are secure. A person seriously bent on mischief will have no difficulty in discovering a file's password. The password must be typed as part of any command that uses the file, so a bit of unobtrusive peeping over the operator's shoulder will reveal it. A clever programmer can circumvent the file system and read the disk directly, bypassing all the checks.

Treat Diskettes as Paper. Remember that computers don't create new kinds of crime, only new opportunities. Data security is a matter of controlling those opportunities so that the level of risk is no worse than it was in the paper system the machine replaced. One way to do this is to treat data and diskettes exactly as you would treat the same information if it were on paper. If simply locking the office door at night would be security enough for the paper, then it's security enough for the data. If papers with that information would be locked in your desk or in a safe, then do the same with the diskettes.

There might be papers—personnel information, say—that ought to be seen by only a few people. If such information is on diskette, that diskette should be handled as the paper file would be: kept under the personal control of the person responsible for it. This is one area in which categorizing diskettes by their use (see Chapter 8) pays off.

Security with a Hard Disk. The use of a hard disk interferes with this scheme because the data can't be carried away from the machine and so remain accessible to any user. Security may be achieved by carrying away on diskette something that is essential to viewing the data. If the data are encrypted (encryption programs can be bought for CP/M), the decrypting program can be kept on diskette in the control of one person. Or perhaps the programs that access the data can be kept on diskette; the trouble of locating and modifying a file without the aid of the program that built it might be deterrent enough.

Computer Crimes

The great opportunity that a computer affords to a criminal is the ease with which data can be copied. A diskette can be duplicated in minutes; it might take hours to copy the same data on paper. Equally important, a copy of a computer file is indistinguishable from the original. One can imagine a dishonest bookkeeper who has a CP/M system at home. It would be easy to duplicate an office diskette, take the copy home where the files could be "cooked" in safety, and substitute the copy for the legitimate diskette next day. Backup copies are potentially more valuable to a thief than are the originals. They can be borrowed for an extended period without being missed.

As the proprietor of a CP/M system your only defenses against such capers are to enforce sensible precautions concerning the handling of diskettes, to choose your employees carefully and pay them well, and to keep a constant watch, sharpened by the exercise of creative paranoia, for signs of incipient wrongdoing.

Chapter 5

Common Commands

This chapter introduces the most common CP/M commands, the ones that all users need every day. Anyone new to CP/M should read it, although if you are used to working with computers you may find parts of it elementary.

This chapter is meant to be read while you are near the machine. The presentation assumes that you'll go to the keyboard and try out the examples as you encounter them. If you work the examples, you will be teaching not only your mind but your fingers and eyes; you'll remember the material much better, and boost your confidence in yourself and the system as well.

LEARNING THE KEYBOARD

If you aren't familiar with the keyboard of your terminal, look at it now. If, despite our recommendation, you aren't near your machine, look at Figure 5-1, and compare it with your own keyboard soon.

Important Keys. Locate the following keys:

the alphabetic keys
the numeric keys
the spacebar
the tab key
the backspace key
the shift keys
the linefeed key
the return key

FIGURE 5-1
A typical terminal keyboard, with the control, backspace, and return keys in the usual locations.

If you've never used this terminal before, have someone disconnect it from the processor ("take it off-line") and then try all the keys out. Remember to reconnect it ("put it on-line") afterward.

THE RETURN KEY. That last key, return, is an important one. It is used to end all commands. The system won't do anything about what you've typed until you indicate that you are done typing with a return. On a few terminals the return key is marked "enter." At least one terminal has both a "return" and an "enter"; if that's the case, ignore "enter" and use "return."

RETURN KEY IN EXAMPLES. In the examples you'll see later, each separate line is to be ended with a press of the return key, unless you're explicitly told otherwise. Sometimes a line in an example consists of nothing but a press of the return key. Rather than risk confusing the printer (and the reader) with blank lines, we'll indicate that the return key should be pressed at that point by writing *return*. That means "press the return key and nothing else at this point."

THE CONTROL KEY. Locate one more key, the control key. It is marked with some abbreviation of the word control: "ctl," "ctrl," or the like (one make of terminal marks it "alt"). The control key is like a shift key in that it gives different values to the alphabetic keys. As with a shift key, you hold it down while pressing another key. The value that results is not printable, but CP/M has a way of showing what control letter was typed.

DISPLAY OF CONTROL LETTERS. Since the control letters aren't really printable, special action must be taken to show on the screen that one was typed. In many cases CP/M will display a control letter using the "ˆX" convention: an up-arrow (↑) or circumflex (ˆ), whichever one your terminal uses, followed by the letter for that key. Thus when you type control-z, CP/M might show ˆZ on the screen.

CONTROL LETTERS IN EXAMPLES. CP/M makes heavy use of the control letters as signals. When referring to a control letter in the text we'll say, for instance, "control-p". When in an example you should use a control-letter as a signal, you'll see this: ˆP. That means "at this point, hold control down and press P".

INITIALIZING CP/M

The First Time

Computer fans say "bringing up the system" to refer to the whole process of turning the machinery on and getting it ready for use. It's hard to give instructions for bringing up CP/M when the hardware comes in so many arrangements. Presumably you've seen your dealer do it; it isn't hard. There are just two things you need to know about the machine, other than how to turn on the power.

FIND THE A-DRIVE. The first thing to know is: Which diskette drive is the A-drive? The A-drive is the drive from which the hardware will attempt to load the CP/M Monitor (the part of CP/M always resident in working storage). Your drives ought to be labeled "A" and "B" (and "C". . . how many have you?). If they aren't marked, you'll have to find out which is which from someone who knows (then label them).

Find the Reset Control. The second thing you need to know is the location of the *reset*. This is usually a push button or a key. It may be located in an awkward place on the back of the processor cabinet. When the reset signal is given, the hardware is completely reset to its initial state. Then the disk hardware automatically selects the A-drive and tries to load the Monitor into working storage. This is called *bootstrap load*, or simply *boot*.

Practice Diskettes. Once you've found reset and the A-drive, obtain two diskettes with files on them. The files should not be important ones; if they are important you might be overcautious when experimenting with commands. Have copies made of two diskettes and use the copies. Be sure to have the diskettes made *bootable*. That means that there is a copy of the Monitor on each, for the hardware to load upon reset.

Turn the system on, put a practice diskette in the A-drive, and reset. The A-drive will be selected, and a moment later a message will appear on the screen. This *sign-on* message describes your version of CP/M (as in Example 5-1). It states the size of working storage and the version number of CP/M. The examples in this book were taken from CP/M version 2.2. Your system may use a different version (see "Versions of CP/M" in Chapter 3).

The CCP Prompt. Below the CP/M message will appear a prompt from the Console Command Processor, or CCP. Most programs that read from the keyboard issue a *prompt*; that is, a short message indicating that they are ready for you to type. The CCP uses "A>" as a prompt.

Initializing with Reset

The Effect of Reset. Reset completely refreshes the state of both hardware and software. It halts all activity in the system instantly. Then it causes the disk I/O interface circuits to load a copy of the first sector of the first track of the diskette in the A-drive into working storage.

Those data ought to be a small machine-language program that contains the logic

EXAMPLE 5-1
A typical CP/M logon message, displayed at the end of a cold start operation, contains both the size of working storage and the version number of CP/M.

```
64K CP/M vers 2.2
A>_
```

needed to load the rest of the Monitor. The Monitor program's instructions occupy the rest of the first few tracks of the diskette.

Bootstrap. The one-sector program loaded by the hardware is called a *bootstrap loader*, after the old saying "to lift yourself by your own bootstraps." The loader is the bootstrap by which the system loads itself. From that name has come the use of "bootstrap" to mean the process of initializing the resident part of an operating system. If you are asked to "boot the system," that means to "press the reset button."

Cold Start. The bootstrap provided by reset refreshes all of the Monitor, and has come to be called a *cold start* (or even a "cold boot") because afterward the system starts out cold, from the beginning.

Hazards of Reset. Reset is not to be used lightly! It can be used to get the system going after a hang-up of some kind, and it can be a very convenient panic button. But think before you use it. Any program executing will have to be run again from scratch. If a disk drive is selected and writing at the moment you reset, the data being written will be scrambled. If the data are the file directory, files may be lost. You should use reset either when nothing is going on in the system, or when the system is irretrievably fouled up.

Initializing with Control-c

A partial bootstrap can be obtained almost any time by entering a control-c at the keyboard (hold the control key and type "c"—see the section on "Learning the Keyboard"). This is called a *warm start* (or, heaven help us, a "warm boot"). It causes a reset of the software by the software. A warm start does not reset the hardware, so it cannot cause bad data to be written to disk. It does end any running program. It causes the Monitor to be reloaded from the A-drive, in case the storage copy of it had been damaged.

Because it is less severe, a warm start with control-c is to be preferred to a cold start with reset. Use the latter only when the system doesn't react to the former.

THE COMMAND PROCESS

Let's repeat some information from Chapter 3. Whenever your CP/M system is idling between jobs, it is under control of the Console Command Processor (CCP). The CCP is waiting for a command to be typed by you. You type the command using certain aids we'll describe shortly, and you signal that it is complete by pressing return.

Form of a Command. The form of command accepted by CCP is:

```
verb operands
```

where the verb is separated from the operands (and the operands from each other) by spaces. Here is an example command:

```
stat beesabig.bug
```

The verb is stat and the only operand is beesabig.bug.

THE COMMAND PROCESS. When the CCP receives the command it assumes that the verb is the name of a program. The CCP locates a program file of that name, loads (copies) it into working storage, and calls the program. The CCP leaves the operands of the command in a known location in working storage for the command program to find.

The command program performs whatever work it is meant to do, short and simple or long and complicated. When the program is done it returns control of the machine to the CCP. The CCP then waits for another command from you.

COMMAND = PROGRAM = FILE. This is CP/M's command process: wait for a command, load the program named by its verb, call the program, wait again. The process is repeated each time you enter a command. A program, of course, is also a file—a file of machine-language instructions. So, in CP/M, a command is a program is a file.

There's one exception to this. There are a few commands that are used so frequently that they have been incorporated into the CCP. This saves the time of loading them from disk. Except that they needn't be loaded, the process of calling these commands is the same. You'll be able to identify these resident commands in two ways. They respond instantly, whereas ordinary commands take a second to load. And you won't be able to see their names in a file directory.

CCP COMMENTS. If the line you type begins with a semicolon (;), the CCP ignores that whole line. This gives you a way of making notes on the screen as you go. We'll find a use for comment lines at the end of the chapter.

Typing Commands

YOUR FIRST COMMAND. Get your system initialized and ready for a command. CP/M is ready for a command when the CCP is in control and waiting; this is signaled by the appearance of the prompt A> at the left margin of the screen.

Type the command

```
dir
```

remembering to end it with return. The DIR command is absolutely safe; there is no way you can hurt the system with it. CP/M will make one of two responses. Either it will reply NO FILE as in Example 5-2a or it will reply with a list of names in four columns similar to Example 5-2b. A CP/M 1.4 system will respond with NO FILE or with a single

EXAMPLE 5-2
Responses of the DIR command, first when there are no files on the diskette and, second, a display of files on a typical diskette.

```
A>dir
NO FILE
A>_


A>dir
A: STAT     COM : SYSGEN   COM : CCSINIT  COM : DDT      COM
A: ED       COM : LOAD     COM : ASM      COM : SUBMIT   COM
A: DUMP     ASM : TESTIT   BAS : XSUB     COM
A>_
```

column of names. Anything else indicates that you misspelled the command verb, which doesn't seem likely. If you got the NO FILE response, then the diskette in your A-drive has no files on it; obtain a better practice diskette.

Response to Unknown Commands. Now pretend to make an error while typing dir. Type

door

(and return). It is very unlikely that your diskette has a command program named "door" on it, so the response should be as shown in Example 5-3. This is the normal CCP response when it can't find a command program to match your verb. The CCP caused the Monitor to search the directory of the diskette, looking for a program named "door." There was none. That being the case, the CCP gave you its equivalent of "Huh?," which is to repeat the command verb with a question mark after it.

Correcting with Control-x. Now pretend again to make a typing error, but this time catch the error before pressing return. Type

dirivel

and DO NOT press return. Instead, type control-x (that's typing the x key while holding

EXAMPLE 5-3
When given a command verb for which it can find no matching command file, the CCP responds with the verb and a question mark.

```
A>door
DOOR?
A>_
```

down the control key, remember?). The command disappears from the screen! Control-x is a start-over signal to the CCP. When CCP gets the control-x it erases everything typed so far and both you and the CCP start over. Use control-x anytime you've fouled up a command line and want to start over.

Correcting with Control-u. Try that again. Type

    dirigible

and DO NOT press return. Instead type control-u. That has the same effect as control-x, except that the old command line, the one you're giving up on, remains on the screen so that you can refer to it if you want to. The result will resemble Example 5-4.

Correcting with Backspace. Once more let's pretend that you are having trouble typing dir. Type

    direemee

and DO NOT press return. Instead, use the backspace key. (If your terminal lacks a backspace key, then use control-h for now; later, file a strong protest with the person who bought a terminal without a backspace.) You'll notice that each time you press backspace (or control-h), the rightmost letter vanishes and the cursor backs up. Backspace is invaluable; whenever you feel yourself making a typo just back up and type again.

Uppercase and Lowercase

You may type CP/M commands in uppercase, lowercase, or a mixture of the two, as you please. The CCP will convert everything you type in the command line to uppercase. When you typed "door" the error message that came back was DOOR? because the CCP had turned it into uppercase.

Since the CCP doesn't care, you might like to enter all commands in lowercase. That's how we'll show them in examples. Your command lines will stand out from the system's uppercase responses.

Not all programs are as forgiving as the CCP, although all of them ought to be. All

EXAMPLE 5-4
Result of using control-u to cancel a command line. The line remains on the screen for reference, but user and CPP start over.

```
A>dirigible#
  darn it#
  dir_
```

CP/M system programs accept lowercase and treat it as uppercase (except for ED; see Chapter 7), but some application programs may not. If you are running an application program and get unexpected results, try giving it input in uppercase.

INTRODUCING THE FILE SYSTEM

Everything that CP/M does revolves around files and the file system. Most commands work on files and the majority of command operands are names of files.

Filerefs: Naming Files

Because files are so important, it isn't surprising that CP/M has a carefully defined system for naming files. The names of files must be typed according to a set of rules. You may write a file's name on paper, or carry it in your mind, in any form you like. To name a file in a command you must use the CP/M format. When we want to talk about the full name of a file in the CPM format we'll use the term *fileref.*

A fileref has three parts: a drivecode, a filename, and a filetype (Figure 5-2).

The Drivecode. The drivecode is a single letter between A and P inclusive, followed by a colon. CP/M provides for up to 16 disk drives, and names them A: through P:. The drivecode specifies the disk drive on which the file is currently to be found. When a command calls for a file as input, and that file's drivecode says the file is on B:, then it is on the B-drive that CP/M will look for the file. The directory of the diskette in the B-drive will be searched for the file, and the file's contents will be read from the B-drive.

The Default Drivecode. The drivecode may be omitted from a fileref; when it is, the CCP supplies one. The drivecode that will be supplied is the letter that appears in the CCP's prompt. Immediately after a cold start the prompt is A> and the default drivecode is A:. A: will be put at the head of any fileref where you don't put a drivecode yourself.

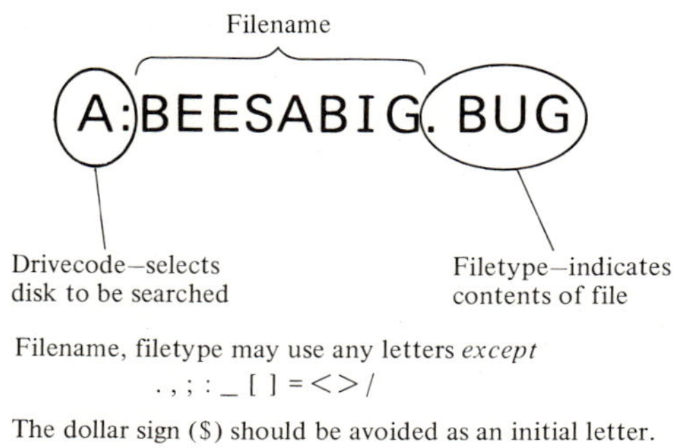

FIGURE 5-2
The parts of a fileref: optional drivecode, filename, optional filetype.

The Filename. The second part of a fileref is the actual name of the file. The filename is a group of from one to eight characters. Most files are given names that are spellable, pronounceable words, such as MYFILE, PAYROLL, or FRED. You are not required to be so prosaic, if you don't want to be. Any printable characters except those shown in Figure 5-2 may be used in a fileref. This lets you give files names like BY+BY, YES&NO, or %OFGROSS. Used carefully, this can be an aid to the memory.

The Filetype. The third part of a fileref is a filetype of one to three characters. This is a short secondary name separated from the filename by a period. The filetype may be anything you choose. It may even be three spaces, that is, omitted entirely. Its letters may be any you wish, except for those listed in Figure 5-2. Certain filetypes are given by convention to certain kinds of files. This convention lets you separate files by the type of their contents.

Table 5-1 shows the filetypes in common use. The only one you should note now is the .COM filetype. This is the conventional filetype for files that contain machine-language programs. .COM stands for command. A .COM file contains a command program, that is, a machine-language program ready to be loaded as a command by the CCP.

When the CCP receives a command, it takes the verb and appends .COM to it. Then

TABLE 5-1
The more important conventional filetypes. Any application package will have its own conventions.

Filetype	Conventional Use
.ASC	Source text of a BASIC program
.ASM	Source text of an assembly language program
.BAK	Original version of an edited file
.BAS	Source text of a BASIC program
.COB	Source text of a COBOL program
.COM	Machine language COMmand, ready to execute
.FOR	Source text of a FORTRAN program
.HEX	Machine-language program in symbolic (hexadecimal characters) form
.INT	Intermediate code produced by CBASIC compiler
.LIB	Collection of source code for inclusion with the MACLIB directive of MAC; collection of relocatable subroutines for linking with LIB.
.LST	File intended for printing
.PAS	Source text of a Pascal program
.PLI	Source text of a PL/I program
.PRN	File intended for printing
.REL	Machine-language program in relocatable form
.SUB	File of commands intended as input to SUBMIT
.SYM	Symbol information written by MAC assembler
.$$$	Temporary file, used by PIP and most editors as the type of the work file

it searches the diskette directory for a file named *verb*.COM, whatever the verb may be. That is the program that the CCP loads and calls, the program that by its logic defines the meaning and effect of the command.

Introducing DIR

The DIR command lists the names of files in a diskette directory. The form of the command is

DIR *fileref*

If the fileref is omitted, DIR lists all files. Example 5-2 shows a sample of its output. Run it again now:

```
dir
```

DIR lists as many as four files on each line it writes. At the left of the line is the drivecode, then comes a filename and a filetype for one file. A colon follows as a divider, then the name and type of the second file, and so on. Compare the response you got with that in Example 5-2. You probably have some of the same files, and some different ones.

DIR will accept an operand consisting of a fileref. Try this:

```
dir a:beesabig.bug
```

The response is probably NO FILE, meaning that the command could find no file with that fileref. Use this form of DIR to find out if a particular file is available without having to scan the whole list.

Ambiguous and Explicit Filerefs

A word that is ambiguous is one that can mean more than one thing. An ambiguous fileref is a fileref that can apply to more than one file. Ambiguous filerefs are very useful, as they provide a way of recalling groups of related files. Some commands allow ambiguous filerefs, whereas others will only work with explicit filerefs, those that apply to only a single file.

THE * REFERENCE. You may substitute an asterisk (*) for either the filename or the filetype (but not for the drivecode) in a fileref. The asterisk means "any." The fileref *.COM means "any file whose type is .COM." The fileref BEESABIG.* means "any file whose name is BEESABIG." The asterisk may be used following other letters. For example, the fileref BEES*.* means "all files whose names begin with BEES..., with any type." Any file whose filename began with BEES would match that reference.

The ? Reference. The question mark (?) can be used in a fileref. When it is used, it means "any single character." The question mark allows you to refer to any group of filerefs that are the same except for one or a few characters. The reference BEE?ABIG.* would match files with names of BEEDABIG, BEEZABIG, BEERABIG, and so forth.

More than one question mark can be used. The fileref ????????.* is the same as *.*; either reference would match files with any name and type. The reference ????.*, however, refers only to files whose names are one, two, three, or four characters long. Longer names wouldn't match.

DIR with Ambiguous Filerefs

The full power of the DIR command becomes clear when you understand the use of ambiguous filerefs. Try

```
dir *.com
```

to list all the commands on your diskette. Then try

```
dir
dir *.*
```

to verify that *.* refers to any name and type.

Exercise the DIR command as much as you can using the files on your diskette. Look at Table 5-2 for ideas.

Using Drivecodes

The CCP prompts you with the name of a drive, and that drivecode is the default; it will be used whenever you omit a drivecode. So far you've only used the A-drive and have had no need of a drivecode. Now get your second diskette and put it into the B-drive. Then do

```
dir b:
```

and DIR will list all the files on that diskette (you could have used dir b:*.*, but DIR assumes "all files" in either case). Compare the result of

```
dir b:*.com
```

with the result of


```
dir a:*.com
```

TABLE 5-2
Some of the many uses of ambiguous filerefs.

Fileref	Will Match
.	All files
q*.*	Any file with name commencing with a Q, from Q alone through QUIETLY.BAS to QZZZZZZZ.ZZZ
wa*.com	Any file of type .COM commencing with WA, such as WASH.COM, WANT.COM, or WAVERLEY.COM
wilt.p*	Any file named WILT with a type beginning P, such as WILT.PLI, WILT.PRN, WILT.PRL, etc.
q.	All files—characters after an asterisk are ignored, so this is equivalent to *.*
wan?	Files with a filetype of three spaces and names of four letters beginning with WAN—WANT, WAND, etc.
w?n?.*	Any file with first letter W, third letter N, total of four letters, any filetype. WANT, WINS.SUB, WONT.GO, but not WINCE.BAS—five-letter names won't match
???????y.*	Eight-letter names ending in Y, any filetype—SUDDENLY.BOO, WAVERLEY.COM
???????.??	File names not exceeding seven letters; types not exceeding two letters.

Drivecodes with Verbs. Think about this problem: When you give a command the CCP searches for a file named *verb*.COM (commands are programs are files!). On what drive does the CCP search? It searches the default drive, the one named in the prompt. In fact, since a command verb is just a filename, the CCP supplies a default drivecode for *verb*.COM exactly as it does for any fileref. If the CCP's prompt is A>, then when it needs to load a command the CCP will search for A:*verb*.COM.

Given that idea—that the CCP supplies a drivecode for the verb just as it does for any other file—think about this: If there were a program named FRED that you wanted to use as a command, and it was on the B-drive, how would you call it? One answer is to move the diskette to the A-drive. A much better answer is to use a drivecode on the command verb, as in b:fred operands. That would cause the CCP to search for B:FRED.COM, which is exactly what is wanted.

With drivecodes you can call a command from the B-disk, giving it as operands a fileref on the A-disk and another on the C-disk, as

```
b:fred a:beesabig.bug c:again.sam.
```

Invalid Drivecodes. If you specify the drivecode of a drive that doesn't exist in your system, CP/M will report an error. Try it now; it won't hurt anything. Find a drive code letter that your system doesn't have (P: is a good bet) and use it:

```
p:fred are you there?
```

The response should resemble Example 5-5. The Monitor tried to select drive P: in order to search its directory for P:FRED.COM. Since there was no drive P: available, an error occurred; the Bdos Err on P: Select message is its way of telling you.

It waits for any input and then performs a warm start. Press the return key. The same message appears again! The CCP is bent on moving to drive P: come hell or high water. Use reset for a cold start; that'll fix things up.

The Drivecode Command

Usually the programs and files that you use during a work session are all together on one diskette. It's handy to make that diskette the default drive. But it isn't always convenient to put that diskette in the A-drive.

The solution is to make some other drive be the default. This is done by giving CCP a command that consists only of a drivecode. Try it now:

```
b:
```

Yes, the command is just the drivecode b: all alone. The next prompt should be B> indicating that the default drivecode is now B:. Try it a few times and verify that the current default drive, named in the prompt, is really supplied on filerefs:

```
dir a:
a:
dir
dir b:
b:
dir
```

When you do a cold start with reset the default drive is set to A:. When you do a warm start with control-c, the default drive remains as it was last set.

Selecting an Empty Drive. If you ask the Monitor to use a drive that is currently empty—by giving a b: drivecode command before you put a diskette in the B-drive, for example, you will probably receive a different error message. Most systems will continue normally if you then insert the diskette and return. If that doesn't wake the system up, do a cold start with reset.

EXAMPLE 5-5
The result of selecting a nonexistent disk drive. Responding with return repeats the problem; a cold start clears it.

```
A>p:
Bdos Err On P: Select
Bdos Err On P: Select

64K CP/M vers 2.2
A>_
```

The STAT Command for File Information

DIR only lists the names of files. STAT gives more information about them. STAT has other functions as well, but for file information the form of the command is

STAT *fileref*

Try it now:

stat *.com

(If you get a response of STAT?, use DIR to find STAT.COM, and use a drivecode command to switch to the disk where it is. If you can't find it, get a diskette that has a copy, load it into the A-drive, and do a control-c warm start.)

The STAT File Report. STAT produces output like that in Example 5-6. It tells you five things about each file that matches the fileref. On the right it gives the explicit fileref, drivecode and all. To the left of that it indicates whether the file may be changed ("R/W" for read-write) or is protected against changes ("R/O" for read-only). In the center under the heading "bytes" it tells the size of the file as a number of kilobytes. The remaining two columns relate to the way that CP/M allocates disk space; this is explored in Chapter 9.

Note that STAT lists the files in alphabetical order. It is the only CP/M command to do so. We'll see later how to use STAT as a convenient way to make a printed record of the contents of a diskette.

STAT for Available Space. STAT can also be used with only a drivecode. In that event it reports on the status of the entire diskette. Try it:

stat a:
stat b:

EXAMPLE 5-6
The result of stat *.com on a typical diskette.

```
A>stat *.com

 Recs  Bytes  Ext Acc
   38     6k    1 R/W A:DDT.COM
    5     2k    1 R/W A:DUMP.COM
   52     8k    1 R/W A:ED.COM
   98    14k    1 R/W A:EDIT.COM
   14     2k    1 R/W A:LOAD.COM
   92    12k    1 R/W A:MAC.COM
  190    24k    2 R/W A:MBASIC.COM
   58     8k    1 R/W A:PIP.COM
  142    18k    2 R/W A:PRINT.COM
   41     6k    1 R/W A:STAT.COM
   10     2k    1 R/W A:SUBMIT.COM
    6     2k    1 R/W A:XSUB.COM
Bytes Remaining on A: 312k

A>_
```

The result should resemble Example 5-7. You are told how many bytes are available for new or expanded files. (If you are using MP/M 2, try the command show space for a similar result.)

STAT FOR DISK STATUS. STAT with no operand reports on all disks that have been used since CP/M was last initialized. Try that:

```
stat
```

This report not only tells you the remaining space but also gives the access state of the disks, that is, whether they can be modified (R/W) or only used for input (R/O). At present your disks should be R/W.

The REN Command to Rename Files

The REN (rename) command changes the name of a file without changing anything else about it. Before trying it out, though, let's create a file that you won't mind losing. We'll make a copy of an existing file, giving it another name. STAT.COM is a small file, so let's copy it. Do this:

```
pip 2bits.com=stat.com
```

The PIP command is described at length in Chapter 6. It makes copies of files. In this case it should have made a copy of STAT.COM and given the copy the name 2BITS.COM. Did it?

```
dir stat.*
dir 2bits.*
stat stat.*
stat 2bits.*
```

EXAMPLE 5-7
The result of STAT for diskette information with typical diskettes.

```
A>stat a:

Bytes Remaining On A: 480k

A>stat b:

Bytes Remaining on B: 142k

A>stat
A: R/W, Space: 480k
B: R/W, Space: 142k

A>_
```

Form of the REN Command. The REN command has the form:

REN *newfileref=oldfileref*

It locates the directory entry for oldfileref and alters it so that the same directory entry is now found under the name newfileref. The contents of a directory entry describe the location of that file's data on the diskette. Since REN doesn't change them, the contents of the file remain the same. Only its name changes. Try it:

```
dir 2bits.*
ren 4bits.com=2bits.com
dir 2bits.*
dir 4bits.*
```

The file that was named 2BITS.COM is now named 4BITS.COM. No other change has taken place.

REN Errors. REN will refuse to work if there is already a file with a name identical to the new fileref. Try it and see:

```
ren stat.com=4bits.com
```

There is already a file STAT.COM, so that can't become the name of another file.

REN also refuses to work if the old fileref doesn't exist. Prove it:

```
ren anewref=notthere
```

There is no file NOTTHERE so REN can't rename it.

Use REN to change 4BITS.COM to SIXBITS.COM, and finally to ADOLLAR.COM (that's inflation!).

The ERA Command to Erase Files

The ERA command removes a file's entry from the directory. It makes the diskette space that was occupied by that file available for use. These actions of ERA can't be revoked! Once erased, the file is gone for good (here's a mnemonic: an ERAsed file is ERAtrievable).

Form of the ERA Command. The form of the ERA command is

ERA *fileref*

where *fileref* may be ambiguous. Let's erase the file ADOLLAR.COM that we built with REN. Before doing so, check its size and the space on the diskette:

```
stat adollar.com
```

Then erase ADOLLAR and check the results:

era adollar.com
stat adollar.*

Your results should resemble Example 5-8. ADOLLAR.COM is gone, and the space that it occupied has been added to the pool of space on the disk.

ERA for Multiple Files. ERA has the ability to erase several files at once. If the fileref given ERA is ambiguous, it will erase all files whose names match the fileref. This is a useful, but potentially dangerous, feature. The best way to tame it is to remember that ERA will erase exactly the files that STAT displays when given the same operand. If STAT with some fileref displays exactly and only the names of files you want to erase, then ERA with the same fileref will erase just those files. We will make use of ERA with an ambiguous fileref later.

Protecting Disks

STAT for Disk Protection. STAT can be used to protect a diskette temporarily against accidental change. To protect a diskette use the form

STAT *drivecode*=R/O

where the drivecode names one of your disk drives, such as A:. Try it now:

stat a:=r/o
stat

EXAMPLE 5-8
When a file is erased, the space it occupied is made available; this shows as an increase in the space reported by STAT.

```
A>stat adollar.*

 Recs  Bytes  Ext Acc
   41     6k    1 R/W A:ADOLLAR.COM
Bytes Remaining on A: 202k

A>era adollar.com
A>stat adollar.com

File Not Found
A>stat
A: R/W, Space: 208k

A>_
```

The display from STAT shows that the A drive has been marked read-only. Any attempt to modify that diskette will produce an error message. This protection is temporary. It lasts only until the next warm start. See for yourself:

```
^C
stat
```

The A-drive is no longer read-only. Protect it again, and try to modify the diskette:

```
stat a:=r/o
ren noway.com=stat.com
```

That should produce BDOS Err on A: R/O. No prompt appears. What now? Just press return. The system will do a warm start, just as if you'd done control-c. Check with DIR; the rename was not done. (In MP/M 2 you may use either STAT or SET; set a:=r/o and stat a:=r/o have the same effect.)

Changed Diskettes Are R/O. If CP/M discovers that you've changed diskettes, it makes the changed diskette read-only. The Monitor takes this precaution because in some cases, if you changed diskettes while a program was running, the program might write in the wrong area of the new diskette. To see it happen you have to change diskettes. First check the status of the A-drive:

```
stat a:
```

Then remove the diskettes from both drives. Put the diskette that was in B: into the A-drive. Make the Monitor look at it, then check its status:

```
dir a:
stat a:
```

It should now be read-only. Put the diskettes back as they were and do a warm start with control-c.

R/O Protection Is Temporary. Disk protection is only temporary. It is done by setting a flag in one of the Monitor's variables. That flag is cleared on a warm start. Most application programs cause a warm start when they end. Therefore, making a diskette read-only usually protects the diskette only for a single command. Still, it is worthwile to protect diskettes while testing a new or unknown program. Permanent protection comes from the write-protect notch in the diskette jacket. Exposing the notch in the jacket of an 8-inch diskette, or covering the notch of a 5-inch diskette, makes it impossible to write on the diskette regardless of its status.

STAT to Change File Status

The STAT command can alter two attributes that are contained in a file's directory entry. The first is the protection attribute, which prevents or allows alteration of the file. The second is the directory display attribute. This controls whether the file will be visible to DIR. The form of the STAT command that sets these attributes is

STAT *fileref* $*attribute*

File Protection. You can give individual files permanent read-only status. The status is recorded in the directory entry for the file. Since the status is recorded on disk with the file, it remains until you change it. In order to see it work, make a file and check its status:

```
pip protect.com=stat.com
stat protect.com
```

Then make the file read-only and verify its new status:

```
stat protect.com $r/o
stat protect.com
```

The response indicates that the file has been protected. Now try to erase or rename the file. The result is an error message BDOS Err on A: File R/O, followed by a warm start when you press return. Any program that tried to erase, rename, or write into this file would be terminated with the same message.

Read-only access can be applied to several files at once by giving STAT an ambiguous fileref. Set all the .COM files read-only:

```
stat *.com $r/o
```

STAT reports on each file as it marks the directory. This is a useful function. As you plan your diskette library (Chapter 8), think about what files ought to be read-only.

STAT will return any file to read-write access in a similar way. Enter

```
stat *.com $r/w
```

and watch the resulting output.

Directory Status. You can hide the names of files so that they don't appear in the output of DIR. This attribute is also set by STAT. Try it:

```
dir protect.com
stat protect.com $sys
dir protect.com
stat protect.com
```

DIR no longer lists the file, even though the file still exists. Note that DIR does not say NO FILE; it just doesn't list the entry. As you can see, when STAT described the file, it showed the name in parentheses to indicate that it had the SYS attribute. The SYS attribute can be removed, restoring the file to visibility, in this way:

```
stat protect.com $dir
dir protect.com
stat protect.com
```

This hiding of files has only one real use. By hiding the names of certain common files that are present on almost all diskettes, you simplify the display written by DIR. If there are many files on a diskette, it is easier to locate the ones of interest if the standard files don't appear.

Summary of STAT

All the variations of STAT appear in the Reference section of this book. Here is a summary of the ones we've looked at so far:

STAT	— disk status
STAT *drivecode* R/O	— protect a disk
STAT *drivecode* R/W	— make a disk alterable
STAT *fileref* $R/O	— make file read-only
STAT *fileref* $R/W	— make file alterable
STAT *fileref* $SYS	— hide file
STAT *fileref* $DIR	— reveal file

In MP/M 2 these functions are available in the SET and SHOW commands as well. If you have MP/M 2 you may prefer those commands to STAT simply because they have fewer forms.

DISPLAYING FILES

In this section you'll be displaying a file in several ways. You'll need a printable file in order to do so. We used a file named TEST.FIL in the examples; its contents are shown in Example 5-9. You could have someone use an editor to make you a file like that. Alternatively, you may use your knowledge of STAT and DIR to locate a small printable file on your practice diskette. Almost any file with a filetype other than .COM or .INT is printable. You want one that is no more than 4K bytes in length. Make a copy of this file under the name TEST.FIL:

```
pip test.fil=whatever-its-name-is
```

filling in the name of the file you found.

EXAMPLE 5-9
A simple test file suitable as a source for experimenting with PIP.

```
This is TEST.FIL line...01
This is TEST.FIL line...02
This is TEST.FIL line...03
This is TEST.FIL line...04
This is TEST.FIL line...05
This is TEST.FIL line...06
This is TEST.FIL line...07
This is TEST.FIL line...08
This is TEST.FIL line...09
This is TEST.FIL line...10
This is TEST.FIL line...11
This is TEST.FIL line...12
This is TEST.FIL line...13
This is TEST.FIL line...14
This is TEST.FIL line...15
This is TEST.FIL line...16
This is TEST.FIL line...17
This is TEST.FIL line...18
This is TEST.FIL line...19
This is TEST.FIL line...20
This is TEST.FIL line...21
This is TEST.FIL line...22
This is TEST.FIL line...23
This is TEST.FIL line...24
This is TEST.FIL line...25
```

The TYPE Command

This is the simplest utility and the one most often used. Its form is

TYPE *fileref*

where *fileref* must be explicit. TYPE gives you a quick look at the named file by typing it at the terminal. It's a very quick look indeed, if your terminal operates at 9600 bps or more; the data stream up the face of the tube faster than the eye can follow. Try it anyway, using your test file:

type test.fil

The contents of the file should flow past. If the file has no more than 22 lines, it will all fit on the screen; if it doesn't, some lines will have scrolled off the top of the screen.

Stopping Output with Control-s

CP/M provides a useful service through the control-s signal. When that character is received, output to the terminal halts and doesn't resume until a key (any key, including control-s) is pressed. This lets you halt the flow of output in order to read it. When you've seen enough, tap any key and let the data roll until you want to stop the flow again.

Enter the type test.fil command again, but don't press return yet. Rest your left pinky on the control-shift key. Rest your left forefinger lightly on the "s" key. Just a small dip of your hand will type control-s. Ready? Press return. See if you can halt the display of TEST.FIL before the first line scrolls out of sight. Give another tap of the "s" key to let output continue.

Control-s can be used to control screen output of most commands. You'll often find yourself controlling output this way, so practice using it a few times. Be sure that you do finally complete the display each time. You can tell it's done when the CCP prompt comes out. Control-s will halt most CP/M output. Try it with the output of STAT *.*.

If you're displaying a very long file and don't want to wait for it to end, type some character other than control-s; the TYPE command will stop instantly.

Console Copy with Control-p

When CP/M receives a control-p signal it begins to echo everything typed at the terminal to the printer. This is called *console copy* and is very handy for getting quick paper copies of files.

Try control-p now. First make sure that your printer is turned on and has paper in it. Then enter a control-p and press return several times. The CCP's prompts of A> should appear at both the terminal and the printer. If nothing happens at either device, then the printer isn't ready or isn't connected to the processor. Use reset to get going again and find out what's wrong. If the output appears at the terminal but not at the printer, or if the system still hangs after you've checked the printer over, then you probably have to make an I/O assignment. Read about assignments in the section on "Other I/O Devices" in the next chapter, and check with your vendor.

When console copy is on, the printer duplicates everything that appears on the screen. You turn console copy off with another control-p. Try it:

ˆP
return (no printer output)
return
ˆP
return (printer displays prompt)
return

You can hear the printer working as it duplicates the prompt.

Set console copy on if it isn't (you can tell by listening to the printer as you press return), then enter the command

```
type test.fil
```

which should display on both the screen and the printer.

Control-s with Control-p. Try it again, and stop the display with control-s. The printer will stop too, and resume again when the display does. The screen display stops the instant you press control-s, but the printer may not. Most printers have a buffer that holds characters until they can be printed. When you press control-s, the processor stops sending data to the printer, but the printer has a backlog of characters already received and not yet written. It doesn't stop printing until it has drained its buffer. At that point the last character printed ought to be the same as the last character typed on the screen.

Evidence of Handshaking. You may have noticed another effect of the interaction between processor and printer. The display, instead of flowing smoothly up the screen, may move, pause, and move again. This is visible evidence of the interaction (called *handshaking*) between processor and printer. When the printer's buffer is nearly full, it signals the processor. The processor waits for a second signal from the printer, indicating that it has nearly caught up, before sending more data. This explains the pauses that occur at the screen while the printer runs full-tilt: the processor is waiting for the printer to catch up.

Avoid Printing "type...". You can avoid having the TYPE command appear at the top of your paper copy. Turn off console copy, then position your printer at the top of the form. Enter the full TYPE command, but before you press return, type a control-p. Then only file data will appear on the printer, except for the CCP prompt that follows the last line. Try it. First make sure console copy is off, then:

type test.fil^P *return*

Printing the File List. Control-p allows you to duplicate any terminal output on the printer. You'll think of many uses for it. Here is one that was promised earlier. Set the printer at the top of the form and then:

```
^P
; the files on my practice diskette as of (date)
stat *.*
^P
```

You've printed a detailed, alphabetical listing of the files on the A-drive diskette, headed by a comment line giving the date. Such a listing should be filed with any important diskette.

Chapter 6

PIP and I/O Devices

PIP and I/O Devices

In this chapter we'll learn the use of PIP, the most important utility command. The command's whole purpose is to move data from one "peripheral" (I/O device) to another. PIP's most frequent use is in moving files from one disk to another; this is what we'll look at first.

PIP can move data from and to devices other than disks. After discussing the way that CP/M names and controls those other devices, we'll practice using PIP to move data between the terminal, printer, and disk drives.

FORMS OF THE PIP COMMAND

The PIP command has two forms. The first is used when you want to call PIP to do a single transfer, then go on to other things:

PIP *destination=source* [*options*]

The format of *destination, source,* and [*options*] will be explained shortly. Use the second form when you want to make several transfers before leaving PIP. Call it by name with no operands and after it has been loaded it will prompt you with an asterisk. Then you may enter a transfer request in the form *destination=source* [*options*]. When that transfer is complete, PIP again prompts with an asterisk; you may continue in this way for as many transfers as you like. Enter return alone to end the command.

PIP FOR DISK FILES

The destination and source of a PIP transfer may be files. In that case the destination and source fields are simply filerefs.

Copying Single Files

Copying on a Single Drive. PIP will transfer files within a single diskette or between drives. We've used the simplest form of the transfer already. Let's do it again to duplicate our test file:

```
pip test2.fil=test.fil
```

This creates a new copy of the source TEST.FIL and names it TEST2.FIL. No options were used. The source in this transfer was TEST.FIL; the destination was TEST2.FIL.

Copying Between Drives. Now make another copy, on the other disk drive. If your A-drive is now active (the CCP prompt is A>), fine. If not, reverse the places of b: and a: in this command:

```
pip b:test.fil=a:test.fil
```

Now there's a file named TEST.FIL on both drives. Did you notice the sound, and possibly the blinking lights, as the processor selected first one drive and then the other? It's hard to miss, unless you're working from a hard-disk drive. If you aren't now working on the A-drive, move to it with a drivecode command so that you'll be in step with the examples.

SEVERAL TRANSFERS IN ONE COMMAND. Use the second form of the command to make several clones of TEST.FIL:

```
pip
t1.fil=test.fil
t2.fil=test.fil
t3.fil=test.fil
```
return

Use DIR and STAT to see what you've done:

```
dir t*.fil
stat t?.fil
```

Notice the usefulness of the question-mark file reference. In this case it lets you pick up only the files that were two characters long, omitting TEST.FIL and TEST2.FIL.

CONCATENATING FILES. There may be several sources in a PIP transfer. The source files are copied in order from left to right, and the destination contains all of their contents. Let's try that:

```
pip t9.fil=t1.fil,t2.fil,t3.fil
stat t?.fil
```

Don't be surprised if the numbers in the STAT display don't add up (as they don't in Example 6-1, for example). STAT reports sizes rounded up to a multiple of kilobytes.

EXAMPLE 6-1
There appear to be discrepancies in the size information when smaller files are merged into a larger one. The explanation lies in the way CP/M allocates storage.

```
A>pip t9.fil=t1.fil,t2.fil,t3.fil

A>stat t?.fil

 Recs  Bytes  Ext Acc
    6     2k    1 R/W A:T1.FIL
    6     2k    1 R/W A:T2.FIL
    6     2k    1 R/W A:T3.FIL
   17     4k    1 R/W A:T9.FIL
Bytes Remaining on A: 184k

A>_
```

The discrepancy in the numbers in the "recs" column has another explanation; we'll look at both of these effects in Chapter 10.

Shorthand Notation. When copying between disks, the source and destination usually differ only in their drivecodes. Since there's no need to type the same information twice, you may omit one of the filerefs, leaving only the drivecode:

```
pip b:=a:t1.fil
pip b:t2.fil=a:
```

Of course you may omit the default drivecode if you wish. The CCP will supply the default drivecode:

```
pip b:=t3.fil
```

Copying Groups of Files

PIP with Ambiguous Filerefs. PIP will accept ambiguous filerefs, but only in certain cases. Source and destination must have different drivecodes, and the complete ambiguous fileref may appear only on one side of the equal sign. You now have four test files with two-letter names. Here is how to move them all to the B-disk:

```
pip b:=a:t?.fil
```

When moving data from one disk to another it's best to be quite specific about drivecodes. It may not make any difference to the system, but you'll feel more comfortable knowing you've said exactly what you meant.

PIP will accept any kind of ambiguous fileref, including *.* meaning "copy everything." When creating groups of related files, plan the names of the files for easy grouping so that it will be easy to copy them, to erase them, and to display their names and status.

Stopping a Copy. PIP checks the terminal as it works. If you press any key, PIP will notice it, report ABORTED, and stop work. Try it now. Enter the command below. When the first transfer is under way, press any key ("X" for instance):

```
pip b:=a:test*.fil
```

After reporting that its work was "aborted" PIP ended, returning control to the CCP. Had you been using the second form of the command, like this:

```
pip
b:=a:test*.fil
```

it would have issued its * prompt and awaited another input.

Telling Which File Didn't Copy. You'll have noticed that when PIP copies a group of files, it reports the names of the files as it moves them. PIP displays a file's name before it begins the transfer. If there is an error, or if PIP is stopped as we just saw how to do, the last name typed tells the file being copied when the PIP stopped.

PIP Options for Disk Files

The V Option. The V option stands for "verify"; it asks PIP to read the destination file after it has been written and check it against the original. This check helps to ensure that what was written can be read. A verified copy takes slightly longer than an unverified one, as more disk operations must be done. The extra time is barely noticeable for short files.

Try a verified copy:

```
pip t4.fil=t1.fil[v]
```

It is a good idea to verify every disk copy you do. We'll use the V option in all our examples from here on.

The R Option. You may recall the feature of STAT by which you could hide the names of files. Hide one of the test files now:

```
dir t?.fil
stat t4.fil $sys
dir t?.fil
```

Now try to copy the hidden file:

```
pip t5.fil=t4.fil[v]
```

PIP responds that the file can't be found.

The R option stands for "read hidden files." When the R option is given, PIP will find the files hidden by STAT:

```
pip t5.fil=t4.fil[rv]
```

The transfer completes; the file was found. Note than when more than one option is given the options may appear in any sequence. Thus [rv] and [vr] are the same.

The W Option. The W option stands for "write over read-only files." Normally, when the destination is the name of a protected file, PIP will not complete the transfer without explicit authorization. Try it:

```
stat t5.fil $r/o
stat t5.fil
pip t5.fil=t1.fil[v]
```

PIP asks for authorization. Tell it n for no; it will reassure you that the file was not deleted.

Had you said y for yes, PIP would have overridden read-only protection and completed the transfer. The W option tells PIP to proceed with the transfer regardless of file protection:

```
pip t5.fil=t1.fil[wv]
stat t5.fil
```

As the STAT display shows, the new file is not protected.

The W option is clearly dangerous for it makes the read-only file attribute useless. It might be useful on some occasions but, since you can always override protection by responding y to PIP's request for authorization, the W option isn't often needed.

The O Option. As we'll see in Chapter 9, the end of a printable file is marked with a special character (control-z). Nonprintable files are not so marked. Usually PIP can tell the difference from the filetype of the file it is copying. If the filetype is one that is conventionally printable, then PIP stops copying when it finds a control-z marker within the file. Once in a long while you might have a file that, because of its filetype, PIP would judge to be printable but which actually has control-z characters as part of its data.

The O option tells PIP to copy every byte of a file, regardless of the presence of control-z characters.

The G Option. Yet another option, G, lets PIP copy files from one user code to another. This option and the use of user codes are covered in Chapter 8.

OTHER I/O DEVICES

Disk files are central to CP/M, but other devices are important too. There is a profusion of devices that could be connected to a CP/M system. In no way could the designers of CP/M provide programming for all of them. Instead, they chose to provide support for a small set of common device types. That left it up to the system's vendors to complete the I/O system with their knowledge of what actually is connected to the machine. The Monitor allows a program to access any four real devices by way of four prototype device names. You choose which real device will play each prototype role before the program is run.

It is necessary to understand the system of I/O assignments in order to make complete use of PIP. However, if you are a computer novice, there is no harm in your skipping the rest of this chapter and returning when you feel more at home with the machine.

The Logical Devices

Logical Devices. The Monitor allows a program to access just four devices over and above disk files (a program can access any number of those). These four devices are named CON:, RDR:, PUN:, and LST:—for console, reader, punch, and list respectively.

I/O Assignments. These devices are called logical devices because they represent classes of devices, not specific hardware. The Monitor will connect each logical device to any of four real devices. These connections may be changed at your command; to do so is to make an *I/O assignment*.

Advantages of Logical Devices. This idea of logical devices provides two benefits. First, it allows programs to be independent of the details of the system configuration. Programs need not be aware of how the CON: device, say, produces data, or of what machine address it has, or of what sequence of machine instructions is needed to make it work. The program makes a service call on the Monitor requesting input from CON:. The Monitor performs the necessary instructions to acquire a character from whatever physical device is currently assigned to CON:. This makes programs independent of the device logic and thus makes it easier to transport programs from one system to another.

The second benefit is that you can change the connections between the logical devices and the real ones. The assignment of LST: to a real device may be changed so that at one time it means the printer and at another time the terminal. The commands that write to the LST: device won't be able to tell the difference.

Meaning of the Logical Device Names. Each of the logical devices has a conventional use and is thought of in certain ways.

CON: is the logical terminal. Almost all CP/M programs assume that CON: has a keyboard operated by human fingers, and they read their primary control input from CON:. Programs assume CON: has a screen that the operator is watching; they write their messages to CON:.

LST: is the logical printer. Most programs write data they expect to print to the LST: device.

RDR: is an unspecified serial input device. PUN: is an unspecified serial output device. Programs that use RDR: and PUN: assume that they are like a paper-tape reader and a paper-tape punch respectively. That is, RDR: is expected to read, and PUN: to write, characters of the ASCII alphabet, one at a time. RDR: and PUN: are the best devices to represent the many exotic I/O boards that will fit the S-100 bus, as sketched at the end of Chapter 2.

The Physical Devices

There are 12 names for physical devices defined in CP/M. They are shown, together with their conventional meanings, in Table 6-1. They are only names; CP/M doesn't enforce any particular relationship between these names and the real devices attached to your system. That relationship is established by the vendor of the system. The vendor knows what devices your system actually has, and will have modified the Monitor so that each device in the system has a name.

The names TTY:, CRT:, and UC1: are meant to apply to terminal-like devices.

TABLE 6-1
The conventional use of the physical-device names—the actual meaning of a name is set by the vendor and is arbitrary.

Name	Conventional Use
	Devices that may be assigned to CON:
TTY:	Typewriter terminal
CRT:	Video display terminal
BAT:	Signals that input requests be diverted to RDR: logical device, output to LST: logical device
UC1:	Another console (human-operated input and output) device
	Devices that may be assigned to RDR:
TTY:	Typewriter terminal
PTR:	Paper-tape (or cassette-tape) input
UR1:	
UR2:	Other serial input devices
	Devices that may be assigned to PUN:
TTY:	Typewriter terminal
PTP:	Paper-tape (or cassette-tape) output
UP1:	
UP2:	Other serial output devices
	Devices that may be assigned to LST:
TTY:	Typewriter terminal
CRT:	Video display terminal
LPT:	A printer
UL1:	Another printer or serial output

TTY: is a conventional name for a typewriter terminal, CRT: is that of a video terminal, and UC1: is left open.

The name PTR: is meant to apply to a paper-tape reader or another serial character input device such as a tape cassette. The names UR1: and UR2: are left open to be applied to any other serial input device you might buy—a cassette drive, a telephone coupler, or even a musical keyboard.

The name PTP: is meant for a paper-tape punch. Like PTR:, it might apply to any serial character output device. If you have a cassette tape, both PTR: and PTP: might apply to it, one for input purposes and one for output. UP1: and UP2: are undefined, except as you and your vendor match them to serial machinery.

LPT: is the conventional name for the main printer in the system. UL1: is an open name available for a second printer-like device.

BAT: is a special name. The designers' intent was that if CON: were assigned to BAT:, then all input requests for CON: would be diverted to RDR: and all output requests diverted to LST:. That would make it possible to prepare a script of commands, place that stream of data on the device assigned to RDR:, and leave the system to run by itself. BAT: thus stands for batch operation. Implementation of this is left to the vendor; the distributed code for CP/M doesn't do anything about BAT:. Systems with a device suitable for assignment to RDR: are in the minority. Hence most systems don't support BAT:, although it could provide a very useful service.

STAT for I/O Device Information

You control the mapping between logical devices and physical device names through the STAT command. Go to the terminal and try two commands:

```
stat val:
stat dev:
```

The results should resemble Example 6-2. STAT VAL: is a convenience provided by STAT. It displays a list of reminders of how to use the STAT command. The bottom four lines of the display list the possible assignments of physical-device names to logical devices. For instance, the CON: device may be assigned to any of TTY:, CRT:, BAT:, or UC1:.

The output of stat dev: is a list of the device assignments that are now in effect. Since you haven't altered them since the last cold start, the assignments that are displayed are the default assignments that are true whenever you initialize the system. This default can be changed. If you find that the default assignments aren't convenient, consult your vendor (or read Chapter 15).

Making an Assignment Chart

One difficulty of explaining device assignment is that we can't know what devices your system has or under what names your vendor defined them. It is important that you know these things about your system.

EXAMPLE 6-2

The STAT VAL: command displays a list of reminders about how to use STAT. The STAT DEV: command shows the current assignments of physical to logical devices.

```
A>stat val:

Temp R/O Disk: d:=R/O
Set Indicator: d:filename.typ $R/O $R/W $SYS $DIR
Disk Status   : DSK: d:DSK:
User Status   : USR:
Iobyte Assign:
CON: = TTY: CRT: BAT: UC1:
RDR: = TTY: PTR: UR1: UR2:
PUN: = TTY: PTP: UP1: UP2:
LST: = TTY: CRT: LPT: UL1:

A>stat dev:
CON: is CRT:
RDR: is TTY:
PUN: is TTY:
LST: is LPT:

A>_
```

Figure 6-1 is an I/O assignment chart filled out for a small CP/M system. The rows of the chart describe the four logical devices. Each column represents one possible assignment to a physical-device name. For instance, the upper left entry is for the assignment of CON: to TTY:.

In each entry of the chart is written the effect of that assignment: the actual device that will be accessed when that assignment is made. The example system has only two devices, a terminal (tube) and a daisy-wheel printer (daisy). The CON: logical device can be assigned to either one. According to the chart, assigning CON: to either TTY: or CRT: will connect it to the video terminal; assigning it to either BAT: or UC1: will connect it to the daisy printer and its keyboard. The BAT: device was not implemented in this system as there was no real device for serial input.

According to the sample assignment chart, if PUN: and LST: are assigned to TTY:, they are connected to "null." This system was set up so that when those assignments were made the output would simply be discarded. This is sometimes useful for testing programs.

You should fill out a chart like this one for your system. Consult your vendor (or read on through Chapter 15) to get the information. There is a blank assignment chart in the Reference section of this book. Fill it in so that the information will be handy.

STAT for Device Assignment

Once you know the vendor-defined meanings of names such as TTY:, LPT:, and PTR:, you can make I/O device assignments to suit yourself. Once more, check the current assignments:

```
stat dev:
```

	TTY:	CRT:	BAT:	UC1:
CON:	tube	tube	daisy	daisy
	TTY:	PTR:	UR1:	UR2:
RDR:	null-eof	tube	daisy	daisy
	TTY:	PTP:	UP1:	UP2:
PUN:	null	tube	daisy	daisy
	TTY:	CRT:	LPT:	UL1:
LST:	null	tube	daisy	daisy

FIGURE 6-1
An I/O assignment chart filled in for a small system with only two devices: a terminal ("tube") and a printer ("daisy"). There's a blank chart in the Reference section; fill in your I/O assignments.

The name presently assigned to CON: is a name for your terminal. If your printer works for console copy (described earlier), then the present assignment of LST: is a name for the printer. Don't be too surprised if both logical devices are assigned to the same name, such as TTY:. One of the most slippery things about the device assignment scheme is that the TTY: you assign to LST: may not mean the same device as the TTY: you assign to CON:. The connections are strictly arbitrary; your only hope of avoiding confusion is to complete the four-by-four grid of the assignment chart and then consult it often. With your assignment chart filled out, find an assignment that will connect the LST: device to the terminal. CRT: is a likely candidate. Then make that assignment with STAT:

```
stat lst:=crt:
stat dev:
```

The display from stat dev: should show that the assignment has been made. Now all output directed to the LST: device will appear at the terminal instead. Let's find out. When console copy is on, console output is duplicated on the LST: device. Try it:

type test.fil^P*return*

Example 6-3 shows what ought to happen. Every output character appears twice (once as written to CON: and once as written to LST:, of course). Turn off this double vision with another control-p and return LST: to its previous assignment. If that was LPT:, say, then the command would be

```
stat lst:=lpt:
```

If you can't remember what it was, do a cold start with reset to get the default settings back.

Ponder your assignment chart. Try to think of ways of using these possible connections. Try also to think of improvements you'd like made in the layout, and what the chart should be like if you added another device to the system.

EXAMPLE 6-3
The result of console copy with the printer assigned to the console device—every output character is duplicated.

```
A>stat lst:=crt:
A>type test.fil (control-p pressed)
TThhiiss  iiss  TTEESSTT..FFIILLEE  lliinnee......11
TThhiiss  iiss  TTEESSTT..FFIILLEE  lliinnee......22
TThhiiss  iiss  TTEESSTT..FFIILLEE  lliinnee......33
TThhiiss  iiss  TTEESSTT..FFIILLEE  lliinnee......44
TThhiiss  iiss  TTEESSTT..FFIILLEE  lliinnee......55
TThhiiss  iiss  (etc)
```

Logical and Physical Devices in MP/M

In many respects MP/M and CP/M are alike as far as the ordinary user can tell. One important difference between them lies in MP/M's treatment of logical devices. The use of CON: is almost the same, but that of the other devices differs.

LST: IN MP/M. In CP/M the printer is all yours, to do with as you wish. Under MP/M you share the printer with any other users who are working at the same time. If your printed lines are not to be mixed up with somebody else's, you have to get exclusive use of it. PIP will do this for you when you specify LST: as the destination of a transfer. Other programs may not seize the printer. There is a way you can do it for them. The control-q signal requests ownership of the printer. If when you type control-q the printer isn't in use, MP/M will reserve it for you and the commands you run. Release the printer later with another control-q.

RDR: AND PUN: IN MP/M. MP/M simply doesn't support the RDR: and PUN: devices. Miscellaneous serial devices are defined as "consoles" to MP/M, and there are a variety of ways in which you can direct I/O to a different "console" than the terminal. You'll find that a CP/M program attempting to use RDR: or PUN: under MP/M in fact will be using the terminal. Such a program will have to be changed to work under MP/M.

PIP FOR LOGICAL DEVICES

PIP will accept the logical device names CON: and RDR: as sources in a transfer. It can use any of the logical devices CON:, LST:, or PUN: as a destination. PIP uses the Monitor for its transfers, so the data will flow between whatever real devices are currently assigned to the logical names.

CON: AS A SOURCE. As an example of using a logical device, let's build a disk file directly from the terminal. When typing data into a PIP transfer, you must remember to end each line with both return and linefeed. In normal command entry the CCP takes care of the linefeed for you, and you only use return.

PIP uses control-z to signal end of transfer. You'll have to enter control-z to stop the operation. Try it. Type carefully!

```
pip my.fil=con:
As long as I type perfectly return linefeed
And never make a slip return linefeed
I'll never need an editor; return linefeed
I can enter files through PIP. return linefeed
^Z
type my.fil
```

As you can see, the data from CON: (the terminal) were placed in the destination, MY.FIL. While typing into PIP this way, you receive none of the typing aids you're used to. If you corrected a typing error by backspacing and typing over, all three characters went into the file: the error, the backspace, and the overstrike. When you display the file with TYPE, the same three characters are typed out, probably too fast for you to see them come. The control-x and control-u error correction aids don't work either.

CONCATENATING LOGICAL DEVICES. A logical device can appear in a list of concatenated files as well. Try this one:

```
pip me2.fil=my.fil,con:,my.fil
```
*linefeed*you can say that again!*return linefeed*
```
^Z
type me2.fil
```

That transfer exposed a problem. How can you tell when PIP is ready to receive data? It doesn't issue a prompt to tell you when it's ready for you to type. The only way you can be sure is to wait for all disk activity to stop. When the select lights are out, or when you hear the click of the head unloading, you know that PIP isn't reading disk data and so it must be waiting for terminal input. If you have a hard disk, there isn't any clear indication. As long as the preceding sources are of reasonable size, waiting 15 seconds or so should be enough to ensure that PIP is listening.

LST: AS A DESTINATION. The logical printer, LST:, can be a PIP destination. Make your printer ready, then try

```
pip lst:=con:
```

Until you enter a control-z, any character you type will be sent to the printer. Your printer may not respond as the terminal does to backspace or tab characters. Try it and see. On the other hand, control-l (also called formfeed) should cause the printer to skip to a new page. Control-l may mean nothing to the terminal, or it may cause the terminal to clear its screen.

DISK FILES TO LST:. The printer is more commonly used as a destination for disk files. Here's the simple form:

```
pip lst:=my.fil
```

but there's nothing to stop you from sending several files:

```
pip lst:=test.fil,my.fil,me2.fil
```

Notice that each file's data follow on the heels of the prior file. In CP/M 2, one way to get each file started on a new page is

```
pip lst:=test.fil,con:,my.fil,con:,me2.fil
```

Each time the printer stops, enter ^L^Z. The printer will feed to a new page, and the next disk file will begin.

PIP Options for Formatting

PIP provides numerous options that regulate the format of the transferred data. In the following examples we'll use the printer and terminal as destinations. This is done here only for simplicity and visible results. All of the formatting options work as well with disk, printer, or any other destination.

THE D*n* OPTION. The D*n* option (the letter d followed by a number) stands for "delete trailing columns"; it causes PIP to truncate each line to the column indicated by the number. Try it:

```
pip
con:=my.fil[d5]
con:=my.fil,my.fil[d3]
return
```

THE P OPTION. The P option stands for "pagination." It causes PIP to insert a formfeed after a certain number of lines of output. If no number of lines is specified, PIP inserts a formfeed every 60 lines. This fits in with the normal use of 11-inch paper spaced at six lines per inch, and results in half-inch margins at top and bottom.

```
pip lst:=test.fil[p5]
```

This begins the listing of the file on a new page, and skips to a new page every five lines thereafter.

Be aware that when sending concatenated files the P option only inserts a formfeed at the head of the first source file. Thus in

```
pip lst:=test.fil[p],my.fil[p]
```

the display of MY.FIL begins immediately after the last line of TEST.FIL. This is true even if the two P options specify different numbers of lines.

THE F OPTION. The F option is used to filter out formfeed characters that might already be in a file. Certain applications create listing files (files of type .PRN or .LST) that contain formfeed characters on the basis of some assumed page size. To print such files on a different size of paper, use the F option to strip the formfeed characters out of the file and the P option to put in new ones at the desired spacing.

THE L AND U OPTIONS. The L and U options change the case of alphabetic characters. The L option makes all alphabetic characters lowercase; the U option makes them all uppercase. Try it:

```
pip con:=my.fil,my.fil[u],my.fil[l]
```

The N and N2 Options. The N and N2 options cause PIP to add a sequence number at the head of each line as it writes. The sequence numbers begin at one and go up by one with each record. The field in which the numbers are placed is six characters wide.

The N option causes PIP to make sequence numbers in which the leading zeroes are converted to blanks, and the number is followed by a colon and a space:

```
pip con:=my.fil[n]
```

The N2 option causes PIP to leave the leading zeroes in the sequence numbers and to follow each with a tab character. With standard CP/M tab stop settings, this places the first data character of the line in column 9, just where the N option put it:

```
pip con:=my.fil[n2]
```

Another example follows.

The T Option. The T option requests PIP to expand tab characters that is, to replace each tab character it finds in the source with some number of spaces. PIP keeps track of the column at which the next destination character will fall. When it finds the next source character to be a tab, PIP writes instead the number of space characters that would be skipped by a tab at that position.

CP/M has a convention that tab stops are set at every eighth position on all output devices (that is, at 9, 17, 25, etc.). Some printers and terminals support settable tab stops; others provide permanent tab stops that may or may not be at every eighth position. And some devices don't support tabs at all.

The T option lets you smooth out these inconsistencies by converting tab characters into spaces on the basis of any tab increment you like. We can test it with the N2 option, which puts a tab after the sequence number:

```
pip
con:=my.fil[n2]
con:=my.fil[n2t]
con:=my.fil[n2t20]
return
```

The first file transfer shows where your terminal places the first tab stop after position six. In the second the tab in each line was replaced by enough spaces to begin the data in column 9, as the T option alone assumes tabs in 9, 17, etc. The third transfer replaces the tab with enough spaces to begin the data in column 21.

Make your printer ready and repeat that series with a destination of LST:. If your printer ignores tabs, or assumes tab stops at some increment other than eight, then the first and second transfers will differ.

The PRN: Device. The P, F, N, and T options let you format data going to any destination, including disk files. PIP supplies a special convenience when the destination is a printer. If you specify the destination as the device name PRN:, PIP writes to the printer and assumes options P60, N, and T8:

```
pip lst:=my.fil
pip prn:=my.fil
```

The S and Q Options. The S and Q options dictate the points at which PIP should Start and Quit copying a source. They let you extract a portion of a source. The extracted portion may be concatenated to other (portions of) files.

In demonstrating these options we will use MY.FIL, the four-line file you entered in the section "CON: as a Source." If you made typing errors in entering that file, or didn't enter it at all, make a good copy of it now.

The S Option.

The S option gives PIP a marker at which to begin extracting data from the source. The marker is the string of characters between S and control-z. Here is an example:

```
pip
con:=my.fil
con:=my.fil[sAnd^Z]
```

The second transfer begins with the word "And" at the head of the second line (don't forget to capitalize "And" exactly as you entered it). PIP ignores all the data that precede the start marker.

The S option is not limited to skipping whole lines:

```
con:=my.fil[stype^Z]
```

causes "As long as I" to be skipped; the transfer commences with the start-string "type."

The Q Option. The Q option is used exactly like the S option:

```
con:=my.fil[qfiles^Z]
```

The transfer begins with the first line and ends with the word "files."

The two options may be combined:

```
con:=my.fil[sAnd^Zqslip^Z]
```

Only the second line is typed.

An extracted file can be concatenated to other data:

```
con:=my.fil[sI'll^Z],my.fil[qslip^Z]
```
return

PIP Options for Serial Transfer

Dozens of kinds of devices can be connected to a CP/M system. Special-purpose devices may have their own software to drive them, but if a device can reasonably be assigned to RDR: or PUN:, PIP can transfer data through it. PIP provides several options that are useful when it is driving serial devices, especially paper-tape and cassette-tape drives.

(If your system lacks such devices, or if you are using MP/M, or if you are new to CP/M, skip this section.)

The B Option. The B option is especially designed for use with paper-tape readers and some cassette recorders. These devices operate at a fixed, and often quite rapid, speed. The tape being read may contain long streams of data. When transferring data to disk, PIP ordinarily reads a fixed amount of data and then writes a disk record. The tape will continue to move while PIP is writing to disk. If PIP takes too long, incoming characters will be lost.

The B option prevents such an overrun by causing PIP to buffer all incoming data in working storage until the device signals end of data with an XOFF character. Only then does PIP write the received data to the destination.

The maximum amount of data that PIP can handle depends on the amount of working storage in your system. For a conservative estimate, subtract a 20K allowance for PIP and the Monitor from the size of your system. A system with 64K of working storage should be able to handle records more than 40 KB long.

The E Option. The E option instructs PIP to echo all transferred data to the console device. This lets you monitor the progress of a transfer between tape and disk. If an error occurs, the last data transferred can be seen on the screen. You can use some unique part of the data as a start marker with the S option when recovering.

The H and I Options. The H and I options are for use when transferring files in the Intel "hex" format, a way of storing machine-language programs in printable form that we'll discuss in Chapter 12. Hex format files are written by the CP/M Assembler; the format is often used to transport programs on tape. The H option causes PIP to check the transferred data for conformity to the format, and to strip out nonessential parts. The I option implies the H option (so both need not be specified), and also strips out program information records allowed by the format.

The Z Option. The Z option causes PIP to zero the parity bit of each byte of data as it is received. Data received via the Monitor from the CON: logical device always have the parity bit set to zero. This isn't true of data from the RDR: device, and that is just as well as some devices that might be assigned to RDR: transfer 8 meaningful bits in each byte.

The Z option gives you control over the parity bit in serial transfers. If the incoming data do not contain useful data in bit 7, specify Z. If all 8 bits are useful, omit Z.

The device assigned to PUN: may require that the parity bits of output data be set to zero. In that case specify the Z option on the source of the transfer.

Special PIP Sources. PIP provides two special device names that may be used as sources in a transfer. The NUL: source stands for 40 ASCII NUL characters. NUL: is used to create a leader or trailer on a paper tape, thus:

```
pip pun:=nul:,my.fil,nul:
```

The EOF: source stands for a control-z character (the ASCII code SUB) which is the CP/M end-of-file mark. PIP automatically sends a control-z at the end of any file transfer it knows to contain ASCII data, but in some circumstances you may want to send one explicitly.

User-Written PIP Code. The PIP program has been designed so that user-written code may be inserted into it. Two user subroutines are allowed, one to be used as a source and the other as a destination. They are designated as INP: and OUT: respectively. The interface between the main PIP program and these user-supplied routines is described in the CP/M documentation. They must be written in assembly language and patched into PIP with the DDT command. We'll look at the use of DDT for patching in Chapter 12.

PIP Summary

This has been a long excursion around the features of PIP. Before going on to another subject you might like to look at the pages on PIP in the Reference section. That will help you to recover a view over the forest after this tour through the trees.

Before leaving this section we should clean up the files we created. That will give us an opportunity to use ERA with ambiguous filerefs. On the A-disk you ought to have several files of type .FIL: T1 through T5, T9, TEST, and TEST2. Some of the files have been copied to the B-disk.

The key to safe use of ERA with an ambiguous fileref is this: The filenames listed by STAT fileref are the files that will be erased by ERA with the same fileref. If a STAT command shows you exactly the files you want erased and no others, then ERA with the same operand will erase those files and no others. Use STAT and ERA in this way to erase all the files created with PIP.

Chapter 7

Using ED

Using ED

Many CP/M users spend more of their terminal time using an editor than any other program. Your editor is the program that lets you create, and then correct, files of all kinds: letters, lists of data, programs, even books on CP/M. The human factors of your editor can be crucial to your productivity.

There are a number of editor programs available for CP/M. Three very popular ones are *Electric Pencil*, *Magic Wand*, and *Word Star*. If you have acquired one of these or another editor, skip this chapter and learn your own editor. If you haven't yet bought another editor, stay with us to learn ED, but plan to investigate some of the others as they are better for many purposes.

A note on the examples in this chapter: When dealing with the CCP it doesn't matter whether you type your commands in uppercase or lowercase. When dealing with ED it matters very much. When doing the examples, type your commands exactly as shown. We'll explain why as we go.

EDITOR CONCEPTS

The Edit Session

Starting the Session. All editors are based on similar concepts. An editor is called as a command and given the name of a file. After it has been loaded by the CCP, the editor loads part or all of the file into working storage; the *edit session* has begun. It waits for you to type an editing command. The command directs the editor to make a change of some kind in its copy of the file. After that change is made, the editor waits again. The edit session continues in this way.

Ending the Session. When you've caused all the changes you want, you give the editor a command that means "OK, finished," and it writes the altered file back to disk. The altered copy has the name of the original file; the old version remains but now has a filetype of .BAK (for backup).

File Handling

How the File Is Moved. During the edit session the editor holds a copy of the file, or part of it, in working storage (Figure 7-1). Sometimes the file to be edited is larger than the space available in working storage. A few editors cannot handle such files, but most provide for this by loading a portion of the file at a time. Only the part of the file in working storage is accessible for editing. When you've finished with the first part of the file, it is written to disk as part of a work file. The next portion of the file is brought into working storage to be edited. When you tell the editor that you're done, any remaining portions of the file are copied to the work file. The original file is then given a filetype of .BAK, and the work file is given the name of the original file.

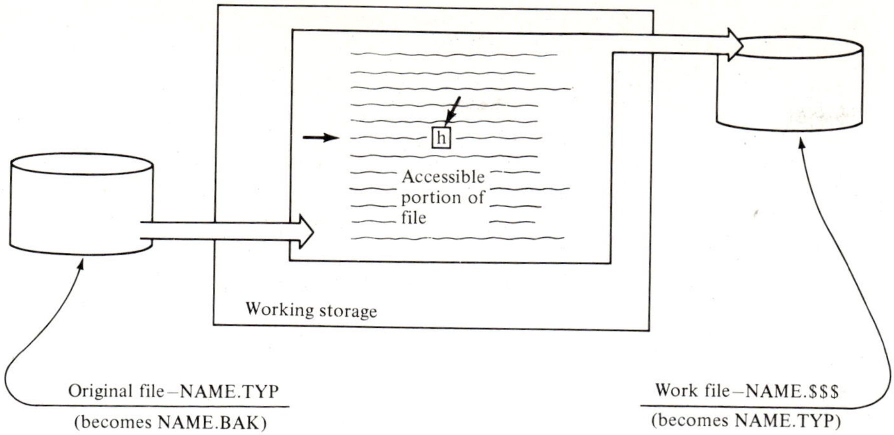

FIGURE 7-1
An editor copies all or part of the original file into working storage where it can be changed. The modified data are written to a work file that eventually acquires the fileref of the original.

The Line Concept. Most editors view the file as a continuous stream of characters, divided into units called lines. By CP/M convention, the marker that ends one line and begins the next is a pair of characters, *return* and *linefeed*.

Lines and Display Lines. A line of text in this sense is not the same as a line of letters across your terminal's screen. A text line may be as short as zero characters (no other characters between one return-linefeed pair and the next), or it may be several thousand characters long. When we want to refer to a line of letters on the screen, we'll speak of a "display line." Otherwise, take "line" to mean "all the characters between one return-linefeed marker and the next."

Current Line and Character. An editor can see only one line at a time and, within that line, only one character at a time. Figure 7-2 shows the first four lines of a file as an editor might see them. The editor is looking at the second line and within it at the initial "h" of "had." The line that the editor sees is called the *current line*; the character it sees is the *current character*. Often the documentation of an editor will talk of the "current line pointer" and the "character pointer"; these can be imagined as the little pointing hands drawn in Figure 7-2.

Types of Editors

Full-Screen Editing. A full-screen editor displays a page of text on the screen of the terminal, then indicates the current character by placing the cursor under it. A full-screen editor allows you to move the cursor with various signals. As you move the cursor the

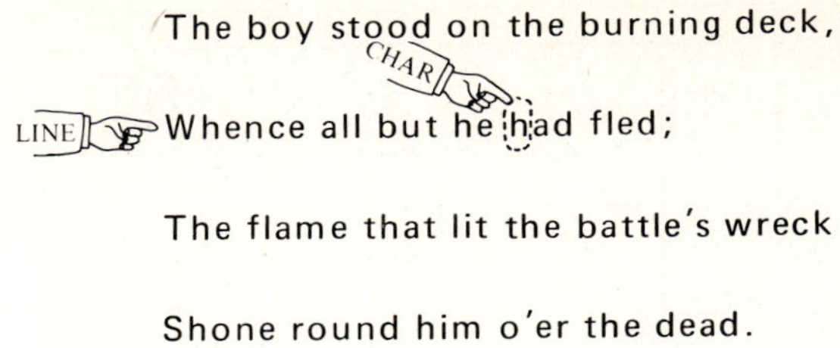

FIGURE 7-2
An editor looks at a single character within a single line. A full-screen editor marks the current character with the terminal cursor; ED reveals the current line with the command 0TT.

editor updates its character pointer accordingly so that it is always looking at the same character that you are. When you type a character it replaces the character at the cursor; the relationship between your input and the rest of the file is always clear.

Line Editing. A line editor such as ED is designed for typewriter-like terminals. It provides commands for moving the character and line pointers about in the file, but the location of the current character isn't so obvious. When using a line editor you have to concentrate a bit harder and have a clear mental picture of those little pointing hands. This quickly becomes automatic.

All editors, then, allow you to load a file into working storage and move a pointer around the lines and characters of the text. All allow you to make changes to the file in the vicinity of the current character, and finally to put the changed file back on disk.

USING ED

ED is a line editor provided as part of CP/M. Here we will introduce many of the parts of ED. Don't expect to learn ED from this demonstration; an editor, like any other complicated tool, is only learned through repeated practice. In this chapter you'll meet the most important parts of ED and learn enough to get you started.

An Initial Session

ED is invoked as a command with an explicit fileref as its operand. Do it now:

```
ed casabian.ca
```

The response is as shown in Example 7-1. If the words NEW FILE don't appear, then a file called CASABIAN.CA already exists; do a control-c warm start, erase it, and repeat the command.

EXAMPLE 7-1
The result when ED is called to create a new file.

```
A>ed casabian.ca

NEW FILE
     : *_
```

Inserting New Text.

Now type the single letter "i" and *return* (be sure to type a lowercase "i"). ED returns as a prompt the line number, 1. At this point it is ready to receive and store anything you type. Take a few minutes to enter the lines of the poem "Casabianca" as shown in Example 7-2. You'll find you can use backspace and control-x to correct typing errors, as when typing commands. End each line with *return*, and use *return* alone to put a blank line between each stanza.

Finishing the File. When you've typed the last line of the poem, enter these things:

```
^Z
b
#t
e
```

When you entered the #T (type all) command, ED displayed the whole file. The E (end) command made ED put the file away on disk. Use STAT and TYPE to verify that it exists.

That was a simple edit session. The file was new, so there was no input file. You had ED accept your input to the file, then displayed the file as ED had it in working storage, and finally stored it away.

Controlling the Edit Session

Put the File Away with E. The edit session is begun by giving the ED command to the CCP. It is ended with one of two commands to ED. The E command writes the complete text into the work file, then changes the directory so that the original file has a filetype of .BAK, and the work file has the main file's name. You used an E in the initial session above.

Quit with No Changes with Q. The Q command tells ED to quit without making any changes. The work file is erased and the original file remains as it was. Any work you've done in the session is nullified. Try it:

```
ed casabian.ca
q
```

ED asks, with a note of disbelief, whether you really mean it. Answer y for yes.

EXAMPLE 7-2
Creating the file CASABIAN.CA with ED. The editor supplies line numbers. Typing correction works. Use the return key alone to enter a blank line.

```
A>ed casabian.ca
NEW FILE
     : *i
    1:      CASABIANCA
    2:
    3: by Felicia Hemans
    4:
    5: The boy stood on the burning deck
    6: From which all but he had fled;
    7: The flame that lit the battle's wreck
    8: Shone round him over the dead.
    9:
   10: Yet beautiful and bright he stood,
   11: As born to rule the storm;
   12: A creature of heroic blood,
   13: A proud, though child-like form.
   14:
   15: The flames rolled on and on -- he would not go
   16: Without his father's word;
   17: That father, faint in death below,
   18: His voice no longer heard.
   19:
   20: He called aloud -- "Say, father, say
   21: If yet my task is done?"
   22: He knew not that the chieftain lay
   23: Unconscious of his son.
   24:
   25: "Speak, father!" once again he cried,
   26: "If I may yet be gone!"
   27: -- And but the booming shots replied,
   28: And fast the flames rolled on.
   29:
   30: Upon his brow he felt their breath,
   31: And in his waving hair;
   32: And looked from that lone post of death,
   33: In still, yet brave despair:
   34:
   35: They wrapt the ship in splendor wild,
   36: They caught the flag on high,
   37: And streamed above the gallant child,
   38: Like banners in the sky.
   39:
   40: (This is an extra stanza, put
   41: Into this stirring verse
   42: So the student may delete it;
   43: The song'll be no worse.)
   44:
   45: Then came a burst of thunder sound --
   46: The boy -- oh! where was he?
   47: -- Ask of the winds that far around
   48: With fragments strew'd the sea!
   49: (press control-z here)
```

Control the Prompt with V. Two other commands control the state of ED during the session. The V (for visible numbers) command controls ED's prompt. When first started, ED prompts with the number of the current line and an asterisk. The command -V shortens the prompt to the asterisk only. You'd only want that if your terminal were slow or noisy (in other words, if your terminal were a typewriter), or if you were driving

ED automatically from a submit file (see Chapter 8). V without the hyphen returns the prompt to normal.

Control Case with U. The U command causes ED to treat all input as uppercase, as the CCP does. This is needed only when entering program text for some programming languages. Otherwise it's better to leave ED in its initial, -U, state so that it stores the letters just as you type them.

ED Error Messages. ED has a very limited vocabulary of error messages. All of them consist of the words BREAK "*x*" AT *z*, where *x* and *z* vary with the circumstances of the message. The word BREAK simply means that ED stopped executing your command, and the character *z* is the last character of the command that it looked at. The character *x* tells the reason it stopped. If *x* is a question mark, ED didn't recognize the command. If it is a greater-than symbol, working storage is full. If it is a sharp sign (#), then ED couldn't repeat the last command as many times as it was told to. That message occurs frequently; it normally just means "finished."

The Form of ED Commands

Commands Are Single Letters. We've seen four examples of ED commands. The B, I, and E commands were typed as single letters, and the #T command took two. ED commands are not at all like CCP commands. First, the verb of an ED command is a single, more or less mnemonic, letter. Second, when an operand is used it is placed in front of the verb, not after it. For instance the T command, as we'll see later, causes ED to type at the terminal. Its preceding operand dictates the number of lines to type.

Numeric Operands. Several ED commands accept numeric operands, and the rules for these operands are consistent. A numeric operand is an integer from zero up to 65535. The sharp character (#) is taken as shorthand for 65535, so that sharp means "any and all." If you omit the operand, ED assumes you mean 1.

Signed Numeric Operands. Some commands allow their numeric operand to have a minus sign in front of it. This means "backward," or "toward the top of the file"; omitting the minus sign means "forward," or "toward the end of the file." For example, T is a command that accepts a numeric operand. The #T command used earlier meant "type all lines from the current one to the end," whereas -2T means "type the two lines before the current one."

Our Notation for Commands. From now on when we refer to commands that, like T, will take signed numeric operands, we'll name them this way: *n*T. Commands that will accept only positive operands we'll refer to like this: *p*A. A few commands will accept only one operand, the minus sign itself with no number. These we will designate *s*B, indicating only a sign is allowed. And those commands that don't allow operands we'll just name by their letter alone.

One other note on naming things and then we'll get on with editing. Some commands head strings of characters. These are much like the marker strings you used with the S and Q options of PIP. After the verb comes a string of any number of characters, and the end of the string is marked with control-z. We'll use the notation *string* to mean "any characters ended by control-z."

Controlling Files and Working Storage

When it is initialized, ED leaves working storage empty. Unlike many editors, ED doesn't read any portion of the text until you tell it to. Observe that when you begin a session:

```
ed casabian.ca
#t
```

ED responds with a blank line number; #T shows nothing. This is so because there is no text in storage, and hence no lines to display.

LOAD TEXT WITH *p*A. The *p*A (for append lines) command brings some number of lines from the source file into working storage:

```
1a
#t
```

The first line of text has been brought in. Its first character is current. The current line, as the prompt tells you, is 1. Then

```
10a
#t
```

brings in 10 more lines; the #T command displays all of them.

Most of the files you edit will fit comfortably in working storage. Use the sharp notation for "all" and bring in the rest of the file:

```
#a
#t
```

CHECK AVAILABLE SPACE WITH 0V. Now let's see how much working storage is available:

```
0v
```

The 0V command produces a display of the number of bytes of storage currently free and the number of bytes in total that ED can use. On a 64K system the response will be something like 37000/38300 (37,000 free bytes out of 38,300 total bytes). Our little Casabianca file has barely scratched working storage.

WRITE TO THE WORK FILE WITH *p*W. Had the source file been a great deal larger, it would have completely filled working storage. When you gave the #A command ED would have reported its cryptic > error, meaning "full." At that point you could make room by writing some of the top lines out to the work file with the *p*W command:

```
35w
#t
```

Note that when the current line (line 1 in this case) is written out, the pointers move down to the first remaining line.

ALTERNATING *p*A AND *p*W. The lines written out are safe, but out of reach for editing. Thus when editing a large file, use *p*A to get a good chunk of data, make changes in that, then use #W to put the data away. Repeat until the whole file is done.

START OVER WITH O. It's inevitable that sooner or later you'll so foul things up that you want to start over. The O (original file) command does that. O is the equivalent of doing Q (quit) followed by calling ED again. It is just the same but a bit quicker. Try it now:

```
o
#a
#t
```

RETURN TO THE TOP WITH H. It's also inevitable that sometimes you'll get half a large file written out and then remember a change you forgot to make at the top. The H command gets you back to the top with all changes intact. It does so by doing exactly what E (end), followed by recalling ED, would do. That is, it makes all the changes done so far permanent, and then starts over on the altered file. In effect H begins a new edit session on the altered file.

Displaying Text

Display commands are the most common ones as one of the common uses of an editor is to browse through a file. ED's display commands are *n*T and *n*P (for type and page—not print—respectively).

USES OF *n*T. *n*T displays some number of lines. To get the full sense of what it does, you have to get the character pointer in the middle of a line in the middle of the file:

```
16l
15c
```

(The *n*L and *n*C commands are described later; they move the pointers.) Now try

```
t
1t
0t
0t1t
0tt
```

and think for a minute. T and 1T are equivalent (an omitted operand is assumed to be 1, so T is assumed to be 1T). Both show the current line from the character pointer through the return-linefeed pair that marks its end. Note carefully that they don't necessarily show the whole line. The current character might be somewhere in midline.

0T shows the current line from the beginning up to, but not including, the current character. If the current character is the first character of the line—as was always the case up until now—then 0T shows nothing, and 1T shows the whole line.

Entry of Multiple Commands. The last two entries show an important feature of ED. You may string together as many ED commands as you like, one after another. 0T1T and its equivalent 0TT say, "Type the start of the line up to the current character, then type from the current character to the end of the line."

0TT Always Shows the Whole Line. 0TT will always type the whole current line, regardless of where in the line the little pointing hand may be. T alone may type the whole line, but only if the current character is the first of the line.

Multiple Lines. Let's get it back to the head of the line and try other versions of *n*T.

```
-15c
-3t
3t
-5t5t
```

The *n*T command displays the n lines preceding the current line, or the current line and $n - 1$ more lines after it.

Display Pages with *n*P. Return to the top of the file and try the *n*P command:

```
b
0p
```

The 0P command displays 23 lines beginning with the current line. Twenty-three is a convenient number of lines. Provided that each text line fits on one display line, which isn't always the case, then 23 text lines just fill the screen, leaving one line on which to enter the next command. Now try


```
p
```

The P command (or 1P, which is the same) advances the line pointer 23 lines, then displays 23 lines starting with that one. The *n*P command allows you to walk through the file in screen-size chunks, forward and backward. It's very convenient for a long file.

Controlling Line and Character Pointers

We've seen how ED is made to load the source file and save it again, and how you get ED to display the source with the *n*T and *n*P commands. In the next section we'll see how to alter the text, but one set of commands must be covered first. That set gives you precise control over the location of the line pointer and character pointer. These pointers mark the only characters of the text that ED can alter.

Go to Top or Bottom with *s*B. We've used one pointer control already, the *s*B command. Try it now:

```
b
t
-b
t
-1t
```

B alone puts the line pointer on the first line in working storage, and T displays it. -B puts the line pointer in limbo; the prompt contains no line number and T displays nothing. What happened? The -1T command shows what happened. The line pointer is aimed at empty space just after the last line in working storage. Displaying the prior line with -1T shows you the last line of the text. This odd behavior has a purpose, as we'll see later.

Move the Line Pointer with *n*L. The *n*L command moves the line pointer *n* lines relative to its present location. Watch the prompt numbers during this sequence:

```
b
5l
-2l
8l
-8l
l
```

The new line number after an *n*L command is the old line number plus *n*.

Move and Display with *n*LT. If you want to see the line to which you've moved, you may append a T command to the *n*L command:

```
b
5lt
9ltlt
```

Whenever you explicitly move the line pointer (with *s*B, *n*P, or *n*L), the character pointer is reset to the first character of the new line. Then T will display a whole line.

Shorthand for *n*LT. As a convenience ED will take a number *n*, alone in the input, to mean "*n*LT." As a further convenience it will take *return* alone as meaning 1, that in turn meaning 1LT. Thus you can walk through a file in small steps very easily:

```
b
5
8
return
return
```

Go to Specific Lines with *num*:. One last way of moving the line pointer is most useful when you know just what line number you want. You might, for example, be working from a printed listing of the file, made by PIP using the N (sequence number) option. Then you might say, "I want to fix lines 16 and 21." Instead of stepping to those lines with *n*L (and doing the mental arithmetic to figure out the right value of *n*) you can simply give the line number as a *num*: command:

```
b
12:t
18:t
6:t
```

The *num*: command moves you directly to the line you name.

Move the Character Pointer with *n*C. You can now move the line pointer anywhere you want it, but in order to change text you must be able to move the character pointer as well. There is only one specific command for that, *n*C.

```
b
0t
19c0t
1c0t
1c0t
-5c0t
0l
0t
t
```

The *n*C command moves the character pointer within the line, *n* characters relative to its present location. The 0T command shows the line from the beginning up to (but not including) the current character.

Get to the Head of the Line with 0L. The text alteration commands usually move the character pointer as well, as a by-product of their work. You can always get the character pointer back to the head of the line by giving any *n*L command, including 0L, which keeps you on the same line but moves the character pointer back to the first character.

Inserting and Deleting Text

We come at last to the purpose of an editor—the alteration of the text that so far we have only loaded and displayed. Text can really only be changed in two ways: You can delete it, and you can insert new text. If you think about it, any change of text, no matter how complicated, can be reduced to deleting erroneous text and inserting correct text. In fact, ED has commands that combine deletion and insertion in one command. They'll come later.

DIFFERENCE BETWEEN I AND i. Let's start with insertion. We've already used line insertion to create our file. At that time you were warned to use a lowercase command letter i. The reason for that was that the I command has an undocumented feature that often causes confusion. If the I command is given in uppercase, it forces all the inserted characters to be uppercase. If it is given in lowercase, it inserts what you type in the case in which you typed it.

INSERT TEXT WITH I. At any rate, two stanzas of the poem were left out of the original copy, one in the middle and one at the end. Using the (lowercase) I command, insert the middle one now:

```
b#t
34lt
i
And shouted but once more aloud,
“My father! must I stay?”
While over him fast, through sail and shroud
The wreathing fires made way.
return
^Z
-8tt
```

INSERTED TEXT PRECEDES THE CURRENT LINE. Notice that the new text went into the file above the current line. That is how the I command operates. It does that so that you can add new lines at the very top of the file. If the current line is 1, you may still insert lines ahead of it. Following the insertion the current line was still the same line as was current before the insertion was done. This is convenient because you can type in some inserted text, end with control-z, look at the text, and then resume the insertion.

INSERTION CHANGES LINE NUMBERS. Notice that the line numbers have changed. The current line was 34 before the insertion; it is numbered 40 now even though the line is the same. ED gives line numbers that reflect their position in the file. If you add lines above the current line, the current line and all after it get larger numbers because they are now farther down in the file than they used to be.

Work from the Bottom Up to Preserve Numbering. This is not a problem unless you are working from a printed listing with line numbers. If you are, and you mean to add 20 lines around line 27 and then make changes near line 250, you will find that by the time you get to it, line 250 has become line 270. This is annoying. The solution is simple. When working from a numbered listing, work from the bottom of the file up! The line numbers at the top of the file won't change regardless of what you do below them.

Inserting at the Bottom. Let's finish inserting that last stanza:

```
-b-1t
i
return
With mast, and helm, and pennon fair,
That well had borne their part—
But the noblest thing that perished there
Was that young faithful heart.
^Z
-6t
```

Now you can see why the -B command puts the line pointer after the last line rather than upon it. The I command inserts text above the current line. If you couldn't get the line pointer below the last line, you couldn't add text at the very end of the file.

Insert Phrases with I*string*. In the original copy the author's middle name was omitted. Insert it now. To do so we'll use a second form of the I command, I*string* (recall that by *string* we mean any characters ended by control-z). This inserts "string" to the left of the current character. Which is the current character? It is the first character that prints on a T command. Make the "H" of "Hemans" be the current character:

```
b2lt
11c
0t
t
```

If the last character printed by 0T (the character left of the asterisk, which is ED's prompt) isn't a space, and the first character printed by T isn't an "H," then adjust the character pointer with *n*L and *n*C commands until these things are true. Then insert the author's middle name:

```
iDorothea ^Z
0tt
```

If you omitted a space after "Dorothea," insert it now, using the same form of the I command.

Delete Lines with *n*K. Deletion, like insertion, can be done by lines or by characters. The *n*K (for kill) command deletes lines. There is an extra stanza in the original copy; take it out now.

```
45:
5t
5k
-2t3t
```

Anticipate Deletion with *n*T. *n*K deletes exactly the lines (or characters) that *n*T types, when the *n*'s are the same. This is a good way to judge a line-delete command before you give it. If *n*T displays exactly and only what you want to delete, then *n*K with the same *n* will delete just that.

Delete Characters with *n*D. Characters are deleted with the *n*D command. *n*D removes *n* characters. When *n* is positive, removal begins with the current character and moves right. When *n* is negative, removal begins just left of the current character and moves left.

There is an excess word in the original copy. Let's take it out:

```
15:t
27c0t
```

Get the letters "and on" just left of the current character (so that they display just left of the asterisk). Then delete them:

```
-7d
0t
0tt
```

Now that you can insert and delete, you can, with some labor, make any kind of correction in a file.

Text Substitution

Replace Phrases with *p*S. The labor of replacing parts of text is reduced by the *p*S (for substitute) command. This command has the form:

*p*S *string string*

You'll recall that *p* means that S accepts a positive operand only. The *p*S command does this: It searches ahead in the text for the first string; when it finds it, it replaces the first string in the text with the second string. It repeats these actions *p* times, or once if *p* is omitted. This saves a lot of *n*L and *n*C moves. *p*S can take the place of *n*D as the second string may be null (consist only of a control-z). Substituting nothing for something amounts to deletion.

The *p*S command, like the I command, behaves differently depending on whether it is typed as a lowercase or uppercase letter. If the command letter is entered as "S", it will treat both strings to uppercase. If it is typed as "s", it will leave them as they were typed.

There is an incorrect word in the second line of the first stanza. The phrase "From which" should be "Whence" and we'll fix it now:

```
b5lt
sFrom which^ZWhence^Z
0tt
```

If ED reports its BREAK "#" AT ^Z message here, it is trying to say that it couldn't locate the first string even once. You probably didn't type "From which" exactly as it appears in the file.

Multiple Substitutions. The *p* in *p*S is another labor-saving device. If there are several places where identical changes are to be made, you can cause them all to happen at once with a single command. For example, Mrs. Hemans preferred to use the poetic "o'er" instead of the "over" used in your copy. We can change both uses of "over" with one command:

```
b
#sover^Zo'er^Z
b#t
```

After doing the replacement twice ED can't find any more instances of the string "over," and reports BREAK "#" AT ^Z.

ED also supports an elaborate *p*J (for Juxtapose) command. When you know ED better you should take a look at that.

Searching for Text

Often you want to locate a specific piece of text. In a short file you can simply walk through with *n*P and *n*T until you find what you want. In a longer file this is a waste of time.

Locate Phrases with *p*F. The *p*F (find) command locates a string of text for you. Its form is

*p*F *string*

and it locates the *p*th occurrence of the string, beginning its search with the current character.

When the search stops the current character is the one immediately following the search string in the text. This sets you up to insert characters just after the string, or to delete it with -*n*D, or to delete the following letters with *n*D.

Like I and *p*S, the *p*F command is sensitive to the case in which you type it. If it is entered in uppercase, it will treat its search string as uppercase and hence can only find an uppercase phrase.

Let's find two occurrences of "flame":

```
b
fflame^Z
0t
0tt
b
2fflame^Z0tt
```

Search the Whole File with *p*N. ED also has a *p*N command that operates just like pF. *p*N has the additional function that when the search reaches the end of working storage, *p*N causes *p*W and *p*A commands to be done to read more of the file from disk. This lets you begin editing a very large file by searching directly to the first editing point.

Macro Commands

In computer jargon a macro is almost any grouping of smaller units, especially commands or instructions grouped for the sake of simplicity. ED allows a macro to be formed from a list of individual commands with the *p*M command. The form of the command is:

> *p*M *any-commands-at-all-except-M*

and it causes the entire command list to be performed *p* times. Here's a simple example of *p*M:

```
-b
10m-1
```

That macro lists the last 10 lines in reverse order. The command -1 (equivalent to -1LT) is performed 10 times.

Mrs. Hemans, the author of "Casabianca," preferred to form the past tense of a verb with "'d" rather than with "ed." The following macro command will use *p*S to change all "ed" words to "'d" and display the changes with 0TT as it goes.

```
b
#msed ^Z'd ^Z0tt
```

It takes some thought and imagination to use *p*M, but the command can be invaluable.

Chapter 8

Library Organization and SUBMIT

Your library of files is central to your system. In this chapter we consider how to care for and organize that library. We'll discuss how to care for diskettes and how to prepare them for use. Then we'll talk about organizing the library on the disks, and how to back it up. Finally, we'll introduce two commands, SUBMIT and XSUB, that can automate these and other tasks.

DISKETTE CARE

Diskette Hazards

Dirt. A diskette is a miracle of precise manufacture that is sent into the world with holes in its jacket. The slightest abrasion or soiling of its surface can make a file unreadable. Murphy's law assures us that this won't be discovered until just when that file is needed most. A diskette should be returned to some kind of protective case the moment it leaves the drive. A diskette left exposed to the cigarette ash, coffee, thumb prints, and cat hairs of this world is a diskette that will let you down.

Heat. The black plastic jacket of a diskette absorbs heat quickly. A dramatic demonstration of this occurred when the photographs shown in Chapter 2 were being taken. An 8-inch diskette was posed under two floodlights while the camera was focused. In less than 5 minutes a pucker appeared in its jacket. As the photographer reached out to rescue the diskette, the jacket wrinkled all over and folded backward under its own weight! Summer sunlight through a window could easily have the same effect.

Magnets. Data are recorded on a diskette in the form of very slight changes in magnetization. A strong magnetic field can alter the recorded data, making the data unreadable. Electric motors, hi-fi speakers, and telephone ringers all emit magnetic fields that can alter a diskette if it approaches them closely enough. Magnetic fields decline rapidly with increasing distance, so a separation of a few inches is probably sufficient protection. However, a separation of a few feet is better.

Pens and Pencils. New diskettes come packed with a set of gummed labels. Stick as many labels as you like on a diskette, as long as you don't cover any of the holes in the jacket. When you write on a label, write lightly with a felt-tip pen or fountain pen. Never use a pencil; dust from the lead might get on the recording surface. Avoid ballpoint pens; it's easy to bruise the plastic surface inside the jacket.

Diskette Accessories

Storage Gadgets. As diskettes have come into wide use, the number of diskette accessories on the market has grown. Those who like gadgets can have a fine time shopping for flip files, special binders, storage boxes, and diskette mailers. Most of these gadgets are useful. Choose some that let you store the diskettes so that they are clean and safe, yet still easy to find. The simplest organizing gadget is also one of the best. It is a clear plastic sleeve punched for an ordinary three-ring binder. Each sleeve holds a diskette in such a way that it can be seen. The binders are inexpensive and easy to store. It's handy to store a diskette in its sleeve in the same binder that holds the program's documentation.

Hole Reinforcers. Several companies sell diskette hole reinforcements (like oversize ring-binder reinforcements) that strengthen the edge of the diskette's center hole. It should not be necessary to reinforce your diskettes. Hole damage is rare and is usually the result of careless handling. Installing the rings is a fussy job that exposes the diskettes to more handling than is desirable.

Head-Cleaning Kits. There are various sorts of head-cleaning kits on the market; all carry high-technology prices. The read-write head in each drive ought to be cleaned a couple of times a year. If you can reach it without disassembling the drive, you can clean it with a cotton swab dipped in isopropyl alcohol—both available cheaply at a drugstore. If you can't get at the head without a lot of work, buy a kit for the time it can save you.

PREPARING A NEW DISKETTE

You can usually pop a brand new diskette into a drive and save files on it at once. That isn't a good idea, but it will work. It's better to put each new diskette through an initialization process. Then you can be confident that all of your diskettes are prepared in the same way.

Mechanical Preparation

Give It an Identity. Every diskette needs a unique identifier, a tag that refers to that diskette alone. The tag should not relate to the diskette's contents because it may be put to many uses in its life. The unique tag lets you relate read errors through the tag to the batch the diskette came in, and to the supplier who sold it.

One Numbering Scheme. One way to give each diskette a unique identity, assuming you don't buy more than 10 boxes a year, is to form a three-digit number that describes the age and source of the diskette. The first digit is the last digit of the year of purchase, the second the number of the box, the third the number of the diskette within the box. The third diskette drawn from the first box bought in 1982 would be numbered 203.

Cover the Write-Protect Notch. If these are 8-inch diskettes, check for a write-protect notch on the lower edge. Not all new diskettes come with notches. If there is one, cover it with a small gummed label. If you forget to, you'll have a puzzling I/O error report from CP/M when you try to format the diskette. A sheet of such labels is usually packed in the diskette box.

Formatting

To *format* a diskette is to write every sector of every track at the sector size and density that you will use. New diskettes are usually formatted at the factory, but the factory's drives and yours might not agree. Formatting ensures that the tracks are laid down in precise alignment with the read-write head in your drive. It also sets the density and the sector size that you will use.

The Formatting Program. Formatting is done with a program that is supplied by the vendor of your system. Each make of disk controller hardware requires a different program to direct formatting. The vendor supplies a formatter as part of the process of customizing CP/M to your hardware. Formatting takes about 30 seconds; afterward the diskette is completely empty of data.

Using the Formatter. Your command dialogue with the formatter will depend on the formatter you have been given. Example 8-1 shows a dialogue with the formatter supplied by one vendor; yours will be similar. Most formatter programs are arranged so that you can format one diskette after another without recalling the program.

Hazards of Formatting. Be very careful with a formatter. It pays no attention to the existing contents of the diskette. You can format a diskette that is full of good data. Most will format the diskette in the A-drive as readily as any other. Formatting is quick. If you start the formatter on the wrong diskette, it will have overwritten the directory before you can hit reset to stop it. It is a good idea to remove the diskettes from the other drives before starting the formatter.

SYSGEN

The Bootstrap Tracks. In Chapter 5 we told you to use practice diskettes that were bootable, that is, diskettes that had a copy of the Monitor on their first (outermost) tracks. That copy is not a file in the usual sense. There is no file directory entry for it, and the space it occupies is not allocated in the file system's usual way. CP/M dedicates the outermost two tracks (three tracks on a 5-inch diskette) to be a place where the code of the Monitor and CCP can be saved, ready for bootstrap loading.

EXAMPLE 8-1
A dialogue with a diskette formatting program as written by a particular vendor—others are similar.

```
A>ddinit
CCS DISK FORMATTER PROGRAM V2.0 - 8 INCH ONLY
WHICH DRIVE (A-D)? B
SINGLE OR DOUBLE DENSITY (S/D)? D  (formatter runs)
WHICH DRIVE (A-D)?_
```

ADVANTAGES OF BOOTABLE DISKETTES. There are advantages to making disks "bootable," that is, to putting a copy of the Monitor on the bootstrap tracks. The space is permanently reserved and can't be used for files whether there's a Monitor copy in it or not. Any bootable diskette can be put into the A-drive and left there. If a diskette without the Monitor is in the A-drive and you call for a warm start, the system will report an I/O error. If you press reset when the A-disk is not bootable, the system will hang. Either of these things can puzzle or frighten an inexperienced user.

A SERIOUS DISADVANTAGE. There's one drawback to making every diskette bootable. The program that is written on the bootstrap tracks—the Monitor—is protected by copyright. Your license agreement with Digital Research permits you to make just five copies of the Monitor or any other part of the CP/M package. That puts you in a bind. The advantages of reproducing the Monitor (and certain commands, such as STAT and PIP) are many, but to do so puts you in violation of the letter of your agreement (which you should have read carefully, and if you haven't done so before, do it now). We'll return to this topic later.

THE SYSGEN COMMAND. The command that places a copy of the Monitor on the reserved tracks of a diskette is called SYSGEN in the standard CP/M system. This program, like the formatter, may have been customized by the vendor and may have a different name. Your CP/M manual contains an example of the use of standard SYSGEN.

USE OF SYSGEN. Example 8-2 shows a dialogue with a version of the program that was modified by a vendor. The program asks for a source from which it can read the Monitor. Normally the source is another bootable diskette (in Chapter 15 we'll see where the original copy comes from). Then it asks for a destination drive, the letter of the drive into which you've loaded the new diskette. When told the destination, the program writes a copy of the Monitor onto the new diskette's reserved tracks and waits again. Like the formatter, the program is arranged to write on one diskette after another without reloading the program. You can run a box of diskettes through formatting and then through SYSGEN, all in a few minutes.

EXAMPLE 8-2
A dialogue with a SYSGEN (Monitor copy) program as written by a particular vendor. See the CP/M documentation for a similar dialogue.

```
A>ccsysgen
CCS SYSTEM GENERATION PROGRAM VERSION 1.0

SOURCE DRIVE: A
SOURCE ON A, THEN TYPE RETURN

DESTINATION DRIVE: B
DESTINATION ON B, THEN TYPE RETURN
   (sysgen program runs)
DESTINATION DRIVE: _
```

Common Commands. There are a few command files that it's convenient to have on every diskette regardless of its use (but see the foregoing comments on copying licensed code). STAT, PIP, and your favorite editor are the most useful ones; you will think of others as you establish patterns of work. These are the commands you use so often that it is an irritation to find them absent, or to have to give an explicit drivecode before the command verb to load them.

Common Commands on the Outer Tracks. Commands in frequent use should be copied onto each new diskette as you initialize it. There is a performance advantage in having the most common commands first on the diskette and first in the directory because CP/M can find and load them more quickly that way. Once copied they might as well be given the SYS attribute so that they won't clutter a directory display, and the R/O attribute so that they can't be erased easily. If you read Chapter 5 carefully, you should be able to work out the list of commands needed to do these things. Don't forget that if the common commands have the SYS (hidden) attribute on the source diskette, PIP won't be able to find them without the R (read hidden files) option. The entire initialization command sequence is shown in Example 8-3. Later we'll see how to automate it.

Receiving Distribution Diskettes

Your library will receive additions from the places that supply you with software. New software comes on diskettes. These distribution diskettes are precious, for they hold the authoritative and original copy of the software.

The first thing to do with any distribution diskette is to write-protect it (cover the notch of a 5-inch diskette, or peel the cover off the notch of an 8-inch one). The second step is to make a copy of all the files onto another, freshly initialized, diskette. This creates a writable working copy of the software and ensures that every file can be read.

The third thing to do with a distribution diskette is to pack it away in a safe place, never to be read again except in the event of a disaster. It's not at all ridiculous to remove it to a different building from the one that houses the computer. If there is tailoring or customization to be done, do it and then file a copy of the tailored version with the original.

Copying Licensed Software. Fee software may be copied again and again around the library onto any diskette where it will be needed. The publishers of fee software would like to control the proliferation of copies of their code, as we noted previously. But achieving a balance between their desires and your convenience is sometimes difficult. The license agreement you sign and return to a software publisher amounts to a legally enforceable contract. The license agreement for one language translator allows "two additional copies only, for backup purposes." And this is for a program that must be present to use any program written in that language! Can you obey the spirit of the agreement—preventing the theft of the publisher's work—while ignoring its letter? Should you do so? Each system owner has to resolve these questions.

EXAMPLE 8-3
Command dialogue used in preparing a new diskette.

```
A>ddinit
CCS DISK FORMATTER PROGRAM V2.0 - 8 INCH ONLY
WHICH DRIVE (A-D)? B
SINGLE OR DOUBLE DENSITY (S/D)? D          (formatter runs)
WHICH DRIVE (A-D)?                         (only return entered)

A>ccsysgen
CCS SYSTEM GENERATION PROGRAM VERSION 1.0

SOURCE DRIVE: A
SOURCE ON A, THEN TYPE RETURN

DESTINATION DRIVE: B
DESTINATION ON B, THEN TYPE RETURN
   (sysgen program runs)
DESTINATION DRIVE:                         (only return entered)

A>pip b:=a:stat.com[vr]

A>pip b:=a:pip.com[vr]

A>pip b:=a:ed.com[vr]

A>stat b:*.com $r/o

STAT.COM Set to R/O
PIP.COM Set to R/O
ED.COM Set to R/O
A>stat b:*.com $sys

STAT.COM Set to SYS
PIP.COM Set to SYS
ED.COM Set to SYS
A>_
```

ORGANIZING THE LIBRARY

People who enjoy organizing things are in their element around a computer system. Nowhere are there so many things in need of organization, or so many ways of organizing them. In this section we'll suggest one of the many lines along which a diskette library might be organized. As time passes you'll develop your own ideas on how it should be done. The important thing is to make the machine do as much of the work as possible.

Categorizing Diskettes

One way of categorizing diskettes is by the kind of use they're given. The way you use a diskette affects the files you put on it and the importance of backing it up.

Distribution Diskettes. One kind of use is that accorded a distribution diskette. It is write protected, copied, and put away. The final version of a program created on your own system might well be put on its own distribution diskette and filed with the fee software.

Work Diskettes. A second kind of usage is accorded what we'll call a *work diskette*. This is one that is used as you would use a chalkboard. On it you can write any file at all for any temporary purpose. A work diskette is the place for casual memos, test versions of programs, the listing file written by a compiler—anything of only transient importance. It should be bootable, of course, and it should have a copy of every command you normally use, set to R/O status.

As a matter of policy any unprotected file on a work diskette should be considered expendable. Anyone who needs space on the diskette may erase anything there, just as anyone who uses a chalkboard may erase it. A file might be marked R/O in the way one might leave a note on a chalkboard to "please save." But since a work diskette won't be backed up, damage to the diskette will cause the loss of whatever files were there.

When the system is used by more than one person, the users may have their own work diskettes, which they can carry away from the machine. It should be clearly announced that any work diskette left in a drive is fair game; important files must be copied on more permanent storage.

Project Diskettes. A project diskette is one that is used as a repository for important files. Each project diskette would contain the files that represent the current state of one project, one unit of the business. You may define a "project" to be anything you like—Accounts Receivable, The Mailing List, My Correspondence 3Q82, and so on.

Because a project diskette contains files related to a single well-defined unit of your computer work, you can always lay your hands on the files that define that work. The scheme has the minor disadvantage that most project subjects won't fill the diskette allotted to them. You might have a lot of project diskettes, with each only partly full. The convenience of knowing where everything is should cover the minor cost of a few more diskettes. Organizing diskettes by projects aids the solution to some data security problems (discussed in Chapter 4).

The files on a project diskette are important in some way to your work. They should never be altered casually. If there is anything dubious about a change, the file should be copied on a work diskette and the change made there. When the change is known to be good, the file can be copied back.

Backup Diskettes. Backup is the computist's word for making copies of important files against the inevitable day when a file is lost. The purpose of making backup copies is to minimize the loss when data are destroyed. People new to computers find it difficult to understand that a magnetic record is not permanent in the way that a paper document is. A paper document can be drenched, torn, and toasted, and still be readable. A magnetic record is robustly there, or it isn't there at all. Blur half the letters on a page, and a person can still make sense of the writing. If one single bit of a sector reads wrong, a disk drive will report an error. And of course it's possible to erase files, or format disks, accidentally—a more thorough erasure than sending papers through a shredder. There are few sensations as sickening as the realization that one has just destroyed an important file. One slip of the finger, one carelessly typed command, and the data are gone, instantly. At such moments it is a great comfort to know that a backup copy exists. If backup is taken on a weekly schedule, then you have lost at most a week's work; if daily, at most a day's. The job of bringing the backup copy up to date is much easier and much less costly than the job of recreating a file from scratch. Given a specific situation, you could analyze the economics of backing up a file—so many hours of work to recreate the file from scratch, so many to make up a week's updates, so many minutes to make regular copies, and some assigned probability of loss. A simpler way to decide on backup frequency is to gauge the panic factor. Pretend to yourself that you've just been told, "The receptionist watered your XYZ project disk along with the Boston fern," and measure the depth of the sinking feeling in the pit of your stomach. For each project diskette, ask yourself, "How badly would it hurt to lose these data? What would it do to my schedule?"

A backup diskette is one that holds nothing but backup copies of files. It need not contain any commands. A backup diskette doesn't have to be limited to a single project; it might hold copies of several partly full project diskettes, provided that all were on the same backup schedule.

You'll have a pool of backup diskettes and a schedule for backing up each project diskette. "Backup every Friday night" might be schedule enough. If the filerefs for a project have been planned carefully, one or two PIP commands will suffice to move the important files to the backup diskette. We'll see later how it can be automated.

Once filled, the backup diskette should be stored away from the rest of the library, in a fireproof safe or in another building. To a business, backup diskettes represent a small security exposure. It's easier to borrow, copy, and return a backup diskette than one in daily use.

ORGANIZING A HARD DISK

A hard disk presents itself to CP/M and MP/M as one or more large, always loaded diskettes. The commands presented in Chapter 5 work the same on a hard disk as they do on diskette. The hard disk simply provides more space and faster access time.

Logical Drives. The hard disk can usually be partitioned into several areas, each of which acts like a single drive. If your system has two diskette drives and a 15 MB hard disk, you can have it set up so that the diskette drives are A and B, whereas areas of the hard disk appear under drivecodes C, D, and E, each with 5 MB of space. C, D, and E are then logical drives ("logical" as an adjective is computer jargon for simulated). The hard disk's space need not be divided evenly among its logical drives.

Problems of Organization. The hard disk presents problems of organization because the data on it can't be loaded and unloaded as diskettes can. You can erase files and copy in new ones, but you cannot conveniently carry one group of files away and load a new group. This implies that the hard disk should play the role assigned to project diskettes. Each logical drive can contain the files representing one (fairly large) unit of work. One logical drive might play the role of work disk for all users.

The User Code

It is easy to place more files on a logical drive than will fit on the terminal's screen when DIR is used. At that point it becomes difficult to keep track of what files are available. It would be convenient to be able to make subsets of the files stored on a large disk so they could be dealt with more conveniently. CP/M offers one aid toward this, a *user code* that qualifies all fileref searches.

THE USER Command. The user code is a number from 0 to 15. There is at all times one active user code. After a cold start, the active user code is 0. The active user code can be changed with the USER command, whose form is

USER *usercode*

OPERATION OF THE USER CODE. When a file is created, the user code active at the time is written in the file's directory entry. When the directory is searched to locate a file, each entry's user code is checked against the code active at the time the search is made. If they are the same, the file is visible. If the active code is different from the code recorded in a directory entry, that file is invisible. DIR will not report on it, nor can any command, with one exception, access it. The effect is to divide the library into subsets, each accessed under its user code.

PROBLEMS OF THE USER CODE. The user code has little value in a system that has only diskette drives. The reason for this is that only the files created under the active user code can be found, and that applies to command files as well. Move from the normal user code of zero to another number and issue the STAT command. The reply will be STAT?, indicating that no such command file exists.

This behavior of CP/M means that in order to work under a user code other than zero you must store a copy of every common command file under each user code. This is not practical in the limited storage capacity of a diskette drive.

User codes become slightly more useful when the large capacity of a hard disk is available. Even so, you might have a program stored under user code 3 and want to run it against a file recorded under user code 0. It can't be done. One file must be copied into the other's user code.

PIP AND USER CODES. PIP is able to copy from one user code to another. The G option of PIP tells it to search for the source under some particular user code. Thus pip a:=b:file[g3] would locate FILE on the B-drive under user code 3 and make a copy on the A-drive under the active user code. One problem remains: How do you make a copy of PIP itself under another user code? The answer for CP/M 2 appears in the Reference section as an example of the SAVE command.

User Codes and the Hard Disk. You could use user codes to partition a large logical drive into as many as 15 different project sets, one under each user code. Users would work under user code 0 most of the time, copying project files to the work drive with PIP and moving to the project's user code to copy them back again.

Hard-Disk Backup

It is absolutely essential to have a backup policy for a hard disk. A hard disk holds as much data as dozens of diskettes. If a diskette is spoiled, you've lost at the most the files of one project; an accident that would wipe out your entire library is very unlikely. With a hard disk, all of your eggs are definitely in a single basket. It is entirely possible that a hardware failure could make everything on a hard disk inaccessible. If there is a failure in the electronics of the drive so that the drive is unusable and must be sent out for repair, you cannot be sure that there will be any data on it when it comes back.

Backup to Diskette. There are two approaches to backing up a hard disk. First, you can arrange to back up individual files or groups of files. As long as each file is small enough to hold on one diskette, such copies can be made on diskette (and automated). This approach might be adopted by one user of the system who wanted to keep backup copies of his or her personal files.

Backup to Tape. The second method is to copy larger units of data onto reels or cartridges of tape. Tape solves the capacity problem; depending on the design of the tape drive and the length of the tape itself, from 1 to 15 MB of data can be copied. Tape introduces a new problem, however. Backup to diskette is done file by file with PIP. Backup to tape is usually done with a special program. To make a lengthy process faster, such programs usually copy entire tracks without regard for file organization. Therefore, a single file can only be recovered by restoring the entire tape, taking all files on that logical drive back to the time the tape was made.

Organizing Under MP/M

An MP/M system is very like a CP/M system. All of the familiar commands work in the same way. The difference is that several users, each with a terminal, can use the system simultaneously. Each user is given an area of working storage and a portion of the machine's attention. All users have access to all drives.

User Codes in MP/M. Under MP/M the user code is a very useful organizing tool. In MP/M each active user has an associated user code. In addition, each user, regardless of his or her active code, can see and access files created under code 0. The commands and files needed by all users can be grouped under user code zero, whereas each user's private files are kept under another number.

Under MP/M 2, access to files under user code 0 has been restricted to files that have the SYS attribute, and then only when they are to be read. This makes user codes an even better organizing tool.

Hard Disks in MP/M. With MP/M a hard disk may be partitioned very nicely into logical drives and, within drives, by user code. The G option of PIP is still needed to move files between user codes, but there is much less need to do so.

Backup in MP/M. MP/M presents a new problem when it is time to take a backup copy from a hard disk. The backup copy will be invalid if any of the copied files are changed while the copy is being made. This could occur if a user at one console is working while the backup is being done at another console. The MP/M command DSKRESET can be used to make logical drives inaccessible while the backup is made.

AUTOMATING WITH SUBMIT AND XSUB

You'll find that system management tasks often involve stereotyped sequences of commands. When initializing new diskettes, for example, the same list of commands must be repeated over and over. The first few times you do it, such a task is a challenge and hence interesting. Later, it's just a chore. SUBMIT is a command that automates the execution of such command sequences. We've put off introducing it to this point so that we could show a real use for it.

The SUBMIT Command

The SUBMIT command causes a file that contains a list of commands to be handed over to the CCP for execution. The CCP will do the commands one by one as they appear in the file, just as if the list were entered command by command from the keyboard. This is a powerful tool for managing the system's work.

The Form of SUBMIT. The form of the SUBMIT command is

SUBMIT *filename parameter-values*

Note that the operand is not a complete fileref, only a filename (and possibly a drivecode). The parameter values will be described later.

Operation of SUBMIT. SUBMIT assumes that the filetype is .SUB and looks for a file of the given name and that type. When SUBMIT finds the file, it copies the data and reformats the data in certain ways. The original file remains; the reformatted copy is placed on the default drive under the name $$$.SUB. If the default drive is A, the command list is executed at once. If not, the list won't have any effect until the diskette it is on is placed in the A-drive.

The CCP Reads the Submitted File. Whenever it begins work after a warm or cold start, the CCP looks at the directory of the diskette in the A-drive to see if a file named $$$.SUB is listed there. If such a file exists, the CCP reads its next command from that file instead of the terminal. Each time it reads a line from $$$.SUB, the CCP deletes the line. Eventually $$$.SUB shrinks to nothing, is erased, and things return to normal.

The net result of SUBMIT is to cause a list of commands from a file to be executed. Thus you can create a complicated list of commands just once by using an editor and run it any number of times, then or later, with little effort.

SUBMIT to Initialize a Diskette. Let's apply SUBMIT to the job of initializing a new diskette. You've worked out the sequence of commands already: the formatter command (whatever it's called in your system), the SYSGEN command (or your vendor's variation), a series of PIP transfers, and two uses of STAT. Example 8-4 shows a file DISKINIT.SUB that would work in one system; it contains exactly the commands that were issued in Example 8-3. Use an editor to prepare a similar file (containing the right commands for your system) and call it DISKINIT.SUB. Be sure to duplicate the dollar signs as shown in the example; we'll see why later.

Put a new, or at least an unimportant, diskette in the B-drive. Then submit DISKINIT:

```
submit diskinit
```

After a bit of activity on the A-drive, the CCP's prompt will appear and after it the first command from the file. When the formatter takes over, respond to its questions as you normally would. When it ends, the CCP will read and display the second command. Respond to SYSGEN as usual. When it ends, the CCP will go on to work its way through the other commands of the file.

Stop a Submitted File with DEL. If you want to stop the execution of a submitted file, you can do it. Each time the CCP gets a new line from the submitted file, it checks the terminal keyboard. If the DEL (or Delete, as it may be marked) key has been pressed,

EXAMPLE 8-4
A simple submit file to carry out the command sequence to initialize a new diskette.

```
A>type diskinit.sub

DDINIT
CCSYSGEN
PIP B:=A:STAT.COM[VR]
PIP B:=A:PIP.COM[VR]
PIP B:=A:ED.COM[VR]
STAT B:*.COM $$R/O
STAT B:*.COM $$SYS
STAT B:
```

the CCP erases $$$.SUB and returns to normal operations. To try this, start DISKINIT .SUB as before. As the first command appears on the screen, press DEL (or Delete). Although the command appears, it won't be executed. The usual CCP prompt will follow it.

You sometimes have a fairly small window of time in which to press DEL. If a submitted command is reading from the terminal, it will receive the DEL character, not the CCP. In this case the window for canceling the submitted file opens following the last input to the command, and closes when the next command is given control, often a matter of only a couple of seconds.

SUBMIT Parameters

Not all command sequences are as stereotyped as that in Example 8-4. Some part of the command list, usually a fileref, will vary from run to run. SUBMIT allows the command list to contain *parameters*, that is, elements whose values are established when the file is submitted.

Effect of Parameters. A parameter is signaled in the file by a dollar sign followed by a digit. The parameter values that follow the filename in the SUBMIT command replace the parameter signals in the file. The first parameter value given in the command line replaces every occurrence of $1 in the file. The second value from the command line replaces every occurrence of $2, and so on up to the ninth value. A signal of $0 is replaced by the name of the submitted file.

Rules for SUBMIT Parameters. If there are parameter values in the command for which no parameter signals appear in the file, the extra values are ignored. On the other hand, if there are parameter signals in the file for which the command contains no values, the unmatched parameters are simply dropped from the file; a programmer would say that they are replaced with the null string. (Note that this paragraph may contradict your CP/M documentation; it is based on experiment whereas the documentation apparently was not.)

An Example of Parameters. Study Example 8-5. It is a submit file similar to the one in Example 8-4. A PIP transfer has been added at the end; the name of the destination file is formed from two parameters, $1 and $2. The first parameter value in the SUBMIT command will replace the filename and the second will replace the filetype. This PIP transfer will create a file whose name (with an initial hyphen) and whose type will be established by the parameter values in the SUBMIT command.

The purpose of this version of DISKINIT is to put a label, in the form of a fileref, into the directory of the initialized diskette. When this is done, the command DIR -*.* will display the unique name of this diskette on the screen. Edit your version of DISKINIT.SUB adding the last two lines of Example 8-5. Then try it:

```
submit diskinit project 203
```

The last two lines of the file will create a file -PROJECT.203 and give it R/O status. In this way you can label the interior of a diskette as well as its exterior jacket. Whenever you wonder which diskette is in a drive—and such moments arise—the command dir -*.* will tell you.

SUBMITTING A DOLLAR SIGN. Look closely at that last STAT command in Example 8-5. Think about the problem faced by SUBMIT: A dollar sign signals a parameter to be replaced, but there are also occasions, as here, when a dollar sign is part of the command. How can SUBMIT distinguish between a dollar sign that is part of the submitted command and one that marks the start of a parameter signal? The solution chosen was to require the user to double the dollar signs that did not signal a parameter. Any single dollar sign is taken by SUBMIT as a parameter signal; a double one means it is to leave a single dollar sign in the submitted command.

SUBMITTING A CONTROL CHARACTER. PIP and ED are often called from submitted files. Both these commands use control characters, especially control-z, in their command operands. SUBMIT allows you to incorporate control characters in a submit file. It uses the same convention we've been using: ^Z in the file stands for control-z, and SUBMIT will replace the ^Z signal with a control-z character in the $$$.SUB file. (In CP/M 2.2 SUBMIT contains a bug that causes it to reject an uppercase signal, but it will accept a lowercase one like ^z. See Chapter 13 where we apply the fix for this problem as an example of using DDT.)

The XSUB Command

XSUB is a command that makes a valuable addition to the functions of SUBMIT. The XSUB command modifies the operation of the Monitor so that lines of program input, as well as commands, may be drawn from a submitted file. This makes it possible to automate the use of some commands that require input from the terminal. The responses you'd have given at the terminal can be placed right in the file.

EXAMPLE 8-5
The previous submit file, parameterized to put a label file on the new diskette. The name of the file is formed from the first two parameter values in the SUBMIT command.

```
A>type diskinit.sub

DDINIT
CCSYSGEN
PIP B:=A:STAT.COM[VR]
PIP B:=A:PIP.COM[VR]
PIP B:=A:ED.COM[VR]
STAT B:*.COM $$R/O
STAT B:*.COM $$SYS
PIP B:-$1.$2=A:STAT.COM
STAT B:
```

An Example of XSUB. Example 8-6 improves on Example 8-5 by supplying the contents of the label file. In Example 8-5 the label file was a copy of STAT under another name. In Example 8-6 we use ED to create a two-line file as the label. The two lines are inserted using the I*string* command so that ED will take them from XSUB. The first line of the file will say THIS IS DISK..., and whatever the label is; the second line will contain an asterisk followed by whatever other parameter values were given in the SUBMIT command. The asterisk in the second line ensures that even if no other parameters are given, there will be a string following the letter I to prevent ED from going into line insert mode.

Set up your version of DISKINIT so that its last lines look like those of Example 8-6. Don't omit the call to XSUB. Then try it:

```
submit diskinit backup 351 initialized 8/4/82
```

When the submitted file calls ED, you will see ED receiving the two I*string* commands and an E command from the submitted file. When the submitted file completes its run, use TYPE to display the label file on the new disk to verify that it looks as you expect it to.

XSUB and the Monitor. In Chapter 13 we explore the Monitor's service requests. For the moment you need to know that the Monitor provides two service requests for console input: byte input and line input. When a program calls for line input the Monitor gathers a complete line of data up to the press of the return key and returns that whole line to the calling program. While it is collecting the line, the Monitor allows the person entering the line to make corrections with backspace, control-x, and control-u.

The byte input service request gets the next character typed and returns it to the calling program. Since the Monitor doesn't see an entire line of input, it can't attempt to handle typing corrections. The character, whatever it was, is handed to the program that asked for it. In general (but not always), if normal typing correction is allowed, your input is being gathered for a line input service request.

EXAMPLE 8-6
The previous submit file, altered to create the label file by calling ED and providing its input with XSUB.

```
A>type diskinit.sub

DDINIT
CCSYSGEN
PIP B:=A:STAT.COM[VR]
PIP B:=A:PIP.COM[VR]
PIP B:=A:ED.COM[VR]
STAT B:*.COM $$R/O
STAT B:*.COM $$SYS
XSUB
ED -$1.$2 B:
ITHIS IS DISK -$1 $2
I* $2 $3 $4 $5 $6 $7 $8 $9
E
STAT B:
```

Programs That Can't Use XSUB. XSUB sets up the Monitor to answer line input requests with a line from the submitted file. It does nothing for byte input requests, for which the Monitor continues to come to the terminal. It is something of an adventure to discover which commands use line input, and hence may be automated with XSUB, and which do not. PIP uses line input to get its commands, but byte input to read from the CON: device as a source. ED uses line input to read commands but, infuriatingly, seems to use byte input for inserted lines even though typing correction works during an insertion.

A Problem with SUBMIT. The SUBMIT command has a problem that further limits XSUB. SUBMIT (in CP/M 2.2) can't cope with a zero-length line. It does some bizarre things if the submitted file contains one. The bug is apparently unfixable; it has been reported more than once but no fix has appeared. As a result you can't use SUBMIT and XSUB to automate a program that, like PIP, requires a null line to signal "end of job."

Uses of SUBMIT

There are two reasons for applying SUBMIT to a task. It may be a stereotyped task done often with only minor variations. Another good reason is that it may be a lengthy task in which many commands must be done in precisely the right order. In that case building the script of commands and submitting it may be a good idea even if the job is to be done only once. Because you think the task out while creating the submit file and proofread it, you lessen the chances of making an error. Even if a task has if-then sorts of decisions (which SUBMIT can't accommodate), it is useful to put the usual sequence in a file.

EXAMPLE 8-7
A submit file used in a real installation to initialize work diskettes. The label file is made first so as to be listed first by DIR. All files are R/O, some are hidden.

```
A>type workinit.sub

XSUB
ED -$1.$2 B:
ITHIS IS DISK -$1.$2
I $3 $4 $5 $6 $7 $8 $9
E
PIP B:=A:VDUMP.COM[VR]
PIP B:=A:STAT.COM[VR]
PIP B:=A:PIP.COM[VR]
PIP B:=A:EDIT.COM[VR]
PIP B:=A:SUBMIT.COM[VR]
PIP B:=A:XSUB.COM[VR]
STAT B:*.COM $$SYS
PIP B:=A:DDT.COM[V]
PIP B:=A:DIVIL1.BAS[V]
PIP B:=A:LOAD.COM[V]
PIP B:=A:MAC.COM[V]
PIP B:=A:PRINT.COM[V]
PIP B:=A:/.COM[V]
STAT B:*.* $$R/O
```

When the task is to be done, edit the file and alter it to fit the situation before submitting it. The burden of remembering the steps and their sequence is left to the system, while the creative work is left to you—an application of the slogan, "Machines should work, people should think."

Example 8-7 shows the contents of WORKINIT.SUB as used in the author's system to initialize work diskettes. The formatting and SYSGEN steps are omitted because it was more convenient to run a box of diskettes through each of those programs by hand. Other than that, Example 8-7 is an expansion of Example 8-6. Certain very common commands are installed on the new diskette and hidden with the SYS attribute; a longer list of commands is moved in and left visible.

The task of making a backup copy of a project disk can be automated very well. You might place a file named BACKUP.SUB on each project diskette. Put in it the commands needed to copy the important files of that disk to a backup diskette. The procedure to take a backup then is: Place the project diskette in the A-drive and a backup diskette in the B-drive. Warm start. Enter submit backup. Remove the diskettes when done.

Chapter 9

The Representation of Data

This chapter is for the CP/M user who has just launched into programming. In it we'll review the fundamental ideas of computer data storage and see how those ideas are applied by the language translators available for CP/M. This isn't a book on programming, and so we look into these interesting matters just deeply enough to gain an understanding of the common practice in CP/M software.

MEANING IS A HUMAN CONCEPT

In earlier chapters we have referred to numbers and characters as if the machine could read and understand symbols as we do. Of course that isn't the case; the processor can handle only patterns of bits. Everything that is to be processed by the machine must be represented in that form.

It's important that you understand that it is we, the humans who use the system, who attach meaning to these patterns. All bit patterns are equally meaningful—or equally meaningless—to the hardware. It is people, and primarily programmers, who decide that one group of bits means "A," that another means 65, and that yet another is the machine instruction MOV A,B. These examples are not chosen at random; all have the same pattern of bits. Meaning is a matter of human perception and of context.

BINARY DATA

Binary Units

Bits. The fundamental unit of computer storage is called the *bit*. A bit can be implemented using anything that will take on only one of two states: a tiny circuit on a chip that can be charged or not charged, or a tiny spot in a magnetic coating that can be magnetized north or south. A single bit can be made to stand for anything that has but two values. Most commonly it stands for one digit of a binary number. In that case its states represent the value 1 or 0.

Bytes. It is convenient for both machine designers and programmers to treat bits in groups of eight. A group of 8 bits has come to be called a *byte*. The byte is a handy unit for human comprehension. It can contain any one of 256 possible combinations of 0 and 1 bits. The combinations can be interpreted in different ways as the need arises: as small numbers, as characters, or as instructions to the machine.

Number Systems

Most beginning texts on programming start with an introduction to the binary number system. As a programmer you have to be familiar with it, not because you use binary numbers in programs (for you rarely do), but because that understanding is basic to understanding the machine representation of data.

Number Theory. Any number system has a base value and a set of digit symbols that stand for the quantities from zero up to one less than the base (think of the decimal system with its base of 10 and digits 0 to 9). The value of a multidigit number is formed by multiplying each digit by the base value raised to some power, and adding the results. If the base is b, then the right-most digit is multiplied by b^0, or 1 (any number to the zero power is equal to 1). The next digit left is multiplied by b^1 (the base), the next by b^2, and so on.

It works out that a number composed of n digits can represent any of b^n different values, including zero. For example, a three-digit decimal number can represent any of 10^3, or 1000, different values (000 to 999).

Binary Numbers. In a binary number the base is 2 and the only digits are 0 and 1. The value of a binary number is the right-most digit—or bit—times 1, plus the next times 2, plus the next times 4, plus the next times 8, and so on. A binary number of n digits can represent any of 2^n different values. For example, a four-digit binary number can represent 2^4, or 16, values from 0000 through 1111. A byte, which has 8 bits, can represent any of 2^8 or 256 values.

Hexadecimal Numbers. *Hexadecimal* is a number system with the base value of 16. Hexa- is the combining form of the Greek word for six and decimal is a Latin tag for ten, so the coined word "hexadecimal" can be read as "the 6-10 system." The digits used in hexadecimal are 0 through 9 with their expected values, plus the letters A, B, C, D, E, and F standing for the quantities of 10, 11, 12, 13, 14, and 15 respectively. A two-digit hexadecimal number can represent any of 16^2, or 256, different values from 00 through FF.

The Uses of Hexadecimal. Hexadecimal is very useful for discussions of binary storage. It is closely related to the binary number system. Any binary number can easily be converted into a hexadecimal number and vice versa. A group of 4 bits can represent any of 16 values, and so can a single hexadecimal digit. With practice it becomes automatic to convert, say, the digit C into the bit pattern 1100, or the bits 1001 into the digit 9. Any of the 256 possible values of a byte can be noted in 2 hexadecimal digits, and this compact notation is often used in program documentation of the more technical sort. A 16-bit binary number, nearly impossible to write out in binary without error, is easy to state in 4 hexadecimal digits.

There is one small drawback to hexadecimal numbers. On paper it is possible to confuse some hexadecimal numbers with decimal numbers. In this book we always add the suffix "h" to any hexadecimal number, like this: 40h, 01A2h.

Numbering the Bits of a Byte. Sometimes it is necessary to talk about the individual bits of a group. The usual convention is to number the bits of a group according to the power of 2 that they represent in a binary number. The right-most bit, which represents 2^0 (i.e., 1), is named bit 0. Its value has the least effect on the value of the binary number, so it is also called the least significant bit. The next bit to the left represents 2^1 (i.e., 2) and is named bit 1; the left-most bit of a byte represents 2^7 (i.e.,

128) and is called bit 7. Bit 7 has the most weight in the binary value of a byte, and is called the most significant bit.

Other Conventions. This convention for naming the bits of a byte is not universal. It is the one in common use in CP/M software, but some organizations (notably IBM) chose to adopt exactly the opposite method and designated the bits from left to right. The terms "most significant" and "least significant" are always understood, as are the equivalent terms "high order" and "low order."

REPRESENTATION OF NUMBERS

There are several ways to represent numbers in computer storage. Each has its advantages and limitations. You need to understand them in order to make a choice among language translators that support different methods.

Binary Integers

An integer is a whole number, one with no fractional part. Any group of bits may be treated as an integer. A byte can be thought of as representing an integer between 00h and FFh, or 0 to 255 in decimal. This is not enough for useful arithmetic. The next logical step is to a 16-bit, or 2-byte, integer. A group of 16 bits can represent any of 2^{16}, or 65,536, values. The processors used by CP/M have machine instructions for doing arithmetic on 16-bit integers, making computation rapid. All CP/M programming language translators support 16-bit integers.

Unsigned Integers. A binary integer may be thought of as an *unsigned* value, one that represents numbers beginning at 0 and running up to 65,535 (or 0000h to FFFFh). That interpretation of an integer is used mostly at the hardware level and in systems programs.

Signed Integers. More commonly a 16-bit integer is interpreted as being a *signed* value, containing a number from -32,768 through 0 to +32,767 (or 8000h to 7FFFh). As stored in binary those values whose left-most bit is 1 are interpreted as negative; those with a left-most bit of 0 are considered positive. The left-most bit is called the *sign bit*.

Precision. The *precision* of an integer is the number of distinct values it can represent. This is usually given as the number of digits in the largest possible value. That can be stated in bits or, less accurately, in decimal digits. A byte has 8-bit precision, which is just another way of saying it can represent 2^8 or 256 different values. You could say it had about 2.4 decimal digits of precision as it can represent about $10^{2.4}$, or about 250 different values. If you have a pocket calculator handy, you can easily calculate the decimal precision of a binary integer by raising 2 to the power of the number of bits in the integer and taking the base-10 log of that number.

Highest and Lowest Value. The precision of a number format is not the same as the highest value that can be stored in it. Precision is a measure of the number of different values that can be represented in that format. The 16-bit integer format can represent 2^{16}, or 65,536, different values, whether it is treated as signed or unsigned. However, an unsigned 16-bit integer can represent the numbers from zero to 65,535 whereas a signed one can represent the numbers from -32,768 through zero to 32,767. The highest value of a signed integer is just half that of an unsigned integer, although both can encode the same number of distinct values.

Overflow. The decimal precision of a 16-bit binary integer is less than five digits. That range is wide enough for a program loop counter, or for work with simple graphics and games, but it is not sufficient for most computation. Even the most elementary business arithmetic involves numbers having more than five digits. If the machine is asked to add 35,000 and 35,000, both represented as 16-bit integers, the computation will *overflow*. Overflow occurs when the number of bits required to represent the result is larger than the number of bits in the integer that receives the result. What happens then depends on the language translator. A few of them insert code to check for overflow; the program will stop and report an error. Most CP/M translators ignore overflow and store a meaningless result.

Binary-Coded Decimal

A group of 4 bits can represent any of 16 values, but not all 16 combinations need be used. If the range of values is restricted to 10, a 4-bit group can be thought of as representing a decimal digit from 0 to 9. A byte may represent two such digits, and a sequence of bytes may stand for a decimal integer of any precision. This representation is called *binary-coded decimal*, or BCD for short.

All processors used by CP/M have machine instructions for doing arithmetic in BCD 1 byte at a time, and so BCD arithmetic is moderately fast. BCD is convenient because it is easy to convert between the BCD values and printable characters. The precision of BCD numbers is up to the designers of the language translator. Language translators that support BCD usually allow a generous number of digits.

Floating-Point Representation

The Problem of Large Numbers. Scientific applications often require numbers with a very wide range of magnitudes, from tiny fractions to vast quantities, while demanding little in the way of precision. For example, the distance from the earth to the sun is about 1.5 times 10^8 kilometers, and Planck's constant is 6.625 times 10^{-27}. Such numbers would require many BCD digits or huge binary integers to represent them, but most of the digits in such a representation would be zero. The precision needed is small; it is the magnitudes that are of interest. Either number could be represented in a 16-bit binary integer if the magnitude, the power of 10 by which it is multiplied, could be expressed separately.

Floating-Point Numbers. That is precisely what *floating-point* representation allows. A floating-point number is composed of two integers. The shorter part, usually a single byte, contains the magnitude, the power of 10 to be multiplied with the number. The longer part, commonly 24 bits, represents a fraction between 0 and 1 that is to be multiplied by that magnitude. The magnitude part of a floating-point number is called its *exponent*; the fraction is called the *mantissa*, or simply "the fraction."

Speed of Floating-Point Arithmetic. Floating-point arithmetic has two disadvantages. The first, and less important, is that most CP/M processors have no machine instructions for such arithmetic. They perform floating-point computations with long sequences of instructions. As a result the computations are fairly slow and take several times as long as computations involving integers. Floating-point hardware units are available for some machines, but they require support in the language translator and this can't always be arranged.

Hazards of Floating Point. The more serious drawback of floating-point representation is that it can yield inaccurate results when used in situations where it isn't appropriate. The precision of a 24-bit fraction is less than seven decimal digits. In other words, the numbers 12,345.67 and 12,345.68 might be the same when encoded in floating-point form. Such small inaccuracies accumulate over a series of computations. For most scientific work a difference of one part in one million is not significant. But in a commercial program where the quantity represented is money, the difference between the two numbers is a penny and is always significant whatever the size of the numbers. A penny's difference in a million dollar account will keep the books from balancing. A penny rounded the wrong way in a tax computation will bring a complaint from the employee who gets the check.

As a general rule floating-point representation should never be used for the calculation of money. If it is necessary to do so, then the precision of the representation must be at least two digits greater than the most precise number to be stored, preferably several digits greater.

REPRESENTATION OF CHARACTERS: ASCII

The 256 values that a byte takes on can be interpreted as standing for characters. Such an interpretation is strictly arbitrary; there is no relationship between bytes and printed letters except as people agree on one. People have agreed on a relationship between certain byte values and certain characters. That agreement, the most widely respected standard in the industry, was established by a committee of the American National Standards Institute (ANSI) and is called the American Standard Code for Information Interchange, or ASCII (the acronym has become a word in its own right, and is pronounced "as'-key"). ASCII has been adopted with only tiny changes by the International Standards Organization, and is in use on all computers (barring only IBM machines) throughout the world. The ASCII code is shown in Figure 9-1.

	ϕ 000	1 001	2 010	3 011	4 100	5 101	6 110	7 111
ϕ 0000	NUL / 00 / 0	DLE / 10 / 16 / P	Space / 20 / 32	ϕ / 30 / 48	@ / 40 / 64	P / 50 / 80 / DLE	` / 60 / 96	p / 70 / 112
1 0001	SOH / 01 / 1 / A	DC1 / 11 / 17 / Q	! / 21 / 33	1 / 31 / 49	A / 41 / 65 / SOH	Q / 51 / 81 / DC1	a / 61 / 97	q / 71 / 113
2 0010	STX / 02 / 2 / B	DC2 / 12 / 18 / R	" / 22 / 34	2 / 32 / 50	B / 42 / 66 / STX	R / 52 / 82 / DC2	b / 62 / 98	r / 72 / 114
3 0011	ETX / 03 / 3 / C	DC3 / 13 / 19 / S	# / 23 / 35	3 / 33 / 51	C / 43 / 67 / ETX	S / 53 / 83 / DC3	c / 63 / 99	s / 73 / 115
4 0100	EOT / 04 / 4 / D	DC4 / 14 / 20 / T	$ / 24 / 36	4 / 34 / 52	D / 44 / 68 / EOT	T / 54 / 84 / DC4	d / 64 / 100	t / 74 / 116
5 0101	ENQ / 05 / 5 / E	NAK / 15 / 21 / U	% / 25 / 37	5 / 35 / 53	E / 45 / 69 / ENQ	U / 55 / 85 / NAK	e / 65 / 101	u / 75 / 117
6 0110	ACK / 06 / 6 / F	SYN / 16 / 22 / V	& / 26 / 38	6 / 36 / 54	F / 46 / 70 / ACK	V / 56 / 86 / SYN	f / 66 / 102	v / 76 / 118
7 0111	BEL / 07 / 7 / G	ETB / 17 / 23 / W	' / 27 / 39	7 / 37 / 55	G / 47 / 71 / BEL	W / 57 / 87 / ETB	g / 67 / 103	w / 77 / 119
8 1000	BS / 08 / 8 / H	CAN / 18 / 24 / X	(/ 28 / 40	8 / 38 / 56	H / 48 / 72 / BS	X / 58 / 88 / CAN	h / 68 / 104	x / 78 / 120
9 1001	HT / 09 / 9 / I	EM / 19 / 25 / Y	) / 29 / 41	9 / 39 / 57	I / 49 / 73 / HT	Y / 59 / 89 / EM	i / 69 / 105	y / 79 / 121
A 1010	LF / 0A / 10 / J	SUB / 1A / 26 / Z	* / 2A / 42	: / 3A / 58	J / 4A / 74 / LF	Z / 5A / 90 / SUB	j / 6A / 106	z / 7A / 122
B 1011	VT / 0B / 11 / K	ESC / 1B / 27 / [	+ / 2B / 43	; / 3B / 59	K / 4B / 75 / VT	[/ 5B / 91 / ESC	k / 6B / 107	{ / 7B / 123
C 1100	FF / 0C / 12 / L	FS / 1C / 28 / \	, / 2C / 44	< / 3C / 60	L / 4C / 76 / FF	\ / 5C / 92 / FS	l / 6C / 108	| / 7C / 124
D 1101	CR / 0D / 13 / M	GS / 1D / 29 /]	— / 2D / 45	= / 3D / 61	M / 4D / 77 / CR	] / 5D / 93 / GS	m / 6D / 109	} / 7D / 125
E 1110	SO / 0E / 14 / N	RS / 1E / 30 / ^	. / 2E / 46	> / 3E / 62	N / 4E / 78 / SO	∧ / 5E / 94 / RS	n / 6E / 110	~ / 7E / 126
F 1111	SI / 0F / 15 / O	US / 1F / 31 / _	/ / 2F / 47	? / 3F / 63	O / 4F / 79 / SI	_ / 5F / 95 / US	o / 6F / 111	DEL / 7F / 127

FIGURE 9-1
The ASCII code displayed. Each square shows one character with its hexadecimal value at the upper right and its decimal value at the lower left. The first two columns contain control characters.

The 7-Bit Code. Every feature of ASCII is the result of careful compromise. One such feature is the size of the code table. It has only 128 elements from 00h to 7Fh, and so can be represented in groups of 7 bits. That length was a compromise between the 6-bit codes in use when the standard was formed and the 8-bit machines then on the horizon.

ASCII in the 8-Bit Byte. Since the creation of the standard the 8-bit byte has become normal. The standard states that an ASCII character, when stored or transmitted in an 8-bit byte, will be stored in the least significant 7 bits with the most significant bit set to zero.

The Parity Bit. When transmitted between machines, an ASCII character may have a *parity bit* added in the most significant position. A parity bit is a check bit that enables many transmission errors to be recognized and caught. The CP/M monitor assumes that the most significant bit of any byte it receives from a terminal is a parity bit, and sets it to zero before delivering the character to the program that requested it. When a program asks the Monitor to transmit a byte to a terminal, the Monitor assumes that the byte is an ASCII character, and sets the most significant bit to zero. The I/O code supplied by the vendor may or may not set it to a parity value.

Printable Characters

The Alphabet. ASCII contains two complete alphabets, one of uppercase letters and one of lowercase letters. The code was devised so that it would be easy to convert from one to the other. Note in Figure 9-1 that the difference between an uppercase letter and its lowercase partner is only in 1 bit. If bit 5 is set to 0, the letter is uppercase; if set to 1, it is lowercase.

Punctuation. ASCII has a rich set of punctuation and special characters, most of which should be present on your terminal and your printer. One, whose byte value is 5Eh, can have two different printable forms. Newer terminals will render this character as a caret or circumflex (^), but some will display it as an up-pointing arrow. Either form is permitted by the standard. This was a compromise between the domestic U.S. code (which used the up-arrow) and the European code (which required the circumflex as a mark of punctuation). Some programming languages use the up-arrow as a symbol for exponentiation. They also will accept the caret. The byte value used by the program is the same in either case.

Non-English Punctuation. The punctuation of most languages is present in ASCII. Items such as the tilde (~) may present difficulties, because the output device must backspace and overstrike, and may have to index up or down. This is impossible with display terminals and some printers.

Collating Sequence. "A" and "a" in ASCII are two different letters with different byte values. This is true in any computer character code, and it causes problems for applications that involve alphabetizing. A person setting up a card index would realize that ADAM, Adam, and adam were all the same word, and that Apple followed all three. A computer would not; based on the values of ASCII it would sort them into the order ADAM, Adam, Apple, and then adam. There are other things about the collating sequence that ASCII establishes that might cause trouble: the numeric characters precede the letters, so that "120A Main" will collate after "1200 Main," and some of the punctuation is oddly scattered. The result is that you must give careful thought to the design of records that are to be sorted.

Control Characters

The Use of Control Characters. The first 32 ASCII codes (00h through 1Fh) and the last (7Fh) are control characters. These have no printable shape; they are used to regulate the transmission of data between two devices. A number of the characters are useful only for teleprocessing (sending data between computers over telephone lines), but several serve useful functions within a system.

Relation to Printable Characters. Each control character is paired with a printable character by a 1-bit change. If bit 6 of a byte containing a control character is set to 1, a printable character results. This was done so that it would be easy for designers to provide a control shift key on keyboards. The relation is clear in Figure 9-1. To find the letter linked to a control code, look four columns to the right in the table. All CP/M terminals have a control shift key (we used it often in the exercises of Chapter 5). The control key links each control character to a normal key button. Control-a thus transmits 01h, the character named SOH, and control-underscore transmits 1Fh, the character US.

Most programming languages provide some way to specify the control characters within a program. BASIC, for instance, has the CHR$ function.

Format Effectors. Seven of the control characters are defined as format effectors—characters that control the format, rather than the content, of the data. The seven are listed in Table 9-1. You should verify which of these characters are supported by your terminal and printer. Your printer may not respond to a backspace (BS) but should support the formfeed (FF); your terminal probably does just the opposite.

CR and LF in CP/M Files. The carriage return (CR) and linefeed (LF) characters are important in CP/M. A pair of bytes CR, LF is used to end each record of a file of ASCII text. Neither CR nor LF alone represents a record boundary, but CR and LF, adjacent and in that order, do.

Device Controls. Thirteen of the ASCII control codes are miscellaneous device controls. These are summarized in Table 9-2. When received by any terminal (and some

TABLE 9-1
The ASCII format effectors, control characters defined to control the format of data rather than its content.

Character Name	Value as Dec.	Value as Hex.	Control Shift	Meaning and Use
CR	13	0Dh	M	Carriage return—return print head or cursor to left margin.
LF	10	0Ah	J	Linefeed—move print head or cursor down one line with respect to the paper or screen display.
BS	8	08h	H	Backspace—move print head or cursor left one character position.
HT	9	09h	I	Horizontal tab—move print head or cursor right to the next defined tab stop. CPM assumes tab stops are set at every eighth position, e.g., 9, 17, 25.
FF	12	0Ch	L	Formfeed—move print head to top of next sheet of paper. Some terminals will clear the screen and others will ignore the formfeed.
VT	11	0Bh	K	Vertical tab—move print head down to the next vertical tab stop.

printers), BEL will cause a beep or chime to sound. The cancel (CAN) character is used by the Console Command Processor as a signal to clear its input line and start over; you've used it often as control-x. CAN would be a logical choice if you needed a special character to mark a deleted record in a file.

SUB IN CP/M FILES. The designers of CP/M chose the substitute (SUB) character to mark the end of a file of ASCII text, and to mark the end of strings in the command languages of PIP and ED. They may have been attracted to it by the mnemonic value of using control-z to signal "the end," but it is curious that they didn't make the more logical choice of the end-of-medium (EM) control character. EM is the character that the standard has set aside to mark the end of active data on some medium, which is precisely the purpose for which CP/M uses SUB. At any rate you must be careful never to write a SUB code as part of a file of ASCII text as CP/M commands won't read past it; any data that follow will be unreachable. The exception is PIP; it will read past a SUB if given its O option.

ESC AND ESCAPE SEQUENCES. The escape (ESC) character is important. It signals that one or more characters following it are to be interpreted in some special way. ASCII devices with special features usually rely on sequences beginning with ESC to control

TABLE 9-2
ASCII device control characters provide a variety of useful functions. Unfortunately their use by equipment designers has not always been consistent or in the spirit of the standard.

Character Name	Value as Dec.	Value as Hex.	Control Shift	Meaning and Use
NUL	0	00h	(none)	Null—used to fill time between data transmissions; has no information content.
BEL	7	07h	G	Bell—sounds an audible alarm.
SO	14	0Eh	N	Shift out—change to an alternate font of printable characters.
SI	15	0Fh	O	Shift in—return to standard printable characters. SO and SI are the logical choices to control screen graphics, but no terminal maker uses them so.
DC1	17	11h	Q	Device control 1—once called XON for transmit on, used to start a unit of a remote device. Some printers emit DC1 when they are ready to receive data.
DC2	18	12h	R	Device control 2—used to start a unit of a remote device.
DC3	19	13h	S	Device control 3—once called XOFF for transmit off, used to stop a unit of a remote device. Some printers emit DC3 when their buffers are nearly full.
DC4	20	14h	T	Device control 4—used to stop a unit of a remote device.
CAN	24	18h	X	Cancel—the data accompanying this character are to be disregarded. Logical choice to mark a deleted record.
EM	25	19h	Y	End of medium—meant to mark the end of active data on a tape or other medium.
SUB	26	1Ah	Z	Substitute—replaces a character known to have been garbled in transmission. CPM uses SUB to mark end of file.
ESC	27	1Bh		Escape—marks the following one to four characters as special controls.
DEL	127	7Fh	(none)	Delete—once called rubout; like null, has no information content. On paper tape a character can be erased by punching all its holes, resulting in DEL.

those special features. For example, some terminals will accept an escape sequence that directs them to move the cursor to a particular spot on the screen. An attempt has been made by ANSI to standardize the design of escape sequences, with little effect. You will find that your terminal's repertoire of special features is controlled by escape sequences different from those used by terminals from other makers.

WORKING STORAGE

The computer's primary storage medium is working storage. It is composed of a large array of integrated circuits, each holding a collection of bits. The array is organized into bytes and each byte can be accessed individually by the processor. The bytes are just bytes to the hardware; it is CP/M and the programmer that impose structure and meaning on them.

Speed of Working Storage. Working storage responds to access requests very quickly. Such speed is essential because all of the instructions and all the data that they act on are held in working storage. If the processor is to keep running at its rated speed, working storage has to deliver data at very high speed.

Addresses. Working storage is organized as an array of 8-bit bytes. Each byte is numbered. The number is called its *address*—it serves the same function as a street address on a house. The first byte in working storage is numbered 0, the next 1, and so on to the limit of the machine.

Address Notation. In CP/M machines addresses are given as 16-bit integers, interpreted as numbers in the range of 0...65,535. A 16-bit integer can be represented as 4 hexadecimal digits, and that is how we'll name specific addresses from now on. Once you are accustomed to it, addresses make better sense in hexadecimal than in decimal as the powers of 2 into which storage naturally divides come out as more suggestive numbers in hexadecimal. For example, the last byte available in a machine with the maximum amount of storage has the address FFFFh, a clearer indication that it is the last than the decimal number 65,535.

Processor Input. In order to read working storage, the processor emits the bit pattern of an address on a set of address lines. The circuits of working storage decode the address to select one of all the bytes they hold, and emit the bit pattern held in that byte on a set of data lines. The processor accepts the bit pattern and proceeds with its operations.

Processor Output. In order to write into working storage, the processor emits both an address value and the data value, and also sets a circuit to indicate that it is writing. The working storage circuitry decodes the address, accepts the bit pattern of the data, and impresses it upon that byte, thus replacing whatever was there. Either process can be accomplished in less than half a microsecond.

Processor Indifference to Meaning. To the hardware, all bytes of working storage are alike. The processor is as willing to fetch an operation code from location 0000h as it is to write a character into the byte at FFFFh. Any location may contain any bit pattern, and the processor is willing to interpret the bits in a location in any way the programmer instructs it to: as a character, as part of a number, or as an instruction.

Chapter 10

The File System

The File System

In this chapter we examine the file system as it is used by a programmer working in a high-level language such as BASIC or Pascal. We will expose the workings of the Monitor in enough detail to enable you to make sense of the STAT command's displays. Then we'll observe the operation of the system as a BASIC program writes a file and reads it back. We discuss the file system in more detail in Chapter 13.

CONTROL OF THE DISKS

A disk is organized at three levels. There is the physical organization of tracks and sectors, which is managed by code supplied by the vendor of the system. On this, CP/M builds an organization of files composed of extents, allocation blocks, and records. The programmer, working through a programming language, imposes his or her view of the stored data on that structure.

Physical Organization

Physical Units. In Chapter 2 we described how a diskette or rigid disk is divided into tracks by the stepping motion of the access arm, and the tracks into sectors by the drive electronics. The number of tracks, the number of sectors per track, and the size of a sector are all matters that vary with the type of drive and the way the disk is formatted. It is possible to have several different disk configurations active at once. The A-drive might have a double-density, 8-inch diskette with eight 1024-byte sectors on each of its 77 tracks whereas the B-drive might have a single-density diskette with twenty-six 128-byte sectors per track. Yet another drive might be a portion of a hard disk with still other dimensions.

The BIOS and the BDOS. This variety is controlled and managed by a part of the Monitor known as the Basic I/O System, or BIOS. This is the part of the Monitor that is written by the system's vendor. Its primary function is to move data to and from I/O devices, especially the disks, at the command of the standard part of the Monitor (which is called the Basic Disk Operating System, or BDOS). We'll have a lot more to say about the BDOS and BIOS in later chapters.

Role of the BIOS. The BIOS is the only part of the Monitor that is aware of the physical organization of the disks. The BIOS manages the disk interface circuits, commanding the access arm to move from track to track and ordering sectors to be read or written. The Monitor makes requests of the BIOS in terms of records of a standard size, 128 bytes. The record might be a sector or only part of a sector. In the latter case the BIOS must read a complete physical sector (disks only read and write complete sectors) and then pass the right 128-byte portion of it to the Monitor.

ROLE OF THE BDOS. The BDOS, the standard part of the Monitor, views all disks as having some number of tracks, each of which contains 128-byte records. CP/M 1.4 only supports disks whose sectors are 128 bytes in length, and so the Monitor's records corresponded exactly to sectors. With version 2.0 of CP/M that relationship was broken. CP/M continues to view all disks as being laid out in 128-byte records, but it relies on the BIOS to relate those standard records to the physical layout of the disk. The BDOS learns such things about a disk as how many tracks it has, or how many standard records fit on a track, by asking the BIOS.

DISK ORGANIZATION

The STAT DSK: Display

The STAT command will display what the BDOS knows about any disk. The form of STAT for that display is

STAT *drivecode*:DSK:

Example 10-1 shows two typical displays for 8-inch diskettes that were formatted just before the displays were made.

Reserved Tracks and Data Tracks

RESERVED TRACKS. The last line of the STAT display gives the number of reserved tracks. Some of the lower numbered (outermost) tracks of a disk are reserved and do not

EXAMPLE 10-1
The STAT disk information display shows everything that the BDOS knows about a disk. The BIOS supplies the information.

```
A>; with single-density diskette...
A>stat b:dsk:

    B: Drive Characteristics
 1944: 128 Byte Record Capacity
  243: Kilobyte Drive Capacity
   64: 32  Byte Directory Entries
   64: Checked  Directory Entries
  128: Records/ Extent
    8: Records/ Block
   26: Sectors/ Track
    2: Reserved Tracks

A>stat b:

Bytes Remaining on B: 241k
```

```
A>; with double-density diskette...
A>stat b:dsk:

    B: Drive Characteristics
 4800: 128 Byte Record Capacity
  600: Kilobyte Drive Capacity
  128: 32  Byte Directory Entries
  128: Checked  Directory Entries
  128: Records/ Extent
   16: Records/ Block
   64: Sectors/ Track
    2: Reserved Tracks

A>stat b:

Bytes Remaining on B: 596k
```

contain data. These are the tracks that contain the image of the Monitor and CCP that is loaded on a warm or cold start. There are usually two reserved tracks. On a 5-inch diskette it may require three tracks to hold the Monitor image. On a rigid disk the number of reserved tracks may be very large; we'll see the reason for that in Chapter 14.

Data Tracks. The remaining tracks on a disk are used for data, except for a section that is reserved for the file directory. The STAT display does not show the count of data tracks directly. Its first line gives the total number of standard records that the drive will hold, and the next to last line gives the number of standard records (confusingly, and incorrectly, reported as "sectors") on each data track. Divide the number of records per track into the total number of records to obtain the number of data tracks.

The File Directory

The file directory is a table of all the files on a disk. The directory contains the name and type of each file and a record of where on the disk each file's data are kept.

Directory Size. The first records of the first (outermost) data track are used by the Monitor to contain the file directory. The size of the directory is a vendor option, reported to the Monitor by the BIOS. The directory size is displayed by STAT in the third line of the display. Each directory entry is 32 bytes long, and the display gives the directory size in terms of entries. Divide by four to learn how many 128-byte standard records are allocated to the directory. Subtract that number from the count of all records in the first line of the display to discover how many of the disk's records are available for data.

A Disk Space Discrepancy. We can now explain one seeming discrepancy in the STAT displays in Example 10-1. The disks were newly formatted and all records should have been available. Yet the disk information display reports a different capacity in kilobytes than the normal STAT display does. The disk information display reports drive capacity as 128 bytes times the total count of standard records. The normal STAT display reports the available data space, which is the total less the records allocated to the directory. When a disk is freshly formatted, the difference between the two quantities is the size of the directory in bytes.

Allocation Blocks

CP/M allocates file space in *allocation blocks*, each containing some number of standard records. An allocation block is the smallest unit of space that CP/M can allocate to a file.

Regardless of its exact size, a file will always have reserved to it some number of allocation blocks. The records contained in a block are adjacent to each other on the disk.

ALLOCATION BLOCK SIZE. The third from last line of the disk information display shows the number of records included in each allocation block. The first information display in Example 10-1 shows that there are 16 records (i.e., 16*128 = 2048 bytes) in each allocation block. On such a disk 16 records is the smallest allocation unit. Files from 1 byte to 2048 bytes in length will have one block of 16 records allocated to them. Files containing from 2049 to 4096 bytes will have two blocks, or 32 records, allocated to them, and so forth. The disk described by the second report in Example 10-1 uses eight records, or 1024 bytes, per allocation block.

A PUZZLE FROM CHAPTER 5. The fact that CP/M allocates space in blocks of several records explains a small puzzle left unexplained in Chapter 5. There we used PIP to create T9.FIL by concatenating three smaller files. According to STAT, each small file occupied 2 KB, but their concatenation occupied only 4 KB. Now it should be clear that the small files were considerably less than 2K bytes each, but each had received an allocation of 2K bytes regardless. The concatenation of their data added to just over 2K bytes and so received two allocation blocks totaling 4K.

USE OF ALLOCATION BLOCK SIZE. It is useful to know the size of an allocation block. You need never estimate the expected size of a file more closely than to the nearest block. There's no point in trying to economize on file space unless the file in question is larger than one allocation block, and unless the economy to be applied will result in savings greater than one block.

Directory Entries and Extents

DIRECTORY USE IN CP/M 1.4. Each entry in the directory can describe a fixed number of allocation blocks. In earlier versions of CP/M the allocation block size was always eight records or 1024 bytes, and a directory entry could describe 16 such blocks. Therefore, a directory entry could describe 16K bytes of space. That amount of space was called an *extent*, and everyone assumed that "extent" meant "the amount of space described by one directory entry, which is 16K bytes."

DIRECTORY USE IN CP/M 2. Version 2 of CP/M extended the file system so that vendors could specify larger allocation blocks. This improved the system's performance and made it possible to use disks of greater capacity. It also complicated the terminology of the file system. With current versions of CP/M (and MP/M) a single directory entry might describe as much as 256K bytes of space. That would be an unusual case, but it is common for disks to be configured so that one directory entry describes 32K or 64K bytes.

Logical and Physical Extents. What, then, does the word "extent" mean? Is it the amount of space controlled by one directory entry? Or does it mean 16K bytes of space (in which case a single directory entry might describe several "extents")? The CP/M documentation uses the term in both ways. We will use the term *logical extent* when we mean a unit of 16K bytes of data. The unqualified term *extent* will refer to the amount of space that can be described by one directory entry on a particular disk. That will be some multiple of a logical extent (some multiple of 16K bytes), depending on the size of an allocation block.

Logical Extents from STAT DSK:. To discover the number of logical extents per directory entry, refer to the STAT disk information display. It shows the number of "records/extent," and in that line, the word "extent" refers to the space described by one directory entry. Divide the number of records shown by 128 (the number of records in 16K of data) to find out how many logical extents a directory entry contains. In both displays in Example 10-1 there are 128 records in an extent, so for those disks a logical extent is equal to a physical one.

Files Larger than One Extent. A directory entry can describe only a limited amount of space—usually 16K bytes and never more than 256K bytes. CP/M allows files to be as large as 8M bytes (8 megabytes). Files of that size can't possibly be described by a single entry in the disk directory.

A file that exceeds the size described by one directory entry has more directory entries allocated to it. A file may have many directory entries, each describing part of the space it occupies. Indeed, if there is only one file on a disk and it fills the disk, then all of the entries in the disk directory are needed to describe that file.

File Allocation

Once you've swallowed that lump of background information, you'll find it easy to understand how CP/M allocates space to files. When data are first put into a file, the Monitor selects an unused directory entry and initializes it. Then it chooses an unused allocation block and records it in the directory entry. The records of that block now belong to the file. As the program produces data, the data are stored in the records of that block. When all the records of the block have been filled, the Monitor selects another block to be recorded in the directory and filled. If a file grows until it has filled all the blocks that can be recorded in an extent, then another directory entry is chosen and the process continues.

In later chapters we examine how the Monitor keeps track of used and unused blocks and directory entries, and how the entries that represent successive extents of a file are linked together. For the purpose of writing application programs, it is enough to know how to decode STAT's disk information display, and to understand the three units controlled by the Monitor: standard 128-byte records, allocation blocks, and extents.

The STAT File Report

Example 10-2 shows the display produced by the stat *fileref* command. In Chapter 5 we sidestepped the job of explaining all the columns, but now that you understand file allocation you can decode them.

NUMBER OF RECORDS IN A FILE. The first column, headed "Recs," is the count of standard 128-byte records that actually contain data for the file. It does not include records that have been allocated as part of a block but not yet used. This is the nearest approximation to the true size of the file that you can get from STAT. The file size in bytes is 128 times the count of records in it. That might be exactly right, or it might be off by as much as 127 bytes.

SPACE ALLOCATED TO A FILE. The second column, headed "Bytes," is a count of the total amount of space allocated to the file; that is, it is the size of an allocation block times the number of blocks that have been allocated. This is not exactly the size of the file—that is better described by the "Recs" column—but it does describe the amount of disk space that this file controls, the amount that would be made available if the file were erased.

LOGICAL EXTENTS IN A FILE. You might guess that the third column, headed "Ext," is a count of the number of extents—that is, directory entries—controlled by the file. In most cases you would be right. This column is a count of the 16-KB *logical* extents owned by the file. To determine the number of *physical* extents, and hence directory

EXAMPLE 10-2
The STAT file display: Recs are 128-byte standard records, Bytes is the space allocated to the file, Ext is the number of 16 KB logical extents and usually the number of directory entries.

```
A>stat *.com

 Recs  Bytes  Ext Acc
   38     6k    1 R/W A:DDT.COM
    5     2k    1 R/W A:DUMP.COM
   52     8k    1 R/W A:ED.COM
   98    14k    1 R/W A:EDIT.COM
   14     2k    1 R/W A:LOAD.COM
   92    12k    1 R/W A:MAC.COM
  190    24k    2 R/W A:MBASIC.COM
   58     8k    1 R/W A:PIP.COM
  142    18k    2 R/W A:PRINT.COM
   41     6k    1 R/W A:STAT.COM
   10     2k    1 R/W A:SUBMIT.COM
    6     2k    1 R/W A:XSUB.COM

A>_
```

entries, used by the file, you must divide by the number of logical extents described by each directory entry.

SEQUENTIAL FILE ACCESS

Let's study the operations of the Monitor as a file is written and then read again. Let's assume that you've written a program that will acquire data from some source and write the data into a new file, one that doesn't yet exist. Afterward the program will read the file back and display it at the terminal. Figure 10-1 shows a simple BASIC program that will do just that.

Creating the File

Opening the File. The program begins by *opening* the file. Anywhere in data processing, to open a file is to locate the file and prepare it for access. Most programming languages provide a statement that opens a file, usually with provision for the name of the file and an indication of whether the program will be reading (in which case the file must already exist) or writing (in which case it shouldn't exist).

Erasing an Existing File. Here we are opening the file for output, and these actions will ensue. First the Monitor will be asked to see if the file exists. If it does, then the Monitor will be requested to erase the file, because it will be replaced. (Some languages leave it up to the programmer to check for an existing file of the same name and erase it.)

The Initial Directory Entry. Once the file is known not to exist, the Monitor is asked to create an initial directory entry for the file. This service request locates an unused directory entry and initializes it with the name of the file. The entry will not show any space allocation. As far as the Monitor is concerned the file has zero length.

Use of the File Control Block. A copy of the directory entry, called the File Control Block (FCB), is kept by the program and passed as an operand of all subsequent service requests. This copy of a directory entry reflects the true state of the file; it contains the current allocation information as the file grows. The directory entry on disk will not change; it will continue to indicate that the file has zero length for some time. If the program halts or is canceled (by control-c or reset) before the directory on disk is updated, the file will have zero length as far as anyone can tell.

Writing to the File

Data Records and Standard Records. It's important to realize that the standard records written by the Monitor bear no relation at all to what the programmer knows as a record. As a programmer you should think in terms of the units of data that are natural to

```
1000 REM A simple program to create a file.  The syntax
1100 REM is correct for Microsoft Basic; small changes are
1200 REM needed for other translators.
1300 REM
1400 REM 1. Establish the on-error routine
1500 REM
1600      ON ERROR GOTO 5100
1700 REM
1800 REM 2. Open the file for output
1900 REM
2000      OPEN "O",#1,"TEST.FIL"
2100 REM
2200 REM 3. Ask the operator how many records to write
2300 REM
2400      INPUT "How many records"; NREC
2500 REM
2600 REM 4. Write NREC records all of the form:
2700 REM      This is TEST.FIL line...,(number)
2800 REM
2900      THIS$ = "This is TEST.FIL line...,"
3000 REM
3100      FOR J = 1 TO NREC
3200        PRINT#1, THIS$;J
3300      NEXT J
3400 REM
3500 REM 5. Close the file and open it again for input
3600 REM
3700      CLOSE#1
3800      OPEN "I",#1,"TEST.FIL"
3900 REM
4000 REM 6. Read back all NREC lines and type them
4100 REM
4200      FOR J = 1 TO NREC
4300        INPUT#1,THIS$,K
4400        PRINT THIS$,K
4500      NEXT J
4600 REM
4700      END
4800 REM
4900 REM ** error trapping routine -- just display the number
5000 REM
5100     PRINT
5200     PRINT "Trapped on error ";ERR;"..."
5300     PRINT "   in line ";ERL;", doing record ";J
5400     PRINT
5500 END
```

FIGURE 10-1
A simple program in BASIC illustrates one language translator's method of bringing CP/M file operations to the programmer.

the problem you are solving. For example, you might be writing a record that consists of a name, a street address, a city, a state, and a zip code. As represented by the programming language, those items might add up to 66 bytes, or 102, or any other number. That is the data record size and the only unit of data worth your attention. It is the job of the language translator to collect those units into 128-byte records, and the job of the Monitor to store the records on disk. Only when you use assembly language does the burden of handling both kinds of records fall on you.

Collecting a Standard Record. The program begins to generate data and specify that the data be written to the file. (In BASIC this is done with a PRINT# statement.) The Monitor has a write service request, but it accepts only units of 128 bytes of data.

The language translator (or the programmer, in assembly language) must provide the code to collect data until exactly 128 bytes are ready. Then a service request is made to write that 128-byte standard record to the file.

Allocating Space. The first time this service request is made, the Monitor will see from the FCB that no space has been allocated to the file. It will select an unused allocation block, record it in the FCB, then write the data to disk in the first record controlled by that allocation block. Subsequent write requests cause the Monitor to write in the following records of that block until the block is filled; then another block is allocated. The block numbers and the count of records written to the latest block are recorded in the FCB. The Monitor keeps no information about the file; everything that is known about the file is recorded in the FCB, which is in the keeping of the program.

Allocating Extents. As writing continues the FCB will become filled with block numbers. When the last record of the last block is written, the Monitor will copy the FCB into the directory on disk. That makes the allocation done in the first extent permanent. If the program is canceled after this point, the file will appear to have exactly one extent of data.

After updating the directory the Monitor, assuming that more data are to come, finds and initializes another directory entry, and initializes the FCB in the program to show that the current extent is empty. Writing may continue in this way, record by record, block by block, and extent by extent as needed.

Completing the File

Closing the File. Anywhere in data processing to *close* a file is to complete the last access to it, make it permanent, and release it. Most programming languages provide an explicit close request; some close all files automatically at the end of the run. The Monitor provides a close service request.

Writing the Last Record. The language translator buffers data in 128-byte records. When the program calls for the file to be closed, there may be a partial record left. That has to be written with a write service request. Then the program asks the Monitor to close the file. The Monitor copies the FCB into the directory on disk, and all the allocation information becomes permanent.

Reading the File

Opening the File for Input. In order to read a file it must be opened. The Monitor is asked to find the file and copy its directory entry into an FCB. There is a count in the FCB of the number of records that have been read; this is set to zero.

Reading a Data Record. The program contains a request for a data record (an INPUT# statement in BASIC). When this is executed, the program calls on the Monitor to provide the next 128-byte standard record. The Monitor reads the record from disk and copies it to a buffer supplied by the program. The FCB is updated to indicate that one record has been read.

Data Records versus Standard Records. The data record needed by the program probably will not be exactly 128 bytes long. It may be completely contained in a standard record, with data left over. In that case the following data must be saved and used to satisfy the next input command. The data record might span two or more standard records, in which case more records have to be read until the complete data record has been provided.

Succeeding Extents. When the last standard record of an extent has been read, the Monitor searches the disk directory for the directory record of the next extent. A copy of that extent entry is placed in the FCB, and reading continues.

Closing an Input File. Under CP/M it is not necessary to close an input file. There is no need to update the disk directory after input. Some operating systems hold information on active files outside the program space and so need a close call as a signal that the operating system may clean up its tables. That is not the case with CP/M; all information on the state of the file is in the FCB, which is held by the program.

It is still a good idea to close input files. There are two reasons for this. First, the code generated by the language translator may benefit from knowing that a file is not in use. It may have buffer space or tables that it can release. The second reason is that MP/M does keep track of open files. When you open a file under MP/M 1, the operating system notes that that disk is active. Until you close the file, MP/M will not allow the system operator to change that disk. MP/M 2 keeps track of each open file so that it can protect one program's files from the actions of other programs.

DIRECT FILE ACCESS

The common way to access a file is sequentially, from first record to last. CP/M offers a second way to access a file: direct access to any standard record in the file. Direct access is useful for many applications and absolutely essential for a few. With it you can retrieve any records you want, in any sequence.

Direct Access in CP/M 1.4. True direct access was added to CP/M with release 2.0. A limited form of it was available in earlier versions. Most of the language translators for CP/M were written for earlier releases of the system and not all of them have been updated to take advantage of direct access. Such packages will limit the size of a directly accessed file to 256K bytes and may not be able to handle direct access on double-density disks.

Input with Direct Access

Reading a file with direct access is slightly more complicated than reading one sequentially. The language will require a different form of input command. In it you will be asked to provide a record number.

Data Records versus Standard Records. Usually the language will require all data records in a direct file to be of the same length—so that the number of the standard record that is wanted can be computed by multiplying the length of one data record by its record number, and then dividing by 128. The result is the number of the standard record in the file in which the data record lies (or at least the one in which it begins).

Reading a Standard Record. With that information the program can call on the Monitor for a direct read of that standard record. If the record lies in a different extent than the one in use, the Monitor will have to search the directory to find the entry that describes the extent that is needed. Then it can find out which block contains the record and so learn where on the disk that record lies.

Output with Direct Access

Allocation with Direct Access. File allocation works differently when a file is created with direct access. The Monitor allocates blocks and extents as you write to them. You need not write every record. If you skip over an extent's worth of records, the space will not be allocated. If you skip over a block's worth, the block will not be allocated.

Files with Holes. It is possible with direct access to create a file that has holes (large areas of undefined space) in it. If such a file is read sequentially, the Monitor will report end of file when it reaches the first hole. All the data following the first hole will be unreachable for sequential reading. If the file is read with direct access and a nonexistent record is requested, the Monitor returns an error code to the program. What the program does then depends on the rules of that particular programming language. One way to avoid both problems is always to create files sequentially and use direct access only for retrieval and update.

STAT and Direct Access

When a file contains holes, the numbers displayed by the stat *fileref* command have little meaning. The stat *fileref* command has an optional operand $S, which causes it to display, in addition to the usual numbers, the so-called virtual size of the file. That is the size the file would have if it had no holes. A file with holes will show a difference between its virtual number of records and the number in the Recs column.

TYPES OF FILES

As CP/M sees it, there is just one kind of file: a series of standard records, allocated in blocks, described by directory entries. From another point of view, there are two types of files: ASCII files and binary files. From still another point of view there are many conventional file types, each with its own rules.

ASCII Files

A file that contains ASCII text may be edited from the terminal with ED or another editor program. A file of ASCII text can be written directly to the terminal or printer with TYPE, PIP, or any other program; all the bytes it contains are valid characters that such devices can handle in a predictable way.

LOGICAL END OF FILE: SUB. As we noted previously, the data records in a file may have any length. Therefore, the last data record in the file might not end with the 128th byte of the last standard record of the file; its last byte could even be the first byte of the last record, with 127 undefined bytes of garbage following it. SUB is the agreed-upon signal for the end of a file of ASCII text. It is conventional in CP/M to fill the unused bytes of the last record of a file with SUB characters (1Ah, control-z). The input routines of most language translators will check for SUB as they move data from the record buffer into the program's variables during an input operation. When SUB appears, the language will report end-of-file status according to its conventions.

PHYSICAL END OF FILE. The Monitor will report end of file when a program requests the next record and there is no next record (either because there are no more records, or because there is a hole in a file created with direct access). This is called *physical end of file*, as opposed to the appearance of SUB which is a logical end of file. In the event that the last data record exactly fills the last standard record, physical end of file will occur before a SUB is seen.

ASCII LINES. It is also a CP/M convention that the data records of an ASCII file are treated as *lines*. A line is a sequence of characters that ends with a carriage return and a linefeed (or CR, LF as we'll say from now on). The appearance of a pair of characters CR, LF is the agreed signal for end of record. A line need not be restricted to the width of a terminal screen or a printer line; it may be any length at all.

END OF LINE: CR, LF. Most languages that write data in ASCII will insert CR, LF after each unit of output. BASIC, for instance, inserts CR, LF following the data written with a PRINT# statement unless the programmer requests it not to. All editors insert CR, LF to mark the boundary of a line, but different editors define "line" in different ways. If you intend your program to read files created by your editor, you should check the editor's documentation; it and the programming language may place different limits on the maximum length of a line.

Binary Files

Binary files are defined by negatives. They do not contain only ASCII characters, their record boundaries are not marked by CR, LF, and in them the appearance of SUB does not signal end of file. .COM files are binary files; they contain machine-language instructions among which any byte value whatsoever may appear. You may type or print a .COM file, but the results will be peculiar and not useful. Files of intermediate code (.INT) and relocatable program files (.REL) are also binary files.

It is possible to create data files that contain other than ASCII bytes. Many programming languages write data items in their ASCII representation as the normal mode of output. If BASIC is used to write a number into a file, the PRINT# statement will convert the number from its binary representation into ASCII numeric characters. Thus a file written from a BASIC program will normally be an ASCII file. However, most languages allow the programmer to write numbers in their binary or BCD representation. When this is done, the file is a binary one; it will contain bytes that are not meaningful as ASCII. Depending on the conventions of the language, such a file may or may not have its records delimited by CR, LF and may or may not have a SUB as an end-of-file mark.

Chapter 11

Language Translators

A language translator—a compiler or interpreter for a programming language—is your primary programming tool. A translator is a complicated, expensive piece of software, and there are dozens of them on the market. In this chapter we talk about the kinds of translators available for CP/M and how to choose among them.

LANGUAGES AS TOOLS

If you've ever worked with your hands, you know how important it is to have the right tool for a job. A task as simple as loosening a screw can be [illegible]deningly difficult if you don't have a screwdriver of the right size. When the corne[illegible] the screwdriver blade have been rounded, the screwhead chewed up, and the scre[illegible] still firmly set in the wood, you have no one to blame but yourself. A programming [illegible]age is a tool, and the same principle applies. Having the right tool makes hard jobs e[illegible]ing the wrong one can make simple jobs impossible.

The Variety of Translators. There are at least six major pro[illegible]ng languages available for CP/M—a "major" language being one that is both used and available as a well-supported software package—from at least eight di[illegible]ndors. In addition, there are at least a dozen less common languages from a [illegible] smaller sources. Each language gives you a different way of stating the solutio[illegible]ms, a way that may fit well to the problem at hand, or may not. Each impleme[illegible]ach language presents you with a different set of CP/M facilities and a dif[illegible] invoking them.

If you are still learning to program, or are doing it for enjoyment, then us[illegible] of [illegible] language is readily and cheaply available. If you are programming profession[illegible] you are doing that when the application has to do with your work, whether yo[illegible] specifically for programming or not—then you should examine languages [illegible] packages they come in as critically as you'd examine any professional tool.

INTERPRETERS VERSUS COMPILERS

Using an Interpreter

Advantages of Interpreters. Programming is most pleasant when an interpreter is used. You type in a part of the program and run it. If there are errors, or the output is not exactly what you want to see, simply change a line or two and try it again. When it is right, add more code and continue. You move from coding to testing and back as fast as your fingers can follow your thoughts.

Interpreters aid you in debugging. When something unexpected happens you can stop the program, display the contents of variables, and let it continue.

Disadvantages of Interpreted Programs. Some disadvantages follow from the nature of an interpreter. An interpreter must be resident in working storage while the

program executes. That means that the program you've written cannot become a CP/M command. The interpreter is the .COM file whose name is the command verb. The interpreter's .COM file must be available whenever the program is run; this can lead to a conflict with the copying limits of your software license agreement.

Once loaded by the CCP, the interpreter loads the source program. This double load may take longer than the total execution time of a small program. And the person who uses your program first must be taught one more irrelevant thing.

Interpreters Use More Storage. Since the interpreter is present during execution, its size is deducted from the useful size of working storage. With a 64K system this is a problem only for the largest of programs, or for programs that are to operate on very large arrays of data. On the other hand, an interpreted program often takes less disk space than the same program compiled.

Performance of Interpreted Programs. The performance of an interpreted program may not be as fast as that of a compiled program. For every operation the program specifies, the interpreter adds a small overhead cost for scanning and decoding the program text. This is not always significant. There are many cases in which the speed of an interpreted program will be identical to that of the same program compiled.

This is always true of simple programs. Who can tell the difference between an execution time of 500 ms and one of 50 ms? Again, if the speed of the program is limited by its I/O so that it spends most of its time waiting for the typist or the disk drive, there will be no noticeable difference between interpreted and compiled execution. Finally, if the program spends most of its time in floating-point computation, compiling it will produce little improvement in speed. Floating-point arithmetic is usually performed by subroutines, and the subroutines run at the same speed whether called by an interpreter or from compiled code.

Using a Compiler

Disadvantages of a Compiler. A compiler places a barrier between you and your program. You cannot cycle rapidly between coding and testing. After preparing the source program with an editor you call the compiler as a CP/M command. It translates the source program, a process that may take several minutes. If the compiler finds syntax errors, you must return to the editor to fix them, then compile again.

If the compiler produces assembly language as its output, you must call the assembler to translate that file. In all cases a linkage program must be run to link the relocatable object program and form a .COM file. Finally, several minutes after you keyed in the source text you can begin to test the program.

If it does not work correctly (and what program ever did, the first time?), you will have little help in debugging. The cause of an error must be deduced by logic from the symptoms, a challenging mental exercise. When you've identified the error, the entire cycle must be repeated. If you can't find the error by logic, then the cycle must be repeated twice: once to insert diagnostic displays into the program, and again to remove them and fix the error.

Compiled Programs Are Commands. The extra labor spent in developing a compiled program is repaid when the program is complete. Because the end product is a machine-language program, it can be called like any other CP/M command.

Performance of Compiled Programs. The performance of a compiled program will be at least as good as that of an interpreted program. In certain cases, but not all, it will be much better. These cases arise when there is a great deal of processing to be done and the data to be processed are characters and integers.

Partial Compilers

There is a middle ground between interpreters and full compilers (which translate the source into machine language). A partial compiler converts the source program not into machine language, but into a set of integers and constants that are the input to a simple run-time interpreter. The interpreter can be speedy, as most of the work of scanning the source code has been done by the compiler. But the compiler can be simpler, as the code it must generate is closely related to the source program's language. For the designer of the package, then, a partial compiler is a good compromise.

For the programmer and the user the partial compiler is a compromise that has the advantages of neither approach. It is as difficult to test and debug with a partial compiler as with a full one. The run-time interpreter is the command verb and must be present whenever a program is run. Only in storage use are there benefits. The sum of run-time interpreter and object program is rarely larger than the size of a compiled program and its linked support modules, whereas the file size of the object program is small.

Matched Translators

A few vendors offer matched translators: a compiler and an interpreter for the same language dialect. The programmer who can afford such a matched pair of translators is in an enviable situation. That programmer can enjoy the benefits of an interpreter while developing a program, then use the compiler to produce the final version.

THE REPRESENTATION OF PROGRAMS

Programs, like data, must be represented in computer storage. Programs are special in that they may pass through several transformations, being represented differently at each stage. The only form of program that the machine can handle is the representation known as machine language. People almost never write in machine language. They write programs in symbolic form, store the programs as ASCII text, and have them translated to machine language by a translator program.

Programs as Text. The initial representation of any program is as ASCII characters, typed at a terminal and received by an editor program. The editor might be your normal

one, or it might be part of an interpreter. Either way, the characters that you've used to symbolize the program are stored in ASCII. The lines may be kept in working storage; often they are written to a file. The original, ASCII version of a program is called the *source* program because it is the source of all the later transformations.

Condensed Program Text. An interpreter works with the symbolic form of the program as typed, scanning it and carrying out the actions it calls for. For the sake of speed, the interpreter will probably condense the text to make it easier to scan. Language keywords and function symbols may be reduced to 1-byte integers, and numbers may be converted to their binary or decimal representation. These changes will be made once as the program is entered, and the reverse change will be made if the program has to be listed.

Intermediate Code. A partial compiler does not transform its input into the machine language of the processor. Instead it transforms it into a highly condensed series of binary integers that represent commands for a very simple, very fast interpreter. This *intermediate code* is placed in a file (usually with filetype .INT). When the program is to be executed, the small, fast interpreter is loaded; it loads the intermediate code and scans it to carry out the actions it represents. Intermediate code may be thought of as the machine language of an imaginary processor designed for their own purposes by the people who designed the language translator.

Assembly Language. A program written in assembly language is created as a file of ASCII text, just as any other source program is. Moreover, some compilers for other languages produce as their output a file of assembly language source. That file must be assembled to produce the machine language form of the program. The compiler-designer's job is simplified when assembly language is used as a sort of intermediate code.

.HEX Files. The output of the CP/M assembler, and of some compilers, is a picture of the program in machine language, but not in its final form. Rather than producing the binary values of machine language, the assembler produces a description of those binary values in the form of ASCII characters. Where the machine-language program would have bytes C30500h, the assembler writes the ASCII characters "C30500". Such a file is called a *Hex file* and always has the .HEX filetype. The purpose of this strange procedure is to create a file that can be (1) read by people, (2) punched into paper tape, and (3) sent from machine to machine easily and with little chance of error.

.REL Files. Some compilers and assemblers produce yet another form of near-machine language. These programs write a file that contains the binary values of machine language to which is added more information. The extra information makes it possible to load the machine-language program at any point in storage, rather than at the single starting point for which it was assembled. Such files of *relocatable* code are given the .REL filetype.

Machine Language. A compiled program may move through three transformations before it arrives at an executable form. Eventually it is transformed into the binary values that the processor will recognize as operation codes. This is a machine-language program. It can be stored in a .COM file and called for execution as a CP/M command.

JUDGING A LANGUAGE

Expressive Power. In an ideal world you could choose a programming language only on the basis of how well its style of expression matched your problem and your thinking habits. You have to have used more than one language, and each more than once, before you can properly judge the expressive power of a notation. We won't venture to give criteria for such comparisons; too much depends on the problem you want to solve and on your personal taste (many disputes about language are really disputes over matters of taste). If you are only beginning, don't worry about the matter, but reserve judgement on your first language until you've tried at least two others.

Packaging. In the real world programming languages come in the form of software packages. The package should be judged, like any other software purchase, on its function, its reliability, its support, the quality of its documentation, and its price. A good implementation of a language of mediocre expressive power may well be a better tool than a sloppy implementation of a very elegant language.

Language Compatibility. One of the criteria for judging a software package—its function—takes a special twist when a programming language is being judged. Most languages have a formal or informal standard that specifies the form and meaning of the language's statements. Those who design language translators seem to feel an irresistible urge to tamper with these standards. If there are two translators for a given language, you may be sure that there are small differences between them in the syntax and sometimes the meaning of statements. From these differences arise software incompatibilities; that is, programs that are valid according to one translator but that produce errors from another, or worse, produce no errors but execute differently. It is hard to find out about these problems in advance. Sometimes incompatible features are touted as enhancements but more often they are mentioned in passing in the back pages of the manuals. Occasionally they arise from errors, and so are not documented at all.

Common Use. There are several advantages to working with a widely used language. There will be more published programs for you to use or to read for your edification. There will be more people to whom you can turn for help. A large market tends to stabilize the language, discouraging incompatible innovations and attracting more publishers to produce more and better implementations.

Portability. When a language is supported by translators that run on several different makes of processor, or under several different operating systems, programs in that language become portable. Portability is very desirable. You can bring portable programs along when you upgrade to a bigger processor, and you stand a better chance of selling portable programs for a profit. Programs written to run on other machines may run on yours with little change.

Language incompatibilities work against portability. The translator that runs on another machine probably came from a different publisher, and the odds are good that there are at least minor differences between that version of the language and yours. And, of course, if you exploit the special features of your own hardware, or step outside the standard language by using things like the PEEK and POKE statements of BASIC, you defeat the idea of portability.

PERFORMANCE. Performance, expressed either as speed of translation or speed of execution, is almost entirely an attribute of the package. A fast translator can be built for any language, and any language can be translated into fast machine code, but both are not likely to be true of the same translator. In order to get a quantitative measure of the speed of a translator, you must try it out on a number of cases. This is the expensive and lengthy process called *benchmarking*. If the language is both common and portable, performance is less a concern. If speed of execution becomes a severe problem, you can move to another translator or to a faster machine without having to rewrite all your programs.

TRANSLATOR CASE STUDIES

Here are brief case studies of a sample of the language translators available for CP/M. The sample includes a rudimentary interpreter, a sophisticated interpreter, a partial compiler, and two full compilers. They illustrate the great variety of translators available, show the many ways in which CP/M's facilities are presented to the programmer, and give an example of how translators can be compared. We'll look at only a few of the translators on the market. By the time you read this some of these packages will have been revised and expanded, and so you should not use these studies as an up-to-date shopping guide.

tiny c

tiny c (always in lowercase) is the product of tiny c associates of Holmdel, New Jersey. It is a small, simple interpreter that supports a subset of the C programming language. The aim of its designers was to supply a modern programming language in a package so small and inexpensive that it could be brought up by hobbyists on the most rudimentary hardware.

DATA REPRESENTATION. tiny c provides only two data formats: 16-bit binary integers (which may be interpreted either as signed integers or as addresses) and characters.

FILE HANDLING. It supports only sequential files of 128-byte standard records; the programmer is responsible for handling data record boundaries, for extracting fields of records, and for detecting end of file. The CP/M version of the package was built for

CP/M release 1.4, before direct access was available. The designers made an unfortunate choice in the way they handled the FCB, which effectively blocks the use of direct access. The user is encouraged to modify the package, so this oversight can be fixed—but only at the price of introducing a language incompatibility with other tiny c users.

Language Power and Portability. Despite the simplicity of the language that it implements, tiny c's expressive power is great. tiny c encourages modular design and extension of the language by the creation of a library of subroutines. If these features are applied carefully, tiny c can be used to state almost any programming problem clearly and simply. In practice such extensions are limited by the speed of the interpreter. Portability is almost nil; the tiny c language is implemented only by this translator.

Performance, Function, etc. By design, tiny c has a limited amount of function. Its documentation is copious and well written. Its price is reasonable. The interpreter is extremely simple and so is relatively slow. A matching tiny c compiler was announced late in 1980; its use should solve most performance problems.

Microsoft Disk BASIC 5.0

The Microsoft Company of Bellevue, Washington, has produced BASIC interpreters for several home computers. As a result the Microsoft dialect of the language is in very wide use.

Data Representation. Disk BASIC 5.0 provides three representations for numbers. It uses 16-bit signed binary integers and two different precisions of binary floating point. The shorter of these is the default; it has a 24-bit fraction (six and a fraction decimal digits). So-called double-precision numbers have a 7-byte fraction, giving 16 decimal digits of precision. It is safe to use the longer form of floating point for commercial arithmetic. Variables must be explicitly declared to have the longer precision; take care not to let a default short-precision number slip into a commercial computation.

File Handling. Disk BASIC allows access to all of CP/M's file capabilities. The translator handles data record boundaries. Sequential files are ASCII files; the CR, LF markers are used to delimit data records. Files may be accessed at random by using an entirely different, and much more awkward, set of language statements than those used for sequential access. When these statements are used, all records must have the same length. The binary representation of numbers can be placed in the records when direct access is used; such items can't be read with the sequential statements.

Language Power and Portability. Several features of the Microsoft syntax differ from that supported by other publishers' BASICs, so almost any program will require editing before it can be transported. On the other hand, programs in Microsoft's version of BASIC can be moved with only trivial changes between any of the systems for which

Microsoft has built a translator, including CP/M-86 for the Intel 8086. BASIC is not an elegant programming language. Especially in a full-blown implementation such as this, every statement of the language seems to be a special case with its own rules of formation. Nevertheless, there are millions of BASIC programs running on hundreds of thousands of machines. It is clearly possible, if not easy, to state most problems in it.

Function, Performance, etc. Disk BASIC lacks function only in the area of tracing and debugging tools, where its capabilities are scarcely better than those of tiny c. Its documentation is adequate. Disk BASIC is a sophisticated interpreter. It converts the program to an internal representation in which language keywords, function symbols, and numeric constants are stored in binary for fast scanning. Execution is fast enough for most applications. A compiler for the same BASIC dialect is available from the same publisher.

CBASIC

If not the first compiler available for CP/M, CBASIC by Compiler Systems, Inc., of Sierra Madre, California, was certainly one of the first. It is a partial compiler. It reads a BASIC source program and writes a file of intermediate code. That file is executed by a fast, simple, run-time interpreter. Because it was on the market early, CBASIC was used by several publishers of commercial software. As a result it is now very common.

Data Representation. CBASIC supports two representations of numbers: 16-bit signed integers and floating point. The floating-point numbers are stored in 8 bytes, of which the first is the exponent. The fraction in the remaining 7 bytes of the number is carried in BCD rather than in binary form, and so has 14 decimal digits of precision.

File Handling. CBASIC file access uses ASCII text only. There is no way, aside from tricky coding, to place binary data in a file. As this is written, CBASIC does not use the direct access feature of CP/M version 2. Unless updated, it will not allow direct access to very large files or files on disks where a physical extent is not the same as a logical extent.

Professional Aids. The CBASIC compiler supports a %INCLUDE directive that causes it to include another file of source text in the program being compiled. This feature can be very helpful. It allows you to develop a library of subroutines and standard code, and then include these in any program as you need them. Proper use of the %INCLUDE feature can make it much easier to develop large programs.

Language Power and Portability. There are a number of serious language incompatibilities between CBASIC and Microsoft Disk BASIC 5.0. For example, in CBASIC the FOR loop always executes at least once; in Disk BASIC it may execute zero times. Therefore, some programs that run correctly with one translator will run incorrectly with the other. There are several differences in the I/O statements; the statements that request direct access are especially incompatible.

Pascal/Z

Pascal/Z, a product of Ithaca Intersystems, Ithaca, New York, is a full compiler for the Pascal language. The "Z" in its trademark signifies that it generates code for the Zilog Z80 CPU. Programs translated by Pascal/Z will run only on a Z80 processor; they cannot be executed on an 8080 processor. Pascal/Z translates a source program in Pascal into a file of assembly language statements. That file must be translated by a Z80 assembler (one is included with the package) to produce a .REL file of relocatable machine language. That file is then given to a linkage program that merges it with support programs from a library of relocatable subroutines. The end result is a .COM file that can be called as a command.

Data Representation. Pascal/Z supports 8-bit unsigned integers, 16-bit signed integers, and binary floating-point numbers with a 24-bit fraction. Linkable subroutines that will perform decimal arithmetic of any precision are included in the package. These subroutines make it possible to use Pascal/Z for commercial work, but the performance of such arithmetic is not likely to be as good, or the using code as clear, as they would be if a more precise representation were built into the implementation.

File Handling. Pascal/Z supports both sequential and direct access to disk files. Files may contain ASCII text in which data items are read and written much as they are in BASIC. Files may also contain data items that are Pascal record variables; in that case the record units are read and written in their binary representations.

Language Power and Portability. Pascal is a language of good expressive power and most programming problems can be stated clearly and simply in it. Pascal programs are at least as portable as BASIC programs. There are Pascal compilers for many small and medium-sized machines (and, since mid-1980, for the IBM 370). Pascal is widely used in both Europe and the United States, but its use on large machines is concentrated in universities.

The I/O statements supported by Pascal/Z are not entirely compatible with those of other Pascal translators. There are also minor incompatibilities in the handling of character strings and of external references.

Professional Aids. Pascal/Z has a source-inclusion feature like that of CBASIC. It aids the programmer in another way by allowing subroutines to be written separately from the main code. These external subroutines are then combined with the main program by the linkage program. Thus two kinds of common libraries can be built up: one of standard code sections, especially data declarations, and one of precompiled subroutines. The subroutines need not be written in Pascal; they may be in assembly language. This allows the programmer to handle hardware dependencies in the way that harms portability the least.

Digital Research PL/I

The PL/I language was developed in the early 1960s by IBM as an alternative to both COBOL and FORTRAN, then as now the dominant programming languages for large machines. Despite the fact that it was used as the basis for the M.I.T. Multics system (built on GE computers), PL/I was identified as an IBM captive language for many years. In recent years a PL/I standard has been issued by ANSI, the language has acquired respectability in academic circles, and it is receiving support from other computer makers, especially the makers of middle-sized machines.

Digital Research, the same company that produces CP/M, makes a PL/I compiler for CP/M. The package includes RMAC, a relocating assembler, and LIB, a linkage program. The compiler produces a .REL file as its output without the need for an assembly step. The relocatable object program is then linked with support subroutines from a library to form a .COM file. Subroutines assembled with RMAC can be linked with PL/I programs, so machine and system dependencies may be isolated from the main program.

Data Representation. PL/I handles 8-bit unsigned and 16-bit signed integers, floating-point numbers with a 24-bit binary fraction, and BCD numbers with up to 15 digits of precision. BCD numbers are handled as fixed-point values; that is, each number has a fixed number of digits on each side of the decimal point. That format is particularly convenient for commercial work.

File Handling. All the CP/M file facilities are accessible from PL/I. Data items can be transferred as ASCII text with the translator converting between ASCII and the internal representation. Data structures can be read or written, in which case the file will contain the internal, binary, representation.

Professional Aids. PL/I supports both source inclusion and linkable subroutines. It also has a limited text substitution ability.

Language Power and Portability. PL/I is a good programming notation; the choice between it and Pascal is largely a matter of individual taste. A full implementation of PL/I will have more built-in functions and more elaborate I/O facilities than Pascal provides, but in its standard subset for small machines its capabilities are almost identical to those of Pascal. Direct access I/O and variable-length strings are a standard part of the PL/I language definition, which is not true of Pascal.

The PL/I community is large but consists primarily of users of large machines. PL/I programs should be at least as portable as Pascal programs, but the sets of machines served by the two languages are entirely different. PL/I programs can generally be exchanged with users of large machines, and Pascal programs with users of small and middle-sized ones. If you employ your CP/M system within a large company, PL/I may give you the opportunity to exchange programs between your system and its big cousin down the hall, or to call on the company's programmers for advice.

Chapter 12

Assembly Language Programming

Sometimes it is necessary to write applications, or parts of them, in assembly language. Some applications won't run fast enough even with compiled code, others require features of the hardware or of CP/M that aren't available in your programming language.

This chapter is for those who must use assembly language under CP/M. We will talk about the use of ASM, the assembler that comes with CP/M, and MAC, a macro assembler from Digital Research. We'll cover CP/M's programming conventions and the basics of using DDT. The presentation assumes that you know something about the assembly language of the 8080 (or Z80) CPU.

EVALUATING ASSEMBLY LANGUAGE

We can judge assembly language just as we judged other languages. An assembler is no easier to use than a compiler. Debugging is more difficult than with a compiled language because small errors can cause things to happen that defy all analysis. A compiler takes care of dozens of trivial housekeeping matters for you, such as the use of the registers and the stack and the details of 16-bit arithmetic. Errors in such things simply don't occur; the errors that do occur are related in some way to the problem and your algorithm for solving it. With assembly language all these details are left to you. Not only do they burden the mental energies that you need for solving the problem at hand, but errors in such code take as long or longer to find than the inevitable errors in the algorithm itself.

The portability of assembly language is nil. An assembled program will run only on the hardware and under the operating system for which it was written. You can't upgrade your hardware or move to another operating system without a rewrite.

At present assembly language is widely used for CP/M applications. However, the population of CP/M users is growing rapidly, and most of the newcomers are not systems-oriented hobbyists but people who, if they know programming at all, know only a high-level language.

The expressive power of assembly language is very low; every problem is difficult and tedious to state. However, performance is as good as can be obtained. The translators run quickly and the resulting code is as efficient as your ingenuity can make it. Every feature of the system is accessible. It is these two features that keep assembly language in use for applications.

USING ASSEMBLY LANGUAGE

The Assembly Process

The process of making an assembled program is very much like the process of making a compiled program. You prepare the source program with an editor and store it in a file as *name*.ASM. Then you invoke the assembler as a command, giving the filename of the source file as its operand. The assembler reads the source program and produces a listing file and an object file. The listing displays the source statements opposite the instruction bytes they generate. The object file contains the byte values of the machine-language program itself. It must be converted into a .COM file before it can be run.

The .ASM File. The source of the assembly language program is built with an editor and stored in a file of type .ASM. The source program contains two kinds of statements. Instruction statements cause the assembler to generate machine instructions. *Directives* direct the assembler in its own operations, telling it to reserve space, test a condition, or define a macro.

The .PRN File. The assembler produces a listing in which it displays the source statements and the resulting object code. The listing can be directed to a file, which is given the filename of the source program and the filetype of .PRN. The listing may be directed to the terminal or printer instead of a file.

The .HEX File. The object code—the bytes that represent machine instructions—is placed in a file that has the filename of the source program and a filetype of .HEX. The .HEX file is an ASCII file; it contains a picture of the object code bytes, with each hexadecimal digit represented by an ASCII character. Each line of the .HEX file represents from 1 to 255 bytes of object code. Each line begins with a count of the bytes in the line, and the location at which the bytes are meant to be loaded. Each line ends with a check sum so that the line can be verified for correct transmission. PIP will verify the check sums if told to do so with the H or I option.

The .SYM File. The MAC assembler produces one additional file, *name*.SYM. This contains a list of the labels in the program with their addresses. The .SYM file is sometimes called (erroneously) a cross-reference file. It can be used with another Digital Research product, the debugging aid SID. The .SYM file is useful in a small way as a documentation aid.

Making a .COM File

Program Addresses. Any assembled program must deal with addresses. Jump and call instructions contain addresses as operands; they instruct the machine to begin execution at those addresses. Your program may contain address constants, 16-bit fields that contain the addresses of data areas or points in the program. In the source program you specify such addresses as labels. At the time of writing you don't care about the value of these addresses, only that they refer to the part of the program you intend. At execution time the machine must be given a specific address. A jump instruction must contain a 16-bit integer that is the address of the target of the jump.

The Origin Problem. The value of that address depends on two things: the *origin* of the program, that is, the address of its first byte, and an offset, that is, the length of program that precedes the location in question. The address wanted is the sum of those two things, the origin and an offset. In order to put the address into the program, both pieces of information must be known. The offset is easy; the assembler simply counts the bytes it has generated up to the point of assembling the labeled item. The value of the origin must be supplied.

Absolute Assembly. With an absolute assembler such as ASM or MAC, you are required to tell the assembler the value of the origin. The assembler can then generate addresses as the sum of that origin and its knowledge of the offset. These absolute addresses are placed in the .HEX file. Once there, they can't be changed; you can only reassemble with a different origin value.

Since the program contains addresses computed on the basis of a certain origin, it must be loaded for execution at that origin and no other. Suppose the assembler was told that the origin was to be 0100h, and on that basis it assembled the first jump with a target address of 0340h. If the program were then loaded into storage at 1000h, it would run correctly up to that jump. Thereupon it would jump to 0340h, regardless of the fact that the target instruction was not there. Something would be there, perhaps a fragment of an old program. Strange things would happen.

Loading a .HEX File. Once the *name*.HEX file has been created it is a simple matter to convert it to a *name*.COM file. The LOAD command performs this task. Its form is:

LOAD *filename*

Only a filename is given; the filetype is assumed to be .HEX. The LOAD command reads the named .HEX file and places the bytes that file describes into storage at their assembled origin. Having created an exact image of the machine-language program, LOAD opens and writes a file using the stored program as the data. The file has the name given as LOAD's operand and the filetype of .COM; it is an exact copy of the program, ready to be loaded by the CCP and run.

Relocating Assembly

An absolute assembler requires you to decide the program's origin in advance and to state that origin in the source file. It's possible to defer a decision on the program's origin until after it has been assembled. An assembler that lets the origin go undefined is a *relocating assembler*. The act of defining a program's origin after assembly is called *relocation*.

Relocating Assemblers. Relocating assemblers usually come as part of a package with a compiler. Digital Research PL/I comes with RMAC; Pascal/Z is delivered with ASMBL. A relocating assembler ducks the whole question of the program's origin. It does not do a complete job of assembling addresses. It places in the object program only the offset values, not the sum of origin and offset.

The .REL File. A relocating assembler doesn't write a .HEX file. It places the object code, in binary, in a file of type .REL. .REL files are not ASCII files; they may contain any byte value. The assembler puts extra information in the file, naming all the points in the program at which incomplete addresses occur. The extra information enables a different program, a linkage editor or linker, to relocate the program.

Relocation and Linking. Relocation is the job of going through a .REL file and adding an origin value into all the incomplete addresses. The origin is supplied at the time of linking, not at the time of assembling. This means that a relocatable program can be set up to run at any origin without reassembly. At the same time the .REL files of a number of programs can be linked together.

Entries and External References. A relocating assembler has one other feature that an absolute assembler does not. It allows the program to declare a label within the program as an *entry point*, and to declare a label that is not defined in the program as an *external reference*. An entry is a label within the program that may be referenced by some other program, one assembled at a different time. An external reference tells the assembler that the label so declared is not part of this program, but is, or will be, defined as an entry in some other program.

For an entry the assembler puts the name of the entry point and its offset within the program into the .REL file, with a flag stating that it is an entry point.

For an external reference the assembler puts in the .REL file the name of the external label, and the offset of every instruction in the program that referenced that name. The addresses in those instructions can't be assembled because the assembler doesn't know what the value of the external label will be. It only knows, or rather it takes on faith, that the value of the external label will be defined later.

Linkers. A relocatable program with its incomplete addresses, relocation information, entry labels, and external references is obviously not ready to be loaded and made into a command. Too much information is missing. Supplying the missing information—the program's actual origin and the value of its external references—is the job of a linker. Linkers too come as part of a package with a compiler. The Microsoft COBOL and BASIC compilers come with LINK-80; Digital Research PL/I comes with LIB.

All work in the same way. A linker is given the name of a main program (a .REL file) and the names of one or more libraries of subroutines, which are also in relocatable form. It is told, or assumes, some origin for the program. The linker proceeds as described in the following.

Loading the .REL File. It loads the .REL file and goes through it, resolving all addresses by adding the origin to them. It notes the names of all entry points. It notes all external references. It then searches the library for subroutines that contain entries matching the main program's external references.

Resolving External References. When it finds a subroutine, it loads it following the main program. The first subroutine's origin will be the byte following the end of the main program. The linker must relocate all the subroutine's addresses by adding this origin to them. Wherever the main program contained a reference to the subroutine, the assembler could only leave zeros. The subroutine's address is now known and the linker can fill in these addresses.

Many subroutines may be loaded, and each may have its own external references that cause the linker to search for yet other entry points. Each subroutine provides an entry (or several entries) that satisfies the external references of other programs. The linker weaves all these interprogram references together, filling in all the information that was not known at the time of assembly. The linked code is then written as a .COM file.

Uses of Relocation and Linking. Since relocating assemblers and linkers are distributed with compilers, you might infer that they are useful only with compilers. That isn't the case. The work of a compiler's designer is certainly made easier by the presence of a linker. The designer can create a library of many small subroutines, each of which performs a simple task needed by compiled programs: one for each floating-point operation, for example. The compiler, on encountering a floating-point operation, need only generate a call to an external routine instead of all the code to do the operation. A compiled program will have dozens of external references to be resolved by the linker.

If you have a relocating assembler and linker, you can—and certainly should—apply them to your own work. They allow you to adopt a modular style of programming. You can create a set of preassembled subroutines that provide you with some of the convenience of using a compiler. You might even use some of the compiler's subroutines as your own. You can isolate device- and system-dependent parts of your application to separate subroutines. For a program that uses advanced features of the terminal you can specify one subroutine for each special terminal function, such as clearing the screen. Then to make the program work with a different kind of terminal, you need only revise the subroutines and relink.

ASSEMBLER FEATURES

All CP/M assemblers support directives that let you manipulate the source program. The simplest way is conditional assembly, which lets you skip over or assemble a portion of code, depending on some condition. Macro assemblers offer more.

Conditional Assembly

Macro assemblers commonly contain some means of conditional assembly; that is, statements that allow you to control the assembly of the program by the value of symbols. Both ASM and MAC (and most other assemblers) provide an IF directive that allows alternate parts of the program to be skipped under some condition. MAC includes loop directives so that a part of the program can be assembled repeatedly.

The IF Directive. The IF directive is used to skip or include parts of a program according to the value of an expression. The text that is skipped or included can be another assembler directive, including another conditional statement or, in MAC, a part of a macro. The expression is usually a simple label but may be any arithmetic combination of constants and labels. Under ASM the normal use of IF is to skip over parts of the program that are not wanted in a particular version of the program. Example 12-1 shows the form of this use of IF.

The ELSE Directive. MAC allows an IF directive to be paired with a matching ELSE directive so that a choice between alternate code sections can be made.

Repeated Assembly. MAC offers three looping directives. The REPT directive repeats the assembly of a section of code a certain number of times. It is normally used to

EXAMPLE 12-1
A sketch of the typical use of the IF directive: the true (nonzero) or false (zero) value of an expression selects statements for assembly (ELSE is supported by MAC but not by ASM).

```
            .
            .
            .
TRUE    EQU     -1      ; GIVE NAMES TO
FALSE   EQU     0       ; ..BOOLEAN VALUES
            .
            .
            .
LONG$MESSAGE EQU FALSE
NOVICE  EQU     TRUE
            .
            .
            .
      IF      NOVICE
TIMEOUT EQU     60      ; NOVICE GETS 60 SECONDS
      ELSE
TIMEOUT EQU     15      ; EXPERTS ONLY GET 15
      ENDIF
        LXI     D,TIMEOUT
        CALL    SETTIME ; START ANSWER CLOCK
            .
            .
            .
      IF      NOVICE OR LONG$MESSAGE
        DB      'You waited too long to answer,'
        DB      ' the penalty is 10 points'
      ELSE
        DB      'Timeout, -10'
      ENDIF
        DB      CR,LF,'$'
```

initialize tables and other repetitive arrays of constants. The IRP directive repeats a section of code once for each of a list of operands, substituting a different operand from the list on each pass. IRP is used to create a series of instruction groups, each parameterized differently.

The IRPC directive repeats a sequence of code once for each character in its operand, allowing substitution of a different, single character on each pass. IRPC finds its greatest use within macros, as it is the only way MAC provides of examining the letters of a single operand—something that the author of a macro often needs to do.

The Macro Concept

As we said in Chapter 7, "macro" is a term that implies any grouping of statements for the sake of simplicity. In programming the term implies more. At a general level it is almost a synonym for the concept of *abstraction*, the most powerful notion in the programmer's armory. In practice, as in the MAC assembler, it also implies the concept of *substitution*.

ABSTRACTION. All of us have practiced abstraction from earliest childhood. A child learning to speak points to a thing and is told that it is a "cup." Later the same child points to a thing of different color and shape and again is told that it is a "cup." Most babies need only a few repetitions of that experience before they form an abstraction: "cup" becomes the name of a *class* of things that are hollow and hold liquid for drinking.

To form an abstraction is to define a class of things that have characteristics in common. Our brains are clearly designed to deal with abstractions, and the value of that is also clear. Once we've formed an abstraction we've made a powerful simplification in our view of the world. The baby can learn responses to the class "cup" as a whole; as soon as a new thing can be placed in the cup class the baby knows how to deal with it. (Once in a while we put things in the wrong class and so deal with them inappropriately, but that's another story.)

Uses of Abstraction. There are endless uses of abstraction in programming. A large part of the developing science of software is the application of abstraction in different forms. Modular programming deals with abstracting single functions of a program, defining those functions in isolated subroutines, and then treating the subroutines as unitary things, or abstractions (relocation and linking are a great aid to this). Top-down programming involves breaking a large task into ever smaller steps, each of which is treated as an abstraction at one level and defined in terms of narrower abstractions at the next.

Macros as Abstractions. In assembly language programming a macro is a means of converting a sequence of assembler instructions into a single instruction, so that the group may be treated as an abstraction. Used properly, this allows great simplification in the task of programming.

All macro assemblers provide a form for macro definition. An example of how MAC does it appears in Figure 12-1. That sequence of assembler instructions defines a macro whose name is PROLOG. The body of PROLOG consists of the statements between the MACRO statement and the ENDM statement. The MACRO statement, besides declaring the macro's name and marking the start of its text, declares that PROLOG has two parameters, named ?SIZE and ?MAIN.

PROLOG is one programmer's abstraction of the class of things "entering a program under CP/M"; when made a macro, the abstraction can be called with a single line of code. Provided the code works in all cases, the programmer can forget the details of program entry and think about things more relevant to the problem at hand.

Substitution. We met the idea of substitution when talking about submit files in Chapter 8. Substitution is the process of replacing one string of characters with another one. A macro assembler does two kinds of substitution. It replaces a call to a macro with the whole text of the macro it names. And within a macro's text it substitutes for parameters the values given in the macro instruction.

Calling a Macro. After having read the definition of PROLOG, MAC will watch for the occurrence of that word in the program text. An occurrence of PROLOG and any operands following it constitute a macro call. When it finds a macro call for PROLOG, MAC will replace the call with the entire body of PROLOG and continue assembling. The instructions contained in PROLOG will become part of the program at that point.

```
; PROGRAM ENTRY MACRO : BUILD LOCAL STACK, SAVE CCP'S STACK
; ON IT.  HANDLE RETURN TO CCP IF MAIN RETURNS HERE.
PROLOG  MACRO    ?SIZE,?MAIN
        LOCAL    STKSIZE
      IF        NUL ?SIZE
STKSIZE SET      16
      ELSE
STKSIZE SET      ?SIZE
      ENDIF
        ORG      0100H              ; START AT T.P.A.
        LXI      H,0
        DAD      SP                 ; HL = CCP STACK PTR
        LXI      SP,STDSTACK        ; SET OUR STACK PTR
        PUSH     H                  ; SAVE CCP PTR FOR EXIT
      IF        NUL ?MAIN
        CALL     MAIN               ; CALL MAINLINE CODE
      ELSE
        CALL     ?MAIN              ; CALL MAINLINE CODE
      ENDIF
;
; ON NORMAL EXIT, MAIN LINE WILL RETURN TO HERE
;
EPILOG  POP      H                  ; RECOVER CCP'S STACK PTR,
        SPHL                        ; ..ACTIVATE IT, AND
        RET                         ; ..RETURN TO CCP
;
        DS       2*STKSIZE ;RESERVE STACK SPACE
STDSTACK EQU     $
        ENDM
```

FIGURE 12-1
The PROLOG macro, typical of assembly macros under MAC. It abstracts the idea of program entry and exit for a simple CP/M command.

Note that MAC isn't choosy about where it finds a macro call. PROLOG was written under the assumption that its call would have the form of a machine instruction, with the macro name in the opcode position. If the word appears as a label or as the operand of an instruction, MAC will replace it there just as readily (with erroneous results).

Macro Parameters. The second substitution a macro assembler performs is to take parameter values from the macro call and substitute them for parameter names in the text of the macro. PROLOG has two parameters, ?SIZE and ?MAIN. Whatever characters occupy the first operand position in the macro call will replace every occurrence of ?SIZE in the body of the macro as it is substituted. The characters in the second operand position of the call will replace ?MAIN. If there are no characters in an operand position, the corresponding parameter name will be replaced by the null string (it will vanish). Note that there is no requirement that a parameter name begin with "?"; that was done so that the parameter names would stand out in the code.

IF in a Macro Definition. The PROLOG macro in Figure 12-1 contains several uses of IF. In each case it tests to see if one of its parameters has no value (has been replaced by the null string). If the ?SIZE parameter is null, PROLOG will supply a default size of 16 words of stack space. If the ?MAIN parameter is null, it will start the program by calling a label MAIN; otherwise it will call the label defined by the parameter.

Macro Libraries

Sometimes a macro is useful only within the program for which it is written. You'd type the definition of such a macro at the top of the source program, call it where it was needed, and that would be that.

A macro often represents the abstraction of something that is useful in many programs. The PROLOG macro in Figure 12-1 could be useful in many assembly programs. Such macros are better kept outside any program and included wherever they are wanted. Most macro assemblers have some way of bringing in code from another file. MAC's method is the MACLIB directive.

The MACLIB Directive. When MAC runs across a MACLIB directive in the source program, it opens the file named in the directive and incorporates the lines of that file in the source program at that point. The MACLIB statement is very like a macro call: the directive is replaced by the contents of the macro library.

MACLIB for Including Source. The term "macro library" used by the MAC documentation is confusing because such files aren't libraries in the usual sense. They are sections of assembler source text that are kept in separate files. If it weren't for a restriction on its use, MACLIB could be used exactly as you'd use the %INCLUDE statement of CBASIC—as a way of including prewritten chunks of code in your program.

Unfortunately MAC can't handle source inclusion in that general form. The assembler text brought in by a MACLIB directive is not allowed to contain any assembler statements that generate machine language. It may contain only statements that define names to the assembler: equate and set statements and the definitions of macros.

MACLIB for Declarations. Even with that restriction, MACLIB is still useful as a way of bringing in a block of prewritten code. There are a couple of dozen values that appear in most CP/M assembly code—values that define important locations in low storage, names for the important ASCII control characters, and the like. Figure 12-2 shows the text of a file called CPMEQU.LIB. Such a file could be included in any program to define these common names.

This source inclusion is especially useful when you are building a suite of related programs. Such programs will have a set of common items that should be named consistently in all. That consistency is best achieved by putting the equates that define those names in a library file and including it in each program. Then if a name must be changed, it need be changed only once, in the library, after which all the programs would be reassembled. If you are using a relocating assembler to create a library of subroutines, the same technique can be used for names that are common to the main program and all its subroutines.

MACLIB for Macro Definitions. The expected use of MACLIB is to bring in the definitions of a set of related macros. There's nothing magic about a macro library; the assembler sees no difference between a macro that is defined in the source program and

```
; * * * * *  CPMEQU.LIB: EQUATE NAMES USEFUL IN ASSEMBLY CODE
;
;        IMPORTANT ADDRESSES
;
BOOT     EQU     0000H    ; WARM-START EXIT POINT
BDOS     EQU     0005H    ; SERVICE REQUEST ENTRY
CPMFCB   EQU     005CH    ; FCB SET UP BY CCP
TPA      EQU     0100H    ; STANDARD PROGRAM ORIGIN
CPMBUFF  EQU     0080H    ; DEFAULT I/O BUFFER
;
;        ASCII CHARACTER SET NAMES
;
BEL      EQU     07H      ; BELL OR BEEP
BS       EQU     08H      ; BACKSPACE
HT       EQU     09H      ; HORIZONTAL TAB
LF       EQU     0AH      ; LINEFEED
VT       EQU     0BH      ; VERTICAL TAB
FF       EQU     0CH      ; FORMFEED
CR       EQU     0DH      ; CARRIAGE RETURN
EOF      EQU     1AH      ; END OF FILE FLAG (SUB)
ESC      EQU     1BH      ; ESCAPE
BLANK    EQU     20H      ; BLANK
UCASE    EQU     0FFH-020H ; 'AND' LOWER CASE TO UPPER
CCASE    EQU     40H      ; 'OR' CONTROL TO CHARACTER
;
; * * * * *      END OF CPMEQU.LIB
```

FIGURE 12-2
The CPMEQU.LIB file can be included in almost any program to define names for locations and values often used in CP/M.

one that is brought into the source program with MACLIB. It is simply more convenient to place common macro definitions in a file external to the programs that use them. If a macro definition needs changing, it is changed only in the library; all assemblies that include it will pick up the new definition.

MACLIB **for Common Code.** MACLIB can't handle statements that generate code. It isn't possible to put the text of a group of common subroutines in a file and then include them at the appropriate place in your program with a MACLIB directive. Assembler error messages will result.

There is a way to get the same effect. If the common subroutines are surrounded by MACRO and ENDM statements, the file can be read by MACLIB. The subroutine code is saved in storage as the definition of a macro. At the point in the program where you want the subroutines to appear, place a macro call to the subroutine macro. Figure 13-3 shows the contents of a library of console output subroutines that is organized this way.

The subroutines of Figure 13-3 bring up the matter of styles of abstraction. They represent one way of abstracting the idea of console output. Another way, espoused by the authors of the MAC manual, is to have a console output macro that you call wherever in the code you need it. The macro call is used instead of a call to a subroutine. The first time it is expanded the macro generates a small subroutine in line with the code; on subsequent calls it generates only a call to that subroutine. A third style of abstracting the idea of console output is to make the subroutine an external one and link it to the program after assembly. All three methods are valid.

CP/M PROGRAMMING CONVENTIONS

In order to write assembly language programs for CP/M you must understand the programming conventions used within CP/M. When you use a compiler or interpreter, all these details are handled for you by the language translator. With assembly language you must work with them directly. The conventions cover three areas: the use of low storage, the method of making service requests, and the use of the File Control Block, or FCB.

From now on we must use more precise terms than "Monitor" for the resident part of CP/M. We'll still refer to the Monitor when we are talking about all of the CP/M code in high storage, but we have to distinguish between the Console Command Processor (CCP), the Basic Disk Operating System (BDOS) which resides above the CCP and handles service requests, and the Basic I/O System (BIOS), which sits at the very top of storage and operates the devices.

Standard and Nonstandard Addresses

Discussions of CP/M's use of storage are complicated by the fact that not all CP/M variants use the same addresses. CP/M has been adapted to a number of machines; in a few of them the hardware design forced the adapters to use addresses different from those we describe here. We'll describe standard CP/M, in which low storage is located at address 0000h, commands are loaded at 0100h, and the Monitor resides at the top of storage.

Low Storage

The first 256 locations of working storage, from 00h through FFh, are reserved by the Monitor to hold system information and to act as an interface between your program and the BDOS. It contains a disk buffer, information on the command that called the program, and the route to the BDOS for service requests. There is a map of low storage in Figure 12-3. We'll tour the main points of interest on that map, from low addresses to high, in the discussion that follows.

The address immediately after low storage, 0100h, is the point at which all command programs are loaded. That is the origin of the Transient Program Area ("transient" because commands are loaded into it one after another), or TPA. The address 0100h is usually equated to TPA and used as the origin of absolute assemblies.

00h: The Warm Start Jump. The first 3 bytes of storage contain a jump to a routine in the BIOS that performs warm start initialization. If your program branches to 00h, it will be terminated and a warm start will occur. The CCP and BDOS will be reloaded from the reserved tracks of the A-disk (if the A-disk isn't bootable, the system will

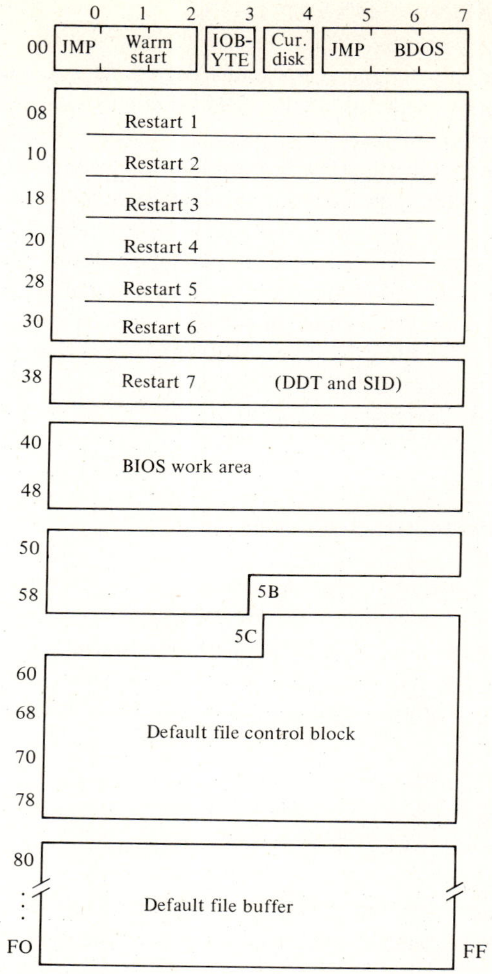

FIGURE 12-3
A map of low storage from address 0000h through address 00FFh.

hang). If your program was called from within a submit file, the next submitted command will be executed. If it wasn't, the user will see the normal CCP prompt.

A jump to 00h is the conventional way to end a CP/M program, and certainly the best way to end after an error of some kind.

03h: THE IOBYTE. The next byte (at 03h) is called the IOBYTE. It contains four 2-bit groups that specify the current assignment of logical to physical device names. There are service requests (numbers 7 and 8) for getting and setting the current values of the IOBYTE. If you want to check or alter the IOBYTE, you should use these requests, even though the byte is easily accessible in CP/M. The byte at 03h might not be up to date under MP/M, whereas under CP/M-86 the IOBYTE is kept elsewhere.

04h: Default Disk and User Code. The byte at 04h contains two 4-bit numbers. The least significant 4 bits hold the drive number of the current default drive, as encoded by service request 25 (see next chapter). The most significant 4 bits contain the active user code, as set by the USER command. As with the IOBYTE, both of these values can be checked or set through service requests. And also, as with the IOBYTE, the values are stored here only under CP/M; MP/M and CP/M-86 are different.

05h: The Service Request Jump. At location 05h there is another jump instruction. This one points to the BDOS, where service requests are handled. Your program issues a service request by preparing parameters in the registers and calling (not jumping to) location 05h.

SIZE OF STORAGE. The address in the service request jump is the lowest address of the BDOS and the address of the byte following the CCP in storage. If your program needs to use all available storage, it may use all the space from 0100 up to (but not including) the byte addressed by the service request jump. If it does so, it will overwrite the CCP. In that case the program must end with a warm start so the CCP will be reloaded. If your program does not require all of storage, it might subtract 810h from the address in location 06h and use storage only to that point. That will leave the CCP (which is just over 800h bytes long) intact.

THE RESTART LOCATIONS. The 8080 and Z80 hardware provides a restart instruction that is like a very concise jump to one of eight locations in low storage. These locations coincide with the storage reserved by CP/M. A restart zero instruction will transfer control to location 00h, the warm start jump, and so cause a warm start.

Restarts 1 through 7 transfer control to locations 08h, 10h, 18h, and so on up to 38h. These same locations may receive control during a device interrupt. The 8-byte areas for restarts 1 through 5 are not defined by CP/M. Unless you are writing an interrupt handler, you should avoid them also. It is tempting to think of using a restart instruction in some clever way to get around in your program, but to do so is to make your program nonportable. Someone else's system might have a hardware use for those locations.

CP/M has reserved restart location 6 (30h) for an unspecified purpose and never used it. Nonetheless, it should be avoided.

The DDT and SID debugging programs use restart location 7 (38h). If your program alters the area from 38h to 3Fh, it cannot be tested with those tools. Under MP/M the DDT program can be configured to use any of the restart locations for its work.

Restart location 7 was probably chosen because a RST 7 instruction has the bit pattern FFh. That's the value that most hardware will return when the CPU reads from nonexistent storage. If a program branches to a nonexistent address, the CPU will fetch an operation code of FFh and do an RST 7.

40h: The BIOS Work Area. The BIOS that handles disk and other I/O has been given the 16 bytes from 40h through 4Fh as a work area. If you are doing systems programming and get deep into the logic of the BIOS, you may discover what this area is used for (its use varies from vendor to vendor). Otherwise leave it strictly alone; alterations could be catastrophic for the file system.

5Ch: The Default FCB. The space from 5Ch to 7Fh always contains an FCB. This FCB is set up by the CCP as it prepares to load a command. In later chapters we will make a lot of use of the default FCB.

80h: The Default Buffer. The 128 bytes from 80h to FFh have two purposes. First, this space makes a convenient buffer for simple file operations. Most standard commands use it for this purpose. Second, when a command begins operation it will find a copy of the command line as typed by the user in the default buffer.

CCP Services for Command Programs

The CCP performs two helpful services for command programs, services that make it easier to write commands. It sets up the default FCB, and it prepares the command line in the default buffer, ready for inspection.

The Command Tail. Before it transfers control to a command, the CCP copies the characters of the command line into the default buffer, beginning at 81h. The characters of the verb are omitted. All the characters that followed the verb are retained. This line is called the command tail (it follows the verb that was at the head of the line). Lowercase characters are translated into uppercase characters, but otherwise the line is exactly as the user typed it. It will begin with at least one space, and may contain any number of spaces between operands and following the last operand. A byte of 00h will follow.

The CCP places the length of the command tail, excluding the 00h byte at the end, in the byte at 80h.

Fileref Operands. The CCP assumes that the first two command operands are filerefs. It places each in the default FCB. The first fileref is set up at the head of the FCB; that file can be opened and accessed using the FCB just as the program finds it. The second fileref, if there is one, is set up in FCB format in the second half of the default FCB beginning at 6Ch. If it is a fileref, it must be copied elsewhere before the FCB is used, because opening a file causes the second half of the FCB to be overwritten. The CCP is very generous about what it will treat as a fileref. If it finds a string of 20 characters in the first operand position, it will place the first eight of them in the default FCB as a filename.

Ambiguous Filerefs. The CCP sets up ambiguous filerefs just as it does unique ones. However, it does not permit an asterisk reference to be put into the default FCB. If it sees an asterisk in a filename or filetype, the CCP deletes it and fills to the end of the field with question marks. If the user typed X*.ASM as the first operand, then the fileref at 5Ch will contain X???????.ASM. In designing a command you must remember that the user can pass you an ambiguous fileref.

Program Entry and Exit

A command program is loaded at 0100h, the start of the TPA. After preparing the default FCB and the command tail, the CCP transfers control to the start of the TPA at 0100h. Your program must initialize itself, and later terminate in an orderly way. You have several options as to how you can handle entry and exit. Most of the considerations center on how the stack pointer register is to be handled.

Simple Programs. When control arrives at your program's first instruction, the stack pointer addresses space in the CCP sufficient to handle eight nested calls (or interrupts). Because of that a simple program can be written as a subroutine of the CCP. Such a program just executes until it is finished, then issues a return instruction.

If you write such a program, you will find that when it ends the CCP's prompt comes out instantly. When you run most applications there is a pause of 1 or 2 seconds while the warm start takes place. No warm start occurs when a program terminates by returning to the CCP. That's why the prompt comes out so quickly at the end of a simple program.

Typical Programs. Very simple programs can be coded quickly as subroutines of the CCP, but this design creates two problems. The first is that larger programs need more stack space than the CCP provides. The stack pointer register must be set up to address an area local to the program.

The second problem is that (in CP/M 2) the CCP doesn't handle submitted files correctly unless each submitted command ends in a warm start. This is a pity, because the quick response obtained by avoiding a warm start is very nice. The fact remains that, to be useful in a submit file, a program must end in a warm start rather than just return to the CCP.

The PROLOG Macro. The PROLOG macro in Figure 12-4 shows how this can be handled. It is meant to be used with a program organized like the sketch in Example 12-2: the prolog code lowest in storage, then variables and constants, then the main routine, and subroutines last. The main routine should return to its caller even though the return is to a JMP BOOT instruction. It might seem simpler to put the warm start jump in the main routine, but there are debugging advantages to having a single, known, exit point from the program.

Elaborate Programs. Two more needs commonly arise. First, a more elaborate

```
;
; PROGRAM ENTRY MACRO FOR COMPLEX PROGRAMS: FIND BOTTOM OF
; CCP AND SET STACK THERE, CALL MAIN WITH HL=END OF STORAGE.
;
PROLOG2 MACRO   ?MAIN
        ORG     0100H               ; START AT T.P.A.
        LHLD    BDOS+1              ; HL --> BDOS
        SPHL                        ; STACK STARTS UNDER BDOS
        LXI     D,0-128             ; NEGATIVE STACK SIZE
        DAD     D                   ; HL --> STACK BOTTOM
        DCX     H                   ; HL --> LAST USABLE BYTE
        IF      NUL ?MAIN
        CALL    MAIN                ; CALL MAINLINE CODE
        ELSE
        CALL    ?MAIN               ; CALL MAINLINE CODE
        ENDIF
;
; ON ANY EXIT, CONTROL WILL RETURN HERE
;
EPILOG  JMP     BOOT                ; DO A WARM START
;
; ERROR EXIT TO ISSUE MESSAGE ADDRESSED BY DE, ERASE
; ACTIVE SUBMIT FILE (IF ANY).
;
ERROREXIT EQU   $
        MVI     C,9                 ; PRINT LINE TO '$'
        CALL    BDOS
;
; ERROR EXIT TO TERMINATE SUBMIT ONLY
;
ERROROUT EQU    $
        LXI     D,SUBMITFCB
        MVI     C,19                ; ERASE FILE IN FCB
        CALL    BDOS
        JMP     EPILOG              ; EXIT BY SINGLE POINT
;
; FCB USED FOR ERASING SUBMIT FILE 'A:$$$.SUB' -- ONLY
; FIRST 16 BYTES ARE SIGNIFICANT.
;
SUBMITFCB EQU   $
        DB      1,'$$$     SUB',0,0,0,0
        ENDM
```

FIGURE 12-4
The PROLOG2 macro does four things needed in a complex program: it provides a large stack, sizes storage, provides for a terminating error message, and cancels an active submit file on an error.

program may need to allocate all possible storage, rather than confine itself to areas defined in the program. Second, an elaborate program will usually have checks for many different error conditions, and for each it will have a message to be typed at the terminal.

An elaborate program should be written with the assumption that it may be called from a submitted file. If it stops because of some fatal error, it should take steps to cancel the execution of the submitted file that (may have) called it. The official way to cancel a submitted file is to erase $$$.SUB.

THE PROLOG2 MACRO. The PROLOG2 macro in Figure 12-4 handles all these matters. It finds the size of storage up to the bottom of the BDOS, and sets the program's stack there. It deducts 128 bytes (allowing for up to 64 nested calls) and passes that address to the main routine in the HL register pair. This address may be saved and used as the limit of storage allocation.

EXAMPLE 12-2
General layout of a program that uses PROLOG. The macro must jump over the stack it defines, so it's convenient to place the program's variables just after the stack.

```
                    .
                    .
               (MACLIB directives)
                    .
                    .
               (macros defined in this program)
                    .
                    .
                    PROLOG nn,name
                    .
               (program variables, FCBs, buffers)
                    .
          name      EQU      $
                    .
                    .
               (body of main program)
                    .
                    .
               (subroutines for this program)
                    .
                    .
               (common subroutines from libraries
                    .
                    END
```

The Error Exit. PROLOG2 provides two ways to end the program. If the main routine ends normally, it will simply return to EPILOG, where a warm start is done. The macro also supplies a label ERROREXIT. If a fatal error occurs, the program may load the DE pair to address an error message and jump to the error exit. There the macro provides code to display the error message and to erase the active submit file if there is one. The two service requests it uses will be described in the next chapter. (Note that this method of ending a submitted file will not work in MP/M, where each user's active submit file has a different name.)

DEBUGGING AIDS

Debugging an assembly language program can be an extraordinarily frustrating job. A debugging aid is a program that lets you exercise a program under your direct control, stopping it at critical points and displaying the machine registers and the contents of storage. One such aid, DDT, is part of CP/M. It has many uses in the maintenance of programs. Another, SID, is available as a separate product from Digital Research, and other debugging tools are sold by other publishers.

Using DDT

DDT, and its bigger brother SID, act in many ways like interpreters of machine language. They control the machine and execute the machine instructions of the program being tested one or a few steps at a time. Because the program is under the debugging aid's control, you may stop it or step along one instruction at a time, pausing when you like to examine the state of working storage. These are invaluable aids to finding the errors in a program; even the most experienced assembly language programmers need them and the novice would be helpless without them.

DDT is called as a command and will accept the name of a program file it is to load for testing:

DDT *fileref*

The operand may be omitted; if it is given it must be a complete fileref naming a .HEX or .COM file.

DDT loads itself over the CCP, just below the BDOS in working storage. It changes the BDOS jump address at location 05h to point to its own beginning, so that programs that use all of storage won't use the storage DDT is in. It then loads the named program at its usual origin and awaits further commands.

DDT supports commands to display the contents of storage as machine instructions or as bytes and characters, commands to trace one or several steps of the program, and commands to run the program until it reaches some particular address. The CP/M document *CP/M Dynamic Debugging Tool User's Guide* contains a good introduction to the commands that DDT supports, as well as a worked example of how DDT can be used to trace and debug a program. If you've never used DDT, it would pay you to type in that example program and work through the example at the terminal.

Applying Patches

DDT is the command that is used to apply fixes to programs for which you do not have the source. Such fixes are stated as changes to be made in the byte values of a program; you learn of them from the publisher of the program.

In order to apply a patch you call DDT with the name of the program to be fixed. You then display the locations that are supposed to be changed and verify that they contain what the publisher said they should contain. You then use DDT commands to replace those values with the corrected values, and end DDT. The result is that the copy of the program now in storage is corrected, whereas the program in the .COM file on disk is still in error.

THE SAVE COMMAND. After you've used DDT to prepare the corrected version of a program, the altered program remains in storage. It will be overwritten by the next command to be loaded into the TPA. Before that happens you must save the new version of the program with the SAVE command, whose form is

SAVE *size fileref*

The SAVE command is part of the CCP (if it had to be loaded from disk, it would wipe out the altered command in storage). Its first operand is the size of the program to be saved. The size is a decimal number of pages, where one page is a unit of 256 bytes. The size is easily calculated. It is the decimal equivalent of the most significant byte of the program's ending address, or one less than that if the address ends in 00h. DDT displays the program's ending address when it loads the program.

The SAVE command writes the given number of pages (i.e., twice that number of standard 128-byte records) to the file given as its second operand. It begins writing with location 0100h, the start of the TPA. The result is a new file containing a copy of the program as you altered it with DDT.

EXAMPLE 12-3
DDT used to patch a message in the STAT command. After the program has been altered in storage, the SAVE command is used to write a copy of it to a new .COM file.

```
A>stat a:dsk:

    A: Drive Characteristics
 4800: 128 Byte Record Capacity
  600: Kilobyte Drive Capacity
  128: 32  Byte Directory Entries
  128: Checked  Directory Entries
  128: Records/ Extent
   16: Records/ Block
   64: Sectors/ Track
    2: Reserved Tracks

A>ddt stat.com
DDT VERS 2.2
NEXT  PC
1580 0100
-d028e,0294
028E 53 65 Se
0290 63 74 6F 72 73 ctors
-s028e
028E 53 52
028F 65
0290 63
0291 74 6f
0292 6F 72
0293 72 64
0294 73 .
-d028e,0294
028E 52 65 Re
0290 63 6F 72 64 73 cords
-g0

A>save 21 nstat.com
A>nstat a:dsk:

    A: Drive Characteristics
 4800: 128 Byte Record Capacity
  600: Kilobyte Drive Capacity
  128: 32  Byte Directory Entries
  128: Checked  Directory Entries
  128: Records/ Extent
   16: Records/ Block
   64: Records/ Track          (note change)
    2: Reserved Tracks

A>_
```

An Example of a Patch. Earlier we commented that the STAT command's disk information display says Sectors/Track when it really is displaying the number of 128-byte standard records per track—not necessarily the same thing. The message text is a constant in the body of the STAT program, and we can change it with DDT. Here are the instructions for the patch:

Around location 028E find the ASCII bytes for "Sectors" (in hexadecimal, 53 65 63 74 6F 72 73). Change those bytes to read "Records" (52 65 63 6F 72 64 73).

The complete process of applying the patch is shown in Example 12-3. The STAT command is tried out, for reference. DDT is called with STAT.COM as its operand. After loading the file DDT reports that the next available byte in working storage (the address of the byte after the last byte of STAT) is 1580h.

DDT's display command is used to verify that the expected values are present, then its substitute command is used to replace them with new values. The go-to-zero command ends DDT.

Since the end of the program was at 1580h, we need to save 21 (the decimal equivalent of 15h) pages. In order to test the change before making it permanent, we want to save the altered program under a different name. Hence the SAVE command is given operands of 21 and NSTAT.COM. The newly created NSTAT command works as expected.

Patching a Real Problem. Here's a second patch example. In CP/M 2.2 the SUBMIT command rejects a file if it contains a control character signal like "^Z." SUBMIT is supposed to convert that into a control-z byte in the submitted command. It turns out that SUBMIT will accept "^z," but that isn't compatible with previous versions of the system or with MP/M or CP/M-86.

This is the official fix for the problem. Use DDT to load SUBMIT.COM. Use the L subcommand to display the instructions beginning at 0441h. It should show

```
0441 SUI 61
0443 STA 0E7D
 .etc
```

(If it does not, don't continue with the patch.) Use the S subcommand to alter the byte at 0442h from 61h to 41h. End DDT and save the updated command.

It's best to save the altered command under a different name and test it. When you're sure that the patch worked and didn't cause any new problems, you can erase the original command and rename the patched version.

Chapter 13

BDOS Services for Applications

This chapter describes the BDOS service requests that are useful in writing application programs. After looking at the programming conventions used in making service requests, we'll examine the requests for console I/O and file I/O in detail.

SERVICE REQUEST CONVENTIONS

SERVICE REQUEST NUMBERS. CP/M 2.2 provides 38 different service requests. They are numbered sequentially from 1 to 37, plus 40 (38 and 39 exist only in MP/M). MP/M 2 adds 15 more (numbers 41-48 and 100-106). The CP/NET software, when installed in a CP/M system, adds six more requests (numbers 64-69). CP/M-86 contains 10 unique requests (50-59). All these requests are described in the Reference section of this book.

MAKING SERVICE REQUESTS. All requests are accessed in the same way: the number of the request is set in register C, a parameter is placed in the DE register pair, and a call is made to the BDOS jump at location 0005h. A few calls need no parameter in DE. When control returns to the program there is usually a return value in register A. A few requests return a value in the HL pair as well.

MAKING REQUESTS IN CP/M-86. The method of making a service request in CP/M-86 is only slightly different. The number of the request is placed in BL and the parameter is passed in DX. The BDOS returns byte values in AL and word values in BX. A CP/M-86 program calls the BDOS by executing INT 224 rather than by a jump.

REGISTER PRESERVATION. The BDOS does not preserve the contents of any register. You cannot assume anything about the contents of the registers following a service call, except for those specified to contain a return value. This makes it awkward to place service calls in the main line of your code. Often you'll have allocated registers carefully to certain functions and a service call upsets those plans.

One approach to the problem is to enclose a call to BDOS within a subroutine that also saves some registers by pushing them on the stack before making the service request. But that is a lot of trouble to achieve a few push and pop instructions.

The SERVICE Macro. Figure 13-1 shows another approach. The SERVICE macro makes it possible to place service requests at any point in a program without worrying about register preservation. It saves the BC and DE registers, and the HL register as well, except for the five services that return values in it. If a second operand is given, the macro assumes that it names a value that should become the parameter of the service call. In that case it loads the DE register with the parameter value. If no operand appears, the macro assumes you have loaded the parameter into DE already. Following the service request it restores the registers it saved.

The Z80 Registers. The BDOS is written in 8080 machine language and will never alter the index and alternate registers that are unique to the Z80 CPU. Normally the BIOS doesn't alter those registers either, or it preserves them if it does. You should check with your vendor; it is likely that your BIOS does not change the Z80 registers. If so, you need not preserve them over a service call.

CONSOLE INPUT REQUESTS

Many useful applications can be built that require no console I/O at all. When it is required, console input should be designed with consideration for the operator in mind. Programs such as the disk formatter used as an example in Chapter 8, which require the user to type one-character responses to crucial questions and can't be automated with XSUB, are the bane of the experienced user's life. Abused though it may be, console

```
;
;   SERVICE MACRO: CALL BDOS FOR A SERVICE, SAVING
;   ALL REGISTERS EXCEPT A AND SOMETIMES HL.  LOAD
;   DE REGISTER WITH PARAMETER IF ONE IS GIVEN.
;
SERVICE MACRO   ?S,?DE
        PUSH    B           ; SAVE BC AND ..
        PUSH    D           ; ..DE ALWAYS.
  IF (?S NE 12) AND (?S NE 24) AND (?S NE 27) AND (?S NE 29) AND (?S NE 31)
        PUSH    H           ; SAVE HL WHEN BDOS DOESNT RETURN IT
  ENDIF
  IF NOT NUL ?DE
        LXI     D,?DE       ; LOAD PARAMETER
  ENDIF
        MVI     C,?S        ; SET SERVICE NUMBER
        CALL    0005H       ; AND CALL BDOS
  IF (?S NE 12) AND (?S NE 24) AND (?S NE 27) AND (?S NE 29) AND (?S NE 31)
        POP     H           ; RESTORE HL IF IT DOESNT HAVE THE RESULT
  ENDIF
        POP     D           ; RESTORE DE, BC ALWAYS
        POP     B
        ENDM
```

FIGURE 13-1
The SERVICE macro makes it simpler to issue a service request, and it handles register preservation.

input is sometimes necessary, and the several service requests that deal with it make a good introduction to service requests in general.

Service 1: Get a Byte

Operation of Service 1. Service 1 is simplicity itself. Call the BDOS with 01h in register C, and receive the next character typed in register A. The system will be suspended until the user presses a key.

Service 1 and Control Characters. According to the CP/M documentation the BDOS checks the received character for control-p or control-s (console copy or stop scrolling respectively). CP/M 2.2 may check; if so, it does nothing with what it finds. This is easily shown with a program so simple you might enter it with DDT:

```
ORG   0100H (in DDT, a100)
MVI   C,1
CALL  5
JMP   100H
END
```

The program simply soaks up console input. If you run it, you'll find that none of the usual control characters have any effect. Control-p does not switch on console copy. Control-c does not cancel the program with a warm start; you'll have to use reset to kill it. If you add output to the program (as we'll soon see how to do), you can demonstrate that control-s doesn't suspend it.

Use of Service 1. The user doesn't get a chance to correct a typing error. If the wrong character is typed, your program will have the data and be off and running long before the operator's finger has reached the bottom of the keystroke. Therefore, it is good practice not to initiate anything irrevocable in response to input from Service 1. Ask for confirmation with another input, or use Service 10 in the first place.

Service 10: Get a Line

Service 10 requests line input. It requires the address of a line input buffer as a parameter in register DE. This buffer consists of a byte giving the maximum amount of data the buffer will hold, a byte in which the BDOS will return the amount actually received, and a series of bytes in which a complete line of user input will be placed.

Operation of Service 10. When called for service 10, the BDOS will begin collecting characters from the CON: logical device and placing them in the buffer. During this process the BDOS will note and respond to all of the usual control characters. When the user enters either a CR or an LF, the line is complete. The count of bytes is placed in the buffer and control returns. The terminating character (CR or LF) is not placed in the buffer nor is it counted in the data.

Use of Service 10. Service 10 allows the user to correct typing errors with control-x and backspace, and to control the system with control-p, -s, and -c. It is the only service that can receive a line of input from a submit file via the XSUB program. Service 10 is therefore the preferred console input method for all applications. The only exceptions would be those that require detailed control of the terminal, such as full-screen editors and games.

Service 11: Console Status

If your application engages in a lengthy spell of processing (say, reading a file of several thousand records), it would be nice to have some way of making it stop. The reset key will do it, of course, but it doesn't give the program a chance to clean up. If the reset button is the only way to stop your program, some day that button will be pressed at just the right time to demolish a file directory.

Operation of Service 11. Service 11 offers a way to check the keyboard for an abort request; it is undoubtedly the way that PIP checks for one. Upon return from service 11 register A contains 00h if no key has been pressed since the last console input. If a key has been pressed, the BDOS returns a nonzero value (the CP/M documentation says the value is FFh, but the author has seen one system that returned 01h).

Use of Service 11. You can imbed a call to service 11 at the center of your processing loop. If a key has been pressed, you may either abort as PIP does (tidying up all files behind you), or call a routine that asks if the user really meant it, going on with the program if the user did not. The latter course has two advantages. First, the program can't be aborted by an accidental brush of the keyboard. Second, it lets the nervous user punch a key just to make sure the program is still alive. It's often hard to tell a hung program from one that is just working hard.

The CISUB Library

Figure 13-2 shows the contents of CISUB, a macro library whose contents illustrate the use of the console input services. It contains no aids for service 1 (that is easily done with a SERVICE 1 macro call). It does contain a macro aid to the use of service 11. CITEST takes as its operand a label to be called in the event that a character has been typed. That routine would handle the abort procedure, returning if no abort was necessary.

CISUB also illustrates the use of service 10. It contains a macro, CIBUFF, that constructs a line input buffer with an additional byte ahead of it. The CISUBM macro generates three subroutines. The first, CIREAD, issues service request 11 to fill a buffer

```
; * * * * *   CISUB.LIB : CONSOLE INPUT AIDS
;
;       MACRO TO CREATE A LINE BUFFER WITH ONE ADDITIONAL
;       BYTE USED BY THE CIGETC SUBROUTINE
;
CIBUFF  MACRO   ?SIZE
        DB      0       ; INDEX FOR CIGETC
        DB      ?SIZE   ; BUFFER SIZE FOR BDOS
        DB      0       ; RETURNED LENGTH OF DATA
        DS      ?SIZE   ; SPACE FOR THE DATA
        ENDM
;
;       MACRO TO TEST IF A KEY HAS BEEN PRESSED AT THE
;       TERMINAL.  OPERAND IS THE LABEL OF A TERMINATION
;       OR USER-COMMUNICATION ROUTINE.
;
CITEST  MACRO   ?CALL
        SERVICE 11
        ORA     A       ; HAS A KEY BEEN HIT?
        CNZ     ?CALL   ; IF SO, CALL GIVEN ROUTINE.
        ENDM
;
;       SET OF SUBROUTINES FOR CONSOLE LINE INPUT
;
CISUBM  MACRO
;
; CILINE: READ A LINE OF INPUT TO A LINE BUFFER (DECLARED WITH
;               THE CIBUFF MACRO)
; INPUT:  HL --> THE LINE BUFFER  (PRESERVED)
; OUTPUT: BUFFER FILLED.  A = NUMBER OF BYTES, Z-FLAG SET IF
;           THE INPUT WAS A NULL LINE.
;
CILINE  EQU     $
        PUSH    H       ; SAVE BUFFER ADDRESS
        MVI     M,00    ; ZERO INDEX BYTE FOR CIGETC.
        INX     H       ; HL --> BUFFER FOR BDOS
        XCHG            ; PUT IN DE FOR BDOS,
        SERVICE 10      ; ..FILL THE BUFFER
        XCHG            ; RECOVER CALLER´S DE
        INX     H       ; HL --> LENGTH OF DATA
        MOV     A,M     ; ..PUT IT IN A
        ORA     A       ; SET Z-FLAG FROM LENGTH
        POP     H       ; RESTORE HL-->BUFFER
        RET
;
; CIGETC: GET NEXT BYTE FROM A LINE BUFFER
; INPUT:  HL --> THE LINE BUFFER (PRESERVED)
; OUTPUT: A = NEXT BYTE.  IF THERE IS NONE, A = CR AND
;            THE Z-FLAG IS SET.
;
CIGETC  EQU     $
        PUSH    B       ; SAVE A WORK REGISTER
        PUSH    H       ; AND THE BUFFER ADDRESS
        MOV     A,M     ; COPY INDEX BYTE,
        INR     M       ; ..AND STEP IT FOR NEXT TIME
        INX  H ! INX  H ; HL --> LENGTH OF DATA
        CMP     M       ; INDEX < LENGTH?
        JC      CIGETC2 ; (YES, DATA REMAINS)
        MVI     A,CR    ; NO, RETURN A CR
        JMP     CIGETC3
CIGETC2 MOV     C,A     ; COMPUTE OFFSET TO DATA FROM HL:
        MVI     B,0     ; (HL+1)-->FIRST BYTE IN BUFFER
        INX     B
        DAD     B       ; HL --> WANTED BYTE
```

FIGURE 13-2

CISUB.LIB contains subroutines that simplify the use of service request 10 (read a line from the console), and macro CITEST that uses service 11 for an abort test based on console status.

```
         MOV      A,M       ; PICK IT UP
CIGETC3  CPI      CR        ; SET Z-FLAG FOR END OF LINE
         POP   H ! POP B    ; RECOVER REGISTERS.
         RET
;
; CIGETNB: GET NEXT NON-BLANK FROM A LINE BUFFER
; INPUT:   HL --> BUFFER (PRESERVED)
; OUTPUT:  AS FOR CIGETC, BUT NEVER A BLANK.
;
CIGETNB  EQU      $
         CALL     CIGETC    ; GET A BYTE,
         RZ                 ; ..EXIT IF END OF LINE
         CPI      BLANK     ; IF IT ISN'T BLANK,
         RNZ                ; ..RETURN
         JMP      CIGETNB
;
; * * * * *       END OF CISUB.LIB
         ENDM
```

FIGURE 13-2 (Continued)

built by the CIBUFF macro. The second, CIGET, returns the next byte from that buffer, or a CR character and the Z flag set if there are no more.

The CIGETNB subroutine takes bytes from the buffer until it finds one that is not blank (or finds the end of the input). It allows you to ignore blanks in the input line.

CONSOLE OUTPUT REQUESTS

Unlike console input, console output is needed in almost every program, if only to tell the user that something has gone wrong. The console output requests are easy to use.

Service 2: Write a Byte

Operation of Service 2. Service request 2 takes as its parameter a single byte in the E register (the contents of D are ignored). That character is displayed at the device currently assigned as CON:. If the character is a tab, the BDOS expands it into a string of one to eight spaces according to its knowledge of where the cursor is relative to the standard 8-column tab stops. It is possible for the BDOS to be wrong about this. If you've been moving the cursor about with escape sequences (which the BDOS, being device independent, doesn't recognize), then tab expansion will be in error. Avoid writing tabs in that case.

Service 2 and Control Characters. The effect of control-s and control-p during service 2 output can best be explained by an example. Assemble this program:

```
       ORG   0100H
TOP    MVI   E,'X'
       MVI   C,2
       CALL  5
       LXI   H,0
```

```
SPIN  DCX   H
      MOV   A,L
      ORA   H
      JZ    TOP
      JMP   SPIN
```

The program types Xs at the terminal with a pause between each. Run it and experiment with control characters. You'll find that control-s, if it is the first input, suspends output as it should. While output is suspended control-c will cancel the program. If you enter any character other than control-s, it is ignored, and thereafter control-s has no effect. This odd behavior is not what the CP/M documentation might lead one to expect. At any rate, while service 2 output is under way control-p will not initiate console copy, nor will control-c alone cancel the program.

Service 9: Write a String

Operation of Service 9. Service 9 provides an easy way to write a complete message to the console. The parameter in register DE is taken to be the address of a sequence of characters terminated by the ASCII value 24h (a dollar sign in the United States, or another currency symbol elsewhere). The string, up to but not including the terminator, is sent to CON:. The effect of control characters during output is much the same as with service 2.

Use of Services 2 and 9. The user can't cancel the program with control-c while it is writing to the console. A program that writes a lot of data to the terminal without pausing for service 10 input ought to include an abort test (such as the CITEST macro).

String Terminators. The choice of 24h as a string terminator was an unfortunate one; as a result, service 9 can never be used to write a string that contains a currency symbol as part of the data. You might wonder why that terminator was chosen when there were at least four other choices that could have been made (the null byte 00h or the EM, ETX, or SUB control characters). Such speculation is irrelevant, inasmuch as the choice *was* made and couldn't be changed now without causing immense problems for existing programs.

Two other conventions have arisen among CP/M programs for terminating strings of output. One convention, probably deriving from the practices of the C programming language, terminates strings with the null byte, 00h. The second marks the last character of a string by setting its most significant bit to 1. Each has its advantages, and each requires a subroutine in the program to handle it.

The COSUB Library

Figure 13-3 shows the contents of a macro library that contains a set of console output subroutines. A call to the COSUBM macro will generate the subroutines at that point in the program.

```
COSUBM  MACRO
; * * * *       COSUB.LIB -- CONSOLE OUTPUT SUBROUTINES
;
;       SUBROUTINE TO WRITE [A] TO CONSOLE
;       ALTERS ONLY A AND F
;
COUT    EQU     $
        PUSH B  ! PUSH D   ! PUSH H
        ANI     7FH      ; CP/M EXPECTS BIT 7 = 0
        MOV     E,A      ; PUT DATA WHERE CP/M EXPECTS
        MVI     C,2      ; CONSOLE OUTPUT FUNCTION
        CALL    0005H
        POP   H  ! POP   D   ! POP B
        RET
;
;       SUBROUTINE TO WRITE RETURN, LINEFEED TO CONSOLE
;       ALTERS NO REGISTERS
;
COCRLF  EQU     $
        PUSH    PSW
        MVI     A,CR             ; THE RETURN..
        CALL    COUT
        MVI     A,LF             ; ..THE LINEFEED.
        CALL    COUT
        POP     PSW
        RET
;
;       SUBROUTINE TO WRITE A SPACE TO THE CONSOLE
;       ALTERS NO REGISTERS
;
COSPACE EQU     $
        PUSH    PSW
        MVI     A,BLANK
        CALL    COUT
        POP     PSW
        RET
;
;       SUBROUTINE TO WRITE BYTES ADDRESSED BY HL,
;       UP TO AND INCLUDING ONE WITH BIT 7 = 1
;       ALTERS A&F, STEPS HL TO LAST BYTE OF STRING.
;
COSTR   EQU     $
        MOV     A,M      ; PICK UP BYTE TO GO
        CALL    COUT     ; PRINT IT
        MOV     A,M      ; LOOK AGAIN, AND
        RLC              ;  ..CHECK BIT 7:
        RC               ;  ..RETURN IF ON
        INX     H        ; ELSE POINT TO NEXT,
        JMP     COSTR    ;  .. AND CONTINUE
;
; * * * * *     END OF COSUB.LIB
        ENDM
```

FIGURE 13-3
COSUB.LIB contains routines to simplify console output. The COSTR routine illustrates the use of a convention for ending strings other than the one used by service request 9.

The COUT subroutine is nothing but a call on service 1, except that the character to be displayed is passed in the A register. That is usually more convenient than using the E register as the service request requires. COUT preserves all registers.

The COSPACE and COCRLF subroutines allow you to write those most common characters, a space and a CR, LF pair, without modifying any registers at all.

The COSTR subroutine writes a string that is terminated by a byte whose most significant bit is set to 1.

FILE-HANDLING CONCEPTS

The greatest number of CP/M service calls are concerned with operations on the file system. The parameter for each of these calls is the address of an FCB, a 36-byte field that reflects the state of a particular file. After reviewing an important CP/M concept, we'll talk about the use of that data structure.

The Idea of the Default Drive

Back in Chapter 5 we spoke of the default drive. That was the drive that was named in the CCP's prompt, and whose drivecode was used wherever the user didn't supply one. The concept of the default drive runs throughout all your dealings with the file system.

When you operate on a file with one of the service requests we'll look at later, the file is assumed to exist on the drive that is currently the default. You may specify another drive in the FCB; if you do, the drive you name is made the default before anything else is done. In other words, the BDOS looks at only one drive at a time, and that drive is automatically made the default.

Service 25: Get Default Drive

Service 25 returns a number indicating the current default drivecode in register A. This can be used to find out which drive the user knows as the default, or saved to reset the correct drive at the end of the program. The returned number encodes the drive; 0 stands for A:, 1 for B:, and so on to 0Fh for P:. This is different from a similar code in the FCB, as we'll see.

Service 14: Set Default Drive

Service 14 sets the drive that is to be the default, exactly as a drivecode command does. The parameter to service 14 is a drive number in register E. The number returned by service 25 may be used for the parameter.

The File Control Block

The FCB holds a copy of the information contained in a file's directory entry. Its initial byte and the 4 bytes at the end are not part of the directory; they are used only within programs. There is a map of the FCB in Figure 13-4. Let's take a tour of its fields.

00h: THE DRIVECODE. The first byte of an FCB is a drivecode byte. If its value is 00h, then any operation using that FCB will be directed to the drive that is currently the default. If the byte is not zero, the operation will go to a specific drive. The drive is coded as a number: 1 stands for A:, 2 for B:, and so on. 1+'X'-'A' is an assembler expression

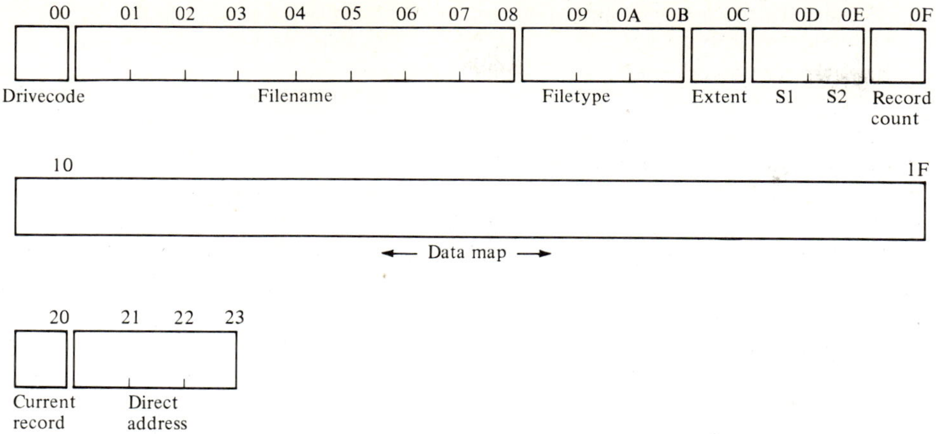

FIGURE 13-4
A map of the File Control Block (FCB), the storage copy of a directory entry used in most file service requests.

that will produce this code for any drive letter X. Note that this encoding of the drive is one greater than the code used by services 25 and 14.

01h TO 08h: THE FILENAME. The filename comes next, as eight ASCII characters. The name is left justified in the field and padded on the right with blanks. The most significant bit of each of these characters is ordinarily zero, as with any ASCII byte. However, those bits are sometimes used as indicators, as we'll see in a later chapter.

09h TO 0Bh: THE FILETYPE. The filetype follows the filename (there is no dot between them in the FCB). The filetype is left justified and padded with blanks. Therefore, a file with no filetype actually has a filetype of three blank characters. The most significant bits of each filetype character are normally 0, but in some advanced service requests we'll look at later they are used by CP/M as indicators.

0Ch: THE EXTENT NUMBER. We discussed file extents in an earlier chapter. We said that one directory entry can control a certain amount of space (usually 16 KB). Files larger than that have a directory entry for each extent. Byte 0Ch contains the number of the file extent currently being processed. It is 00h in the first extent of a file, 01h in the next, and so on up to 1Fh. That provides for 32 extents, the maximum in CP/M 1.4. CP/M 2 can handle more than 32 extents. In extents with higher numbers the overflow beyond 1Fh is kept elsewhere in the FCB.

0Dh: THE S1 AND S2 NUMBERS. The 2 bytes at 0Dh and 0Eh in the FCB are used by BDOS for its own purposes. The uses to which these bytes are put are not defined, may change in future versions of the system, and probably differ between CP/M and MP/M.

0Fh: THE RECORD COUNT. The byte at 0Fh contains a count of the number of standard records controlled by this extent. The STAT command computes the number of records in a file by adding up the record count field of each directory entry for the file. If a file is built with direct access writes and contains holes (unallocated space), the record count byte may be inaccurate.

10h TO 1Fh: THE DATA MAP. The 16 bytes from 10h to 1Fh contain a list of the allocation blocks controlled by this extent of the file. This is the most important information in the FCB. These numbers specify the disk locations where the file's data are to be found. The data map should be left strictly alone. If you alter the map before closing the file, the results can be catastrophic. The information from the directory ends here; following bytes exist in storage only.

20h: THE CURRENT RECORD. The byte 20h into the FCB is used by the BDOS as a count of the number of standard records that have been read or written in this extent of the file.

You are expected to set the current record number to 00h when opening a file for sequential access. Then the first access will produce the first record of the extent. The current record byte will be incremented to 01h, which will cause the next service request to access the second record, and so on. When the current record equals the record count byte (on input) or the capacity of the extent (on output), the BDOS knows that the extent is finished.

21h TO 23h: RECORD ADDRESS. The last 3 bytes of the FCB were added in CP/M 2. Programs written for earlier versions may not have provided for this extra space (tiny c, for instance, dedicated these bytes to other purposes). Such programs cannot use the direct access service requests.

Direct access to any standard record of a file is done by setting a 24-bit integer in bytes 21h, 22h, and 23h. 21h is the least significant byte and 23h is the most significant. This is the reverse of what you might expect, but it fits well with the operation of the 8080's instructions. After the address has been set a request for a direct access operation is made; the BDOS reads or writes the record whose number is specified.

In CP/M 2 there cannot be more than 65,536 records in a file. In that system the byte at 23h is always zero. MP/M 2 supports larger files. It will allow the third, most significant, byte to contain a value as large as 03h.

FILE INPUT REQUESTS

Reading from a file can be almost as simple as reading from the console. Three steps are required: open the file, read its data, and recognize the end of the data.

Service 15: Open Existing File

OPERATION OF SERVICE 15. Service 15 requires the address of an FCB in register DE. The BDOS uses the drivecode byte to select a drive. It looks up a directory entry for the file and extent named in the FCB. If it is found, the data map from that directory entry is copied into the FCB and the file is ready for reading.

THE DIRECTORY SEARCH. The first 15 bytes of the FCB affect the directory search. The drivecode decides which drive's directory will be searched. If it is 00h, the directory of the current default drive will be used. If not, the drive specified by the drivecode byte will be made the default drive.

AMBIGUOUS FILEREFS. The filename and filetype must have been set up properly (left justified and padded with blanks). The search will fail if they are not. However, the fileref in the FCB may be ambiguous. If it contains question marks, the BDOS will open the first directory entry whose fileref matches the reference. This is true only in CP/M and MP/M 1. In MP/M 2 the fileref must be explicit.

THE EXTENT NUMBER. The extent number byte takes part in the directory search as well. You should set this byte to 00h before the service request so that the first extent entry will be found. You could set it to, say, 01h and so open the second extent of the file (assuming there is one) instead of the first. This is how direct access was done prior to version 2.0 of CP/M. However, the highest extent you can open in this way is the 32nd. It makes more sense (and yields better performance) to use the direct access services now.

THE S1 AND S2 BYTES. The S1 and S2 bytes participate in the file search. The only thing that you may be sure of about the function of these bytes is that, if they are zero, the first extent will be found.

Opening the Default FCB

If your program takes a fileref as its first operand, you may use the FCB prepared at 5Ch in low storage. The CCP sets it up ready to open. Check that the byte at 5Dh—the first byte of the filename—isn't blank (if it is, no operand was given). Then simply request service 15, passing the address of the default FCB in register DE. This convenient feature makes it very easy to write programs that process a single file.

Service 26: Set Buffer Address

Before reading a file you must tell the BDOS where the data are to be put. This is done with service 26, which takes the address of a record buffer in register DE. Until another service 26 is done all file access requests will use that buffer.

USING THE DEFAULT BUFFER. The CCP sets location 80h as the buffer address before entering your program. If you don't change the buffer address with a service 26, all file accesses will use that buffer from 80h to FFh. This feature simplifies the job of writing simple programs. You must remember to process any operands from the command tail before doing any file accesses through the default buffer, as that is also the place where the CCP stored the command tail.

Service 20: Sequential Read

Operation of Service 20. Once the file has been opened and the buffer address set, you may read data. Service 20 requests a standard record from a file. The address of the FCB is passed in register DE and a return code is returned in register A (if your CP/M or MP/M documentation says a "directory code" is returned in register A, correct it; that is not the case).

The Return Code. If the return code is 00h, then a copy of the current record has been placed in the buffer, ready for processing. The current record byte has been incremented and, if that made it equal to the record count byte, the BDOS has opened the next extent of the file and copied its data map into the FCB. If the code in register A is nonzero (don't assume it will be FFh), no more records are available. This is physical end of file; it can happen on the first read request because a file can contain zero records.

End of File

Physical End of File. CP/M has two conventions for end of file. The first is the physical end of file, which is signaled by a nonzero value in register A following service 20. That means that there is no next record in sequence. That could happen because there are no more records in the file, or it might be that this file was created with direct access and has a hole in it (a sequence of records that have never been written and hence were never allocated).

Logical End of File. In a file of ASCII text the SUB control character signals the end of data. SUB usually occurs in the last standard record of the file, but it might occur in the next to last record, or indeed anywhere. Many programs fill each output buffer with SUB characters before putting data in it. The result is that the last part of the last record of a file is filled completely with SUB bytes. That is not always done; sometimes there is only a single SUB character, followed by unpredictable values to the end of the record.

If the last useful byte of an ASCII file is also the last byte of a record, some programs don't bother to write an additional record containing a SUB. Therefore, the end of an ASCII file can be signaled either by physical end of file or by the appearance of a SUB character in the data.

The TF Command

Figure 13-5 shows the complete source of a simple program TF (for Type File). It does what the TYPE command does: it writes the contents of an ASCII file at the console. TF

```
; * * * *          TF : A PROGRAM TO TYPE FILES
;
           MACLIB   CPMEQU   ; INCLUDE STANDARD NAMES
           MACLIB   PROG     ; PROLOG, SERVICE MACROS
           MACLIB   COSUB    ; CONSOLE OUTPUT ROUTINES
           MACLIB   CISUB    ; CISUB FOR CITEST MACRO
;
           PROLOG   20,TF    ; SET UP STACK
;
TF         EQU      $
           LDA      CPMFCB+1; FIRST FILENAME BYTE:
           CPI      BLANK    ; NO OPERAND GIVEN?
           RZ                ; ALL DONE IF SO.
;
           SERVICE 15,CPMFCB ; OPEN THE FILE
           INR      A        ; CHECK FOR ERROR (FFH)
           RZ                ; EXIT IF OPEN FAILED
;
TFTOP      EQU      $
           SERVICE 20,CPMFCB ; READ A RECORD TO 0080H
           ORA      A        ; ..IF THERE IS ANOTHER
           RNZ               ;   (THERE WASN'T -- EXIT)
;
           CITEST   TFABORT ; ABORT IF A KEY'S BEEN HIT
;
           LXI      H,CPMBUFF ; START OF BUFFER,
           MVI      B,128    ;     ..AND ITS LENGTH.
;
TFLOOP     MOV      A,M      ; NEXT FILE BYTE..
           CPI      EOF      ; IS IT AN EOF MARK?
           RZ                ; QUIT IF SO,
           CALL     COUT     ; ..ELSE TYPE IT AND
           INX      H        ; POINT TO NEXT BYTE.
           DCR      B
           JNZ      TFLOOP   ; DO ANOTHER IF THERE IS ONE,
           JMP      TFTOP    ; ..OR GET NEXT RECORD
;
TFABORT RET                  ; EXIT WHEN CITEST FINDS A KEY HIT.
;
; SUBROUTINES:
           COSUBM
           END
```

FIGURE 13-5
The TF (for Type a File) command demonstrates sequential input using the default FCB and default record buffer, and the use of CITEST for an abort test.

uses the default FCB prepared by the CCP and the default I/O buffer. It uses the macro libraries shown earlier; the PROG library contains the PROLOG2 and SERVICE macros seen earlier. TF watches for both end-of-file signals and terminates when either occurs.

FILE OUTPUT REQUESTS

Deleting an Existing File

File output is more involved than input. Complications occur upon opening of the file. If a file of the same name presently exists, it must be erased—otherwise the data written would simply replace what are already there. If your program wrote more data than the file held originally, all would be well. If it wrote less, some old data would remain, at best taking up space to no purpose, and at worst causing errors in the program that reads the data.

Deletion Policies. File deletion is just as permanent an action as the ERA command. Generally speaking, it is not a good idea for a program to erase any file unless it can be sure that doing so will cause no harm. PIP and the CP/M editors have policies that makes file deletion safer.

It is a CP/M convention that any file whose filetype is .$$$ is a temporary file that can be erased without warning. Set up the output FCB with the filename requested by the user, but with a filetype of .$$$. Your program can delete that fileref without worry.

At the end of the program when the output file has been built and closed, the program may delete the original file if it exists, and then rename the new output file to give it the correct filetype. That is the sequence PIP uses. Editors don't delete an existing file; they rename it so that it has a filetype of .BAK before they rename the new file to its correct type.

Another policy is possible: a program can simply refuse to take the responsibility for file deletion. Such a program would check to see if its output file existed. If it did, the program would terminate with a message. It would then be up to the user to do the erasing.

Service 19: Delete a File. Service 19 takes an FCB and erases the file named in it. It returns a signal in the A register, indicating whether or not the file existed (that hardly seems useful—whether or not the file *did* exist, it doesn't afterward!).

Service 23: Rename a File. Service 23 renames a file, just as the REN command does. The present name of the file is given in the FCB in the normal way. Its new name must be placed in the same format in the data map space of the FCB, from bytes 11h to 1Bh. The new filename is taken from bytes 11h through 18h, and the new filetype from bytes 19h through 1Bh.

Service 22: Make a File

After any existing file has been erased, and before output begins, a directory entry must be created for the file. This is done with service 22. For that service register DE addresses an FCB with the drivecode, filename, and filetype filled in as usual and other fields set to zero.

Operation of Service 22. The BDOS selects an unused entry in the directory and fills it in from the FCB. The data map in the new directory entry is filled with zeros and its record count byte contains zero. This indicates that although the new file exists (it can be listed by DIR and STAT) no space has been allocated to it. If your program terminates at that point, the file will remain in the directory and STAT will show that it has no records. Such a file can be opened for input; end of file will be signaled on the first read request.

Use of Service 22. It is absolutely essential to use service 22 before writing to a file. During output the BDOS does not check to see if a directory entry exists. You can write to an unmade FCB with apparent success for one extent. When the extent must be closed, either because of a close request or because it is full, an error will occur and the file will not be recorded in the directory. In MP/M 2 the BDOS will refuse to write to an unmade FCB.

Service 21: Sequential Write

Once the file has been made, the current record byte set to zero, and the buffer address set (service 26), you may write in the file. This is done with service 21. Prepare a standard record of 128 bytes in the current buffer, put the address of the FCB in register DE, and issue the request.

Allocating a New Extent. The BDOS increments the record count of the FCB. If that becomes greater than the capacity of an extent, the BDOS updates the directory by copying the FCB's data map into the directory entry prepared when the file was made. It then allocates a new directory entry, clears its data map, gives it an extent number one higher than the prior extent, and copies it into the FCB.

Allocating a New Block. If the record to be written is the first of a new allocation block, the BDOS allocates a block and records its number in the data map of the FCB. With these allocation matters taken care of, the BDOS will copy the record from the current buffer onto disk and return to the program.

Errors During Sequential Write. If all this goes correctly, register A will be returned with a value of 00h (if your CP/M or MP/M book says it will contain a "directory code," correct it). Two things can go wrong with a sequential write. The BDOS may want to open a new extent only to find that there are no free directory entries. Or, it may look for a new allocation block and find that none are available (that is, that the disk is full). If either of these things happens, it will return a nonzero value in register A. (Under CP/M 2.2, a value of 01h says that there are no free directory entries and a value of 02h says that there is no disk space. MP/M and CP/M-86 may return different codes.)

Service 16: Close a File

Having written to a file, you must close it. Service 16 closes the file. It requires an FCB address in register DE. The BDOS looks up the directory entry that matches the FCB (the one with the same filename, filetype, and extent number) and copies the data map from the storage FCB into it. Only at that time is the space allocation for the last extent made permanent.

RESULT OF NOT CLOSING. If you do not close the file (if, for example, your program is aborted with control-c), the last, or only, directory entry will not be updated to show the data space allocated to it. The file will exist, provided it was recorded by service 22, but all data written into the last, or only, extent will be lost. The space written to in that extent will be available for reuse by another file.

The FT Command

Figure 13-6 shows the source of a command called FT (for File Typer). It makes the file named in the command, then uses the CISUB library shown earlier to read lines of input from the console. Each input line is copied into a record buffer. When 128 bytes have been collected, a record is written to the file. When the operator types a null line, FT closes the file and returns to the CCP. Any of several errors cause it to exit via the ERROREXIT label defined by the PROLOG2 macro.

The FT command could stand improvement. You might like to enhance it by making it issue a prompt character before reading each line. You might change the way it handles existing files; as given, it adopts the simple policy of refusing to erase a file.

```
; * * * * *     FT : BUILDS FILES BY TYPING
;
        MACLIB  CPMEQU   ; DEFINE IMPORTANT NAMES
        MACLIB  PROG     ; PROLOG2, SERVICE MACROS
        MACLIB  CISUB    ; CONSOLE INPUT ROUTINES
        MACLIB  COSUB    ; AND OUTPUT FOR COCRLF ONLY
;
        PROLOG2 FT       ; SET UP STACK, GO TO FT
;
; * * * ERROR MESSAGES
;
CCMSG   DB      'Can''t close the file',cr,lf,'$'
CWMSG   DB      'Error on write',cr,lf,'$'
CMMSG   DB      'Can''t make the file',cr,lf,'$'
FEMSG   DB      'File exists -- you erase it',cr,lf,'$'
;
INPUT   CIBUFF  128      ; DEFINE LINE INPUT BUFFER
;
FT      EQU     $        ; START OF PROGRAM
        LDA     CPMFCB+1
        CPI     BLANK    ; ANY OPERAND GIVEN?
        RZ               ; DONE IF NOT
;
        SERVICE 15,CPMFCB ; OPEN FILE AS FOR INPUT
        INR     A        ; DOES FILE EXIST?
        JZ      FT2      ; NO, CONTINUE.
        LXI     D,FEMSG  ; YES, QUIT WITH A MESSAGE.
        JMP     ERROREXIT
```

FIGURE 13-6
FT (for File Typer) takes lines from the console and puts them in a disk file. The many errors that can be found make it more complicated than TF (FIGURE 13-5). The PROLOG2 macro simplifies things.

```
;
FT2     SERVICE 22,CPMFCB ; NEW FILE.  MAKE IT.
        INR     A       ; DID THAT WORK?
        JNZ     FT3     ; YES, CONTINUE.
        LXI     D,CMMSG ; NO, QUIT WITH A MESSAGE.
        JMP     ERROREXIT
;
FT3     LXI     D,CPMBUFF ; DE INDEXES DISK BUFFER
        MVI     B,00      ; B COUNTS BYTES IN IT
;
FTOP    EQU     $       ; HERE FOR EACH CONSOLE LINE
        CALL    COCRLF  ; CURSOR TO NEXT SCREEN LINE
        LXI     H,INPUT
        CALL    CILINE  ; SERVICE 10 GETS INPUT LINE
        JZ      FTCLOSE ; ALL DONE IF NULL LINE
;
FTLOOP  CALL    CIGETC  ; NEXT INBYTE
        JZ      FTEOL   ; (END OF LINE)
        CALL    FTPUT   ; GOT A BYTE, PUT IT IN FILE
        JMP     FTLOOP  ; ..AND GET NEXT
;
FTEOL   MVI     A,CR    ; END OF INPUT LINE, PUT
        CALL    FTPUT   ; ..CR, LF INTO
        MVI     A,LF    ; ..THE FILE
        CALL    FTPUT
        JMP     FTOP    ; THEN GET NEXT LINE
;
; WHEN A NULL LINE IS RECEIVED FILL THE REST OF THE
; BUFFER WITH EOF MARKS, WRITE IT, AND CLOSE FILE.
;
FTCLOSE MVI     A,EOF   ; FILL DISK RECORD WITH SUBS
        STAX    D
        INX     D
        INR     B
        JP      FTCLOSE
        SERVICE 21,CPMFCB ; THEN WRITE LAST RECORD
        ORA     A         ; DID IT WORK?
        JNZ     CANT$WRITE
        SERVICE 16,CPMFCB ; CLOSE THE FILE
        INR     A       ; CHECK SUCCESS,
        RNZ             ; RETURN TO EPILOG IF OK
        LXI     D,CCMSG
        JMP     ERROREXIT
;
; SUBROUTINE TO STOW THE BYTE IN A IN THE DISK BUFFER.
; DE-->BUFFER, BC COUNTS BYTES IN IT.  WRITE THE BUFFER
; WHEN IT FILLS UP.
;
FTPUT   STAX    D       ; PUT BYTE IN BUFFER,
        INX     D       ; STEP BUFFER INDEX,
        INR     B       ; COUNT BYTES IN THIS RECORD
        RP              ; RETURN IF NOT UP TO 128
        LXI     D,CPMBUFF; RESET BUFFER PTR,
        MVI     B,00    ; ..AND BYTE COUNT
        SERVICE 21,CPMFCB ; THEN WRITE RECORD
        ORA     A       ; ..AND IF IT WORKED
        RZ              ; ..CONTINUE IN PROGRAM
CANT$WRITE EQU  $
        LXI     D,CWMSG ; IF IT DID NOT,
        JMP     ERROREXIT ; ..QUIT WITH MESSAGE.
;
;  COMMON SUBROUTINES
;
        CISUBM
        COSUBM
        END
```

FIGURE 13-6 (Continued)

The SEQIO Library

MAC, Digital Research's macro assembler, is distributed with a macro library called SEQIO.LIB. This macro library contains a number of aids to the use of sequential files. The library is described at length in the MAC documentation. It will repay study, as will any exercise in reading other people's programs. Although you may not care for its rather convoluted style, SEQIO.LIB can serve as the basis for a set of sequential file macros that will make file access nearly as simple as console access.

DIRECT ACCESS

The steps of opening, making, and closing files are the same for direct access as for sequential operations. Only the operations of reading and writing differ.

Service 34: Direct Write

With service 34 your program may write any standard record that it wishes. The file must have been opened with service 16 or made with service 22, ensuring that at least one directory entry exists for it. The record must have been prepared and the buffer address aimed at it with service 26. Once all this has been set up, your program need only store a 24-bit record number in the direct address bytes 21h to 23h of the FCB and request service 34. Under CP/M 2, and for all but the largest files under MP/M 2, the record address will be a 16-bit number and byte 23h will contain zero.

Locating the Extent. When it receives a direct write request, the BDOS studies the direct address number in the FCB. From the number it determines the extent of the file in which that record must fall. If that is not the extent currently open (that is, not the one reflected by the FCB), the BDOS writes the current extent record back to the directory from the FCB. It then locates the proper extent record in the directory. If no such extent record exists, it selects an unused directory entry and initializes it with the fileref and a data map showing zero space allocation. The desired extent record, new or existing, is then copied into the FCB.

Locating the Block. Once the right extent of the file has been found, the BDOS determines in which of the allocation blocks in the extent's data map the record should fall. If no block has been allocated at that position, the BDOS chooses one and records it in the FCB.

Writing. Finally, the BDOS writes the data record onto disk in the right allocation block. If that record existed before, its data are replaced.

Files with Holes

It should be clear from the description that a file written with service 34 could have holes in it. A file might have 10 extent records, each controlling just one allocation block in each of which you have written just one record. Most of the file simply wouldn't exist. The display produced by the STAT command would show peculiar numbers that would have little meaning. It is best, and usually no more difficult, to create a direct access file with no holes in it.

The STAT command has an optional operand, $S, which causes it to show the so-called virtual size of a file, that is, the size the file would have if all of its records existed.

Service 33: Direct Read

You may read a record from an open file with a direct read. Direct reads and direct writes may be done alternately to the same file (the same is true of sequential reads and writes, but there's no point to doing that). To read a record directly set the buffer address, place a record number in the direct address bytes of the FCB, and request service 33.

Locating the Extent. The BDOS determines the extent in which that record must fall. If it is not the current extent (the one reflected in the FCB), the BDOS must locate the proper extent record and copy it into the FCB. Before doing so it checks to see if the current extent has been modified. If that's the case, the BDOS must first update the directory entry for the current extent.

Locating the Block. Having found the extent, the BDOS figures out the allocation block into which the wanted record must fall and looks at that entry in the extent data map. From that information it can find the record on disk and read it into the buffer.

Nonexistent Records. If either the extent or the block that is needed has not been allocated, the BDOS returns an error code in register A. That might be a normal event when using direct access; it means that the record you tried to read has never been written.

A Hazard of Direct Input

There is one case in which a direct read might return garbage. Suppose that at some time the first record of an allocation block had been written. That block of records will have been reserved to the file and the first position in it will have been filled with a record's data. However, if service 34 was used to write the record, then nothing can be said about the other records in the allocation block. If the block has ever been part of another file, they might contain any sort of garbage.

Now suppose that your program requests a direct read of a record that falls as record 2 of the same allocation block. Will the BDOS inform you that the record you want does not exist? It will not! The BDOS cannot tell; its directory information tells it only that a certain allocation block has been made part of this file. It has no record of whether or not all the records of that block were written.

When a file is written sequentially, or written directly but without holes, this problem cannot occur because all allocation blocks except the last are filled. The BDOS can tell the number of records in the last block by taking the remainder after dividing the record count by the number of records in a block. Such a computation has no meaning for a file written directly.

Service 40: Write with Zero Fill

Service 40 can be used to prevent the problem just described. If service 40 instead of service 34 is used for direct writes, the BDOS adds one more feature to the operation. If it has to allocate a new block in order to write the record, it writes all of the rest of the records in the block as well, filling them with binary zeros. When a file is written this way, a direct read that hits upon an unwritten record of an existing block will return a buffer full of binary zeros. The program that reads the file can test some field of the record that ought not to be zero to find out whether the record exists.

Service 36: Get Direct Address

The Concept of an Index. Suppose a file was built with sequential writes, and you'd now like to process it with direct reads. Let's say that the data records aren't necessarily multiples of 128 bytes in length; they might start anywhere in the file. It won't be practical to make direct reads without more information. You can't give the standard record number of a data record whose position you don't know.

What is wanted in such a case is an *index*, a table that gives the starting position of each data record in the file. An index is a two-column table that gives the value of some *key value* for each record, and opposite the key value the position in the file of the record that contains that key.

Operation of Service 36. Service 36 allows you to build such an index while reading an existing file sequentially. What service 36 does is compute the standard record number of the last record read (sequentially) from the file, and return that number in the direct address bytes of the FCB.

Use of Service 36. To build an index, read the file sequentially. For each data record note the key value and, through service 36, the file position. Record these items in the index. Each data record's position requires four bytes—a 3-byte record address, and a 1-byte offset of its first byte within the record. Having built an index, you can now look up the position of any record and retrieve it with service 33.

Chapter 14

Services for System Programming

In this chapter we plunge deeper into the file system. We'll examine the disk directory in minute detail and find out how to read and write it from a command program. Then we'll study the disk space management method of CP/M 2 and see how to interpret its parameters from a program. The chapter includes several programs that can reveal the internal workings of CP/M.

TWO USEFUL LIBRARIES

This chapter is illustrated with several programs, written for the MAC assembler. They rely on two new macro libraries in addition to the COSUB, CPMEQU, and PROG libraries we met in the prior chapters.

The HEXSUB Library

The HEXSUB library (Figure 14-1) contains a set of subroutines that display data in hexadecimal. Its central routines are COHEX, which types the ASCII image of a hex byte at the console, and HEXBYTE, which returns the ASCII image of a byte in the A and C registers so it can be inserted in another message. HEXLINE displays some number of bytes, first in hex and then as characters. HEXDUMP prefixes the display line with a display of the address of the first displayed byte.

The DPSUB Library

The DPSUB library, shown in Figure 14-2, contains a few routines that manipulate the 16-bit registers of an 8080. As we'll see, disk space allocation is controlled by parameters that are often 16-bit integers. Our example programs become shorter and clearer when the necessary routines are moved to a library. The DP$ADAD and DP$ADAH routines add the contents of the A register into the DE and HL register pairs respectively. DP$LDHA performs an indirect load of the DE register from an address that is the sum of the A and HL registers. DP$SRLD does a logical right shift of the contents of the DE register. Many other routines could be added to such a library, but these are the only ones needed by the example programs.

The XCMD Program

Figure 14-3 contains an example program of the sort we'll use throughout this chapter. This program, XCMD, uses the HEXSUB routines to display the default FCB and the

```
HEXSUBM MACRO
; * * * *  HEXSUB.LIB -- HEX DISPLAY ROUTINES FOR MAC ASSEMBLER
;                     -- ASSUMES PRESENCE OF COSUB.LIB ROUTINES.
;
; SUBROUTINE TO DO AN ADDRESSED DUMP OF ONE LINE.  HL-->DATA,
;    B HAS LENGTH (SHOULDN'T EXCEED 16 OR SO).
; HL IS INCREMENTED SO SUCCESSIVE LINES CAN BE DUMPED,
;    BC, DE ARE PRESERVED, AF IS TRASHED.
;
HEXDUMP EQU     $
        CALL    HEXADDR ; DISPLAY HL CONTENTS IN HEX,
        MVI     A,':'   ; THEN A COLON,
        CALL    COUT
        CALL    COSPACE ; ..A BLANK, AND ...
;                         ..FALL INTO HEXLINE
;
; SUBROUTINE TO DUMP B BYTES OF HL-->DATA TO CONSOLE
;    REGISTERS USED AS FOR 'HEXDUMP'.
;
HEXLINE EQU     $
        PUSH    B       ; SAVE PARAMETERS FOR
        PUSH    H       ; ..RE-USE WITH ALPHA PART.
;
HEXL2   MOV     A,M     ; CURRENT BYTE..
        CALL    COHEX   ; ..PRINTED IN HEX
        CALL    COSPACE ; ..AND A BLANK AFTER.
        INX     H       ; STEP TO NEXT BYTE,
        DCR     B       ; IF ANY,
        JNZ     HEXL2   ;  (THERE IS)
;
        CALL    COSPACE ; TWO BLANKS AFTER HEX DISPLAY.
        CALL    COSPACE
        POP     H       ; RETRIEVE DATA ADDRESS
        POP     B       ; ..AND COUNT
        PUSH    B       ; PRESERVE COUNT FOR CALLER.
;
HEXL3   MOV     A,M     ; CURRENT BYTE..
        ANI     7FH     ;  (LESS ITS BIT 7)
        CPI     20H     ; ..IS IT CONTROL?
        JC      HEXL4   ; (YES)
        CPI     7FH     ; IS IT DEL?
        JNZ     HEXL5   ; (NO)
HEXL4   MVI     A,'.'   ; UNPRINTABLE BYTE, USE A DOT.
HEXL5   CALL    COUT    ; PRINT BYTE OR DOT
        INX     H       ; STEP TO NEXT,
        DCR     B       ; ..IF ANY
        JNZ     HEXL3
;
        POP     B       ; RESTORE CALLER'S COUNT
        RET
;
;       SUBROUTINE TO PRINT HL AS AN ADDRESS IN HEX.
;       ALTERS ONLY A, F.
;
HEXADDR EQU     $
        MOV     A,H
        CALL    COHEX
        MOV     A,L
        CALL    COHEX
        RET
;
;       SUBROUTINE TO PRINT THE HEX BYTE IN A
;       ALTERS ONLY A, F
;
```

FIGURE 14-1
HEXSUB.LIB contains subroutines for displaying data in hexadecimal; it is included in most of the example programs that follow.

```
COHEX    EQU     $
         PUSH    PSW      ; SAVE THE BYTE,
         CALL    HEXLEFT  ; GET AND
         CALL    COUT     ;  ..PRINT LEFT HALF,
         POP     PSW      ; RETRIEVE BYTE,
         CALL    HEXRIGHT;  ..DO RIGHT HALF
         CALL    COUT
         RET
;
HEXLEFT  EQU     $        ; SET UP FOR LEFT NYBBLE
         RAR ! RAR ! RAR ! RAR
HEXRIGHT EQU      $        ; DO NYBBLE NOW ON RIGHT
         ANI     0FH      ; ISOLATE 4 BITS
         CPI     0AH      ; CHECK ALPHA CASE
         JC      HEXLR    ; [A]< 0AH
         ADI     'A'-3AH  ; CORRECT FOR ALPHA
HEXLR    ADI     '0'      ; CONVERT TO PRINTABLE
         RET
;
;        SUBROUTINE TO RETURN THE HEX VALUES OF A,
;        LEAST SIGNIFICANT HALF IN C, MOST SIGNIFICANT
;        IN A.  USED WHEN ASCII-HEX IS TO BE STORED.
;
HEXBYTE  EQU     $
         PUSH    PSW      ; SAVE THE BYTE,
         CALL    HEXRIGHT; ..PUT THE RIGHT HALF
         MOV     C,A      ; ..INTO C REG
         POP     PSW
         CALL    HEXLEFT  ; AND THE LEFT HALF
         RET              ; ..INTO A.
; * * * * * END OF XSUB.LIB
         ENDM
```

FIGURE 14-1 (Continued)

command tail as it received them. XCMD is very useful for learning the exact details of how the CCP sets up low storage before loading a command program—something every systems programmer needs to know. Example 14-1 shows XCMD in operation.

STYLE OF EXAMPLE PROGRAMS. XCMD is typical of the examples to follow. All of them place variables and message constants between the PROLOG macro and the main code, and put subroutines at the end. All will work under CP/NET; most should work under MP/M but haven't been tested under it. All were written to optimize clarity of logic rather than speed or program size.

THE DISK DIRECTORY

The disk directory is the heart of CP/M's file system. The directory is really a keyed direct access file composed of extent records. There are endless ways in which these records could be collated, listed, and reported on, if we could just get at them. In fact there are service requests that allow us to read the directory easily—requests that are supported under CP/M, MP/M, and CP/M-86.

Reviewing the Directory

DIRECTORY RECORDS. Let's go over what we learned about directory operations in prior chapters. Directory records are 32 bytes long. Each contains most of the data of an FCB, notably a fileref, an extent number, a record count, and a data map.

```
DPSUBM  MACRO
; * * * * * 16-BIT REGISTER SUBROUTINES
;
;       SUBROUTINE TO LOAD DE FROM M[HL+A]
;       ALTERS ONLY DE, FLAGS.
;
DP$LDHA EQU     $
        PUSH    H
        MOV     E,A     ; MAKE 16-BIT OFFSET
        MVI     D,0
        DAD     D       ; ADD OFFSET TO BASE
        MOV     E,M     ; PICK UP L.S. BYTE
        INX     H
        MOV     D,M     ; GET M.S. BYTE
        POP     H
        RET
;
;       SUBROUTINE TO SHIFT-RIGHT-LOGICAL DE
;       ALTERS A,F (A = L.S. BYTE. Z,C FLAGS SET)
;
DP$SRLD EQU     $
        ORA     A       ; CLEAR CARRY
        MOV  A,D  ! RAR ! MOV D,A
        MOV  A,E  ! RAR ! MOV E,A
        RET
;
;       SUBROUTINE TO ADD A TO DE
;       ALTERS A,F (A=M.S. BYTE, Z,C FLAGS SET)
;
DP$ADAD EQU     $
        ADD     E
        MOV     E,A
        MOV     A,D
        ACI     0
        MOV     D,A
        RET
;
;       SUBROUTINE TO ADD A TO HL, AS ABOVE
;
DP$ADAH EQU     $
        ADD     L
        MOV     L,A
        MOV     A,H
        ACI     0
        MOV     H,A
        RET
;
;       SUBROUTINE TO DO AN UNSIGNED COMPARISON
;       OF (B,C) :: (H,L).  ALTERS A, LEAVES
;       FLAGS SET AS FOR THE COMPARE INSTRUCTION.
;
DP$CPBH EQU     $
        MOV  A,B ! CMP H
        RNZ      ; EXIT IF M.S. BYTES DIFFER
        MOV  A,C ! CMP L
        RET      ; B=H, EXIT WITH C:L FLAGS
;
; * * * * * END OF DPSUB.LIB
        ENDM
```

FIGURE 14-2
DPSUB.LIB contains convenience routines for working with the 16-bit register pairs of the 8080. Use of the routines clarifies the logic of the example programs.

```
; * * * * *  XCMD -- EXAMINE THE COMMAND OPERANDS
;
        MACLIB  CPMEQU   ; STANDARD NAMES
        MACLIB  PROG     ; PROLOG, SERVICE MACROS
        MACLIB  HEXSUB   ; HEX DISPLAY ROUTINES
        MACLIB  COSUB    ; CONSOLE OUTPUT
;
        PROLOG  20,XCMD
;
FCBMSG  DB      'Default FCB --',CR,LF,CR,LF+80H
TAILMSG DB      CR,LF,'Command tail --',CR,LF,CR,LF+80H
;
XCMD    EQU     $
        LXI     H,FCBMSG ; PRINT FCB HEADING
        CALL    COSTR
        LXI     H,CPMFCB
        MVI     B,16     ; DUMP DEFAULT FCB
        CALL    HEXDUMP  ; ..IN TWO LINES
        CALL    COCRLF
        CALL    HEXDUMP ! CALL COCRLF
;
        LXI     H,TAILMSG ; PRINT TAIL HEADING
        CALL    COSTR
        LXI     H,CPMBUFF
        MOV     A,M      ; GET LENGTH OF TAIL AND
        ADI     00FH     ; ..ROUND TO MULTIPLE OF
        ANI     0F0H     ; ..SIXTEEN.
        RZ               ; (EXIT IF NO OPERANDS)
XCMD2   MOV     C,A      ; ..SAVE LENGTH IN C
        CALL    HEXDUMP  ; DUMP 16 BYTES OF TAIL
        CALL    COCRLF
        MOV  A,C ! SUB B ;COUNT 16 BYTES,
        JNZ     XCMD2    ; ..CONTINUE IF MORE
        RET
;
; COMMON SUBROUTINES
;
        HEXSUBM
        COSUBM
        END
```

FIGURE 14-3
The XCMD command displays the low-storage operands as the CCP leaves them. The program allows checking out the way the CCP sets up operands.

Space Allocation. File space is allocated in blocks. The size of an allocation block is a vendor option that may be different on different disks. The data map in a directory entry is a list of the allocation blocks controlled by that entry. The sum of the space controlled by one entry is called a physical extent, or just an extent. A logical extent is 16K bytes of space. A physical extent is equal to one or more logical extents.

Directory Use. A file that is larger than one physical extent has more than one directory entry. Each entry for the file contains the same fileref but differs in its extent number (and possibly in the S1 and S2 bytes, but that isn't defined and might change from one version of CP/M to another). We've said that the BDOS allocates directory entries as they are needed. We didn't say so, but you've probably guessed that the entries for a file may appear in any sequence in the directory.

CONTENTS OF DIRECTORY ENTRIES

The directory occupies one or more allocation blocks. These are always the first allocation blocks on the disk. Later we'll see how they are reserved. Each standard

EXAMPLE 14-1
Running the XCMD program. 03h in the record count of the FCB is probably residual from loading XCMD. Such unexpected effects can be discovered by simple display programs.

```
A>xcmd
Default FCB --

005C: 00 20 20 20 20 20 20 20 20 20 20 20 00 00 00 03   .           ....
006C: 00 20 20 20 20 20 20 20 20 20 20 20 00 00 00 00   .           ....

Command tail --


A>xcmd A:*.com this-is-too-long-to-be-a-fileref
Default FCB --

005C: 01 3F 3F 3F 3F 3F 3F 3F 3F 43 4F 4D 00 00 00 03   .????????COM....
006C: 00 54 48 49 53 2D 49 53 2D 20 20 20 00 00 00 00   .THIS-IS-   ....

Command tail --

0080: 20 20 41 3A 2A 2E 43 4F 4D 20 54 48 49 53 2D 49   ) A:*.COM THIS-I
0090: 53 2D 54 4F 4F 2D 4C 4F 4E 47 2D 54 4F 2D 42 45   S-TOO-LONG-TO-BE
00A0: 2D 41 2D 46 49 4C 45 52 45 46 00 20 20 20 20 20   -A-FILEREF.

A>_
```

(128-byte) record in the directory contains four 32-byte directory entries. Although they are blocked in groups of four, each entry is independent of the others. Let's look at the data in a directory entry (Figure 14-4).

The User Code

INACTIVE ENTRIES. The first byte of a directory entry, the one that corresponds to the drivecode of an FCB, contains a user code, which is also an activity code. An inactive directory entry contains E5h, which is usually the value to which a disk formatter initializes every byte of every sector (but see the comments on disk formatting at the end of the chapter).

ACTIVE ENTRIES. An active directory entry contains the user number, from 0 to 15 (00h to 0Fh). In prior versions of CP/M this value was always 00h. Version 2 (and MP/M) added the concept of a user code and the activity byte was chosen to hold it.

THE USER CODE IN MP/M 2. In CP/M 2 and MP/M 1 the user code byte contains either E5h or a number in the range of 0 to 15. Two new directory entry types have been added in MP/M 2. Both are distinguished by values in their user code bytes. The Directory Label entry is marked by a user code byte of 20h. An Extended FCB (XFCB) is marked with 1*x*h, where *x* is a user code number.

The Attribute Bits

The fileref portion (the filename and filetype fields) of a directory entry is laid out just like the same part of an FCB. This area is defined to hold ASCII characters. That means

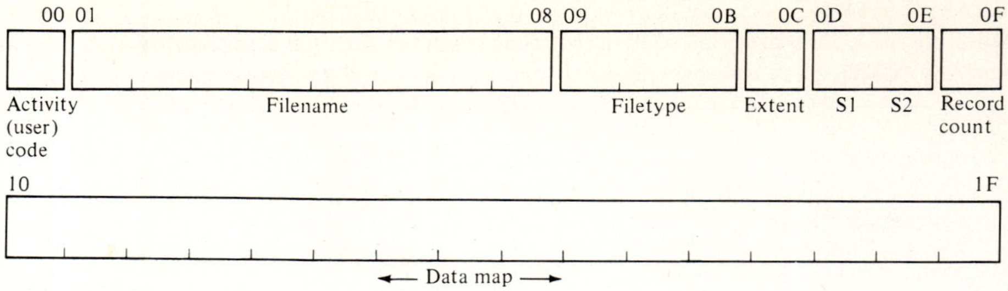

FIGURE 14-4
A map showing the layout of a directory entry. Compare it with the layout of an FCB (Figure 13-4).

that the most significant bits are unused. It's no surprise that these bits have had meanings assigned to them. When comparing the fileref of a directory entry to a constant, or to another directory entry, you must be sure to mask off the most significant bit of each byte.

Attribute Notation. The CPM documentation refers to each of these bits by naming its byte followed by a prime mark (apostrophe). The attribute bit in the first byte of the filename is called f1' (f1 prime), the bit in the third filetype byte is t3' or (t3 prime), and so on.

The Read-Only Attribute. Bit 7 of the first filetype byte (t1') represents the read-only file attribute. When a file is made R/O with the STAT command, STAT sets this bit to 1 in all extents of the file.

The System Attribute. Bit 7 of the second filetype byte (t2') represents the System (no directory display) attribute. When the STAT command gives a file the SYS attribute it sets this bit to 1 in all extent entries for the file.

The Archive Attribute. Bit 7 of the third filetype byte (t3') is used to signal a change in a file. The BDOS sets t3' to 0 whenever it updates a directory entry, that is, whenever the data map of an extent is altered. We'll see later that a command program can cause the bit to be set to 1. If that is done, and the bit is later found to be 0, then that extent of the file must have been changed.

Using the Archive Attribute. Attribute t3' is intended for use by an archiving program, that is, a backup program that backs up only files that have changed since the last backup run. Such a backup scheme is much more economical than whole-disk backup, as usually only a small number of files change over a backup period. An archive program would have logic like this:

```
for each active directory entry do:
   if not(t3') then do:
      open this extent as an FCB;
      copy this extent to backup;
      record the extent in an archive catalog;
      set t3' to 1 in the directory
   end
end
```

It would make use of the fact that any extent, not just the first one, can be opened with service request 15. The other services needed are covered in this chapter. In MP/M 2 the A option of PIP implements exactly this logic.

Reserved Attribute Bits. Bit 7 of each of the 4 right-hand filename bytes (f5' through f8') has been reserved by Digital Research. We can assume that a use eventually will be found for those bits.

Free Attribute Bits. In an act of unprecedented generosity Digital Research explicitly set aside bit 7 in each of the 4 left-hand filename bytes (f1' through f4') for the use of application programs. This creates a problem. There are only 4 bits and an endless number of application programs. There is no central agency to record the use of the bits, much less standardize it. Perhaps Digital Research will act in that capacity. If you are writing a program for public distribution and want to use a file attribute bit, you might contact Digital Research to see if anyone else has used your bit. No matter what anyone does, these bits will either go unused or there will be incompatible uses.

Service 30: Set Attribute Bits. It is not necessary to have write access to the directory in order to set the file attribute bits. Service 30 takes an FCB address as its parameter, finds the matching directory entry, and copies the file attributes from the FCB onto the directory entry. Service 30 changes all the attribute bits at once. If you want to change only 1 bit while leaving all the others alone, the FCB should really be a directory entry. Find the directory entry (see below), alter the bit of interest, and use the directory entry as the FCB for service 30.

You can set or reset any of the 11 bits in this way, including the read-only attribute. Considering that the read-only attribute is the only way to protect a file from destruction, resetting that bit would be unfriendly, at the very least.

The Extent Number

Use of the Extent Number. The extent number of a directory entry links all the entries for one file together. The first entry for the file is extent number zero, and the rest have higher numbers. If the file is built sequentially, all extents through the last will exist and all data maps save the last one will be full. If the file is built with direct writes, some extent numbers may be absent. Extent entries don't necessarily appear in sequence in the directory, although they will more often than not.

Extents Beyond the 32nd. CP/M supports files as large as 8 MB (32 MB in MP/M 2). If a directory entry controls the minimum amount of space, 16 KB, 512 entries are needed to describe an 8 MB file. There is a conflict here, because the extent number byte won't hold that large a number. As we'll see later, the extent number byte is allowed to have an ASCII question mark in it on certain service requests. Therefore it can't be allowed to have a normal extent number of 3Eh as that is a question mark. The largest value allowed in the extent number byte has been set at 1Fh, allowing 32 distinct extent numbers, from 00h to 1Fh. That was good enough in earlier versions of CP/M; 32 extents of 16 KB make a 512-KB file, the limit of a normal diskette.

Extent Overflow. CP/M and MP/M now support large drives and files. How are the additional extents recorded? The Digital Research documentation doesn't say. We can assume that the extent number is somehow split between the extent number byte and the S1 or S2 byte, but we don't know which of those bytes is used or how the split is accomplished. Anything that is not documented can't be relied on. What isn't documented may be changed in a later version, and so even if you find out how the larger extent numbers are handled, you risk version dependency if you write code that relies on it.

The Record Count

Use of the Record Count. The record count byte is normally the sum of the standard records controlled by the directory entry. It has two purposes. During sequential access the BDOS can compare the current record byte with the record count; when they become equal it is time to open the next extent of the file. Second, the record count, modulo by the number of records in a block, yields the number of records used in the last block allocated.

Files with Holes. The first use is undependable when the file has been created with holes by direct access writes. Then the record count can be used to compute the number of records in the last block allocated to the directory entry but may be higher than the number of records owned by the entry.

The Data Map

Use of the Data Map. The data map is simply a list of allocation block numbers. A value of zero indicates that no block has been allocated (there is a block numbered zero, but it is always allocated to the directory, and thus zero can be used to mean that no block exists). Normally the nonzero block numbers are filled in from the left of the map, and the only zero values are at the right end. However, a file with direct access holes may have block numbers of zero, representing unallocated space, at any point in the map.

Data Map Format. Some disks can hold more than 255 allocation blocks. In that case a block number must be a 16-bit integer, and only eight of them can be recorded in the data map. When the disk holds less than 256 allocation blocks, a block number will fit in a byte. Then the data map can hold 16 block numbers. Later we'll find out how to tell which case holds for any particular disk.

THE SEARCH SERVICES

Two service requests give access to the directory entries in a way that is both device independent and supported in CP/M, MP/M, and CP/M-86. These are requests 17 and 18, Search First and Search Next. Each requires the address of an FCB in the DE register pair. Each returns a directory entry in the current record buffer.

Service 17: Search First

When your program requests service 17, the BDOS searches the directory for the first entry that matches the fileref and extent number in your FCB. It places the matching directory entry at one of four offsets in the current record buffer. Register A contains 0, 1, 2, or 3 to indicate the buffer offset. The offset is 32 times register A (add the register to itself five times). The FCB used in the service is not changed.

Service 18: Search Next

Service 18 does exactly what service 17 does, except that the search for a directory entry to match the FCB begins where the preceding search stopped. The next matching entry will be returned. If either request fails to find a matching entry, it returns FFh in register A to indicate failure.

Using the Search Requests

Buffer Contents. The directory entry may appear in the buffer at an offset of 0, 32, 64, or 96 bytes. The reason for this is plain: the directory is written as 128-byte standard records, each containing four directory entries. Under CP/M the BDOS moves the record containing the matching entry into the buffer; the entry you want is at some offset because it is one of the four entries in that record.

Buffer Contents Under CP/NET. You should not assume that the BDOS always moves a complete directory record into the buffer. Under CP/NET the data may have come over the network from another machine. CP/NET, in order to minimize the amount of data transferred, might send only the wanted entry, leaving the rest of the buffer undefined. You can rely only on the exact letter of the specification: search promises to return a single directory entry only.

Search Restrictions. The BDOS remembers its position by noting its stopping point in a variable within the BDOS. The same variable is used during an open or make request, and possibly during other file operations. Therefore, you should not request any other file services between one search and the next; the BDOS might lose its position. (It is likely that some CP/M commands take advantage of this. It may be possible to open a file under an ambiguous name, read it, then request a Search Next to find the next file to read. This is not a documented feature of CP/M; like all such features you cannot rely on it to be version or system independent.)

Searching for Unique Filerefs. The search requests may, of course, be used to look for specific filerefs. For example, if you wanted to alter one attribute bit, you would use a search request to find that file's first directory entry. Alter the single attribute bit in the entry and use the entry itself as the FCB given as input to service 30. That technique preserves the settings of the other 10 attribute bits.

Searching for Ambiguous Filerefs. The true usefulness of the search requests comes from the fact that the fileref you pass may be ambiguous. The asterisk reference is not allowed, but the fileref may contain any number of question marks. The first directory entry that matches the fileref by the usual rules is returned by the search.

The HEXDIR Program. Figure 14-5 contains the source of a command called HEXDIR. This program accepts an optional drivecode as its operand. It displays the first directory entry of every file on the selected drive. The entries are sent to the console in hexadecimal. The files displayed by HEXDIR are the same, and appear in the same order, as the names displayed by the DIR command with the same operand. The only exception is that HEXDIR will display names that have the SYS attribute and DIR will not. Example 14-2 shows the output of HEXDIR.

Searching for Ambiguous Extents. The search requests will accept a question mark in the extent number position of the FCB. The HEXDIR program has a zero in the extent number of its FCB. Accordingly, the search operations return only the entries that have a zero in their extent number field. When the extent number is ambiguous, the search functions return every directory entry of the files whose filerefs match the FCB. If the fileref in the FCB is all question marks, every directory entry that is in use will be returned.

The ACTDIR Program. The ACTDIR program (Figure 14-6) takes advantage of extent ambiguity to display all active directory entries. It differs from HEXDIR only in its heading message and the question mark in the extent number of the FCB. Run ACTDIR against different disks with files of various sizes and note everything you can about the way directory entries appear. If your system has a hard disk, build a file of 2 or 3 megabytes and display its directory entries. How is the extent number handled? Build a file with direct access holes and look at its extents. Example 14-3 shows the output of ACTDIR.

EXAMPLE 14-2
Running HEXDIR against a disk that held only a few files. The second entry is full; there must be other extents for it. Note that allocation block numbers are two bytes each.

```
A>hexdir b:
Extent-zero directory entries, drive B

00 48 45 58 44 49 42 20 20 43 4F 4D 00 00 00 04    .HEXDIR  COM....
02 00 00 00 00 00 00 00 00 00 00 00 00 00 00 00    ................

00 50 52 49 4E 54 20 20 20 43 4F 4D 00 00 00 80    .PRINT   COM....
03 00 04 00 05 00 06 00 07 00 08 00 09 00 0A 00    ................

00 48 45 58 44 49 52 20 20 41 53 4D 00 00 00 0D    .HEXDIR  ASM....
0C 00 00 00 00 00 00 00 00 00 00 00 00 00 00 00    ................


A>_
```

```
; * * * * *  HEXDIR -- DISPLAY EXTENT-0 DIRECTORY ENTRIES
;
        MACLIB  CPMEQU   ; STANDARD NAMES,
        MACLIB  PROG     ; PROLOG, SERVICE MACROS
        MACLIB  HEXSUB   ; HEX DISPLAY ROUTINES
        MACLIB  COSUB    ; CONSOLE OUTPUT ROUTINES
        MACLIB  DPSUB    ; 16-BIT ROUTINES
;
        PROLOG  30,HEXDIR
;
HEADING DB      'Extent-zero directory entries, drive '
DRIVE   DB      0,CR,LF,CR,LF+80H
;
THEFCB  DB      0                 ; DRIVE ALREADY SELECTED
        DB      '????????'        ; FILENAME
        DB      '???'             ; FILETYPE
        DB      0                 ; EXTENT ZERO ENTRIES
        DB      0,0,0             ; S1, S2, RECORD COUNT
        DW      0,0,0,0,0,0,0,0 ; DATA MAP
        DW      0,0               ; CURRENT RECORD, DIRECT ADDR
;
HEXDIR  EQU     $
        LDA     CPMFCB   ; SEE IF A DRIVECODE WAS GIVEN
        DCR     A        ; CONVERT A=1 INTO A=0
        JP      DIR2     ; (RESULT NOT FF -- CODE GIVEN)
        SERVICE 25       ; OMITTED, GET CURRENT DRIVE
DIR2    MOV     E,A      ; SAVE DRIVE FOR SERVICE 14
        ADI     'A'      ; MAKE PRINTABLE,
        STA     DRIVE    ; ..PUT IN MESSAGE,
        LXI     H,HEADING
        CALL    COSTR    ; ..PRINT HEADING.
        SERVICE 14       ; SELECT DRIVE (CODE IN REG E)
        SERVICE 17,THEFCB ; GET FIRST ACTIVE ENTRY
;
DIRLOOP ORA     A        ; ANY ENTRIES LEFT?
        RM               ; (BACK TO CCP IF NOT)
        CALL    DIRDUMP ; YES, DUMP THIS ONE IN HEX
        SERVICE 18,THEFCB
        JMP     DIRLOOP ; DO NEXT ENTRY, IF ANY
;
; DUMP THE DIRECTORY ENTRY WHOSE NUMBER IS IN A,
;     FROM THE CURRENT RECORD IN THE BUFFER.
;
DIRDUMP LXI     H,CPMBUFF
        ADD     A        ; CONVERT 0,1,2,3 --> 0,32,64,96
        ADD   A ! ADD  A
        ADD   A ! ADD  A
        CALL    DP$ADAH ; ..AND ADD TO BUFFER ADDRESS
        MVI     B,16     ; AMOUNT TO DUMP IN EACH LINE
        CALL    HEXLINE ! CALL COCRLF    ; 1ST LINE
        CALL    HEXLINE ! CALL COCRLF    ; 2ND LINE
        CALL    COCRLF                   ; BLANK LINE
        RET
;
; COMMON SUBROUTINES
;
        HEXSUBM
        COSUBM
        DPSUBM
        END
```

FIGURE 14-5
HEXDIR displays the first directory entry for each file in the directory, including those that have the SYS attribute.

```
; * * * * *  ACTDIR -- DISPLAY ALL ACTIVE DIRECTORY ENTRIES
;
        MACLIB  CPMEQU  ; STANDARD NAMES,
        MACLIB  PROG    ; PROLOG, SERVICE MACROS
        MACLIB  HEXSUB  ; HEX DISPLAY ROUTINES
        MACLIB  COSUB   ; CONSOLE OUTPUT ROUTINES
        MACLIB  DPSUB   ; 16-BIT ROUTINES
;
        PROLOG  30,ACTDIR
;
HEADING DB      'Active directory entries, drive '
DRIVE   DB      0,CR,LF,CR,LF+80H
;
THEFCB  DB      0                ; DRIVE ALREADY SELECTED
        DB      '????????'       ; FILENAME
        DB      '???'            ; FILETYPE
        DB      '?'              ; ** ALL EXTENT NUMBERS **
        DB      0,0,0            ; S1, S2, RECORD COUNT
        DW      0,0,0,0,0,0,0,0  ; DATA MAP
        DW      0,0              ; CURRENT RECORD, DIRECT ADDR
;
ACTDIR  EQU     $
        LDA     CPMFCB  ; SEE IF A DRIVECODE WAS GIVEN
        DCR     A ....
        .
        .
        .
```

FIGURE 14-6
ACTDIR shows all directory entries for all existing files. The remainder of the program is identical to HEXDIR (Figure 14-5).

Searching All Entries. Both HEXDIR and ACTDIR are limited to displaying active directory entries that were created under the current user code. When a question mark is placed in the drivecode position of the FCB, the search operations return every entry, whether active or not, under any user code. The only directory entries that are not returned in this case are entries that have never been used.

EXAMPLE 14-3
Running ACTDIR against the disk of Example 14-2. The second extent of PRINT.COM is revealed; it controls only 14 records (0Eh in the record count) of one block.

```
A>actdir b:
Active directory entries, drive B

00 48 45 58 44 49 52 20 20 43 4F 4D 00 00 00 04   .HEXDIR  COM....
02 00 00 00 00 00 00 00 00 00 00 00 00 00 00 00   ................

00 50 52 49 4E 54 20 20 20 43 4F 4D 00 00 00 80   .PRINT   COM....
03 00 04 00 05 00 06 00 07 00 08 00 09 00 0A 00   ................

00 50 52 49 4E 54 20 20 20 43 4F 4D 01 00 00 0E   .PRINT   COM....
0B 00 00 00 00 00 00 00 00 00 00 00 00 00 00 00   ................

00 48 45 58 44 49 52 20 20 41 53 4D 00 00 00 0D   .HEXDIR  ASM....
0C 00 00 00 00 00 00 00 00 00 00 00 00 00 00 00   ................


A>_
```

The ALLDIR Program. Figure 14-7 shows the ALLDIR program. ALLDIR differs from HEXDIR and ACTDIR only in its heading message and in the question mark in the first byte of its FCB. When ALLDIR is run, it displays all directory entries except those that have never been used (see the section on disk formatting for the meaning of "never been used"). Usually some entries are inactive (have E5h in their first byte). The rest of an inactive entry is unchanged from its last use. The fileref and data map will reflect the state of that extent at the time the file was deleted. Example 14-4 shows the result of running ALLDIR. Under MP/M 2 ALLDIR will display the Directory Label and any XFCB entries that exist.

DISK SPACE MANAGEMENT

CP/M 2 can manage file space on almost any sort of disk from a single-density 5-inch diskette to a multimegabyte hard disk. New disk models appear on the market almost weekly. Each new model has its own set of dimensions, that is, its own number of heads and tracks, range of sector sizes, and total capacity. The responsibility for managing these device characteristics is placed on the BIOS. Only a few characteristics of a disk are relevant to space management. The BDOS requires the BIOS to tell it the value of these few parameters. Your programs can view the same parameters and so handle many disk tasks while remaining as independent of hardware details as the BDOS is.

Fundamental Parameters

CP/M asks the BIOS to tell it three fundamental things about any disk. The most important parameter is the size of an allocation block. This parameter is chosen by the

```
; * * * * *  ALLDIR -- DISPLAY ALL DIRECTORY ENTRIES
;
         MACLIB  CPMEQU   ; STANDARD NAMES,
         MACLIB  PROG     ; PROLOG, SERVICE MACROS
         MACLIB  HEXSUB   ; HEX DISPLAY ROUTINES
         MACLIB  COSUB    ; CONSOLE OUTPUT ROUTINES
         MACLIB  DPSUB    ; 16-BIT ROUTINES
;
         PROLOG  30,ALLDIR
;
HEADING DB      'All directory entries, drive '
DRIVE   DB      0,CR,LF,CR,LF+80H
;
THEFCB  DB      '?'               ; ** ALL ** ENTRIES
        DB      '????????'        ; FILENAME
        DB      '???'             ; FILETYPE
        DB      '?'               ; ** ALL EXTENT NUMBERS **
        DB      0,0,0             ; S1, S2, RECORD COUNT
        DW      0,0,0,0,0,0,0,0 ; DATA MAP
        DW      0,0               ; CURRENT RECORD, DIRECT ADDR
;
ALLDIR  EQU     $
        LDA     CPMFCB  ; SEE IF A DRIVECODE WAS GIVEN
        DCR     A ....
```

FIGURE 14-7
ALLDIR shows all directory entries, including those for erased files and those created under other user codes. It does not show never-used entries. The program continues identically to HEXDIR.

EXAMPLE 14-4
Running ALLDIR against the disk of Example 14-2. It reveals an erased file and one stored under user code 2. Note that never used entries do not appear.

```
A>alldir b:
All directory entries, drive B

00 48 45 58 44 49 52 20 20 43 4F 4D 00 00 00 04   .HEXDIR  COM....
02 00 00 00 00 00 00 00 00 00 00 00 00 00 00 00   ................

00 50 52 49 4E 54 20 20 20 43 4F 4D 00 00 00 80   .PRINT   COM....
03 00 04 00 05 00 06 00 07 00 08 00 09 00 0A 00   ................

00 50 52 49 4E 54 20 20 20 43 4F 4D 01 00 00 0E   .PRINT   COM....
0B 00 C0 00 00 00 00 00 00 00 00 00 00 00 00 00   ................

00 48 45 58 44 49 52 20 20 41 53 4D 00 00 00 0D   .HEXDIR  ASM....
0C 00 00 00 00 00 00 00 00 00 00 00 00 00 00 00   ................

E5 45 52 41 53 45 44 20 20 46 49 4C 00 00 00 80   eERASED  FIL....
0D 00 0E 00 0F 00 10 00 11 00 12 00 13 00 14 00   ................

E5 45 52 41 53 45 44 20 20 46 49 4C 01 00 00 80   eERASED  FIL....
15 00 16 00 17 00 18 00 19 00 1A 00 1B 00 1C 00   ................

E5 45 52 41 53 45 44 20 20 46 49 4C 02 00 00 7E   eERASED  FIL....
1D 00 1E 00 1F 00 20 00 21 00 22 00 23 00 24 00   ...... .!.".#.$.

02 55 53 45 52 2D 32 20 20 46 49 4C 00 00 00 80   .USER-2  FIL....
25 00 26 00 27 00 28 00 29 00 2A 00 2B 00 2C 00   %..´.(.).*.+.,.

02 55 53 45 52 2D 32 20 20 46 49 4C 01 00 00 0E   .USER-2  FIL....
2D 00 00 00 00 00 00 00 00 00 00 00 00 00 00 00   -...............


A>_
```

author of the BIOS (usually the vendor of the disk system), and the choice has many consequences. The BDOS must also know the capacity of the disk in allocation block units and the number of standard 128-byte records that will fit on one track of the disk. These three things are all that the BDOS needs to know in order to manage the disk.

Allocation Block Size. The allocation block size may take any of five values. Those values are the integral powers of 2 from 2^{10} (i.e., 1024) to 2^{14} (16,384). Note that the size of an allocation block has nothing to do with the size of a disk sector. An allocation block must contain an integral number of sectors; except for that stipulation it is simply a quantity used by the BDOS for space allocation. The BIOS manages physical sectors and is only indirectly concerned with allocation blocks.

Block Size and Space Efficiency. The allocation block size affects the file system in several ways. The first effect is on the efficiency with which the disk space is used. Since file space is allocated in whole blocks, the designer can expect that, on the average, half of the last block in each file will be unused. The larger the block size, the greater this unused space will be. The size of the disk must be considered, as well as the number of files likely to be on it. The smaller the disk, and the greater the number of files, the smaller the block size ought to be.

Block Size and the Data Map. CP/M knows the capacity of a disk only in terms of how many allocation blocks it will hold (its size in terms of sectors and tracks is the business of the BIOS). If the disk will hold fewer than 257 allocation blocks, then a block number will fit in a single byte; the BDOS can record 16 block numbers in the data map of each directory entry. If the disk holds more than 256 allocation blocks, then each block number must be recorded as a 2-byte integer and the data map can hold only eight numbers.

This is the second effect of the allocation block size: together with the disk capacity it decides how many block numbers will fit in a data map. By making the block size large enough that there are fewer than 256 blocks on the disk, the designer allows more blocks to be named by each directory entry. This economizes on the number of entries needed for large files, but it conflicts with the need for space efficiency.

Block Size and Extent Size. The block size and the disk capacity determine the amount of space that can be described by one directory entry's data map. That amount will be either 8 or 16 times the size of a block. It will also be a multiple of 16,384, the size of a logical extent. (There is one case that would violate this rule. If the block size were 1024 and there were more than 255 blocks, a directory entry could only describe 8K of data. This case is not allowed; 1K blocks may only be used on disks that hold less than 256 KB of data.)

This is the third result of the choice of a block size. It determines the relation of a physical extent (the space described by one directory entry) to a logical extent. The larger a physical extent, the smaller the number of directory entries needed to describe a large file. This affects the system's performance because it takes time to locate and open a new extent record (a seek to the directory track is required). The larger a physical extent, the less time it takes to process large files. This is especially important for direct access processing. On the other hand, large extents require a large block size that results in inefficient use of space.

Block Size and Directory Size. The choice of allocation block size has one more effect. The smaller the block size, the greater the number of directory entries it takes to describe all the space on the disk. Designers must consider two extremes. At one extreme they must imagine that a single file fills the disk. The absolute minimum number of entries in the directory is the number of entries required to describe that file. If the directory were smaller, it would never be possible to use the space on the disk. At the other extreme, the disk might be filled with a large number of small files, each using only one or two blocks of space but requiring its own directory entry to describe it.

In general the smaller the block size is, the larger the directory must be. As we'll see, there can't be more than 16 allocation blocks devoted to the directory, so for large disks the choice of block size is sometimes dictated by the need to have a directory of reasonable size.

Blocks Per Disk. The BDOS expects the BIOS to tell it the total number of allocation blocks that the disk will hold. This number is the capacity of the disk for space allocation; when all of the blocks are in use, the disk is full.

Records Per Track. The BDOS does not concern itself with the size of a disk sector; that is purely the affair of the BIOS. However, the interface between BDOS and BIOS (which we'll examine in the next chapter) requires that the BDOS ask for disk operations in terms of tracks and records, rather than in terms of records alone. The BDOS can compute which standard record it wants to read or write. However, in order to know which track that record is on, the BDOS has to know how many standard records there are on one track. Then it can divide the record number by that amount and so learn what track to ask for.

The Disk Parameter Block

The important disk parameters that control space management are passed from the BIOS to the BDOS in a 15-byte structure called the Disk Parameter Block (DPB). Service request 31 returns the address of the DPB for the disk that is currently selected. You can make use of some of the fields in it. Figure 14-8 shows a map of the DPB; we'll tour that map in the following paragraphs. Table 14-1 shows all the possible combinations of allocation block size and disk capacity, with the resulting DPB parameter values.

The XDPB Program. The XDPB program in Figure 14-9 will display the DPB for the default disk or (if a drivecode is given as its operand) for some other disk. Example 14-5 shows the result of running XDPB in a system that supported both single- and double-density diskettes. Note that the most important parameter, the size of a block, does not appear in the DPB. It affects all the other parameters and can be derived from them.

SPT: Standard Records Per Track. Your CP/M documentation refers to the first field in the DPB by the name SPT, which stands for "sectors per track." That name

TABLE 14-1

All possible combinations of allocation block size and disk size, and the effect of each combination on the other disk parameters. The first row describes the only combination allowed prior to CPM 2.0.

Block Size	Block Shift	Block Mask	Blocks per Disk	Blocks in Data Map	Extent Size	Logical Extents	Extent Mask
1024	03h	07h	<256	16	16K	1	00h
			>255		(not allowed)		
2048	04h	0Fh	<256	16	32K	2	01h
			>255	8	16K	1	00h
4096	05h	1Fh	<256	16	64K	4	03h
			>255	8	32K	2	01h
8192	06h	3Fh	<256	16	128K	8	07h
			>255	8	64K	4	03h
16384	07h	7Fh	<256	16	256K	16	0Fh
			>255	8	128K	8	07h

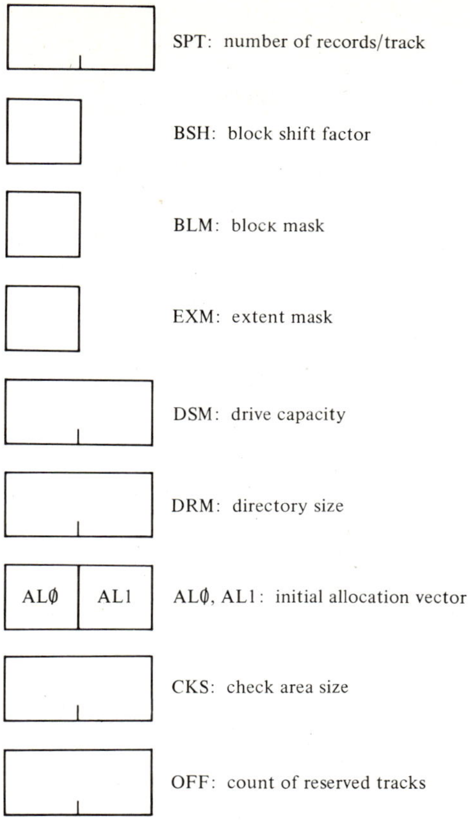

FIGURE 14-8
A map of the Disk Parameter Block (DPB), whose address is returned by service request 31.

reflects a confusion that runs through all the CP/M manuals. In CP/M 1.4, 128 bytes was the only disk sector size supported by CP/M. People who worked with CP/M quite reasonably thought "sector" when they meant "a unit of 128 bytes of data." Unfortunately the habit has stuck even though a disk sector may now have any of a number of sizes, with 128 bytes becoming less and less common.

The first DPB field contains the number of standard 128-byte records that will fit on a track of the disk. A single-density soft-sectored diskette may have 128-byte sectors (the second display in Example 14-5 describes such a disk), although that is not certain. For all formats other than the "exchange format" this number will be some multiple of the actual number of physical sectors on a track.

Note that this field of the DPB is a 16-bit integer. CP/M is prepared to handle disks that hold more than 255 records per track. If the BDOS knows the number of the standard record it wants, then it can compute what track it wants by dividing that record number by DPB.SPT.

BSH, BLM: The Block Shift and Block Mask. The BSH (Block Shift) byte of the DPB contains the number of times that a record number should be shifted to the right to obtain its allocation block number. The BLM (Block Mask) byte contains a mask,

```
; * * * *  XDPB -- DISPLAY THE DISK PARAMETER BLOCK
;
         MACLIB  CPMEQU   ; STANDARD NAMES,
         MACLIB  PROG     ; PROLOG, SERVICE MACROS
         MACLIB  HEXSUB   ; HEX CONVERT & DISPLAY
         MACLIB  COSUB    ; CONSOLE OUTPUT
;
         PROLOG  30,DPB
;
DISPLAY EQU      $        ; ENTIRE REPORT FORM
        DB       'Disk Parameter Block for drive '
DRIVE   DS       1       ! DB CR,LF
        DB       'SPT: '
SPT     DS       4       ! DB ' records per track',CR,LF
        DB       'BSH: '
BSH     DS       2       ! DB '    recno >> BSH = block number',CR,LF
        DB       'BLM: '
BLM     DS       2       ! DB '    recno AND BLM = record in block',CR,LF
        DB       'EXM: '
EXM     DS       2       ! DB '    logical extent versus physical',CR,LF

        DB       'DSM: '
DSM     DS       4       ! DB ' highest block number (origin 0)',CR,LF
        DB       'DRM: '
DRM     DS       4       ! DB ' highest directory number (origin 0)',CR,LF
        DB       'ALV: '
ALV     DS       4       ! DB ' bits reserving directory blocks',CR,LF
        DB       'CKS: '
CKS     DS       4       ! DB ' size of check vector in bytes',CR,LF
        DB       'OFF: '
OFF     DS       4       ! DB ' number of reserved tracks',CR,LF+80H
;
DPB     EQU      $
        LDA      CPMFCB   ; DRIVECODE GIVEN?
        DCR      A        ; CONVERT A=01 INTO A=00
        JP       DPB2     ; (YES, ONE WAS GIVEN)
        SERVICE  25       ; NO DRIVECODE, GET CURRENT DISK
DPB2    MOV      E,A      ; SAVE FOR SELECT SERVICE
        ADI      'A'      ; MAKE DRIVECODE PRINTABLE,
        STA      DRIVE    ; ..PUT INTO DISPLAY
        SERVICE  14       ; ..AND SELECT IT
        SERVICE  31       ; HL --> DPB FOR CURRENT DISK
        PUSH     H        ; (SAVE IT FOR DUMP)
;
        LXI      D,SPT    ; DE --> FIELD IN DISPLAY,
        CALL     CVT2     ; MAKE PRINTABLE, ADVANCE HL & DE
;
        LXI      D,BSH    ! CALL CVT1
        LXI      D,BLM    ! CALL CVT1
        LXI      D,EXM    ! CALL CVT1
        LXI      D,DSM    ! CALL CVT2
        LXI      D,DRM    ! CALL CVT2
        LXI      D,ALV    ! CALL CVT1 ! CALL CVT1
        LXI      D,CKS    ! CALL CVT2
        LXI      D,OFF    ! CALL CVT2
        LXI      H,DISPLAY
        CALL     COSTR    ; PRINT THE WHOLE THING
        POP      H        ; THEN DUMP IT ALL IN HEX
        MVI      B,15
        CALL     HEXDUMP ! CALL COCRLF
;
        RET               ; RETURN TO CCP
```

FIGURE 14-9
XDPB **displays the Disk Parameter Block, the structure from which the BDOS gets all its information about a disk.**

```
;
CVT2     EQU     $         ; DISPLAY 16-BIT INTEGER
; (8080 FORM -- FIRST BYTE IS THE LEAST-SIGNIFICANT)
         PUSH    H         ; SAVE -->L.S. BYTE
         INX     H         ; HL -->M.S. BYTE
         CALL    CVT1      ; ..CONVERT, STORE THAT
         XTHL              ; SAVE HL, HL -->L.S.B.
         CALL    CVT1      ; ..CONVERT, STORE THAT
         POP     H         ; HL-->NEXT DATA
         RET
;
CVT1     EQU     $         ; DISPLAY BYTE AT HL++
         MOV     A,M       ; GET BYTE,
         INX     H         ; ..ADVANCE HL
CVT1A    CALL    HEXBYTE   ; A,C = ASCII DISPLAY
         STAX    D         ; PUT LEFT IN DISPLAY
         INX     D
         MOV     A,C       ; PUT RIGHT IN DISPLAY
         STAX    D
         INX     D
         RET
;
; * * * * * COMMON SUBROUTINES
;
         HEXSUBM
         COSUBM
         END
```

FIGURE 14-9 (Continued)

which, if ANDed with a record number, will produce the relative number of the record within its allocation block.

The size of an allocation block can be determined from BSH. Initialize a register pair to the value 128. Then double the register contents (either with a left shift or with an add) BSH times.

EXM: The Extent Mask. The EXM (Extent Mask) field of the DPB gives the relationship between a physical extent and a logical extent. A logical extent number results from dividing a record number by 128. The corresponding physical extent number can be computed from the logical extent number using EXM. However, the physical extent number can also be computed directly from the record number and BSH (shift the record number right BSH times to yield a relative block position, and divide the result by 8 or 16 depending on the number of blocks in a data map). It is not clear what role EXM plays in the BDOS's calculations.

DSM: Highest Block Number. The DSM (Disk Space Maximum) field of the DPB gives the highest valid allocation block number for the disk. Allocation blocks are numbered from zero, so DSM is one less than the number of blocks on the disk. If the most significant (right-most, as the 8080 stores it) byte of DSM is zero, then there are 16 block numbers in a data map. If it is not zero, then a data map must contain eight numbers of 2 bytes each.

The capacity of the disk in kilobyte units can be computed from DSM and BSH. Initialize a register pair with DSM+1. Double that value BSH–3 times. Double the value BSH times to find the disk capacity in records. Note that the disk capacity in bytes (DSM+1 doubled BSH+7 times) is likely to overflow a 16-bit register.

EXAMPLE 14-5
The output of XDPB, as run against double-density and single-density diskettes. The DPB provides the STAT command with most of the information it displays in the disk status report.

```
A>dpb
Disk Parameter Block for drive A
SPT: 0040 records per track
BSH: 04   recno >> BSH = block number
BLM: 0F   recno AND BLM = record in block
EXM: 00   logical extent versus physical
DSM: 012B highest block number (origin 0)
DRM: 007F highest directory number (origin 0)
ALV: C000 bits reserving directory blocks
CKS: 0020 size of check vector in bytes
OFF: 0002 number of reserved tracks
F777: 40 00 04 0F 00 2B 01 7F 00 C0 00 20 00 02 00    @....+...@. ...

A>dpb b:
Disk Parameter Block for drive B
SPT: 001A records per track
BSH: 03   recno >> BSH = block number
BLM: 07   recno AND BLM = record in block
EXM: 00   logical extent versus physical
DSM: 00F2 highest block number (origin 0)
DRM: 003F highest directory number (origin 0)
ALV: C000 bits reserving directory blocks
CKS: 0010 size of check vector in bytes
OFF: 0002 number of reserved tracks
F71D: 1A 00 03 07 00 F2 00 3F 00 C0 00 10 00 02 00    .....r.?.@.....
```

DRM: Size of Directory. The DRM (Directory Maximum) field of the DPB gives the highest numbered entry in the disk directory. The entries are numbered from zero, so there are DRM+1 entries in the directory. Note that DRM is a 2-byte field; CP/M is prepared to handle directories with more than 256 entries.

Recall that directory entries are stored four per standard record. Therefore, DRM+1 will be a multiple of four and DRM+1 shifted right twice will yield the number of standard records in the directory.

ALV: Allocation Vector. The BDOS keeps an allocation vector for each active disk. This is a string of DSM+1 bits, one bit per allocation block, in which a 1-bit means that the related block is in use. The two ALV bytes of the DPB are the initial value for this allocation vector. They become the leading bytes of the full vector. Some number of leading bits in the ALV bytes are set to 1 so as permanently to reserve that many allocation blocks to contain the directory.

CKS: Directory Check Size. When the BDOS selects a drive it can check to see if the disk on that drive has been changed since the last warm start. If the volume has been changed, the drive is made read only.

The CKS (Check Size) field of the DPB determines if this will or will not be done. If it is zero, then no check will be made. This is usually the case only for drives whose disks cannot be removed. If CKS is not zero, checking will be done. In that case CKS is usually given the value (DRM+1)/4, the number of standard records in the directory. CKS might be smaller than (DRM+1)/4, but then not all entries would be checked; there would be a small possibility that a disk change could go undetected.

In MP/M 2 the most significant bit of CKS is used as a flag. If that bit is 1, the drive described by this DPB has fixed disks. If the bit is 0, the disk can be removed from the drive.

OFF: Track Offset. Most disks have reserved tracks. Diskettes have two or three tracks reserved for the image of the Monitor that is loaded on a warm or cold start. The OFF field of the DPB tells how many tracks are reserved on this particular disk. The BDOS will add this value to the track number it computes using the record number and the SPT field, before requesting that the BIOS seek to that track. Since the first blocks on the disk are reserved to the directory, and since disk tracks are numbered from zero, the value in OFF is also the number of the track that contains the directory.

Large Offset Values. The OFF field is 2 bytes long. CP/M is prepared to handle disks that have more than 255 reserved tracks. This might seem peculiar. Why should so many tracks be reserved? The answer is that the OFF value can be used to partition a large disk into several smaller logical drives. Imagine a large disk with 512 tracks. It could be presented to the BDOS as four separate disks, each with its own DPB. The capacity values of the drives might be equal, each reflecting the capacity of 128 tracks of the disk. The offset value of the first would be zero, of the second 128, of the third 256, and of the fourth 384. As far as the BDOS would be able to tell four different drives would exist. The BIOS would know that there was only one.

A Hypothetical Disk

Parameters of the Disk. Pretend we're designers, preparing to interface a new disk to CP/M. The disk is a hard disk with four recording surfaces under four read-write heads and 128 tracks per surface. CP/M and MP/M don't have the concept of multiple read-write heads, so we will simply treat it as a 512-track disk; in our BIOS we will translate BDOS track requests into cylinder and head requests.

Each track of the disk holds 32 sectors of 512 bytes, for a total of 16,384 bytes per track. The total capacity of the disk is 8 MB and we'll present it to CP/M as a single logical drive. But what disk parameters shall we use? Let's get out our pocket calculators and try some numbers.

Finding the Block Size. An allocation block size of 1024 is clearly out of the question. It yields 8192 blocks in total; block numbers would be 2 bytes, and a physical extent would be less than a logical extent. That isn't allowed.

Try again with a block size of 2048. There are then 4096 blocks; each directory entry can control 16K. If a single file filled the disk, it would occupy (8 MB divided by 16 KB) 512 extent entries. That is the minimum size of the directory, which requires 128 records or 8 blocks to hold it. The ALV bytes would be `FF00h` (refer to Table 14-1 for the other DPB values).

Extremes of the Directory. However, there is another extreme to consider. The disk might be filled with 4096 one-block files. It would require 4096 entries, or 1024 directory records, or 64 blocks, to hold such a directory. Nobody would have so many little files, but this design is short on directory entries. Suppose there were 256 two-block files on the disk. Each uses up a directory entry. There would be 3584 unused blocks left, and only 256 directory entries left to describe them. It would take 448 directory entries to describe that space, so we clearly risk running out of directory entries before we run out of allocation blocks.

A Balanced Design. Try once more with a block size of 4096. Then the disk accomodates 2048 blocks in total. The eight entries in a data map will describe 32 KB. If the disk is completely filled with a single file, that file will be described in 256 directory entries. Let's allow 512 directory entries instead. Now if there are 256 two-block files (or even 256 one-block files), enough entries remain to describe all the remaining space. The directory will fit in four blocks (ALV is F000h).

This last design seems the best. Each file will contain half a block, or 2048 bytes, of wasted space, but that can't be avoided. If there are 512 files, there'll be 1 MB of wasted space. That is only 12 percent of the total; the actual amount of wasted space will probably never approach that.

The Record Count Problem. When, as in this example, the physical extent exceeds 16 KB, a directory entry will control 256 or more records. How can these large numbers be counted in the single FCB byte used for a record count? The documentation doesn't say. It seems likely that the byte contains, not the number of records in the whole extent, but the number of records in the last logical extent used within it. The record count would be the actual count modulo 128, or would be set to 128 to indicate that the last logical extent was full. This might explain the BDOS's need for the EXM field, which is redundant otherwise.

Activating a Drive

The first time a drive is used following a warm or cold start the BDOS must perform two chores. The CP/M documentation refers to these as "logging in" the drive. The two chores are to build the allocation vector for the disk, and to build its directory check vector. These vectors are built in space provided by the BIOS.

The Allocation Vector. The allocation vector is a bit map, an array of bits each of which corresponds to one allocation block. Therefore, the size of the allocation vector is DSM bits (rounded up to a byte). The BIOS is required to contain space for an allocation vector for each drive that it supports. As we'll see, the address of this area is returned during a BIOS call.

When a disk is activated, its allocation vector is initialized to all 0-bits. Then the ALV bytes from the DPB are installed in the first bytes of the vector. That ensures that the blocks used for the directory are reserved. Finally, the BDOS reads all the directory records. Each time it finds an active directory entry it reads the data map in that entry. For each nonzero block number in the data map it sets the corresponding bit of the allocation vector to 1.

THE XALV PROGRAM. Service request 27 returns the address of the allocation vector for the disk that is currently selected. The XALV program in Figure 14-10 will display the allocation vector of the default disk or (if a drivecode is its operand) another disk. The vector is displayed as a list of 1's and 0's, 64 per line. Run XALV, then erase a file and run it again. Copy a large file with PIP and run XALV once more. Example 14-6 shows what XALV's output looks like.

THE DIRECTORY CHECK VECTOR. The BIOS is required to provide space for a directory check vector for each drive it supports. That vector is an array of bytes, 1 byte for each standard record in the directory, or (DRM+1)/4 bytes.

The BDOS builds the check vector while it builds the allocation vector. It forms a 1-byte hash code for each standard record in the directory and places that hash code in the check vector. Thereafter every time it scans the directory for some extent record it again forms a hash code as it reads each record. If a hash code fails to match the one formed when the disk was activated, the BDOS assumes that the disk volume has been changed. It marks the drive read-only. Each time a directory entry is updated because of a file access its standard record's hash code must be updated as well.

Space Allocation

ALLOCATING A BLOCK. Once you understand the space management parameters, you can probably work out the logic of space allocation for yourself. When the BDOS needs to give a new allocation block to a file, it scans that drive's allocation map from left to right. The first 0-bit found corresponds to the first free allocation block. That bit's (and block's) number is placed in the FCB for the file.

ALLOCATING AN EXTENT ENTRY. When the BDOS needs a new extent record, it reads the directory and scans for the first inactive entry (the first with E5h in the user code byte). That is the entry that it initializes with the current user number, the fileref from the FCB, an extent number one greater than that in the FCB, and a data map of zeros.

ORDER OF ALLOCATION. Both of these allocation schemes use (or reuse) the lowest numbered space first. This tends to keep active directory entries compressed to the front

EXAMPLE 14-6
The output of XALV, run against a double-density diskette. The pattern shows CP/M's preference for allocation on the outermost tracks. Patches of 000 in the first rows show erased files.

```
A>xalv
Allocation vector of disk A

11111111000011111111111111111111111111111111111111111111111111111
11111111111111111111101111111111111111010110001101111111111111111
11111111111111100000001111111111111111110000000000000000000011111
11111111111100000000000001111111111000000000000000000000000000000
000000000000000000000000000000000000000000000000
A>_
```

```
; * * * * * XALV -- EXAMINE THE ALLOCATION VECTOR
;
        MACLIB  CPMEQU  ; STANDARD NAMES
        MACLIB  PROG    ; PROLOG, SERVICE MACROS
        MACLIB  DPSUB   ; 16-BIT ROUTINES
        MACLIB  COSUB   ; CONSOLE OUTPUT
;
        PROLOG  30,XALV
;
DPB$DSM EQU     5       ; OFFSET TO 'DSM' IN D.P.B.
HEADING DB      'Allocation vector of disk '
DRIVE   DB      0,CR,LF,CR,LF+80H
;
XALV    EQU     $
        LDA     CPMFCB  ; DRIVECODE GIVEN?
        DCR     A       ; FCB FORM TO SERVICE 14 FORM
        JP      XAL2    ; (DRIVECODE SPECIFIED)
        SERVICE 25      ; OMITTED, GET CURRENT DRIVE
XAL2    MOV     E,A     ; SAVE FOR SERVICE 14
        ADI     'A'     ; MAKE PRINTABLE,
        STA     DRIVE   ; ..PUT DRIVE IN HEADING,
        LXI     H,HEADING
        CALL    COSTR   ; ..AND PRINT IT.
        SERVICE 14      ; SELECT WANTED DRIVE
;
        SERVICE 31      ; HL --> DISK PARAMETERS
        MVI     A,DPB$DSM ; OFFSET TO DPB.DSM
        CALL    DP$LDHA ; LOAD THAT TO DE
        MVI     A,7     ; ROUND DSM UP TO
        CALL    DP$ADAD ; ..A MULTIPLE OF 8
        MVI     B,3     ; ..THEN DIVIDE IT BY 8
XALSR   CALL    DP$SRLD ; ..BY SHIFTING DE RIGHT
        DCR     B  ! JNZ XALSR
; DE = NUMBER OF BYTES IN THE ALLOCATION VECTOR
        SERVICE 27      ; HL --> ALLOCATION VECTOR
        MVI     B,8     ; B = BYTES PER LINE
;
XALOOP  CALL    XALBYTE ; DISPLAY 8 BITS,
        DCX     D       ; ..COUNT IT,
        MOV A,E ! ORA D ; ..CHECK FOR ZERO,
        RZ              ; ..BACK TO CCP IF THAT'S IT
        DCR     B       ; SEE IF THAT WAS 64 BITS
        JNZ     XALOOP  ; (CONTINUE IF NOT)
        CALL    COCRLF  ; NEW LINE AFTER 64 BITS
        MVI     B,8
        JMP     XALOOP  ; CONTINUE
;
; SUBROUTINE TO PRINT THE 8 BITS OF THE BYTE AT [HL]
; INCREMENTS HL TO NEXT BYTE, ALTERS AF.
;
XALBYTE PUSH    B       ; SAVE A WORK REG
        MVI     C,8     ; C HAS THE LOOP COUNT,
        MOV     B,M     ; ..B THE BYTE ITSELF.
        INX     H       ; INCREMENT DATA POINTER
;
XB1     MOV     A,B     ; CURRENT BIT TO CARRY AND
        RAL    !  MOV B,A
        MVI     A,'0'   ; ..PRINT A ZERO OR
        ACI     00      ; ..A ONE, DEPENDING ON CARRY
        CALL    COUT
        DCR     C ! JNZ XB1
;
        POP     B
        RET
;
;  COMMON SUBROUTINES
;
        DPSUBM
        COSUBM
        END
```

FIGURE 14-10
XALV displays the allocation vector for a disk. Each bit stands for an allocation block; 1 means the block is in use.

of the directory, and files compacted toward the outer edge of the disk. It means that the track of a diskette that receives the most wear is the track that carries the directory, followed by the rest of the tracks in ascending numerical order. In normal use an unreadable disk sector on one of the innermost tracks may go undetected for weeks, whereas a bad sector on an outer track will be discovered very quickly.

DISK FORMATTING AND THE DIRECTORY

The Directory High-Water Mark

The logic of the BDOS's directory scan depends on finding E5h in the first byte of an inactive entry. Some simple tests with a newly formatted diskette and a stopwatch revealed that the dependency goes even deeper. The time it takes the BDOS to log in a disk does not vary with the number of active files on a disk. It varies with the maximum number of directory entries that have *ever* been used, whether or not those entries are presently active.

The CP/M documentation asserts that a program like ALLDIR will see every directory entry. If the documentation were correct, ALLDIR would always display the number of entries given by the DRM field of the Disk Parameter Block. In fact, it does not. ALLDIR will display every directory entry that has ever been used, but it will not display a directory entry that has *never* been used.

Both these facts imply that the BDOS has some way of detecting the high-water mark of its use of the directory. Presumably it stops reading the directory at the high-water mark. There can't be an active entry past the high-water mark because the BDOS always allocates the earliest unused entry.

But what is the high-water mark? E5h in the first byte signals an inactive entry. The documentation doesn't say, but we can hypothesize that E5h in the second byte signals an entry that has never been used. This is reasonable, because filenames are (supposedly) always uppercase. A second byte of E5h could only result from a filename beginning with "e," with its f1' attribute bit set.

The Reason for E5h

Why does CP/M have this reliance on the byte value E5h? That is the sector formatting character specified by the IBM standard for single-density diskettes. CP/M was originally designed to support single-density, "IBM-compatible" diskette drives. A freshly formatted single-density diskette will contain E5h in every byte of every sector, and especially in the directory sectors. Since E5h signals an inactive entry, an initialized diskette automatically has an empty directory. If E5h indeed signals the high-water mark, then an initialized diskette has its high-water mark set automatically as well.

The Fill-Character Dilemma

E5h is not a universal constant, nor was its choice as the format fill character arbitrary. The format fill character is chosen to have a bit pattern that optimizes the action of the drive electronics. Not surprisingly the fill character specified by IBM for its double-density drives is different: 4Eh. The fill character recommended for a hard disk will be different still. A disk formatter that fills double-density sectors with E5h is not "IBM compatible." On the other hand, a CP/M disk formatter that fills sectors with 4Eh is asking for trouble. The BDOS will think that the directory of such a diskette is full!

That can be circumvented by requiring the user to issue ERA *.* after formatting a diskette. That will put E5h in all the user code bytes, making all entries appear inactive. It probably won't, however, reset the high-water mark by writing E5h in every second byte. On such a diskette ALLDIR ought to display every directory entry, and log-in time should not vary with directory use.

Most disk vendors bow to necessity and use the E5 fill character for all disk formats, accepting a slight loss of disk reliability in return for CP/M compatibility. A few formatters attempt to compromise by writing E5 in every 32nd byte and the optimum fill character elsewhere, in effect doing ERA *.* for the user.

Chapter 15

The BIOS and System Generation

This chapter covers the BIOS, the part of the Monitor that is supplied by the vendor to handle the I/O devices. We'll examine its functions and how they are called. Then we'll go over the procedure for modifying the BIOS, linking it to the BDOS, and putting the updated Monitor on the bootstrap tracks of a diskette. The presentation assumes that you've had considerable experience with both assembly language and CP/M.

THE BIOS

The BIOS contains all the device-dependent code in the Monitor. Its interface to the BDOS is the same for CP/M and MP/M. That interface may be used by ordinary commands, although there is rarely any need to do so.

The BIOS must be customized to the hardware of a particular system. The bulk of the code in it is concerned with handling the disks, and is usually provided by the vendor of the disk system. The rest of the BIOS, usually less than a fifth of it, operates the serial I/O devices. This part too may have been provided by the party who sold the system, or the job of tailoring the serial I/O code may have been left up to you. It is this part of the BIOS that most often needs changing because serial devices are often added or replaced.

The BIOS Interface—CP/M and MP/M

In CP/M and MP/M the BIOS resides just above the BDOS, in the highest addresses of working storage. The first dozen instructions in the BIOS constitute a jump table, a list of jump instructions each of which leads to a service routine that provides a single function. We'll call this list of jump instructions the entry table. Table 15-1 lists all the entries.

The address at location 00h in storage is a jump to the second jump of the entry table, an entry that produces the service of a warm start of CP/M. The first entry, the cold start service, is only needed during a cold start. The other entries are divided between disk services and serial I/O services. Of the latter all except the List Status function are available as BDOS services.

The BIOSCALL Library. Figure 15-1 shows the contents of a macro library, BIOSCALL.LIB. This library contains equate statements to define the entry table and a subroutine named BIOS that calls the BIOS service indexed by register A. We'll use this library in the examples that follow.

The BIOS Interface—CP/M-86

CP/M-86 provides an interface to the BIOS by way of a BDOS service request. A program under CP/M-86 requests a BIOS function by requesting BDOS service 50.

Consult the Reference section of this book for the parameters to be passed with service 50. In essence, the program supplies the offset into the BIOS entry table and the contents of the BIOS argument registers. Although the calling sequence is different, the BIOS functions of CP/M-86 are the same as those of CP/M.

TABLE 15-1
The functions of the BIOS, with their offsets in the BIOS entry table. The entry table is found from the address in low storage at 0001h. The disk functions cannot be called from a command program under MP/M 2.

Name of Function	Entry index,	Table offset	Purpose
			Start Functions
BOOT	-1,	-03h	Finish initializing the system after the bootstrap load has been completed.
WBOOT	0,	00h	Refresh the CCP and BDOS images at the end of a command; refresh low-storage jumps.
			Disk Functions
SELDSK	8,	18h	Select the disk to which following disk functions refer.
SETTRK	9,	1Bh	Select the track for further operations.
SETSEC	10,	1Eh	Select the standard record (not sector) of the current track for the next operation.
SECTRAN	15,	2Dh	Translate a record position number according to the skew algorithm in effect for the disk.
SETDMA	11,	21h	Establish the address of the record buffer for the next operation.
READ	12,	24h	Read the currently selected record into the current buffer.
WRITE	13,	27h	Write the data from the current buffer into the selected record.
HOME	7,	15h	Equivalent to a call to SETTRK with an argument of zero.
			Serial IO Functions
CONIN	2,	06h	Get the next byte from the logical console.
CONOUT	3,	09h	Write a byte to the logical console.
CONST	1,	03h	Return a signal that there is or is not an input byte ready at the logical console.
LIST	4,	0Ch	Write a byte to the logical printer.
LISTST	14,	2Ah	Return a signal that the logical printer is or is not ready to accept another byte.
READER	6,	12h	Get the next byte from the logical reader.
PUNCH	5,	0Fh	Write a byte to the logical punch.

```
; * * * * BIOSCALL.LIB: CODE FOR CALLING BIOS ENTRIES
;
B$WBOOT     EQU  0*3      ; WARM START
B$CONST     EQU  1*3      ; CONSOLE STATUS
B$CONIN     EQU  2*3      ; CONSOLE INPUT
B$CONOUT    EQU  3*3      ; CONSOLE OUTPUT
B$LIST      EQU  4*3      ; LIST OUTPUT
B$PUNCH     EQU  5*3      ; PUNCH OUTPUT
B$READER    EQU  6*3      ; READER INPUT
B$HOME      EQU  7*3      ; SEEK TO TRACK 00
B$SELDSK    EQU  8*3      ; SELECT DRIVE
B$SETTRK    EQU  9*3      ; SELECT TRACK
B$SETSEC    EQU  10*3     ; SELECT RECORD
B$SETDMA    EQU  11*3     ; SET BUFFER ADDRESS
B$READ      EQU  12*3     ; READ ONE RECORD
B$WRITE     EQU  13*3     ; WRITE ONE RECORD
B$LISTST    EQU  14*3     ; LIST DEVICE STATUS
B$SECTRAN   EQU  15*3     ; SKEW TRANSLATION
;
;       SUBROUTINE TO CALL BIOS AT THE ENTRY TABLE
;       VECTOR WHOSE OFFSET IS IN THE A-REGISTER.
;       ALTERS A&F, AND HL.  PRESERVES BC, DE
;    ** NOTE: ASSUMES BIOS IS ON PAGE BOUNDARY **
;
BIOSM   MACRO
BIOS    EQU     $
        PUSH B ! PUSH D
        LHLD    BOOT+1   ; HL-->WBOOT ENTRY
        ADD     L        ; ADD A TO MAKE ADDRESS
        MOV     L,A      ; HL-->DESIRED BIOS ENTRY
        PUSH    H        ; SAVE THAT, GET
        LXI     H,BIOSRET ;..RETURN ADDRESS
        XTHL             ; STACK RETURN ADDR,
        PCHL             ; ..GO TO BIOS, WHICH
BIOSRET EQU     $        ; RETURNS HERE.
        POP  D ! POP  B
        RET
        ENDM
; * * * * * * END OF BIOSCALL.LIB
```

FIGURE 15-1
BIOSCALL.LIB **demonstrates the code needed to call on BIOS functions. Calling the BIOS is rarely necessary.**

THE BIOS START FUNCTIONS

The BIOS functions fall into three groups: start functions, disk functions, and serial I/O functions. In this section we'll examine the start functions, that is, the work the BIOS does during a cold or warm start.

The Cold Start Entry

The first entry to the BIOS is intended for the use of the bootstrap load program; it initializes the system immediately after the Monitor has been loaded by a bootstrap loader.

Bootstrap Load. In most systems a hardware reset causes a bootstrap load operation. In almost all systems reset enables a segment of read-only storage that contains a bootstrap load program. That program may load the entire image of the Monitor from the reserved tracks of the disk in the A-drive. Or it may only load a one- or two-sector loader from the first track, which in turn loads the rest of the Monitor.

Once the complete Monitor image—CCP, BDOS, and BIOS—has been read into high storage, the bootstrap program transfers control to the Monitor by jumping to the first vector of the entry table.

Initializing the Hardware. When control arrives at the cold start routine of the BIOS, the entire Monitor has just been loaded. The BIOS code may assume that the cold start was initiated by a hardware reset, and that therefore all the serial devices in the system have been reset. One of the purposes of the cold start entry is to initialize these devices. It may have to set the transmission speed of serial device ports, or initialize the buffer of a memory-mapped terminal. If there are interrupt-driven I/O devices, the cold start code should initialize the devices, set up the interrupt vectors, and enable the CPU for interrupts. The cold start code is responsible for typing a log-on message at the terminal.

Initializing Low Storage. The cold start code initializes two low-storage locations that are not changed by warm start. It sets the current disk number to 00h, indicating drive A: and user code zero. It sets the initial value of the IOBYTE, which represents the state of the I/O device assignments. As delivered, most BIOSs initialize the IOBYTE to 00h, which assigns all four logical devices to TTY:. This is not the best setting; new users find it a barrier to understanding the use of STAT for device assignments. A better setting is 81h, which assigns CON: to CRT: and LST: to LPT:.

After initializing devices and the IOBYTE, the cold start code joins the logic of the warm start entry to initialize the jump addresses in low storage and transfer control to the CCP.

Location of the Cold Start Code. Once the cold start is over (that is, once the BIOS is initialized and has entered the CCP), the cold start code is never used again. Because of this single use, some designers place the code in what is, the rest of the time, a BIOS disk buffer. That saves a few bytes of space (the BIOS is always short of space). No command program should ever call the cold start entry; it may end up "executing" a directory entry.

The Warm Start Entry

The second entry table vector leads to the warm start routine. This routine is called at the end of most commands. Its purpose is to refresh the BDOS, CCP, and low storage after a program has, at least possibly, overwritten them. The BIOS itself is only refreshed by a cold start, so if a command overwrites the BIOS then nothing, including warm start, will work until a reset is done.

Warm Start Functions. The first job of warm start is to reload the image of the CCP and the BDOS (but not the BIOS) from the reserved tracks of the disk in the A-drive. To do so it no doubt will use several of the BIOS disk functions as subroutines.

After loading the CCP and BDOS the warm start code will usually refresh the warm start and service request jumps in low storage, and it may initialize variables in the BIOS work area between 40h and 4Fh. Normally no other system variables are reset during a warm start. The IOBYTE, user code, and default drive are left as they were. However, the author has found it useful to check the drive number and, if it is invalid, to zero byte 04h. If a runaway program puts garbage in 04h, the system can be locked in a loop issuing a message such as BDOS Error on k: select.

The jumps in the BIOS entry table are neither reloaded nor refreshed, since DESPOOL or another such program may have modified them.

When everthing is in order, the warm start code must put the default drive and user code (in other words, a copy of byte 04h) in register C and branch to a location 3 bytes into the CCP. The CCP will begin the command process.

The CCP's Autocommand Entry

The CCP can be entered at an offset of 0 bytes instead of the normal offset of 3 bytes. If this happens, the CCP will check the byte at CCP+7; if that is nonzero, it will execute a precoded command as if the user had typed it. The precoded command may be any valid one; it could be, for instance, the name of a command program that is always used when the system starts up. We'll see later how to code the command into the CCP.

The autocommand entry normally would be used only after a cold start rather than after every warm start. This can be arranged by having the cold start code jump to CCP+0 and the warm start code jump to CCP+3. If the two functions join in common code prior to entering the CCP, the unique warm start code can zero the byte at CCP+7, negating the precoded command on all but a cold start.

THE BIOS DISK FUNCTIONS

The BIOS disk functions are designed to serve the needs of the BDOS. The BDOS requests I/O in terms of drives, tracks, and standard 128-byte records. The BIOS translates these requests into disk I/O operations.

Under MP/M 2, the disk functions should never be called from a command program. They will usually be located in a different bank of storage, not in common storage. Calling a disk function will result in a transfer to a meaningless location.

Disk Selection

THE SELDSK FUNCTION. The SELDSK (Select Disk) vector of the BIOS entry table lets the BIOS know that the BDOS is planning to use a particular drive. That is the only drive that the BDOS will be concerned about until it calls SELDSK again. The BIOS will often do nothing about this call except to note the drive number for later functions, because the BDOS may select a disk and then not operate upon it. Depending on a parameter, however, the BIOS may do more.

The BIOS should check the requested drive number against its own knowledge of the number of drives it supports; the BDOS has probably taken the drive number from a program's FCB and has no way of knowing whether or not such a drive exists. The drive number might even be garbage as the result of an error in the program. The BIOS returns zero in the HL register pair if the number is invalid.

The Disk Parameter Header. When the disk number presented to SELDSK is valid, the BIOS returns in the HL register the address of a structure called the Disk Parameter Header (DPH). The DPH is used by the BDOS to locate its disk information. The DPH contains the address of the Disk Parameter Block that we looked at so carefully in the last chapter. It also contains the addresses of the allocation and check vectors for this disk, and a few bytes of storage that the BDOS uses as a scratch pad (this is probably where the BDOS keeps its memory of where to start on a Search Next service, but we can't be sure of that).

The DPH also contains the address of a sector—actually, record—translation table, an address that must be used as a parameter to the SECTRAN function.

SELDSK and Registers DE. The CP/M documentation says that the only parameter of SELDSK is the drive number in register C. The MP/M documentation specifies an additional parameter. There, registers DE are to contain an even number (the least significant bit of register E is to be 0) if this is the first time the given drive has been selected since the BDOS's information about it was initialized. Otherwise DE are to contain 0001h, or at least an odd number.

CP/M Produces the DE Parameter. In fact, at least since version 2.2, the CP/M BDOS has generated the same parameter in the DE pair, and at least one common BIOS expects and uses it. A 0 in bit 0 of register E signifies that the drive is being selected for the first time (1) since a cold or warm start refreshed the BDOS, or (2) since service request 13 reset the BDOS disk information, or (3) since service request 37 reset the BDOS's record of the drive.

Use of the DE Parameter. The BIOS may assume that if register E bit 0 is 0, the diskette in the selected drive may have been changed since the last select of that drive. In that case the BIOS may read the drive to determine the density and sector size of the disk mounted in it. A command program that calls the SELDSK entry can't be sure whether the drive has been used before or not. How can it know what to put in the DE pair? One fail-safe method is to issue service request 14 (select drive) first. The BDOS will call SELDSK with the correct parameter in DE. Then the command program can be sure that the drive has been selected at least once and can pass DE=0001h without fear.

Track Addressing

BDOS Track Computation. The BDOS views a disk as containing some number of tracks, each having some count of standard records that are numbered from zero up to one less than the value in the SPT (standard records per track) field of the DPB. The

BDOS addresses data by computing a track number and a record number on that track. It calls on the BIOS to select the track.

The BDOS does not know, directly, how many tracks the disk has. That information is implicit in the DSM (maximum allocation block number) field of the DPB. The BDOS computes a record number from an allocation block number. It arrives at a track number by dividing the record number by the number of records on a track, and adding the OFF (count of reserved tracks) field of the DPB.

THE SETTRK FUNCTION. Having made these computations, the BDOS calls the BIOS at the SETTRK vector of the entry table. Most BIOSes simply note the track number and return, deferring any disk action until it must be done. If the disk controller interface supports interrupts and asynchronous operation, the BIOS may commence the seek operation at this time so that it can run concurrently with the BDOS's processing.

Record Addressing

The position of the record on the track is found as the remainder after dividing the record number by the number of records per track. It is a value from zero up to one less than the value of the SPT field of the DPB (note: from zero, not from one, despite the conventional numbering of disk sectors). The BDOS must ask the BIOS to select that record, but first it may have to ask the BIOS to translate the record position to allow for skew.

SECTOR SKEW OR INTERLEAVE. It is common, but by no means universal, for the sectors of a disk to be *skewed*. This means that consecutive units of data are not placed in consecutive sectors on the track. Instead, two units of data that ought logically to be adjacent are in fact separated by some number of sectors. The purpose of skew is to improve performance. The expectation is that the processor is more certain to be ready for data when the data rotate under the read-write head. Skew can eliminate one revolution's wait for a missed sector. The effect of skew (or *interleave*, as it's called with hard disks) is to reduce the average latency of the drive.

THE SKEW TABLE ADDRESS. The BDOS finds out whether or not the disk uses skew by checking the first word of the Disk Parameter Header structure (returned by the SELDSK function). If that word is zero, no skew is used; the record position computed from the record number is correct. If the word is not zero, it is the address of a translate table in the BIOS. In this case the disk does use skew and the record position must be translated in some way so that it addresses the correct physical position on the disk.

SKEW TRANSLATION IN CP/M 1.4. Prior to version 2.0 of CP/M, skew translation was a simple matter. CP/M supported only single-density, 8-inch diskettes with 26 sectors per track. A standard skew factor of six sectors was applied. To translate a record position into a sector number the BDOS used the record position as an index into a table of 26 bytes. The indexed byte contained the actual sector number that contained the desired record. Programs written for earlier versions of CP/M, assuming 26 sectors and the standard skew, sometimes do their own skew translation. Such programs are still being published in hobbyist magazines. They won't work in CP/M version 2 because it supports disks that have no skew, disks that skew by more or less than six sectors, and disks with many more than 26 sectors per track and many more than one record per sector.

The Problem of Disk Formats. Skew translation is now more complicated. A disk sector often contains more than one record. The records that share a sector are physically, as well as logically, adjacent, but logically adjacent records that fall into different sectors are separated. Skew translation can still be handled by indexing a table with the record position number. However, the skew table for disks with one sector size is different from that for disks with another sector size. There are four common sector sizes; a drive may be loaded with a diskette that has any of the four sizes. This is why the BIOS must pass the address of a translate table to the BDOS through the Disk Parameter Header. Only the BIOS knows the physical sector size of the diskette currently loaded in a drive; it must tell the BDOS which of four possible tables to use.

The Problem of Disk Capacity. The size of modern disks complicates matters still more. A double-density diskette can hold 64 records per track, a hard disk even more. A BIOS that keeps skew tables for several disk layouts can spend 500 or more bytes on tables alone.

Skew Computation. One way to overcome this problem is by computing the skew translation instead of looking it up. At least one popular BIOS does this. In this BIOS the translate table address in the Disk Parameter Header points only to a short list of parameters for the skew algorithm, instead of pointing to a full look-up table. The implication for command programs is that the first word of the DPH can't be relied upon to point to a complete skew look-up table.

Skew and Diskette Compatibility. The decision of what skew factor to apply to a diskette is left to the BIOS, and each BIOS is the work of a different vendor. Given the same format of density and sector size, two vendors may still choose different skew factors. Diskettes couldn't be exchanged between the two systems because the BIOS of the second system would read the physical sectors in a different order than they were written by the first system. The only standard skew factor is that of 6 used with 8-inch disks in exchange format.

The SECTRAN Function. If the record position must be translated, there will be a nonzero value in the first word of the Disk Parameter Header returned from the SELDSK function. In that case the SECTRAN function of the BIOS must be called. It takes a computed record position as a 16-bit integer in the BC register pair, and the address of a translate table in the DE register pair. It returns the translated record position in the HL register pair. The record position is a 16-bit number and should be saved as such, even if you "know" that there are fewer than 256 records on a track. It might contain a head-select value for a double-sided diskette or multihead hard disk.

Changing the Skew Address. We might ask why the BIOS must pass an address to the BDOS when all the BDOS will do is to pass it back again. The reason for this arrangement is that it allows the system programmer access to the skew translation process. If you want to write a program that accesses data directly through the BIOS, you can do so. Further, it opens the possibility that, to handle a nonstandard disk (one from another operating system, or from a BIOS with different ideas on skew factors), you can get the address of the Disk Parameter Header and change the address of the skew table in it.

The RECTRAN Program. Figure 15-2 shows the source of a program called RECTRAN. It generates all record positions from zero up to the maximum for the selected disk, and passes each through the SECTRAN function of the BIOS. The translated numbers that result are displayed in hexadecimal, eight per line. Example 15-1 shows what the output of RECTRAN looks like.

Run RECTRAN against different disk formats and study the patterns that result. Read through the code of your BIOS to see how it performs the translation. Does it use a table, or does it compute the translation?

The SETSEC Function. Once the record position has been translated (if that was necessary), the BDOS calls the SETSEC function of the BIOS to select the record to be accessed. Most BIOSes simply record the record number, again deferring actual disk operation until it is necessary.

Reading and Writing

Having addressed data by telling the BIOS the disk, the track, and the record, the BDOS may request that the record be read or written. Before doing so it must have set a buffer address.

The SETDMA Function. The SETDMA function of the BIOS does exactly what BDOS service request 26 does: it establishes the storage address of the record buffer for following reads and writes. To a program there is no functional difference between calling service 26 and calling the SETDMA function. The BDOS, of course, must sometimes set a buffer address different from the one being used by a program; when the program opens a file, the BDOS must set a buffer address for directory reading, then reset the program's data address.

A command program should always use BDOS service 26 to set the buffer address. If it calls the SETDMA entry directly, the BDOS and the BIOS will thereafter disagree on the buffer location.

The READ Function. The READ function of the BIOS requests that it read the standard record that has been addressed by previous calls to SELDSK, SETTRK, SECTRAN, and SETSEC. The data are placed in the present buffer address and a success code of zero is returned in the A register. If that code is nonzero, the BIOS had tried several times to read the sector containing the record and failed.

```
; * * * * * RECTRAN -- DISPLAY SKEW TRANSLATION
;
        MACLIB  CPMEQU   ; STANDARD NAMES,
        MACLIB  PROG     ; PROLOG, SERVICE MACROS
        MACLIB  COSUB    ; CONSOLE OUTPUT
        MACLIB  HEXSUB   ; HEX DISPLAYS
        MACLIB  BIOSCALL; BIOS INTERFACE
;
        PROLOG  30,RECTRAN
;
HEADING DB      'Record skew pattern for disk '
DRIVE   DB      0,CR,LF,CR,LF+80H
NOXLATE DB      'that disk needs no translation.',CR,LF+80H
NRECS   DW      0        ; RECORD COUNT FOR LOOP
PLENGTH EQU     16       ; NUMBERS PER LINE
NPRINT  DB      0        ; NUMBERS LEFT ON THIS LINE
;
RECTRAN EQU     $
        MVI     A,PLENGTH
        STA     NPRINT   ; INITIALIZE COUNT OF NUMBERS
        LDA     CPMFCB   ; SEE IF DRIVE SPECIFIED
        DCR     A        ; CONVERT FCB FORM TO SERVICE 14 FORM
        JP      REC2     ; (YES, DRIVE GIVEN)
        SERVICE 25       ; OMITTED, GET CURRENT DRIVE
REC2    MOV     E,A      ; SAVE DRIVE FOR SERVICE 14
        MOV     C,A      ; ..AND FOR BIOS SELDSK CALL
        ADI     'A'      ; MAKE PRINTABLE,
        STA     DRIVE    ; ..PUT IN HEADING & PRINT
        LXI  H,HEADING ! CALL COSTR
        SERVICE 14       ; ESTABLISH DRIVE TO BDOS
        SERVICE 31       ; HL-->DPB, SET DE = SPT
        MOV E,M ! INX H ! MOV D,M
        XCHG             ; SAVE RECORDS/TRACK
        SHLD    NRECS    ; ..FOR LOOP CONTROL
        MVI     A,B$SELDSK
        CALL    BIOS     ; HL-->D.P.H., SET DE-->XLATE TABLE
        MOV E,M ! INX H ! MOV D,M
        MOV     A,E      ; IF THAT ADDRESS IS ZERO,
        ORA     D        ; ..NO TRANSLATION IS DONE.
        JNZ     REC3
        LXI  H,NOXLATE ! CALL COSTR
        RET              ; ..IN WHICH CASE, QUIT.
REC3    LXI     B,0      ; CLEAR RECORD NUMBER
;
RECLOOP MVI     A,B$SECTRAN
        CALL    BIOS     ; HL = XLATE(BC)
        CALL    PRINT    ; DISPLAY THE RESULT
        LHLD    NRECS    ; DECREMENT LOOP VARIABLE
        DCX     H
        MOV  A,L  ! ORA H
        RZ               ; RETURN TO CCP IF DONE
        SHLD    NRECS    ; SAVE LOOP COUNT
        INX     B        ; STEP RECORD NUMBER
        JMP     RECLOOP  ; AND CONTINUE
;
PRINT   CALL    HEXADDR  ; PRINT HL AS HEX WORD
        CALL    COSPACE  ; ..AND A SPACE
        LDA     NPRINT   ; SEE IF END OF LINE
        DCR     A
        STA     NPRINT
        RNZ              ; (NO, CONTINUE)
        MVI     A,PLENGTH
        STA     NPRINT   ; REFRESH LINE COUNT
        CALL    COCRLF   ; START A NEW LINE
        RET
;
; COMMON SUBROUTINES
;
        COSUBM
        HEXSUBM
        BIOSM
        END
```

FIGURE 15-2
RECTRAN displays the record positions that result from skew translation of the sequential numbers from zero up to the number of records on a track.

EXAMPLE 15-1
RECTRAN reveals the skew pattern of a double-density diskette with 1024-byte sectors. Groups of eight records (one sector) are consecutive; sectors are skewed by two.

```
A>rectran
Record skew pattern for disk A

0001 0002 0003 0004 0005 0006 0007 0008 0019 001A 001B 001C 001D 001E 001F 0020
0031 0032 0033 0034 0035 0036 0037 0038 0009 000A 000B 000C 000D 000E 000F 0010
0021 0022 0023 0024 0025 0026 0027 0028 0030 003A 003B 003C 003D 003E 003F 0040
0011 0012 0013 0014 0015 0016 0017 0018 0029 002A 002B 002C 002D 002E 002F 0030

A>_
```

The Effect of Sector Buffering. Note that the BIOS might not do any disk I/O when it is called on to read a record. The BIOS operates on whole sectors. If a sector holds more than one record, and if the wanted record is already in the buffer as the result of a prior read, no disk operation is needed. If the sector buffer is inactive or filled with a prior sector, the BIOS will have to read the needed sector.

The Effect of Write Buffering. The BIOS might have to do two disk operations during a READ function. If it had been writing earlier, it might have a sector of data in its buffer that hasn't yet been written to disk. That sector must be written in order to clear the buffer so that the desired sector may be read.

The READIR Program. The program whose source appears in Figure 15-3 reads the disk directory using direct calls on the BIOS. Its output should be similar to that of the ALLDIR program of Figure 14-7, although the program is quite a bit more complicated

```
; * * * * * READIR -- READ DIRECTORY VIA BIOS CALLS
;
        MACLIB  CPMEQU   ; STANDARD NAMES,
        MACLIB  PROG     ; PROLOG, SERVICE MACROS
        MACLIB  COSUB    ; CONSOLE OUTPUT
        MACLIB  HEXSUB   ; HEX DISPLAYS
        MACLIB  DPSUB    ; 16-BIT ROUTINES
        MACLIB  BIOSCALL; BIOS INTERFACE
;
        PROLOG2 READIR
;
HEADING DB      'Physical directory entries, drive '
DRIVE   DB      0,CR,LF,CR,LF+80H
ERRMSG  DB      CR,LF,'BIOS reports read error.',CR,LF,'$'
DPB$DRM EQU     07H      ; OFFSET OF DRM FIELD IN D.P.B.
DPB$OFF EQU     0DH      ; OFFSET OF OFF FIELD IN D.P.B.
NRECS   DB      0        ; RECORDS LEFT TO GO
;
READIR  EQU     $
        LDA     CPMFCB   ; SEE IF DRIVE SPECIFIED
        DCR     A        ; CONVERT FCB FORM TO SERVICE 14 FORM
        JP      REA2     ; (YES, DRIVE GIVEN)
        SERVICE 25       ; OMITTED, GET CURRENT DRIVE
REA2    MOV     E,A      ; SAVE DRIVE FOR SERVICE 14
        MOV     C,A      ; ..AND FOR BIOS SELDSK CALL
```

FIGURE 15-3
READIR reads all the directory entries on a disk by calling the BIOS. It adds no information to that shown by ALLDIR, but shows the use of the BIOS for nonstandard disk I/O.

```
        ADI      'A'      ; MAKE PRINTABLE,
        STA      DRIVE    ; ..PUT IN HEADING & PRINT
        LXI   H,HEADING ! CALL COSTR
        SERVICE 14        ; ESTABLISH DRIVE TO BDOS
        SERVICE 31        ; HL-->DPB  -  GET DRM, OFF
;
        MVI      A,DPB$DRM
        CALL     DP$LDHA ; DE = LAST DIRECTORY ENTRY NUMBER
        INX      D       ; DE = TRUE COUNT OF ENTRIES
        CALL     DP$SRLD ; DIVIDE IT BY FOUR TO GET
        CALL     DP$SRLD ; ..COUNT OF STANDARD RECORDS.
        MOV      A,E     ; ASSUMING THAT'S < 256,
        STA      NRECS   ; ..SAVE IT FOR LOOP CONTROL
;
        MVI      A,DPB$OFF
        CALL     DP$LDHA ; DE = TRACK OFFSET, WHICH IS
        PUSH     D       ; ..DIRECTORY TRACK.  SAVE IT.
;
        MVI      A,B$SELDSK
        CALL     BIOS    ; HL-->D.P.H., SET DE-->XLATE TABLE
        MOV E,M ! INX H ! MOV D,M  ; ..OR MAYBE 0000
;
        POP      B       ; BC = WANTED TRACK NUMBER
        MVI      A,B$SETTRK
        CALL     BIOS    ; ESTABLISH THE TRACK NUMBER
        LXI      B,0     ; CLEAR RECORD NUMBER
;
RECLOOP PUSH     B       ; SAVE CURRENT RECORD NUMBER
        MOV A,E ! ORA D ; IS TRANSLATION NEEDED?
        JZ       NOXLATE ; (NO)
        MVI      A,B$SECTRAN
        CALL     BIOS    ; HL = XLATE(BC)
        PUSH H ! POP B   ; BC = TRANSLATED RECORD NUMBER
NOXLATE MVI      A,B$SETSEC
        CALL     BIOS    ; ESTABLISH WANTED RECORD
        MVI      A,B$READ
        CALL     BIOS    ; READ THAT RECORD TO CPMBUFF
        POP      B       ; (RECOVER STACKED RECORD NUMBER)
        ORA      A       ; ANY PROBLEMS ON THE READ?
        JZ       REA3    ; ..NO.
        LXI      D,ERRMSG; YES, QUIT
        JMP      ERROREXIT
;
REA3    CALL     PRINT   ; ALL OK, PRINT ENTRIES.
        LDA      NRECS
        DCR      A
        STA      NRECS   ; UPDATE LOOP COUNT,
        RZ               ;  RETURN TO EPILOG IF FINISHED
        INX      B       ; UPDATE RECORD POSITION,
        JMP      RECLOOP ;  CONTINUE.
;
PRINT   EQU      $       ; DISPLAY 4 DIRECTORY ENTRIES
        PUSH     B       ; SAVE MAINLINE'S BC
        LXI      H,CPMBUFF
        MVI      B,16    ; NUMBER OF BYTES PER LINE
        MVI      C,4     ; NUMBER OF RECORDS
PLOOP   CALL     HEXLINE ! CALL COCRLF
        CALL     HEXLINE ! CALL COCRLF
        CALL     COCRLF
        DCR  C ! JNZ PLOOP
        CALL     COCRLF ! CALL COCRLF
        POP      B
        RET
;
; COMMON SUBROUTINES
;
        COSUBM
        HEXSUBM
        DPSUBM
        BIOSM
        END
```

FIGURE 15-3 (Continued)

than ALLDIR. There is no benefit in reading the directory this way, but the same techniques could be used in a program that updated the directory. You could write a program that recovered an erased file by restoring a user code to the first byte of the file's extent records, for instance. Example 15-2 shows the output of READIR.

The WRITE Function. The WRITE function of the BIOS requests that it take the standard record in the buffer and write it into the record position addressed by previous calls on the BIOS. The record is taken by the BIOS and started on its way to the disk.

Sector Buffers and Prereading. The BIOS might have to do two disk operations for a write. When a sector contains more than one record, the BIOS must first read the correct sector, then move the record into it, and finally write the sector back to disk. The initial read of a sector is called a preread, and isn't always needed. Also, the sector write sometimes can be deferred until it is forced by later events.

EXAMPLE 15-2
The output of READIR is identical to that of ALLDIR, save that it shows never used entries. These are completely filled with E5h, the usual formatter fill-character.

```
A>readir b:
Physical directory entries, drive B

00 48 45 58 44 49 52 20 20 43 4F 4D 00 00 00 04    .HEXDIR  COM....
02 00 00 00 00 00 00 00 00 00 00 00 00 00 00 00    ................

00 50 52 49 4E 54 20 20 20 43 4F 4D 00 00 00 80    .PRINT   COM....
03 00 04 00 05 00 06 00 07 00 08 00 09 00 0A 00    ................

00 50 52 49 4E 54 20 20 20 43 4F 4D 01 00 00 0E    .PRINT   COM....
0B 00 00 00 00 00 00 00 00 00 00 00 00 00 00 00    ................

00 48 45 58 44 49 52 20 20 41 53 4D 00 00 00 0D    .HEXDIR  ASM....
0C 00 00 00 00 00 00 00 00 00 00 00 00 00 00 00    ................

E5 45 52 41 53 45 44 20 20 46 49 4C 00 00 00 80    eERASED  FIL....
0D 00 0E 00 0F 00 10 00 11 00 12 00 13 00 14 00    ................

E5 45 52 41 53 45 44 20 20 46 49 4C 01 00 00 80    eERASED  FIL....
15 00 16 00 17 00 18 00 19 00 1A 00 1B 00 1C 00    ................

E5 45 52 41 53 45 44 20 20 46 49 4C 02 00 00 7E    eERASED  FIL....
1D 00 1E 00 1F 00 20 00 21 00 22 00 23 00 24 00    ...... .!.".#.$.

02 55 53 45 52 2D 32 20 20 46 49 4C 00 00 00 80    .USER-2  FIL....
25 00 26 00 27 00 28 00 29 00 2A 00 2B 00 2C 00    %..´.(.).*.+.,.

02 55 53 45 52 2D 32 20 20 46 49 4C 01 00 00 0E    .USER-2  FIL....
2D 00 00 00 00 00 00 00 00 00 00 00 00 00 00 00    -...............

E5 E5 E5 E5 E5 E5 E5 E5 E5 E5 E5 E5 E5 E5 E5 E5    eeeeeeeeeeeeeeee
E5 E5 E5 E5 E5 E5 E5 E5 E5 E5 E5 E5 E5 E5 E5 E5    eeeeeeeeeeeeeeee

E5 E5 E5 E5 E5 ..... (display continues for many lines)

A>_
```

Deferred Writes. Most program output is sequential; there is a high probability that the next write will be directed to the next record in the same sector. In that case deferring the sector write will allow the BIOS to avoid the next preread. On the other hand, if the program alternates reading and writing, the read requests will force out the written sectors so that every write requires a preread and every read forces a write. In that event three disk operations will be done for every two program accesses. This could be avoided by the use of two sector buffers, one for reading and one for writing, but most BIOSes can't afford that much space.

Write Parameters. The WRITE function takes a parameter in register A. That parameter is an indication from the BDOS to the BIOS of the purpose of the write operation. The BIOS can increase the performance and the reliability of the system by recognizing this code. If you write a program that calls on the WRITE function, you must be sure to provide a valid parameter.

Write 2: Unallocated Data. When the write parameter is 2, the record is the first to be written to its allocation block. An allocation block usually corresponds to one or more whole sectors. Usually the sectors that comprise an allocation block are contiguous (logically contiguous; they may span a track boundary, and skew must be considered). When the BIOS knows it is writing the first record of an allocation block, it can skip prereading that sector; the other records of the sector (and of the allocation block) can't have any useful data in them.

Writes Following a Write 2. Write 2 occurs only for the first record of a block; all other records of the block are passed under write 0. The BIOS can verify that each successive write follows sequentially on the prior one. As long as they do, and as long as no reads intervene to force out the buffer contents, the BIOS can collect and write sectors without prereading. The *CP/M 2.2 Alteration Guide* contains an example of this logic.

Write 0: Ordinary Data. When the BDOS is handling any record other than the first of an allocation block (or a direct access write to any record), it passes write parameter 0. If the BIOS finds that the record continues an unbroken series from the last write 2, it can avoid a preread. Otherwise it must read the sector into which the record falls and place the record among the others in the sector. It may then defer writing the sector back to disk in hopes that the next write will fall in the same sector.

Performance Implications. Any command program can be designed to make the most of write buffering. A read will break the chain of buffered writes; so will a write to a different file. Best performance is realized when the program reads and writes data in long bursts. Only a single large buffer is needed for this. The program either may read one record at a time while accumulating output in the large buffer, or it may read records to fill the large buffer and then write single records as they are produced. Either way, it transfers a large amount of data for each file before switching to the other.

Write 1: Directory Data. If the write parameter is 1, then the record is part of the disk directory. A preread has to be done. The sector should be written immediately; a directory write should never be deferred. If the sector write is deferred, a reset signal or program error can prevent the data from reaching the directory. That risk is tolerable for file data—if the program bombs or is aborted, the files are expected to be incomplete—but it is not tolerable for directory data. The sector may remain in the buffer so that a preread can be avoided in the unlikely event that the next access addresses the same sector, but the data should be transferred to disk at once.

THE BIOS SERIAL I/O FUNCTIONS

The BIOS functions that deal with serial I/O are needed to make the BDOS (and all programs) device independent. It is up to the BIOS to direct the flow of serial data according to the current device assignments. With one unimportant exception, all of the serial I/O functions provided by the BIOS are also provided as service requests through the BDOS. There are no advantages, and several disadvantages, to calling directly on the BIOS for serial I/O.

Functions for Logical Devices

The BIOS provides seven functions that deal with the four logical devices of CP/M. Three of these are related to CON:, the logical console; two support LST:, the logical printer; and the remaining two operate the logical reader and punch. Example 15-3 shows the code of these services as it would appear in a typical BIOS.

Console Functions. The three console functions are CONIN, CONOUT, and CONST. CONIN must determine which device is currently assigned as the console, get a byte from it, and return that byte in the A register. It is CONIN's responsibility to clear bit 7, the parity bit, of a received byte to zero.

The CONOUT function is given a character in the C register. It must find out which device is currently assigned as the console and transmit the byte to it. The BDOS always clears bit 7 of the byte before calling on CONOUT.

EXAMPLE 15-3
Code from a typical BIOS, showing support of logical I/O devices. Note the code for the BAT: device. BAT: is useful when a serial input device for RDR: exists (a modem, for example).

```
; THE FOLLOWING ROUTINES DO LOGICAL I/O ACCORDING TO THE IOBYTE.
; 'CRT' IS THE H19 TERMINAL DRIVEN FROM THE 2810 CPU SERIAL PORT,
; 'LPR' IS THE DIABLO 1650 KSR ON THE GODBOUT BOARD AT 2A/2B.
; 'AUX' IS A SERIAL DEVICE ON THE GODBOUT BOARD AT 28/29
;
;
; ROUTINE CONI IS THE CONSOLE INPUT ROUTINE CALLED FROM THE BIOS
; JUMP TABLE UP FRONT.  IT ADDS THE PARITY-STRIP THAT CP/M REQUIRES.
; BIOS ROUTINES CALL 'CI' STRAIGHT.
;
CONI:   CALL    CI      ; GET THE NEXT CHARACTER
        ANI     7FH     ; STRIP OFF THE PARITY BIT
        RET
```

EXAMPLE 15-3 (Continued)

```
;
CONMSK  EQU     03H      ; MASK TO STRIP OUT CON ASSIGNMENT
CONMID  EQU     02H      ; PIVOT VALUE FOR COMPARING
RDRMSK  EQU     0CH      ; MASK TO STRIP OUT RDR ASSIGNMENT
RDRMID  EQU     08H      ; PIVOT VALUE FOR COMPARING
PUNMSK  EQU     30H      ; ETC..
PUNMID  EQU     20H
LSTMSK  EQU     0C0H
LSTMID  EQU     80H
;
CO:     LDA     IOBYTE   ; CONSOLE OUTPUT
        ANI     CONMSK   ; ISOLATE CONSOLE ASSSIGNMENT
        CPI     CONMID
        JM      CRTOUT   ; CON = TTY,CRT = H19
        JNZ     LPROUT   ; CON = UC1 = 1650
;                          CON = BAT = FALL INTO LIST OUT
LO:     LDA     IOBYTE   ; LIST OUTPUT
        ANI     LSTMSK   ; ISOLATE LIST ASSIGNMENT
        JZ      NULOUT   ; LST = TTY = NULL OUTPUT
        CPI     LSTMID
        JM      CRTOUT   ; LST = CRT = H19
        JMP     LPROUT   ; LST = LPT,UL1 = 1650
;
CSTS:   LDA     IOBYTE   ; CONSOLE STATUS
        ANI     CONMSK   ; ISOLATE CONSOLE ASSIGNMENT
        CPI     CONMID
        JM      CRTIST   ; CON = TTY,CRT = H19
        JNZ     LPRIST   ; CON = UC1 = 1650
;                          CON = BAT = FALL INTO RDR STATUS
BATST:  LDA     IOBYTE   ; (USED ONLY FOR CON: = BAT:)
        ANI     RDRMSK   ; ISOLATE READER ASSIGNMENT
        JZ      IOER     ; RDR = TTY = NUL INVALID FOR BAT:
        CPI     RDRMID
        JM      AUXIST   ; RDR = PTR = AUX PORT
        JZ      LPRIST   ; RDR = UR1 = 1650
        JMP     CRTIST   ; RDR = UR2 = H19
CI:     LDA     IOBYTE   ; CONSOLE INPUT
        ANI     CONMSK   ; ISOLATE CONSOLE ASSIGNMENT
        CPI     CONMID
        JM      CRTIN    ; CON = TTY,CRT = H19
        JNZ     LPRIN    ; CON = UC1 = 1650
                         ; CON = BAT = USE RDR..
        LDA     IOBYTE   ; ..IF IT'S VALID
        ANI     RDRMSK
        JZ      IOER     ; RDR = TTY = NUL WRONG FOR BAT:
;
RI:     LDA     IOBYTE   ; READER INPUT
        ANI     RDRMSK   ; ISOLATE READER ASSIGNMENT
        JZ      NULIN    ; RDR = TTY = NUL DEVICE
        CPI     RDRMID
        JM      AUXIN    ; RDR = PTR = AUX DEVICE
        JZ      LPRIN    ; RDR = UR1 = 1650
        JMP     CRTIN    ; RDR = UR2 = H19
;
LSTAT:  LDA     IOBYTE   ; LIST OUTPUT STATUS
        ANI     LSTMSK   ; ISOLATE LIST DEVICE ASSIGNMENT
        JZ      NULOST   ; LST = TTY = NULL DEVICE
        CPI     LSTMID
        JM      CRTOST   ; LST = CRT = H19
        JMP     LPROST   ; LST = LPT,UL1 = 1650
;
PO:     LDA     IOBYTE   ; PUNCH OUTPUT
        ANI     PUNMSK   ; ISOLATE PUNCH ASSIGNMENT
        JZ      NULOUT   ; PUN = TTY = NULL DEVICE
        CPI     PUNMID
        JM      AUXOUT   ; PUN = PTP = AUX DEVICE
        JZ      LPROUT   ; PUN = UP1 = 1650
        JMP     CRTOUT   ; PUN = UP2 = H19
```

The CONST function is called to discover the input status of the console device, that is, whether it has a byte ready for input or not. CONST is expected to return FFh in the A register if a byte is ready, and 00h if one is not.

Console I/O: BDOS versus BIOS. Hobbyist magazines often publish CP/M programs that perform console I/O using these BIOS functions. This is lamentable. The BIOS functions provide none of the user services that are part of the similar service requests provided by the BDOS. Console output sent through CONOUT cannot be suspended with control-s nor can it be copied to the printer with control-p. Console input obtained through CONIN cannot be supplied by XSUB, nor can the user correct typing errors or cancel the program with control-c. The overhead imposed by the BDOS is trivial compared with the human advantages to be gained by using service requests for console I/O.

In the last chapter we noted that control-s and -p aren't always effective during BDOS operations either. That doesn't affect the main point. Control-p can be hit before a command is started. Then any BDOS output the command does will be copied to the printer, but no BIOS output will be.

Printer Functions. The BIOS provides two functions for the logical printer. The first is the LIST function. It is passed a byte in register C. LIST must find out which device is assigned to LST: and send the byte to it. The BDOS always sets the parity bit to 0 before calling the LIST function.

The LISTST function is a convenience for Digital Research's background print utility, DESPOOL. That program gets control whenever a console input service request is issued. It needs to know if the printer is ready to accept a byte or not. If it is ready, DESPOOL will send a byte to the printer before letting the current service request continue. LISTST has the job of finding out whether or not the device now assigned to LST: is ready to receive a byte. LISTST returns the same signals in register A as CONST does.

Reader and Punch Functions. The CP/M BIOS has an entry called READER, which returns a byte from the device currently assigned to RDR:, and an entry called PUNCH, which takes a byte and sends it on to the device assigned to PUN:. The rules for the two entries are identical to the rules for CONIN and CONOUT respectively.

Reader and Punch Under MP/M. Under MP/M these two entries will be null, consisting only of RET instructions. MP/M does not have support for the logical devices RDR: and PUN:. Instead it defines all serial devices as "consoles." Under MP/M, a program that would, under CP/M, use the RDR: and PUN: logical devices must attach a separate process whose console is the device to be operated. That subordinate process can be device independent as the CP/M program can, but the program that uses this technique will be system dependent; it will only work under MP/M.

BIOS Support of the Physical Devices

A BIOS may be written to ignore device assignments. The BDOS calls on the BIOS function that corresponds to the logical device it wants. The BIOS may have a single, fixed mapping from these logical devices to physical devices. In such a system the use of STAT to display and change device assignments is still possible, but it has no effect.

Use of the IOBYTE. It is preferable that the BIOS recognize and support device assignment. When this is done, the code of each logical device function does nothing but determine which physical device is needed and branch to the driver for that device. The active device assignments are encoded in the IOBYTE at 03h in Low Storage. The code in Example 15-3 shows how that byte can be used by the logical device functions. The sequence of tests and branches in these routines determines the meaning of the device assignments. For example, the design of the LIST routine in Example 15-3 determines that if LST: is assigned to TTY:, printer output is to be thrown away; if to CRT:, then printer output is to go to the terminal (not the logical console but the physical terminal). If the assignment is to either PRT: or UL1:, then the output is to go to the physical printer.

Device Drivers. Each physical device is given one or more driver routines of its own. These routines—rarely more than half a dozen instructions—receive control from the logical device routines and return directly to the caller of the BIOS. Example 15-4 shows a typical set of physical device routines such as would be called by the logical device code of Example 15-3.

The device routines don't care what logical device they were called for. The CRTIN routine of Example 15-4 may be called by either the CONIN or the READER routines of Example 15-3. The CRTOUT routine may be called by any of the CONOUT, LIST, or PUNCH routines, depending on the current assignments. A device such as a terminal, which may be assigned to either list or console, must have both an input status routine and an output status routine.

CUSTOMIZING THE BIOS

The BIOS is prepared like any other assembly language program, although its testing requires some care. There are usually a number of ways in which a BIOS can be improved. Such improvements are satisfying, but must be made with care because the whole system depends on their correctness.

Changing the Storage Size

The BIOS Base Address. The simplest BIOS change is a change in the size of working storage. The BIOS resides in the highest possible locations in storage. It is prepared as an absolute assembly with its origin set high enough that the end of the BIOS is as high as possible in working storage. The BIOS base address must allow for the buffers it needs, and for the presence of any fixed ROM or disk hardware windows in storage.

Changing the Base. Probably your BIOS looks much like the example shown in Appendix C of the *CP/M Alteration Guide*, with features from the sector blocking code

EXAMPLE 15-4

Code from a typical BIOS shows the drivers for physical devices, including null ones. Details of device handling will be different in every installation.

```
; THE I/O DRIVERS START HERE.  EACH DATA PATH HAS TWO ROUTINES:
; A STATUS ROUTINE AND A TRANSFER ROUTINE.  INPUT PATHS HAVE A
; ROUTINE 'XXXIST' (INPUT STATUS) AND A ROUTINE 'XXXIN'.  OUTPUT
; PATHS HAVE 'XXXOST' (OUTPUT STATUS) AND 'XXXOUT' -- XXX BEING
; THE DEVICE MONICKER IN ALL CASES.
;
AUXDATA EQU     28H      ; MODEM OR WHATEVER
AUXSTAT EQU     29H
LPRDATA EQU     2AH      ; DIABLO 1650 KSR
LPRSTAT EQU     2BH
;
SERDTR  EQU     04H      ; DATA TERMINAL READY BIT
SERTXBE EQU     01H      ; TRANSMIT BUFFER EMPTY
SERRXBF EQU     02H      ; RECEIVE BUFFER FULL
;
;  THESE ARE THE DRIVERS FOR THE NULL DEVICE
;
NULOST  EQU     $        ; NULL OUTPUT ALWAYS OK
NULIST  ORI     0FFH     ; NULL INPUT ALWAYS READY
        RET
NULIN   MVI     1AH      ; NULL INPUT ALWAYS CTL-Z (EOF)
NULOUT  EQU     $        ; NULL OUTPUT IS A NO-OP
        RET
;
;  THESE ARE THE DRIVERS FOR THE CRT, USING VENDOR'S CODE.
;
CRTIST  IN      SLSTAT   ; GET 8250 LINE STATUS
        ANI     RXRDY    ; RECEIVE BUFFER READY?
        RZ               ;  (NOPE, EXIT A=00)
        ORI     0FFH     ; YES, A=FF
        RET
;
CRTIN   CALL    CRTIST   ; WAIT FOR DATA READY
        JZ      CRTIN
        IN      SDATA    ; READ IT
        RET              ; EXIT, A=XX
;
CRTOST  IN      SLSTAT   ; GET 8250 LINE STATUS
        ANI     TXMTY    ; CHECK TRANSMIT BUFFER
        RZ               ;  (STILL WORKING, A=00)
        ORI     0FFH     ; BUFFER AVAILABLE,
        RET              ;  A=FF
;
CRTOUT  CALL    CRTOST   ; WAIT FOR BUFFER EMPTY
        JZ      CRTOUT
        MOV     A,C      ; OUTBYTE IS IN C
        OUT     SDATA    ;   SEND IT
        RET
;
;  THESE ARE THE DRIVERS FOR THE AUXILIARY GODBOUT PORT
;
AUXIST  IN      AUXSTAT ; GET UART STATUS
        ANI     SERRXBF ; CHECK RECEIVE BUFFER
        RZ              ;  (NO DATA, A=00)
        ORI     0FFH    ; BYTE READY
        RET
;
AUXIN   CALL    AUXIST  ; WAIT FOR A BYTE
        JZ      AUXIN
        IN      AUXDATA ; GET IT
        RET
;
AUXOST  IN      AUXSTAT ; GET UART STATUS
```

EXAMPLE 15-4 (Continued)

```
         ANI      SERDTR  ; CHECK DATA TERMINAL READY
         JZ       AUXOST1 ; (SERDTR=0 MEANS 'READY')
         XRA      A       ; DEVICE UNREADY OR BUSY
         RET              ;   RETURN A=00
AUXOST1  IN       AUXSTAT ; DEVICE IS READY, IS UART?
         ANI      SERTXBE ; CHECK XMIT BUFFER
         RZ               ; (STILL SENDING, A=00)
         ORI      0FFH    ; ALL OK, RETURN A=FF
         RET
;
AUXOUT   CALL     AUXOST  ; WAIT FOR ALL-CLEAR
         JZ       AUXOUT
         MOV      A,C     ; SET UP DATA,
         OUT      AUXDATA ;  SEND IT.
         RET
         PAGE
;  THESE ARE THE DRIVERS FOR THE PORT TIED TO THE 1650
;
LPRIST   IN       LPRSTAT ; GET UART STATUS
         ANI      SERRXBF ; CHECK RECEIVE BUFFER
         RZ               ;  (NO DATA, A=00)
         ORI      0FFH    ; BYTE READY
         RET
;
LPRIN    CALL     LPRIST  ; WAIT FOR A BYTE
         JZ       LPRIN
         IN       LPRDATA ; GET IT
         RET
;
LPROST   IN       LPRSTAT ; GET UART STATUS
         ANI      SERDTR  ; CHECK DATA TERMINAL READY
         JZ       LPROST1 ; (SERDTR=0 MEANS 'READY')
         XRA      A       ; DEVICE UNREADY OR BUSY
         RET              ;   RETURN A=00
LPROST1  IN       LPRSTAT ; DEVICE IS READY, IS UART?
         ANI      SERTXBE ; CHECK XMIT BUFFER
         RZ               ; (STILL SENDING, A=00)
         ORI      0FFH    ; ALL OK, RETURN A=FF
         RET
LPROUT   CALL     LPROST  ; WAIT FOR ALL-CLEAR
         JZ       LPROUT
         MOV      A,C     ; SET UP DATA,
         OUT      LPRDATA ;  SEND IT.
         RET
```

of Appendix G in that book. If that is the case, then all you need to do to change the origin of the BIOS is to change the value of the equate label msize at the front of the source program, and reassemble. If the author of the BIOS didn't follow the Digital Research examples, then you must determine what the assembly origin ought to be and change it. In either case be careful that all of the BIOS, including the buffers and variables at the end of the assembly, fits inside of storage. Both ASM and MAC will allow the assembly location counter to overflow past FFFFh without giving you any warning.

Changing the Disk Functions

The disk functions of a BIOS make an interesting and educational study, but there is rarely any need to alter them. If you do so, you may find it hard to convince your dealer that you have a problem with the disks. The dealer may demand that you demonstrate a failure using a stock BIOS.

Disk Error Reporting. One area that can sometimes be improved with little alteration of the code is that of disk error reporting. Most BIOSes don't display any information about a disk error; they simply tell the BDOS that one occurred. You may be able to find a place to stow the track, sector, and command of the operation that failed so that you can retrieve them with DDT after a failure. You could add code to display that information on the terminal when an error happens, or you might prefer to write a command that retrieves and displays the stored information after the fact.

Soft-Error Statistics. If there is room in the BIOS to store it, it would be nice to keep a count of the number of recoverable errors that occur on each drive. A command could then be written that would display and clear the count, or add it to a file so that you could spot a trend of increasing error frequency and relate it to a specific drive or diskette.

Deleting Unused Tables. Some BIOSes contain tables and code to handle many different kinds of disks. If you have only a few disk types, you can gain space in the BIOS by deleting the unneeded tables. Rather than remove the statements that define them you should use conditional assembly. Surround the unwanted tables and the code that names them with IF statements controlled by equate variables with meaningful names. Then you can change the equates to bring the tables back into the BIOS later.

Changing the Serial I/O Functions

The serial I/O functions must be changed whenever a new device is added to the system and whenever you change the address or controlling board of a serial port. These changes are easy to make and, since they don't affect the integrity of disk files, they are safer and cause less anxiety than disk changes.

IOBYTE Support. There are a lot of convenience features you could add to the serial device functions. An obvious change is to make the BIOS support device assignment, if it doesn't already do so.

Printer Handshaking. If your printer support doesn't shake hands with the printer, you should look into making it do so. Most serial ports can be made to pass the state of the Data Terminal Ready line through to your code, and most printers can be set up to report their status on it. It's very nice to know that when the printer runs out of paper, printing will stop until paper is loaded, then pick up smoothly from where it left off. There is a minor performance advantage in having printer data transferred at the printer's maximum rate, with the BIOS waiting whenever the printer's buffer is full. The advantage is minor because the average transmission rate will be exactly the rate at which the printer puts letters on paper. Only during the last buffer's worth of data is the processor free for other commands.

Interrupt-Driven Terminal I/O. One very useful enhancement is to make the terminal into a buffered, interrupt-driven device. This requires a fair amount of code, perhaps more code than will fit in the BIOS. The cold start function must set up the interrupt vectors and condition the terminal controller for interrupts. There must be an interrupt handler to receive and buffer data, and the output code must send the data if the terminal is idle or buffer the data for the interrupt routine to send if the terminal is active. The user must be given some signal—perhaps the break key, which has no use under CP/M—to cancel any characters typed but not yet processed.

Once this has been done an experienced user can type commands ahead of the system. This is a feature that must be used to be appreciated, but once you've had it you'll never want to be without it.

Testing BIOS Changes

Unless a BIOS change is very simple—a change in the size of storage or the address of an I/O port—you'd be wise to test the change before generating a new system. It isn't easy to give the BIOS a thorough test, but it isn't hard to give it a simple shakedown that will turn up any gross errors. The following technique will work for BIOS changes that don't affect the action of the console.

The testing method relies on the fact that all BIOS calls are made through the BIOS entry table. Prepare a small driver program to issue the service requests that will trigger the changed code of the BIOS. Append the altered BIOS to the end of the driver program source, with its origin set just past the end of the driver code. Assemble the combined program.

Load the assembled driver and the test BIOS under DDT. Use DDT to alter some of the jump instructions in the real BIOS entry table to point to the corresponding entries of the test BIOS. Use the DDT Go command to run the driver program, with breakpoints in the test BIOS (the SID and ZSID debuggers are useful in this case, for they allow you to set multiple, permanent breakpoints). Step the test BIOS through the changed code. At the end of the test don't forget to do a cold start in order to refresh the real BIOS entry table.

SYSTEM GENERATION

When you change the BIOS or the size of working storage, you must generate a new image of the Monitor and store it on the bootstrap tracks of a disk. This is a fairly simple process provided you understand what each step is meant to accomplish.

Be aware that some system vendors have their own versions of the system generation procedure. We can't cover all the variations here. We'll look at how a standard system generation is done. You'll have to find out what extra aids or impediments your system's vendor has added to the procedure.

The Bootstrap Tracks

The aim of system generation is to get a modified version of the Monitor—CCP, BDOS, and BIOS—written onto the bootstrap tracks of a diskette. It's a simple thing in concept but complicated by diskette format.

Standard Bootstrap. The standard diskette for CP/M is a single-density, 8-inch one with twenty-six, 128-byte sectors per track. The first two tracks are always used for bootstrap on such a diskette. That provides 52∗128, or 6656, bytes of space for the image of the Monitor. The standard Monitor comes very near to filling that space.

The Problem of BIOS Size. When a BIOS expands with the addition of sector-buffering logic and IOBYTE support, it often pushes the Monitor size above 6656 bytes. Note that this is only the result of code size. The extra buffer space required for sector buffering affects the location of the Monitor in storage, but the buffers aren't recorded on the bootstrap tracks. All vendors have their own solutions to the problem.

The No-Buffering Solution. Some vendors keep the BIOS simple (and thus small) by handling only 128-byte sectors regardless of disk density. Physical sectors map directly to record numbers. Unfortunately that violates the IBM standard for double density and often leads to reliability problems with double-density recording. It also causes disk incompatibility, as vendors who follow the IBM standard won't read 128-byte sectors at double density.

The Double-Load BIOS Solution. Another solution is to make cold start a two-step operation. The Monitor on the bootstrap tracks is recorded with a small, simple BIOS. The full-function BIOS is recorded together with a relocation program as an ordinary .COM file. The precoded command in the CCP is set up to invoke the command that loads the larger BIOS. During cold start the Monitor loads with a simple BIOS. The precoded command causes the full BIOS to be loaded as a command. The command relocates the BIOS dynamically and moves it into place. The problem is solved, but two disadvantages follow. The full-BIOS command must be present on every bootable diskette, and a cold start (but not a warm one) takes longer.

The Double-Density Solution. An IBM standard double-density diskette has a single-density first track with twenty-six, 128-byte sectors. Its second track is double-density with the number and size of sectors desired. The extra capacity of the second track is usually enough to allow the full Monitor to fit the bootstrap tracks. Systems that use the double-load solution with single-density diskettes may not need it on double-density ones.

Double-Density Track 0. Some vendors format all tracks of the diskette to the desired density. That gives ample space on the two bootstrap tracks, and simplifies the

BIOS as well, for it needn't treat track 0 as a special case. However, such diskettes aren't "IBM standard" (although the vendor may choose to overlook this fine point in the documentation). More to the point, diskettes from "IBM standard" systems can't be read by these systems because they expect the entire diskette to be recorded at the density used on track 0.

The ROM Solution. Some systems incorporate a ROM monitor permanently located in the highest addresses. Since it's there, the BIOS may as well make use of it. Doing so may take enough code out of the BIOS to allow it to fit on any bootstrap tracks.

Other Configurations. None of the foregoing applies to systems that boot from 5-inch diskettes, or from double-sided diskettes of either diameter. Here the arrangement of bootstrap tracks is entirely up to the vendor, although the bootstrap tracks will always be the lowest numbered so that the OFF value of the Disk Parameter Block can account for them.

The MOVCPM File

The CCP and BDOS are distributed as part of a remarkable command called MOVCPM. This command is central to system generation, and we must look at it in detail—first as a file, then in execution as a command. We'll give addresses in MOVCPM as it is loaded in the TPA (assuming a standard TPA at 0100h).

The Function of MOVCPM. The purpose of MOVCPM is to prepare and leave behind in storage an image of the CCP and BDOS, relocated for the storage size of the system. That image can then be written to the bootstrap tracks by a different program.

The Executable Part. MOVCPM contains several parts. At its lowest addresses lies an executable program whose function is to relocate the addresses in the CCP/BDOS image to a different origin. When we speak of MOVCPM as a command we'll be speaking of this program.

The Bit Map. Following its executable part MOVCPM contains a bit map with 1 bit for each byte of the CCP/BDOS image. Where a bit is 1 the corresponding byte is the most significant byte of an address. Relocation is done by adding a page (256-byte unit) offset to each byte of the image that is marked in the map. (The same relocation method is used in MP/M, where such files are given the .PRL—page relocatable—filetype.)

Boot Loader Space. From addresses 0900h through 09FFh, MOVCPM contains space in which the vendor may place a bootstrap loader program. The final Monitor image will be written to disk beginning from 0900h; this space determines the contents of the first and second bootstrap sectors.

Not all boot loaders fill two sectors. If the vendor can fit the loader into 128 bytes, it is placed in 0980h to 09FFh, leaving 0900h through 097Fh cleared to zero. This causes MOVCPM to take special action, as we'll see.

The Vendor's Loader. The vendor will have placed a loader in your copy of MOVCPM. It is an absolute assembly with the origin required by the hardware ROM that loads it, usually 00h or 80h.

The CCP and BDOS Images. From 0A00h through 1FFFh (1600h, or 5632 decimal, bytes), the MOVCPM file contains the image of the CCP and BDOS. The programs have been assembled to some origin. The standard origin is 3400h. The vendor may have replaced the standard programs with programs assembled to a lower origin in order to make room for a larger BIOS. It is usual to move the Monitor down by 2 KB (800h bytes) to make room in storage for sector buffers. Therefore, your CCP/BDOS image may have an origin of 2C00h, 800h lower than the standard.

The Distributed BIOS. At 2000h, following the CCP and BDOS images, MOVCPM contains a BIOS. This may be the BIOS that you can read in Appendix B of the *CP/M Alteration Guide*. If so, it is useless in your system and of no interest. On the other hand, your vendor may have installed a BIOS customized for that vendor's standard hardware configuration. In that case it may be perfectly usable.

The MOVCPM Command

The form of the MOVCPM command is

MOVCPM *size flag*

The first operand, *size*, states the size of storage as a decimal number of kilobytes. It may be given as an asterisk, meaning "measure the present size." The *flag* operand is either an asterisk, or omitted entirely. We'll deal with it later.

When you issue the MOVCPM command, the file is loaded into the TPA and given control as usual.

Serial Number Checks. The command compares the CP/M serial number in the command against the serial number in the active BDOS in high storage. If they aren't the same, it issues an error message and ends. MOVCPM contains safeguards so that it can't be stepped past these checks under DDT. The result is that MOVCPM for one person's system can only be executed under that person's Monitor. You can't run your copy of MOVCPM under a Monitor booted from someone else's disk.

Compressing a Small Loader. If the space from 0900h through 097Fh contains zeros, MOVCPM now copies the code image, from 097Fh to the end, downward by 80h bytes. This ensures that all bootstrap sectors will be in use. If your loader is only 128 bytes (many are), the resulting addresses are

Loader:	0900h to 097Fh
CCP/BDOS:	0980h to 1F7Fh
BIOS:	1F80h for length of BIOS

Relocating CCP and BDOS. MOVCPM uses its first operand to determine the desired system size. If that was given as an asterisk, it tests each byte of storage until it finds one that can't be modified and uses that size.

The command scans the bit map and relocates each marked byte by the difference (in page units) between the standard system size of 24K and the specified size. Note that this relocation factor is independent of the assembly origin of the BDOS and CCP. They presumably are assembled to an origin that leaves adequate BIOS space in a 24K system; the relocation factor is the amount by which they have to be moved up in order to have the same relationship to the end of the existing system.

Modifying the Log-on Message. The MOVCPM command searches through the BIOS area beyond the BDOS image. If it can find the character constant k CP/M vers 2.2, CR, LF, it places two decimal digits—the value of the system size—in the 2 bytes preceding the string. This nice little service sets up the log-on message issued by the BIOS (xxk CP/M vers 2.2) to display the correct storage size.

The Second Operand of MOVCPM. The second, *flag*, operand of MOVCPM determines what it will do after relocating the CCP and BDOS images. If the second operand is omitted, it will copy those images to the proper place in storage so that they are located at the correct address for their new origin. MOVCPM will then jump to the cold start entry point of the newly moved BIOS. Unless your vendor has installed a customized BIOS in MOVCPM, this is not likely to produce any useful result.

The second operand should always be given as an asterisk. That tells MOVCPM to terminate with a warm start, leaving the relocated images behind in storage.

Saving the Relocated CCP and BDOS

After MOVCPM terminates working storage from 0900h through 1F80h contains the image of the bootstrap loader, CCP, and BDOS that you want in your system. It lacks only your BIOS. It should be saved at once with the SAVE command:

```
save 31 name.COM
```

Now you can retrieve those images with DDT. These two steps (MOVCPM and SAVE) can be done once when you receive CP/M; they needn't be repeated unless the size of storage, and hence the origin, is changed.

Adding the BIOS

You have assembled and tested the new BIOS. It has been assembled to the absolute origin it will have when the system is running. All that remains is to attach it to the images of the CCP and BDOS, and put the combined program image on disk.

Load the CCP/BDOS Image. Load the relocated CCP and BIOS (the saved .COM file) under DDT. The BIOS will go into this image beginning at 1F80h and extend for some length. Use the DDT fill command to fill that area with some known value: 00h, or perhaps E5h.

Compute the Load Offset. Your BIOS has its assembled origin, but you want to load it into storage at 1F80h. Use the DDT hex command to find the difference between the two addresses:

h1f80,*origin*

supplying the origin of the BIOS. The difference between the two numbers is the offset that you want DDT to use when loading the .HEX file that contains the BIOS. The difference will be a large hexadecimal number. Load the file:

i*biosname*.hex
r*difference*

Then use the DDT display and list commands to make sure that the BIOS image is in fact now in storage from 1F80 to its end.

The Precoded Command. It's now time to install a precoded CCP command if you'll use one. Use DDT to display the 129 bytes beginning at CCP+7 (0987h-0A07h with a small loader, or 0A07 to 0A87 with a 256-byte loader). The byte at CCP+7 will contain the length of the command string in hex. The command itself is entered into the buffer beginning at CCP+8. It may be 127 bytes long, and must end with a byte of 00h (not counted in the length). The easiest way to prepare the command is as an assembly program:

```
CCP        EQU  0980H   ; — or 0A00h?
           ORG  CCP+7
           DB   CMDEND-CMDSTART
CMDSTART   DB   'THIS IS THE COMMAND'
CMDEND     DB   0
           END
```

Assemble the program beforehand, then load its .HEX file with DDT.

Compute the End Address. Examine the BIOS listing and find the end address that encompasses all code and initialized values but which excludes uninitialized buffers and tables (they won't be written to disk). Add the *difference* value to find the location of the end in the storage image. It will usually agree with the end address displayed by DDT after it loaded the BIOS file.

Save the Monitor Image. Once again, save the merged images as a .COM file. Use the number of pages that will save all of the image through the end of the BIOS.

The SYSGEN Command

SYSGEN's Sources. The purpose of the SYSGEN program (supplied by your vendor) is to write an image of the Monitor onto the reserved tracks of a disk. SYSGEN will obtain the Monitor image in one of two (or possibly three) ways. Most SYSGEN programs take no command operand. Usually the command requests the letter of a drive that contains a diskette from whose bootstrap tracks it can read a Monitor image. If the question is answered with a null line, the command assumes that the image is already in storage where MOVCPM leaves it (0900h and up).

The SYSGEN distributed to vendors by Digital Research has the ability to take a fileref as its operand. If a fileref is given, that SYSGEN will load the named file at 0900h and use it as the Monitor image. You might experiment with your vendor's SYSGEN to see if it has this ability.

Using SYSGEN. The first SYSGEN is done as follows. Prepare a new diskette and mount it. Use DDT to load the saved Monitor file into storage. End DDT. Call SYSGEN and tell it (with a null response) that the image is already in storage. Give it the letter of the drive where the new diskette was mounted. It copies the image, beginning at 0900h, onto the bootstrap tracks of that diskette. The diskette can then be put in the A-drive; a cold start will load the new Monitor.

Later SYSGENs. Once the Monitor is on a disk and has been tested, that disk can be used as the source disk in other SYSGEN operations, as described in Chapter 8. You've changed the Monitor, and the latest version should be transferred to all the bootable diskettes in the library. That's a tedious job; defer it until you are quite sure that the new BIOS works well and no further changes are needed.

Glossary

Address: The location of data in file storage or working storage. Usually an integer that is the index of the storage unit (the byte or the record) in which the addressed data begins.

ALGOL (ALGOrithmic Language): A programming language designed by an international committee in the early 1960's. ALGOL introduced many fundamental concepts to the field. Widely available in Europe but little used in the United States, where it came just too late to supplant FORTRAN.

Algorithm: A step-by-step plan for the solution of a problem. See the first section of Volume I of Knuth's *Art of Computer Programming* for a detailed history and definition of this useful word.

Allocation Block: The smallest unit of disk storage allocated to a file by the CP/M or MP/M Monitor. Ranges in size from 1 to 16 KB.

ANSI (American National Standards Institute): The committee that oversees voluntary manufacturing standards in the United States. ANSI reviews and publishes standards documents written by committees that are usually administered by industry or professional organizations, and represents the United States in the International Standards Organization (ISO). *See* EIA, CBEMA.

APL (A Programming Language): A programming language designed by Kenneth Iverson in the 1960's. Intended for the concise expression of algorithms, especially those relating to arrays of data, APL is an exceptionally elegant language, much loved by those who know it. It is rarely used on small computers due to its special character set and its need for a complex interpreter to achieve reasonable speed.

Application: Any use of a computer not devoted to managing the computer's own affairs. Applications are what computers are all about; they pay the bills.

Architecture: The design of a computer system, in particular its instruction set, but also its interfaces and I/O devices.

ASCII (American Standard Code for Information Interchange): A standard defining the binary values of printable and control characters for computer storage. The ASCII representation of characters is used in all computers except those from IBM.

Assembler: A program that translates the text of a program written in assembly language into a machine-language program.

Assembly Language: A notation used for writing machine-language programs in words and numbers. Each machine design has its own unique assembly language. *See* Assembler; Machine Language.

Backup: Making and preserving copies of files in order to minimize the cost of the loss or destruction of data. As an adjective, the copies so made.

BASIC (Beginner's All-Purpose Symbolic Instruction Code): A programming language designed by John Kemeny at Dartmouth and intended for instructional use. Widely available on small computers because of its supposed simplicity and because of the ease with which a translator can be implemented.

BCD (Binary Coded Decimal): A representation of numbers in computer storage in which each group of four bits represents one digit of a decimal number.

BDOS (Basic Disk Operating System): The hardware-independent part of the CP/M Monitor. The BDOS is always resident in working storage. It executes service requests for programs and manages the file system.

Binary: A number system to the base 2, much used within computer systems. *See* Bit; Byte; Floating Point; Decimal; Hexadecimal.

BIOS (Basic I/O System): The part of the CP/M Monitor that controls the disk drives, terminal, and printer for the rest of the system. The bulk of the BIOS is devoted to handling disks, so the BIOS is usually supplied by the manufacturer of the disk controller circuitry.

Bit: The fundamental unit of computer storage; short for "binary digit." A single bit can represent either the value zero or the value one (true or false, on or off).

Board: *See* Circuit Board

Bootstrap: (1) As a verb, to initialize an operating system. (2) As a noun, the program that loads the resident part of an operating system.

bps (bits per second): A unit of measure for the rate of transmission of data. *See* Transmission Rate.

Bug: An error, especially in a program. A bug is almost always the result of a mistake or oversight on the part of a human being. *See* Debug; Glitch.

Bus: A set of electrical conductors, each with a defined use, so arranged that circuit boards can be plugged into the bus in parallel.

Byte: A unit of computer storage; a group of eight bits. The contents of one byte can represent an integer from 0 to 255, or an integer from -128 to +127, or one character symbol. What the byte's contents really stand for is determined by the program that reads and processes it.

C: Not an acronym, "C" is a programming language designed for use in writing operating systems. Used at Bell Laboratories to write the bulk of the UNIX operating system, C has become available on small machines. C is an excellent alternative to assembly language for systems programming.

CBEMA (Computer and Business Equipment Manufacturer's Association): The trade committee that administers standards committee X3 for ANSI. Committee X3 and its subcommittees have written most of the programming language standards now in effect.

CCP (Console Command Processor): The part of the CP/M Monitor that reads commands from the terminal and initiates them. The comparable program in MP/M is called the Command Line Interpreter (CLI).

Chip: *See* Integrated Circuit.

Circuit Board: A plastic or fiberglass board carrying metal traces that supports and connects integrated circuits and other electronic components. It usually represents one functional unit of a computer.

COBOL (COmmon Business-Oriented Language): A programming language intended for the expression of problems in commercial data processing. Standardized by the American National Standards Institute, COBOL is often required in federal data processing contracts. COBOL compilers are available for CP/M.

Command: A request that may be made by a user of an operating system. In CP/M, most commands are implemented as programs that reside in disk files.

Command language: The set of all commands a program will accept, and the rules for their formation. In CP/M, commands have the form "verb operand(s)."

Compatibility: A characteristic of programs that are different but have the same purpose, such that each can process data prepared for the other. For example, two BASIC interpreters are compatible when each accepts and correctly processes programs written for the other. Compatibility may be "upward," that is, one way only. For example, diskettes recorded under CP/M 1.4 can be read by CP/M 2, but the reverse is not necessarily true; thus CP/M 2 is "upward compatible" with CP/M 1.4.

Compiler: A program that translates the text of a program written in a programming language into a machine-language program. The machine-language program that is the output of the process (the object program) can be stored in a file for later execution.

Computer: A machine that follows a step-by-step program to organize data represented by patterns of electric pulses.

Computer System: A computer and its associated I/O devices and programs; the whole forming a single machine for organizing and presenting information to people.

Control Character: A binary value whose function is to control the form, or regulate the transmission, of data. ASCII defines 32 control characters that can be sent from a terminal keyboard by holding the control shift key while pressing another key.

Correctness: A characteristic of a program that delivers the expected output in the expected format. Much theoretical work has been done on ways to create correct programs from the start, as opposed to debugging them after they have been written. Many good things have come of this work (*see* Structured Programming; Top-down Design) but no magic solutions.

CPU (Central Processing Unit): That part of a computer that executes instructions. In small machines the CPU is usually a single integrated circuit.

Debug: To find, analyze, and correct the errors that will inevitably be present in all but the most trivial of programs. The second most enjoyable, and usually the most time-consuming, part of creating a computer program.

Decimal: A number system to the base 10, used often by human beings and occasionally by computers. *See* Binary; BCD; Hexadecimal.

Delimiter: A marker that separates one unit of a program statement or command from another. Typical delimiters are the space and tab characters, but any punctuation may act as a delimiter, depending on the program that interprets the data.

Directory: A designated area on a disk or diskette in which the operating system keeps a list of all files present on the disk and the location of their contents.

Disk: (1) A rotating disc coated with magnetic material, on which a computer can store data. (2) Casually, the term for any use of disk or diskette, as in "I'll just save this on disk."

Disk Drive: The mechanical device that supports a disk or diskette, rotates it, and reads or writes on it on command from a computer program.

Diskette: A disc of plastic, coated with magnetic material and cased in a jacket, on which a computer can store data. First used by IBM to give their service personnel a portable means of storing diagnostic programs. Widely used with small computers because of the low cost of the disk drive that handles it, despite the fragility of the medium.

Disk Parameter Block (DPB): The data structure, kept by the BIOS, that tells the BDOS all it needs to know about a disk in order to do space management.

Disk Parameter Header (DPH): The data structure, kept by the BIOS, that tells the BDOS where to find the DPB and other areas it needs.

Editor: A program whose purpose is to create or modify files under the immediate control of a human being. A programmer, writer, or clerk is likely to spend more time with an editor than with any other program.

EIA (Electronic Industries Association): A manufacturer's association that administers standards committee C83 for ANSI. That committee wrote standard RS-232-C that specifies the serial data transmission interface used by most terminals and printers.

Exchange Format: The format of 8-inch diskettes that can be read by any CP/M (or MP/M) system—single-density recording with twenty-six, 128-byte sectors per track, 77 tracks, initialized to 0E5h bytes and IBM standard sector addresses.

Extent: A unit of disk storage used by the CP/M or MP/M Monitor. Either 16 KB (a "logical extent") or the amount of space controlled by one directory entry (a physical extent, from 16 to 256 KB).

File: A named collection of data stored in a computer system. In CP/M and MP/M a file consists of one or more directory entries and a series of 128-byte records containing the file's data. *See* File Storage; File System.

File Control Block (FCB): The data structure prepared by the programmer to hold information about a file while the file is open.

File Storage: Any of the more-or-less permanent media for storing computer-readable data, for instance, diskette and tape. Opposed to Working Storage ("RAM").

File System: The component of an operating system that allows the user to create and manipulate files. The file system includes the functions of directory management and disk space management, and sometimes the utility programs that transfer files from device to device.

Floating Point: A representation of a number in which the significant digits of the number are stored as one integer (the fraction), and the magnitude of the number is stored as another integer (the exponent). The magnitude represents a power of the number base (which may be 2, 10, or 16) and may be thought of as the position of the decimal point in the fraction.

Floppy Disk: Casual term for diskette, used because the diskette is flexible, in contrast to the hard metal disk that preceded it.

Format : To write all sectors of a disk or diskette at the desired density and sector size. Minor details of formatting (density of track zero, fill byte value) can cause incompatibilities between systems. *See* Exchange Format.

FORTRAN (FORmula TRANslator): One of the first true programming languages, designed to express mathematical problems. A wonder for its time, now thought to be difficult and error-prone by comparison with, for example, PL/I or Pascal. Very common because of the huge number of existing programs written in it and the relative ease of implementing a compiler for it.

Garbage: Programmer's term for unpredictable or unwanted data, for example the data that follows an end-of-file mark in a file.

Glitch: A transient, unrepeatable error in the operation of a machine, usually an error in the hardware.

Hardware: The mechanical and electronic components of a computer system, as opposed to the software, which is equally, or more, important.

Hexadecimal: (From hexa-, meaning 6, and decimal, thus "the six-ten system.") A number system with the base value 16 and digits 0 to 9 and A to F. A convenient system for programmers, for a group of four binary bits can be represented as a single hexadecimal digit. Binary values are unsayable (e.g., "11010100"), but their hexadecimal form can be written, pronounced, and remembered (e.g., "D4").

Index: A table relating the key values of the records in a file to the addresses of those records within the file. *See* Key.

Input: (1) A signal received by a computer from another device. (2) Data given to a computer system, as "These numbers are the input for that program." (3) (ungrammatical) The act of sending data to a computer, as "I'll just input a control-c here."

Instruction: (1) One of the elementary operations that a particular computer can do. (2) The operation code that invokes that operation.

Instruction Set: The set of all instructions that a CPU can perform. The design of the instruction set is crucial to the speed, ease of programming, and eventual success of the machine.

Integer: A number with no fractional part; in computer storage, a group of bits interpreted as a binary integer. CP/M languages usually support integers of 16 bits, treated as numbers in the range -32768 to 32767. *See* Binary; BCD; Floating Point; Hexadecimal.

Interface: (1) The point at which two different things come into contact. (2) The design of the connection between two electronic devices, such as a computer and an I/O device. (3) The conventions used for passing control and information between two programs. (4) The rules and conventions for the use of a program by a person (the "man-machine interface").

Interpreter: A program that examines the text of a program written in a programming language and carries out the machine-language instructions that the program intends. Both the interpreter and the program being interpreted are present in working storage during the process. *See* Compiler.

I/O: An abbreviation for "Input and Output." Loosely, an abbreviation for all exchanges of data between a computer and the outside world. *See* Input; Output; and I/O Device.

I/O Device: A machine attached to a computer which, by exchanging signals with it, connects the computer to the outside world. For examples *see* Disk Drive; Printer; Terminal.

Key, Key Value: A field within a data record that contains unique information that can distinguish that record from all others in the same file. Used in a file index, where each key value is associated with the address of the record having that key.

KB (Kilobyte): 1024 bytes, a common measure of computer storage. *See* Byte; MB (Megabyte).

KSR (Keyboard Send-Receive): Term for a typewriter printer that has a keyboard.

Latency: The time required for a desired sector of a disk or diskette to rotate under the read-write head. Usually given as one-half the total rotation time.

Linker: A program that converts a relocatable object program into an executable program by supplying an origin and the addresses of its external subroutines.

Load: (1) To copy a file (especially a program) into working storage. (2) to convert a .HEX file into a .COM file with the LOAD command.

Logical: Computer jargon for simulated, as opposed to physical, meaning tangible. For example, CP/M may partition a physical (real), hard disk into smaller, logical (simulated) drives.

Machine Language: Computer operation codes and addresses, especially as represented in storage. A machine-language program is a sequence of bytes that represent operation codes and addresses. *See* Assembly Language.

MB (Megabyte): 1,048,576 (1024 times 1024) bytes, a measure of computer storage. *See* Byte, KB (Kilobyte).

Memory: Poor term for computer storage. One rare and expensive type of computer storage (associative storage) bears a faint resemblance to the organization of human memory, but in general the use of the term encourages the misleading idea that computers can "think."

Memory Bank: A term from the science fiction of the 1950's that has no meaning in modern terminology; often used by journalists unaware of the distinction between working storage and file storage, or of the many kinds of the latter.

Monitor: General term for the part of an operating system that resides permanently in working storage, providing services to other programs. *See* BDOS; BIOS; CCP.

Nybble: A cutesy term for a group of four bits — one-half a byte, or a hex digit.

Object Program: The representation of a program in machine language, as delivered by a compiler. May include relocation information.

Operating System: A collection of programs that apply the computer to the management of the computer and its work.

Operation Code: A number that, when received by a CPU, causes it to do a certain instruction.

Output: (1) A signal sent by a computer to another device. (2) Data received from a computer system, as in "This output looks peculiar." (3) (ungrammatical) The computer's act of sending data, as "It's outputting good stuff now."

Parameter: In software, an element of a command or statement whose value is set from outside the program at the time of execution, rather than being set at the time the program is written (a constant) or being developed from computation (a variable).

Pascal: A programming language designed by Nicolas Wirth for use in the teaching of programming and the design of algorithms. Currently very popular and widely available for small computers. An excellent alternative to BASIC.

Physical: Computer jargon for tangible or real. *See* Logical.

PL/I [Programming Language/I (Roman one)]: A programming language first promoted by IBM as having the best of both COBOL and FORTRAN (i.e., as being good for both commercial and mathematical problems). Now standardized by ANSI and available for small computers. An alternative to Pascal, especially where compatibility with a large computer system is needed.

Precision: The number of digits that can be stored, given a particular representation of numbers. Equivalent to "accuracy." An attempt to store a number with more digits than the precision the representation allows results in a loss of information. A floating-point number drops the least significant digits in that case; an integer representation will lose the most significant digits, resulting in a meaningless value.

Printer: A device that prints on paper under the direction of a computer.

Program: A step-by-step plan meant for computer execution. *See* Programming Language; Algorithm.

Programming Language: An artificial language designed to make it easy to express problems for computer solution. *See* Assembler; ALGOL; APL; BASIC; COBOL; FORTRAN; Pascal; PL/I.

Processor: The CPU with its interface and timing circuits. Usually implemented as a collection of integrated circuits on a single-circuit board.

PROM (Programmable, Read-Only Memory): Like ROM, but its contents can be changed (although usually they are not).

Protocol: An agreed upon set of rules for communication, especially between two machines.

RAM (Random Access Memory): Engineer's term for fast-access computer storage (*See* Working Storage); not used in this book because (a) the readers are not thought to be engineers and (b) the term is imprecise: disk storage is also capable of random access.

Record: One unit of data in a file. In CP/M files, the term has two meanings. A data record is usually a line of characters terminated by a return, linefeed character pair. A record as the CP/M Monitor knows it is a unit of 128 bytes.

RO (Receive Only): A term for a typewriter printer that lacks a keyboard.

R/O (Read Only): The state of a storage medium that is protected against modification.

ROM (Read-Only Memory): Fast-access storage whose contents are fixed at the factory and cannot be changed by the computer. Used in some computers for the part of the operating system that is always resident in working storage, to eliminate the need of loading it. Also used to contain a bootstrap program that loads the operating system and then disables itself.

RS-232: The standard for interconnecting terminals and other serial devices with a computer. *See* EIA.

R/W (Read and Write): The state of a storage medium which the computer can modify.

S-100 Bus: A bus design commonly used in small computers. Originally designed around the Intel 8080 CPU chip, now used with several different CPUs. Standardized by the IEEE (IEEE-696). *See* Bus.

Sector: *See* Track.

Seek: To move the head of a disk drive to the required track.

Seek Time: The time it takes to perform a seek. Given as either "expected" seek time (one-half the time to seek the full width of the disk) or as "track-to-track" seek time.

Service Request: Act of a program in calling upon a Monitor for some service. The service provided by the Monitor.

Skew: An arrangement of data on a diskette such that sectors whose contents would logically be adjacent are in fact separated along the track. The sectors are interleaved so that sector n is separated from sector $n+1$ by some number of other sectors (the number is the skew factor).

Software: Programs, or a program; usually opposed to hardware. The set of programs used with a particular computer system.

Source Program: The representation of a program as a sequence of characters readable by a human being. The form of input to an interpreter or compiler.

Spooling: (from SPOOL, Simultaneous Peripheral Operation On-Line.) An operating system function in which data meant for the printer are collected on disk to be printed later, during the execution of the next program. In small systems the term has been applied incorrectly to the action of a utility such as Digital Research's DESPOOL, which prints disk files concurrently with the execution of other programs. CP/M and MP/M do not have a true spooling function, for they do not collect program output automatically; the user must take special action to direct the output to a named disk file.

Standard: An authoritative, formal definition of an interface or a programming language. *See* S-100 Bus; RS-232; ANSI; ASCII.

Structured Programming: A collection of techniques for programming that arose from theoretical work in program correctness, most of which can be summarized in the words "discipline" and "forethought."

Terminal: Combination of keyboard and display tube (video terminal) or keyboard and print unit (typewriter terminal); the point at which a human interacts with a computer.

Top-down Design: A technique of structured programming in which the program design is stated very simply at the first level, then that statement is expanded into subproblems each of which is stated plainly, then each substatement is in its turn expanded until the statements are at the level of detail supported by the programming language to be used.

Track: An imaginary circle traced over the surface of a disk by its read-write head, along which data is stored. All diskette drives, and some disk drives, divide the track into arc-shaped sectors of equal length, and read or write only complete sectors on any operation.

Transmission Rate: The rate at which bits are sent over a communications line. Measured in bits per second (bps). The standard rates are 110 bps, 300 bps, and successive doubles of 300 through 19,200 bps.

Utility: A program whose purpose is to copy data from one place to another with little or no processing or reformatting.

Variable: A named location in working storage, used to hold values during the execution of a program.

Word: The unit of storage that is natural to a particular machine's architecture. For most small computers the byte (8 bits) is also the word. Almost always a number of bits that is a power of 2 such as 8, 16, or 32, although some machines have used words that were multiples of 6 or 12 bits.

Working Storage: Fast-access storage from which the processor reads its program and in which the programmer saves variables. *See* RAM; ROM; PROM.

Index

Index

Part Two

A Reference for Users and Programmers

Reference

Form and Use of Filerefs

Files are designated by three-part names. They are:

the *drivecode*, a single letter followed by a colon, that designates a disk drive, for example A: or E:

the *filename*, one to eight characters long—if the filename contains an asterisk or a question mark, it is *ambiguous*, otherwise it is *explicit*;

the *filetype*, zero to three characters long—like the filename, the filetype may be ambiguous or explicit.

The valid drive letters are A through P, naming the 16 possible drives that a CP/M system can support.

Neither filename nor filetype is allowed to contain embedded spaces or any of these characters:

. , ; : = [ ] _ < >.

Most commands take *filerefs* as operands. A fileref is

{drivecode}filename{.filetype}

that is, a filename, possibly preceded by a drivecode and possibly followed by a filetype. Some commands accept only the filename, providing an assumed filetype of their own.

When the drivecode is omitted, the system will supply the drivecode of the default drive (the one named in the system's command prompt).

Some commands accept ambiguous filerefs, but most require explicit ones. Each command's requirements are spelled out in its description in this reference.

Effects and Use of Ambiguous Filerefs

Fileref	Will match
.*.*	All files
q*.*	Any file with a name commencing with a Q, from Q alone through QUIETLY.BAS to QZZZZZZZ.ZZZ
wa*.com	Any file of type .COM commencing WA, such as WASH .COM, WANT.COM, or WAVERLEY.COM
wilt.p*	Any file named WILT with a type beginning with a P, such as WILT.PLI, WILT.PRN, WILT.PRL
q.	All files—characters after an asterisk are ignored, so this is equivalent to *.*
wan?	Files with a filetype of three spaces and names of four letters beginning with WAN—WANT, WAND
w?n?.*	Any file with the first letter W, third letter N, a total of four letters, any filetype. WANT, WINS.SUB, WONT.GO, but not WINCE.BAS—five-letter names won't match
???????y.*	Eight-letter names ending in Y, any filetype—SUDDENLY .BOO, WAVERLEY.COM
???????.??	Filenames not exceeding seven letters, types not exceeding two letters

Conventional File Types in CP/M and MP/M

Filetype	ASCII	Conventional Use
.ASC	yes	ASCII source text of some BASIC programs
.ASM	yes	Source text of an assembly language program
.BAK	yes	Original version of an edited file
.BAS	no?	Source text of some BASIC programs; may contain tokenized (compressed numeric) keywords
.CMD	no	CP/M-86 machine language program (command)
.COB	yes	Source text of a COBOL program
.COM	no	CP/M-80 machine language program (command)
.DOC	yes	Program documentation, usually informal
.FOR	yes	Source text of a FORTRAN program
.HEX	yes	Machine language program in symbolic (hexadecimal characters) form; output of ASM, MAC
.INT	no	Intermediate code produced by some compilers
.IRL	no	Indexed relocatable library built by the LIB command
.LIB	yes	Collection of source code for inclusion with MACLIB; collection of relocatable subroutines for linking
.LST	yes	File intended for printing
.MSG	yes	Informal documentation or note
.PAS	yes	Source text of a Pascal program
.PLI	yes	Source text of a PL/I program
.PRL	no	Machine language program in page-relocatable (MP/M)
.PRN	yes	File intended for printing
.REL	no	Machine language program in relocatable form
.RSP	no	Resident system procedure for MP/M (see .PRL)
.SPR	no	System procedure for MP/M (see .PRL)
.SRC	yes	Assembler language source text for some assemblers
.SUB	yes	File of commands intended as input to SUBMIT
.SYM	yes	Symbol information written by MAC assembler
.SYS	no	System file for MP/M
.TEX	yes	File of text with formatting commands, input to the TEX text formatter
.TXT	yes	Informal documentation or note
.$$$	unk.	Temporary file, used by PIP and most editors as the type of the work file

Control Characters Recognized by CP/M and MP/M

Control characters are recognized and acted on by the Monitor when it is reading a command line, or reading a complete line at the request of a command program. Many control characters are not recognized when a command requests its console input one character at a time, and none when it bypasses the Monitor to read the console via the BIOS. The program may then supply its own meanings for the control characters.

Character	Use	Effect When Recognized
		Standard Keys on Most Terminals
backspace	edit	Deletes prior character, backspaces cursor.
delete	edit	Deletes prior character in storage, but types the deleted character at the console.
linefeed	edit	Ends input line, returns cursor to margin.
return	edit	Ends input line, returns cursor to margin.
rubout	edit	(same as delete)
tab	edit	Moves cursor to next eighth position (9, 17, 25, etc.); program receives an ASCII TAB.
		Control-Shift Characters
control-b	control	Terminates and removes DESPOOL.
control-c	control	Terminates command, causes a warm start.
control-d	control	Detaches console from command (MP/M only).
control-e	edit	Moves cursor to new line without ending the input line.
control-f	control	Activates DESPOOL.
control-h	edit	(same as backspace)
control-i	edit	(same as tab)
control-j	edit	(same as linefeed)
control-l	control	Under ED, stands for CR, LF in string search and replacement subcommands
control-m	edit	(same as return)
control-p	control	Starts or stops copying console output to the printer.

Character	Use	Effect When Recognized
control-q	control	Gets exclusive use of the printer (MP/M only).
control-r	edit	Retypes the input line as received so far.
control-s	control	Suspends console output; restart with any key.
control-u	edit	Deletes input so far, moves cursor to new line.
control-x	edit	Deletes input line so far, moves cursor to its starting position.
control-z	control	Flags end of a string to ED or PIP.

Physical Device Names

Name	Conventional Use
	Devices that May Be Assigned to CON:
TTY:	Typewriter terminal
CRT:	Video display terminal
BAT:	Input requests diverted to the RDR: logical device, output to LST: logical device
UC1:	Another console (human-operated input and output) device
	Devices that May Be Assigned to RDR:
TTY:	Typewriter terminal
PTR:	Paper-tape (or cassette-tape) input
UR1:, UR2:	Other serial input devices
	Devices that May Be Assigned to PUN:
TTY:	Typewriter terminal
PTP:	Paper-tape (or cassette-tape) output
UP1:, UP2:	Other serial output devices
	Devices that May Be Assigned to LST:
TTY:	Typewriter terminal
CRT:	Video display terminal
LPT:	A printer
UL1:	Another printer or serial output

Blank Assignment Chart

Determine the effect each of the 16 possible I/O assignments has in your system, and document it here. Rows refer to logical device names, and columns refer to physical device names. If the effect of assigning STAT CON:=TTY: is to direct console I/O to the terminal, you might write "terminal" in the upper left corner cell.

	TTY:	CRT:	BAT:	UC1:
CON:				
	TTY:	PTR:	UR1:	UR2:
RDR:				
	TTY:	PTP:	UP1:	UP2:
PUN:				
	TTY:	CRT:	LPT:	UL1:
LST:				

Commands

Topical Summary of CP/M Commands

Command Syntax	Page	Function
Commands for File Information and Display		
DIR {*fileref*}	313	Display files on a drive
STAT *d*:{ DSK: }	355	Display disk information
STAT *fileref*	359	Display file information
TYPE *fileref*	371	Display file at console
PIP *dev:=fileref*[*options*]	343	Send file to serial device
DUMP *fileref*	317	Display file in hex
Commands for File Alteration		
ED *fileref* {*d*:}	319	Start editing session
ERA *fileref*	325	Erase files
REN *newref=oldref*	349	Rename existing file
STAT *fileref* $*attribute*	361	Alter file attribute
LOAD *fileref*	327	Convert .HEX to .COM file
SAVE *size fileref*	351	Copy storage to .COM file
PIP	339	Start PIP session
PIP *destination=source*[*options*]	341	Transfer single file
PIP *d*:=*fileref*[*options*]	343	Transfer multiple files
Commands for Serial Devices		
PIP *dev:=fileref*[*options*]	343	Send file to serial device
STAT DEV:	363	Display device assignments
STAT VAL:	363	Display STAT operands
STAT *logical=physical*	363	Make device assignments
LOCAL *device*	329	End use of remote device
NETWORK *device=number*	337	Ask use of remote device
Commands for Building Programs		
DDT {*fileref*}	309	Start debugging session
LOAD *fileref*	327	Convert .HEX to .COM file
SAVE *size fileref*	351	Copy storage to .COM file

Command Syntax	Page	Function
		Commands for System Information
STAT DEV:	363	Display device assignments
STAT USR:	365	Display user-code status
STAT VAL:	363	Display STAT operands
CPNETSTS	307	Display network devices
		Commands for System Control
STAT *d*:=R/O	357	Make drive read-only
STAT *logical=physical*	363	Make device assignments
SUBMIT {*d*:}*filename* {*parameters...*}	367	Run command list in file
USER *code*	373	Set active user code
XSUB	375	Supply input from file
DSKRESET {*d*:}	315	Reset local, remote drives
		Commands for System Generation
MOVCPM *size flag*	335	Build relocated Monitor
SYSGEN	369	Copy Monitor image to disk
		CP/NET *Commands*
CPNETLDR	305	Set up CP/NET connection
CPNETSTS	307	Display network devices
DSKRESET {*d*:}	315	Reset local, remote drives
ENDLIST	323	Close remote print file
LOCAL *device*	329	End use of remote device
LOGIN {*pass*} { [*master*] }	331	Ask use of remote system
LOGOFF { [*master*] }	333	End use of remote system
NETWORK *device=number*	337	Ask use of remote device
RCVMAIL { [*master*] }	347	Receive network messages
SNDMAIL [*master*] (*target*) '*message*'	353	Send message on network

The two main components of a CP/M node of a network are the Slave Network I/O Supervisor (SNIOS), a hardware-dependent program that controls the communication link(s), and the Network Disk Operating System (NDOS), which extends the functions of the CP/M Monitor. Each program is kept as a file of type .SPR.

This command need be done only once after a cold start. The network programs remain in storage over a warm start.

Following this command a LOGIN command must be done to open communications with a master network node.

CPNETLDR

The command loads and initializes the code needed to connect a CP/M system to a CP/NET network.

The command searches the default disk for the files SNIOS.SPR and NDOS.SPR; when it finds both it loads them at the top of the Transient Program area and prepares the system to act as a CP/NET node.

The command displays a report showing the starting addresses and length of each of the main components of CP/M.

The CPNETLDR command must have been done before this command can be done. If this system has not been logged in to some master system with the LOGIN command, all devices will be local.

The slave processor ID is the value that a user at another node would use to send a message to this system. You might include it in a message or when reporting a problem to the operator of the master node.

The network status byte is normally 10H. If the first digit is zero, then no LOGIN command has been done. If the second digit is not zero, then a communication error recently tock place. Note the value of the second digit, as it is reset to zero by the command.

A drive shown as LOCAL is simply one that is not accessed via the network; it need not exist. The command reports on all possible disk drives, whether or not they exist in the local system. When a drive is located on some other node, the ID of that node is shown; it might be used to send a message to the operator of that system as in

```
dskreset c:
sndmail (00) "done with your disk G:"
```

CPNETSTS

The command reports the status of the system as a node in a CP/NET network. The report resembles this:

```
CP/NET 1.0 Status
=========================================
Slave Processor ID = 14H
Network Status Byte = 10H
Disk device status:
   Drive A: = LOCAL
   Drive B: = LOCAL
   Drive C: = Drive G: on Network Master ID = 00H
   Drive D: = LOCAL
       ...
       ...
   Drive P: = LOCAL
Console Device = LOCAL
List Device = List #0 on Network Master ID = 00H
```

The status of each device that can be accessed via the network is shown. A LOCAL device is one that is accessed normally as part of the local CP/M system's configuration. Devices accessed at a distance are identified with the system and device name that they represent.

DDT is used to debug programs written in assembly language. It also finds use as a special utility program for building program images, and in applying patches to fix programs.

See the USER command for an example of using DDT to load the image of a command; see Chapter 12 for an example of applying a vendor's patch to a command.

An assembly-language program can be built from different modules, each assembled at a different, known origin. For example, a main program might contain a reserved space for a terminal driver subroutine. Different terminal drivers can be prepared, each customized for a particular terminal type. The correct driver can then be incorporated in the main program with DDT:

ddt main.com	load image of main program
-iterm120.hex	prepare to load driver for Soroq IQ120
-r	read terminal driver to its origin
-g0	warm start, leaving merged program
save 37 main120.com	save customized command program

DDT { *fileref* }

The DDT command initializes a debugging session. The code of the debugger is loaded and moved to the top of the Transient Program Area, replacing the CCP. The address of the end of the Transient Program Area in low storage is changed to protect the debugger.

If *fileref* is specified, that file is loaded into the Transient Program Area. The reference must be explicit and have a filetype of either .HEX or .COM. A .COM file is loaded at 0100h; a .HEX file is loaded at its assembled origin.

The debugger then prompts with a hyphen and waits for a subcommand. A table of DDT subcommands follows this topic.

The command is ended by a warm start. One may be obtained either by typing control-c or by entering the G0 (go to zero, i.e., to the warm start jump) subcommand.

Summary of DDT Subcommands

Syntax	Description
A*start*	Assemble into storage: DDT prompts with successive addresses from *start*. Enter operation names, and register names or hex values as operands. End the process with a null entry.
D{*start*}{,*end*}	Display storage: DDT displays storage in hex and ASCII, 16 bytes per line. The display begins with *start* if given, or where the prior D left off, or with the HL value of the last instruction traced. It ends with *end* if given, or after 12 lines. Use any key to end the display early.
F*start*,*end*,*xx*	Fill storage: DDT replicates *xx* in every byte from *start* through *end*. Caution: DDT will happily fill right over itself and the BDOS if told to do so.
G{*start*}{,*b1*{,*b2*}}	Execute program: DDT transfers control to *start* if given, or to the test program's PC. If one or two break addresses are given, DDT makes each an RST 7 instruction; control returns to DDT if the program reaches one and the instructions are restored.
H*first*,*second*	Hex arithmetic: DDT responds with two numbers, *first*+*second* and *first*–*second*.
I*fileref*	Initialize FCB: *fileref* is set in the default FCB at 5Ch. Any drivecode is ignored. The FCB may be used by the test program; more often it is used by the R subcommand. Use S to set up a drive number.
L{*start*}{,*end*}	List instructions: DDT displays storage as instructions in assembler format, from *start* if given, or where the last L left off, or from the PC address of the last traced instruction. The display ends with *end* if given, or after 11 lines have been typed. Use the delete key to stop the display.
M*start*,*end*,*to*	Copy storage: DDT copies the block of storage from *start* through *end* to the address *to*.
R{*bias*}	Read program: The file named in the default FCB at 5Ch is loaded as a program. The filetype must be .COM (load address is 0100h+*bias*) or must have the .HEX format. In that case the *bias* is added to the load address in each line, causing the file to load away from its assembled origin. The highest load address this session and the current PC value are displayed.

Syntax	Description
S*start*	Modify storage: DDT prompts with the address *start* and that byte's contents in hex. Enter a new value, or CR alone, to leave it unchanged. DDT prompts with the next address; enter period, CR to end.
T{*count*}	Trace program: An instruction is traced. The test program PC provides its address; use X to set it. The register state and the instruction are shown before the instruction is done; use X to see the instruction's effect. If *count* is given, DDT continues for that many instructions; use the delete key to stop it early.
U{*count*}	Trace without display: Instructions are traced as for T but no state display is typed.
X	Display program state: The test program registers and the instruction addressed by its PC are shown.
X*register*	Modify register: DDT prompts with the contents of the named register or flag. Enter CR alone to leave them unchanged, or enter a new value. The registers are A, B, D, H, S (for SP), and P (for PC). Flags are C, Z, M, E, and I.

The command DIR with no operand displays all files with the active user number. Use ambiguous filerefs to see the names of sets of files, for example,

dir *.com	to see all command verbs
dir his???.*	to see six-letter filenames beginning HIS

When DIR produces no output at all, displaying neither a filename nor a message, it is because there is at least one file that matches, but all files that match have the SYS attribute. Use STAT with the same operand to see their names.

When DIR responds NO FILE but you think there ought to be files, check the active user code with STAT USR:. The files you expect might be under a different user code.

DIR should not be used to preview the effect of an ERA command, as was possible in prior systems. DIR does not report files with the SYS attribute but ERA will erase such files. Use STAT to preview ERA; it reveals both system files and those that are read-only.

DIR { *fileref* }

The system searches a disk's directory for files that match *fileref*, and displays the names of those it finds. Only files created under the active user code are examined. Files with the SYS attribute may be found, but their names are not displayed.

If *fileref* includes a drivecode, the system searches the directory of the disk in that drive. If no drivecode is given, it searches the directory in the default drive.

When *fileref* is explicit, only one file can be found. If it is ambiguous, many files may be found to match. Their names are displayed four per line. If *fileref* is omitted, the command assumes an operand of *.*, meaning "all."

If no matching files are found, the message NO FILE is displayed.

The command finds little use for local drives, which are reset by the warm start at the end of the command anyway. It is useful for causing a reset of a drive that is located at another node. Use CPNETSTS to find out the local drivecode for a remote drive. After the operator at the other node has loaded a diskette for you, use the DSKRESET command to cause the remote system to reset its drive so that you can write on it.

(This command is a standard part of an MP/M system, where it replaces the warm start for purposes of resetting disk status. MP/M has no warm start.)

DSKRESET { *drivecode* ... }

The command resets one or more drives, that is, it causes CP/M to forget the check information it uses to detect when a diskette is changed. The diskette in the drive may then be changed without CP/M marking it read-only.

If no *drivecode* is given, all drives used by this node are reset. If a single *drivecode* is given, only that drive is reset. Several *drivecodes* may be specified, separated by commas; each drive is reset.

This command is of most use to programmers who want to see the exact contents of a file, unedited by any of the normal display mechanisms.

The operand is usually an explicit fileref. However, it may be ambiguous, in which case DUMP displays the first file under the active user code that matches the reference. That will also be the first file named by DIR, given the same operand.

DUMP *fileref*

The file named by *fileref* is displayed at the console in hexadecimal format. Each line of the display shows 16 bytes of data, prefixed by the relative address of the data in the file.

See Chapter 7 for a discussion of ED and examples of its use.

The I, F, and S subcommands behave differently depending on the case in which the command letter is typed. The subcommand i accepts input as typed, whereas the subcommand I converts the typed input to uppercase.

ED can be used to inspect an input file that is marked read-only. If the session ends with the Quit subcommand all will be well. If ended with End, ED will attempt to rename the input file, causing BDOS Error on x: File Read-Only and a warm start. ED cannot take its input from a read-only disk drive. The message BDOS Error on x: R/O appears at the start of the session.

ED can be automated with the XSUB program. The script of an entire edit session can be put into a submit file and run without human intervention. In this way a set of complicated but routine changes can be run with only a single command. One exception: the bulk Input subcommand will not accept input via XSUB.

ED *fileref* { *drivecode* }

An edit session is begun on the named file (*fileref* must be explicit). A file of the same filename, but with a filetype of .$$$, is created to be a work file. The program then awaits an edit subcommand from the console. A table of ED subcommands follows this topic.

If the named file does not exist, a NEW FILE is reported. If it does exist, ED prepares to read it. Any existing *filename*.BAK is erased at this time.

The presence of the optional *drivecode* changes the command's operation. If a file named *fileref* exists on that drive, ED terminates with the message FILE EXISTS, ERASE IT. If there is no duplicate filename, the work file is created on that drive.

When the session is ended with an End subcommand, the edited data are written to the work file, which is then given the name *fileref*. The original file is given a new filetype of .BAK. If the command ends with a Quit subcommand, the work file is erased and the original file is unchanged (although a .BAK file of the same name is gone, regardless).

Summary of ED Subcommands

Key: *s* = a sign (blank or –); *n* = an unsigned or negative number;
p = an unsigned number; *string* = letters ending in control-z.

Syntax	Description
n	A number alone has the effect of *n*LT.
p:	Move to the *p*th line in the file.
:*p*	Before a letter, means "the range of lines from the current one to the *p*th one, inclusive."
*p*A	Read *p* lines from the source file and append them to the file copy in storage.
*s*B	Move to the beginning line (B) or bottom (-B) of the file.
*n*C	Move right/down *n* characters (positive), or left/up *n* characters (negative) in the file.
*n*D	Delete *n* characters beginning with the current one and moving right (positive), or delete the *n* characters left of the current one (negative).
E	End the session: write all source text to the work file and rename it; rename the source file to .BAK.
*n*F*string*	Find the *n*th occurrence of *string*. Positive *n* searches down, negative searches up. Treats *string* as uppercase when command is F, as mixed case for f.
H	Start over at the top of the source file, preserving all changes. Do the actions of E, then begin again on the new source file.
I	Start bulk input; all input to a control-z is added before the current character. Input is forced to uppercase if command is I; lowercase is accepted under i.
I*string*	Insert the *string* before the current character.
*n*J*string1string 2string3*	Search for *string1* as for F; insert *string2* as for I; delete following characters up to *string3*. No deletion is done if *string3* can't be found. With empty *string2*, J performs delete from-to; with empty *string1* as well it is delete-to; with impossible *string3* it is insert-after.

Syntax	Description
*n*K	Delete *n* lines starting with the current one and going down (positive), or *n* lines before the current one (negative).
*n*L	Move down (positive) or up (negative) *n* lines.
*p*M*commands*	Repeat the sequence of *commands*, *p* times.
*p*N*string*	Search down for the *p*th occurrence of string, doing W and A actions as needed to scan all lines of the source file.
O	Restart the session with the original file: delete the work file and clear the storage buffer.
*n*P	Page down (positive) or up (negative) *n* multiples of 23; display 23 lines as for T.
Q	Quit the edit with no changes: delete the work file and end the command. Note that any .BAK file is lost.
R{*filename*}	Open *filename*.LIB and insert its contents as for I. When *filename* is omitted, uses $$$$$$$$.LIB (see X).
*n*S*string1string2*	Find *string1* as for F; replace it with *string2*. Treats both strings as uppercase if command is S.
*n*T	Type *n* lines starting with the current one (positive), or the *n* lines above the current one (negative).
*s*U	Force inserted letters to uppercase (U), or allow them to be mixed-case (-U). See note on cases under F, I, S.
*s*V	Use line numbers as a prompt (V), or use only an asterisk (-V), or display free/total storage (0V).
*p*W	Write the top *p* lines of the file copy in storage to the work file (see A).
*p*X	Copy *p* lines starting with the current one to the temporary file $$$$$$$$.LIB (from whence R can read them). 0X clears the temporary library.
*p*Z	Idle for (theoretically) *p* seconds. Actual delay depends on the machine clock speed. Wake it up with any key.

When output written to the LST: logical device is travelling over the network to a printer at a remote node, the ENDLIST command signals that node that the end of a printed file has been reached. If the remote node has been saving the output on disk, it will know it can close the file and schedule it for printing. Use the ENDLIST command at the conclusion of a program so that its printed output will not run together with the output of the next command.

When the printer is a local device, the command has no use, although it will usually cause no harm. It is safe to include ENDLIST in a submit file that may be used with either a local or a remote printer.

ENDLIST

The command writes a single end-of-file character (ASCII SUB control character, or control-z) to the LST: device.

Remember the mnemonic "ERAsed files are ERAtrievable," and use caution when erasing more than one file. In fact, it is possible to write a program that can, in some cases, recover an erased file. Such programs only work when no files are created on the disk following the erasure.

Use ambiguous filerefs to erase sets of related files, for example,

era *.bak	to erase all edit backup files
era his???.*	to erase six-letter filenames starting with "HIS"

Use STAT to anticipate the effects of an ERA command. STAT given the same fileref displays all files ERA will attempt to erase, including those with the SYS attribute and those that are R/O.

When ERA responds NO FILE, but you think there ought to be files, check the active user code with STAT USR:. The files you expect might be under a different user code.

ERA *fileref*

The system searches a disk's directory for files that match *fileref*, and erases those it finds. Only files created under the active user code are examined. Files with the SYS attribute are found and can be erased.

If *fileref* includes a drivecode, the system searches the directory of the disk in that drive. If no drivecode is given, it searches the directory in the default drive.

When *fileref* is explicit, only one file can be erased. If it is ambiguous, many files may be erased. If the *.* reference is used, the command requests confirmation before erasing all files.

If a matched file has the R/O attribute, the message

```
BDOS Error on x: file r/o
```

will be displayed and the system will await any console input, following which a warm start will be done. Some matching files may be erased before the R/O file is encountered.

If *fileref* is omitted, or if no matching files are found, the message NO FILE is displayed.

A .HEX file is the normal output of a (nonrelocating) assembler. It represents each byte of a program with two ASCII characters, one for each hexadecimal digit. Each line of the file is preceded by the address at which the line's data are to be loaded, and followed by a one-byte checksum.

The HEX format was devised as a way to represent a machine language program in standard ASCII characters. Such a representation can be printed and transmitted via media, such as paper tape, that require 7-bit ASCII.

The usual sequence of operations is to create the .HEX file, load it, and try it out:

```
asm testprog
load testprog
testprog operands...
```

DDT's R subcommand will load a .HEX file for testing or as a subcomponent of a larger program:

asm partprog	assemble customizing module
ddt fullprog.com	load major program
-ipartprog.hex	
-r	overlay with customizing module
-g0	
save *nn* fullprog	save customized program

See Chapter 15 for an example of this technique in a CP/M system generation.

LOAD *fileref*

The named file is read and inspected for correct HEX format. The program it represents is formed in working storage at its correct origin. The program image is written to disk under the same filename but with a .COM filetype. The command reports:

FIRST ADDRESS xxxx	starting address of the program
LAST ADDRESS xxxx	ending address of the program
BYTES READ xxxx	count of bytes in the program image
RECORDS WRITTEN xx	128-byte records in the .COM file

If *fileref* includes a drivecode, both input and output take place on that drive. Otherwise both input and output take place on the default drive. If the filetype is omitted from *fileref,* the command supplies a .HEX filetype.

The command will report a number of errors in file handling:

CANNOT OPEN SOURCE	input file not found
NO MORE DIRECTORY SPACE	output file can't be created
CANNOT CLOSE FILE	disk or directory is full

and in the format of the input file:

INVALID HEX DIGIT	input character not in '0'..'F'
CHECK SUM ERROR	each line of input is checked

Following these errors the command reports the load address and the address in the record in which the error occurred.

The CPNETLDR command must have been done before this command can be done. If no LOGIN command has been done, then all devices will be LOCAL already.

When CP/NET is active, the CON: and LST: devices, and any disk drive, may be located on another system, with data passing to and from the local system over the network. Devices are made remote with the NETWORK command. This command reverses the effect of NETWORK for a device. Use CPNETSTS to find out which devices are local and which are remote.

Here is an example of remote I/O:

```
cpnetldr              load the CP/NET support code
login                 connect to the (main or only) master
network c:=g:         drivecode C: to mean master's G-drive
pip a:=c:master.ful   copy file from master's disk to ours
local c:              make drivecode C: local again
```

There need not be a real drive C: on the local system; any drivecodes A...P will do. Using nonexistent drive letters for remote drives helps avoid confusion.

Notice that the command LOCAL CON: is meaningless if given at the local console; if it can be given there, then CON: was local already. LOCAL CON: is useful only when given from the remote console, after which no more commands will be accepted there.

Before making a remote disk local, it's a good idea to reset it with DSKRESET.

LOCAL CON:
LOCAL LST:
LOCAL *drivecode*

The command changes the indicated device from one that is accessed remotely over the CP/NET network to one that is accessed locally as part of the system.

The first form is used to direct I/O for the CON: logical device to the local console instead of a console on a remote system.

The second form directs I/O for the LST: logical device to the local printer instead of a printer on a remote system.

The third form is used to direct disk I/O to a local disk drive instead of a disk drive on a remote system.

The CPNETLDR command must have been run before LOGIN can be done. Once LOGIN has been successful for a particular master system, it need not be repeated unless a LOGOFF command is done.

The LOGIN attempt may fail for any of several reasons. It may be rejected by the master system because the password is incorrect or because the master is overloaded. The CP/NET software may not be active in the master system, or indeed the master system might not be turned on.

More than one LOGIN may be done. The following sequence will copy a file from master system 00 to a disk on master system 02:

cpnetldr	initialize network software
login	log in to master 00
login 02	log in to master 02
network d:=c:	drivecode D: represents master 00 drive C:
network e:=b: [02]	drivecode E: represents master 02 drive B:
pip e:=d:remote.fil	copy file from one master to the other

LOGIN { *password* } { [*idmaster*] }

The command contacts a master system on the CP/NET network and requests the right to use that master's facilities.

If *password*—one to eight letters—is specified, it is sent with the request. Otherwise the letters PASSWORD are used.

If *idmaster* is specified, that master is contacted. Otherwise master 00 is contacted.

It is not clear what the command reports if the LOGIN fails.

The CPNETLDR command must have been done before this command can be done. A successful LOGIN to the same master should have been done, but no harm will come if one has not.

The master system has some resources tied up for each system that has logged in to it. Those resources can only be freed by LOGOFF. The master will not voluntarily free them. It is good practice to use this command whenever a master's services aren't going to be needed.

LOGOFF { [*idmaster*] }

The command contacts a master system on the CP/NET network and informs it that this system no longer needs its facilities.

This command is part of the process of generating a new CP/M 1 or CP/M 2 system, either initially or when the size of working storage is being altered. It is the only means of relocating the Monitor, a necessary step for most systems as the Monitor is distributed with an assembled origin suitable for a system with 20K bytes of working storage. The command is often modified by the system's vendor, and may have a different name to distinguish the customized version from that supplied by Digital Research.

It is a common mistake to omit the *leave* operand. The command then attempts to execute the relocated Monitor. The BIOS contained in the relocated image is usually not the correct one for this system, and the result is a hung system that can only be recovered by a cold start. The command is normally given operands of two asterisks:

```
movcpm * *
```

This causes the Monitor image to be relocated for the size of the machine. At the end of the command the image of the Monitor is in working storage, ready to be saved as a .COM file. The customized BIOS for the system can then be patched into the .COM file and the customized system placed on a disk with SYSGEN.

See the SYSGEN command for the rest of the generation process; see Chapter 15 for further discussion.

MOVCPM *size leave*

The image of the CCP and BDOS contained in the command is relocated for execution in a machine with *size* kilobytes of storage. If any *leave* operand is present, the command ends, leaving the Monitor image in storage. If *leave* is omitted, the Monitor image is moved to its relocated origin and begins execution as if it had been loaded by a cold start.

The *size* operand may be given as a decimal number of kilobytes, or as an asterisk, or omitted. If it is omitted or given as an asterisk, the command uses the size of working storage as it presently exists.

The CPNETLDR command, and a LOGIN for the desired master system, must have been done successfully before this command can be done.

When CP/NET is active, the CON: and LST: devices, and any disk drive, may be located on another system, with data meant for those devices passing to and from the local system over the network. This command makes a device remote. The LOCAL command reverses its effect. Use CPNETSTS to find out which devices are local and which are remote.

Here is an example of remote I/O:

cpnetldr	load the CP/NET support code
login	connect to the (main or only) master
network c:=g:	drivecode C: to mean master's G-drive
pip a:=c:master.ful	copy file from master's disk to ours
local c:	make drivecode C: local again

There need not be a real drive G: on the local system; any drivecode letter A...P will do. Using nonexistent drive letters for remote drives helps avoid confusion.

When the command NETWORK CON: is given, no further commands can be entered at the local terminal; all console I/O will be directed through the network to the master system. The command LOCAL CON: will end the connection and make the local terminal usable again. It must be given from the remote console, after which no more commands will be accepted there.

NETWORK CON:=*number* { [*idmaster*] }
NETWORK LST:=*number* { [*idmaster*] }
NETWORK *drivecode*=*drivecode* { [*idmaster*] }

The command changes the indicated device from one that is accessed locally as part of the system to one that is accessed remotely over the CP/NET network. In each case, *idmaster* is the number of a master node to which this CP/M system is connected. If it is omitted, the number 00 is used.

The first form is used to direct I/O for the CON: logical device to a console on the remote system. *Number* is the MP/M console number of the remote console.

The second form directs I/O for the LST: logical device to a printer on the remote system. *Number* is the MP/M console number of the remote printer device.

The third form is used to direct disk I/O to a disk drive on the remote system. The first *drivecode* is the drivecode that will be used in commands in the local system. The second *drivecode* is the actual drivecode of the disk in the master system.

PIP is used to copy data between disks and between serial devices. It is conventional to speak of "moving" data with PIP. New users should keep in mind that data are not moved but copied; the source of a transfer is never changed. Chapter 6 contains many examples of the use of PIP.

Specify a single transfer as part of the command. When doing two or more, it is faster to call PIP with no operands and specify the transfers after. This avoids the warm start each time PIP ends.

Users of two-drive systems have a problem when copying between two diskettes neither of which has a copy of PIP. The solution is to load PIP and then change the source diskette:

A>pip	load PIP from the A-drive
*	PIP waits; load source diskette in A-drive
b:=a:xyz*	read from A, write to B
*	PIP waits; put system diskette back in A
(return)	end PIP, warm start follows

CP/M notices when a diskette is changed and marks it read-only; therefore you can't change the destination diskette. The changed source diskette must be recorded at the same density and sector size as the one removed.

See the USER command for copying files between user codes.

PIP { *transfer* }

If a *transfer* is specified, it is performed and the command ends.

If no *transfer* is given, the command prompts with an asterisk and awaits the entry of a transfer specification. It performs that transfer and prompts again, until a null line is entered.

If a character is typed at the console while the command is working on a transfer, the transfer stops. PIP reports ABORTED. It then ends, or prompts for another transfer, depending on how it was called.

A *transfer* is given as:

destination=*source*[*options*]...

where *destination* and *source* are the names of devices or files. There are two kinds of transfer: those that create a single file from one or more sources, and those that copy multiple files. The two kinds of transfer are described in the following topics, and summary tables follow them.

Here are examples of single transfers:

```
clone.bas=original.bas[v]
tail.bas=original.bas[s12000^Z]
```

The file CLONE.BAS is a duplicate of ORIGINAL.BAS; TAIL.BAS is a copy of the part of ORIGINAL.BAS that begins with the characters 12000. Single transfers may also move between drives:

```
c:backup.dat=b:master.dat[v]
b:laminate=one.pli,two.pli,three.pli[v]
```

Single transfers are used to write files to the printer when pagination or sequence numbering is wanted (console copy is easier for simple listings; see the TYPE command):

```
lst:=cbios.prn[t8p]
prn:=equ.lib,mac.lib,hex.lib
```

The special device names NUL: and EOF: are designed for use with a paper-tape punch:

```
pun:=nul:,prom1.hex,eof:,nul:,prom2.hex,eof:,nul:
```

In MP/M 2 ambiguous names may be sent to serial devices, as in:

```
prn:=b:*.bas[t8p50]
```

destination=*source* [*options*]...

The *destination* in a single transfer may be an explicit fileref, the name of a logical device like LST:, the name of a physical device like CRT:, or one of two special PIP device names, PRN: or OUT: (a table of all PIP device names follows the next topic).

The *source(s)* in a single transfer may be explicit filerefs, names of logical devices like CON:, names of physical devices like CRT:, or PIP special device names like EOF:. As many *sources*, separated by commas, may be given as will fit in a command line of 128 characters.

Each *source* is read until end of file is reached and its data are written to the *destination*.

This form of transfer is commonly used to create backup copies of files. The names of sets of related files should be designed for easy copying:

b:=a:po0????.dat	numeric purchase orders, not "poorly.dat"
g:=b:gl*.cob	source modules of general ledger system

The W option (override R/O file protection) is at its most dangerous when a group of files is being copied. When copying a single file there is little chance that a wanted file will be destroyed. When ambiguous filerefs are used it is much easier to pick up an unexpected file by mistake.

In MP/M 2 both source and destination filerefs may be ambiguous, provided they are ambiguous in the same way, as:

```
b:*.bak=a:*.asm[va]
```

In this case the destination files will have different names. The new A option is especially useful for backing up a hard disk.

drivecode=*fileref* [*options*]

This form is used to transfer one or a number of files between drives. The source *fileref* may be ambiguous. The source drive must be different from the destination drive. Only one *fileref* may be given.

The file or files that match *fileref* are copied to the destination drive. The copies are given the same names as their sources. When the *fileref* is ambiguous, PIP reports the name of each file at the console. The name is typed as the copy begins, so if the transfer is aborted, it is the last name that was not completely copied.

Summary of PIP Options

Key: n = a number; *string* = any letters ended with control-z

A	Copy only files with the Archive attribute false; make it true afterward (MP/M 2 only).
B	Buffer input until storage is full or an ASCII DC3 (formerly XOFF, 13h) is seen, then write. Lessens chance of overrun.
D*n*	Truncate input lines after the *n*th character.
E	Echo all data at the console as they are copied.
F	Remove formfeeds (ASCII FF, 0Ch) from the input (P may be used to insert others).
G*n*	Look for this file under user code *n*. (MP/M 2: may be given with destination as well.)
H	Check for correct .HEX format; prompt the user if an error is found. Drop inessential bytes (e.g., NUL, DEL).
I	Drop :00 records from the .HEX-format data (includes actions of the H option).
L	Translate uppercase letters into lowercase.
N1	Add sequence numbers of the form " 99:" to each line.
N2	Add sequence numbers "00000099:," TAB, to each line.
O	Not an ASCII file; don't treat SUB (1Ah) as CP/M end of file (assumed when the filetype is .COM).
P*n*	Insert a formfeed (ASCII FF, 0Ch) after every *n* lines. If *n* is omitted, 60 is assumed (see the F option).
Q*string*	Stop copying when the characters *string* are written.
R	Read the file even if it has the SYS (no directory display) file attribute.
S*string*	Skip input data until the characters *string* are seen.
T*n*	Replace tabs with spaces to simulate tab stops set at every *n*th column. Assumes 8 if *n* omitted (CP/M standard tabs).
U	Translate lowercase letters into uppercase.
V	Do a read-back check of the destination disk file.
W	Replace a read-only destination file without asking the user's permission (bad practice).

Device Names Used in PIP Transfers

Key: d = valid as a destination; s = valid as a source

Logical Devices

CON:	d	s	The currently assigned console device
LST:	d		The currently assigned printer device (see also PRN:)
RDR:		s	The currently assigned reader device
PUN:	d		The currently assigned punch device

Special Devices

PRN:	d		Same as LST: with options [t8np] added
NUL:		s	40 ASCII NUL characters (00h) to space a paper tape
EOF:		s	An ASCII SUB character (1Ah) to mark CP/M end of file
INP:		s	Code patched into PIP, reached via CALL 103H
OUT:	d		Code patched into PIP, reached via CALL 106H

Physical Devices (defined by BIOS code)

TTY:	d	s	A hard-copy terminal device
CRT:	d	s	Usually the main terminal device
UC1:	d	s	A special terminal device
LPT:	d		Usually the main printer device
UL1:	d		A special printer device
PTR:		s	An input device
UR1/2:		s	An input device
PTP:	d		An output device
UP1/2:	d		An output device

The CPNETLDR command, and a successful LOGIN for the desired master system, must have been done successfully before this command can be done.

In CP/NET terminology, "mail" is a one-line message sent by the user of one system in the network to the user of another. Mail is sent with the SNDMAIL command and received with this command. Mail may also come from the user of a master system, or be broadcast to all nodes from a master system. Mail is held by the master closest to this system until it is called for with this command. Then it is sent and also deleted from the master system's queue.

Here is what one side of a conversation by mail might look like:

```
sndmail (04) "Elmer, ready for lunch?"
rcvmail
04: YES MEET YOU IN THE LUNCHROOM - E.
```

RCVMAIL { [*idmaster*] }

The command queries a master system in the CP/NET network for any mail (messages from other CP/NET nodes) that it is holding for this system. If there are messages, they are received and displayed at the terminal.

If *idmaster* is specified, that master will be queried; if it is not, then master 00 will be queried.

The system will be suspended until a message is received.

REN can only be used with explicit filerefs. In CP/M 1, CP/M 2, and MP/M 1 it is not possible to rename a set of related files, as:

```
ren oldprog.*=prog.*    only in MP/M 2
```

REN is handy when all but one or two of a set of files are to be erased or copied. Rename the exceptions, then operate on the remaining set with a single command:

```
ren allbut=except.com
pip b:=a:*.com              copy all but EXCEPT.COM
ren except.com=allbut
```

A read-only file cannot be renamed, nor can a file on a read-only drive. A file with the SYS attribute, if renamed, will then appear in directory displays.

REN *newref=oldref*

The command requires a single operand composed of two explicit filerefs linked by an equal sign. The file named *oldref* is renamed *newref*.

Drivecodes must be omitted from both filerefs, or both drivecodes must be the same. If the drivecodes differ, the command reports *oldref*? and ends.

If a file named *newref* already exists, the command reports FILE EXISTS. If the file *oldref* cannot be found, the command reports NO FILE. In either case no action takes place.

The purpose of SAVE is to preserve a copy of a program image that has been prepared in working storage, usually so that it can be executed later as a command. The normal sequence of events is to use DDT to create the program image and SAVE to preserve it:

ddt badprog.com	load program with a bug
...	alter it with DDT subcommands
-g0	return to the CCP
save 28 goodprog.com	copy the altered program to disk

DDT reports the address of the byte following the end of the program as loaded. The number of pages to save is the decimal value of the most significant byte of this address, unless the address ends in 00h when one less page is needed:

end address is 0E3A	save 0Eh, or 14 pages
end address is 2200	save 21h, or 33 pages

A *size* of zero is permitted; SAVE 0 NULL.COM creates a command file of length zero. Such a command has a use; the NULL command that results is equivalent to restarting the last-executed program at address 0100h. Some programs can be restarted in this way and some cannot.

SAVE *size fileref*

The present contents of working storage, beginning at address 0100h, are copied to disk under the name *fileref*. *Size* specifies a decimal number of pages (256-byte units) to be copied.

Fileref must be explicit. If a file *fileref* already exists, it is replaced. If there is not enough disk space for the file, NO SPACE is reported.

The CPNETLDR command, and a successful LOGIN for the desired master, must have been done before this command.

In CP/NET terminology, "mail" is a one-line message sent by the user of one system in the network to the user of another. Mail sent to a slave system travels through the network to the master system closest to its destination. There it is held until the user of the slave system enters the RCVMAIL command.

Here is what one side of a conversation by mail might look like:

```
sndmail (04) "Elmer, ready for lunch?"
rcvmail
04: YES MEET YOU IN THE LUNCHROOM - E.
```

Mail can be sent to a master system by giving the master system's id for *idrecvr*:

```
sndmail [01] (01) "is my listing finished? Ellen."
```

The message will be held at the destined master system until a user of that system enters the MRCVMAIL command.

SNDMAIL { [*idmaster*] } (*idrecvr*) "*message*"

The command passes a message to a master system in the CP/NET network for delivery to another CP/NET node.

If *idmaster* is specified, the message will be sent via that master; if it is not, then master 00 will be used.

It is a common typing error to omit the colon following *drivecode*. In that case STAT assumes you want information on a file. Usually there is no file of that name, and STAT reports NO FILE.

The first form of the command tells the free space on a drive. Use it to see if there is room for some file, and to check the results of erasing files to make room:

stat bigfile	check size of BIGFILE
stat b:	see if there's room on the B-drive
era b:*.prn	clear some space on the B-drive
stat b:	check space again
pip b:=bigfile	copy the file

The report produced by the second form of the command is based on the CP/M Disk Parameter Block. It describes the information used to allocate space to files. Chapter 14 describes the Disk Parameter Block, relates it to STAT's report, and discusses disk space allocation. The report lines indicate:

1. heading
2. total capacity, including directory space, in records
3. total capacity, including directory space, in kilobytes
4. number of directory entries
5. whether CP/M checks for diskette changes: 0 means not
6. space controlled by one directory entry
7. size of an allocation block (minimum space allocation unit)
8. 128-byte records (not disk sectors) per track
9. tracks reserved for monitor (not included in capacity)

STAT { *drivecode* }
STAT *drivecode*DSK:

The first form of the command reports the access status and the amount of free space on disk drives. If no *drivecode* is given, it reports on all drives that have been accessed since the last warm start. When *drivecode* is specified, that drive is accessed and described. The report for each disk resembles:

```
A: R/W, SPACE: 142K
```

The second form reports the facts that CP/M knows about the drive named by *drivecode*. The report resembles:

```
   B: Device Characteristics
4800: 128-Byte Record Capacity
 600: Kilobyte Drive Capacity
 128: 32-Byte Directory Entries
 128: Checked Directory Entries
 128: Records/ Extent
  16: Records/ Block
  64: Sectors/ Track
   2: Reserved Tracks
```

Use this command to give temporary protection to a disk while testing a new command program:

```
pip b:=testdata
stat a:=r/o
newprog b:testdata
```

If NEWPROG goes off the rails and tries to create a file on the A-drive, it will be terminated at once. The protection is only temporary since the next warm start will remove it.

Programs that do disk I/O through the BIOS are not subject to this control; they can write on any drive.

CP/M marks a drive read-only automatically if it finds that the diskette in it has been changed. The check information used for this feature is saved when the drive is first accessed after a warm start. On each following access CP/M compares the check information to the diskette now in the drive and sets read-only status if there is a difference. A warm start resets the status of all drives; new check data is built for each drive as it is used.

STAT *drivecode*=R/O

The disk drive named by *drivecode* is marked read-only. This access status remains in effect until the next warm start.

If a command tries to change a read-only disk in any way, it is terminated with the message Bdos Err on x: R/O. The system waits for any character to be typed, then performs a warm start.

The Recs and Bytes columns tell of the space allocated to a file. Recs is the number of standard 128-byte records the file occupies, and is the closest estimate of a file's actual size. Files of ASCII text may not fill the last record and hence may be as much as 127 bytes shorter than indicated. Bytes is the amount of space allocated to the file, the amount of space that would be made available if the file were erased.

This command is the only one that reports on a file's access attribute (whether it is marked read-only or not). Files are made read-only with the STAT command for file control.

This command is the only one to report whether a file has the DIR or SYS attribute (can or cannot be displayed by DIR). Files with the SYS attribute are displayed with parentheses around the filename and filetype. Files are given the SYS attribute with the STAT command for file control.

Since files are listed in alphabetical order this is a convenient command for making a hard-copy list of a diskette's directory to store with the diskette. Ready the printer. Enter the command

stat *d:**.*

supplying the drivecode of the diskette to be listed. Before pressing return, enter control-p to start console copy. The report will be printed.

STAT *fileref*

The *fileref* may be ambiguous. A drivecode may be part of it; if one is, that drive's directory is scanned. Otherwise the default drive's directory is scanned.

The command produces a report similar to the following, with one line for each file that matches *fileref*:

```
Recs    Bytes   Ext  Acc
  83      12K     1  R/W   B:(BIGGER.PAS)
  17       4K     1  R/O   B:SMALL.PAS

Bytes Remaining On B: 92K
```

The lines of the report are sorted in alphabetical order by fileref. If no file matches, the command reports only NO FILE.

Files with the SYS attribute are indicated with parentheses around the filename.

Setting the R/O (read-only) attribute makes it impossible to alter the marked file in normal use. This is permanent protection (as opposed to making a disk drive read-only, which lasts only until the next warm start). If a command tries to alter a read-only file (tries to erase it, rename it, or write to it), the command is terminated with the message Bdos Err on x: file R/O. When the next character is typed, a warm start occurs.

PIP can override read-only file protection. It will do so only with the operator's approval, unless the W option is specified. In that case, PIP will replace read-only files without any warning. Programs can (but should not) be written to remove read-only protection from a file. Programs that do disk I/O through the BIOS are not subject to any control.

The SYS attribute is used to shorten the output of the DIR command. Files that are always present can be removed from the DIR display by giving them the SYS attribute. The DIR attribute is the reverse of SYS; it makes the file appear in the DIR command's display.

Files with the SYS attribute are displayed only by the STAT command for file information.

STAT *fileref* $R/O
STAT *fileref* $R/W
STAT *fileref* $SYS
STAT *fileref* $DIR

The fileref may be ambiguous. If it includes a drivecode, the directory on that drive is scanned. Otherwise the default drive is scanned. If no file matches *fileref*, the command reports NO FILE and ends.

The stated attribute—R/O, R/W, SYS, or DIR—is set in every file that matches *fileref*. The command reports each fileref it finds, in the order in which they occur.

Since the relationship between physical device names and actual I/O devices is set by the code of the BIOS—usually written by the vendor of the system—the meaning of an assignment will vary from system to system. The meaning of a physical name may differ depending on the logical device to which it is assigned. The TTY: assigned to CON: may mean something different than TTY: as assigned to PUN:.

Find out the exact meaning of each assignment in your system and fill in the assignment chart on page 299. Use pencil, because these meanings can be changed by changing the BIOS when new devices are added.

STAT DEV:
STAT *logical=physical*
STAT VAL:

The first form of the command reports the present device assignments. The report resembles this:

```
CON: = CRT:
RDR: = TTY:
PUN: = TTY:
LST: = LPT:
```

The names on the left are the names of the CP/M logical devices. Those on the right are names of physical devices. The code of the BIOS determines the relationship between physical device names and the actual I/O devices attached to the system.

The second form of the command assigns the logical device name *logical* to the physical device *physical*. *Logical* must be one of the four names on the left side of the report; *physical* must be a physical device name. There is a table of physical device names on page 298, and a blank I/O assignment chart on page 299.

The third form of the command displays a reminder list of all STAT operands, and a list of the physical device names that may be assigned to each logical name.

When DIR or another command unexpectedly returns the message NO FILE, or when the CCP cannot find a command that ought to exist, it is likely that the wrong user code is active. The command USER 0 will return you to user code 0 under which most files are stored. So will a cold start. A warm start should leave the active user code unchanged.

Normally only files created under the active user code can be accessed. PIP can read a file under another user code and store a copy of it under the active code. See the USER command for a discussion of how to initialize a copy of PIP under a particular code.

STAT USR:

The command reports the active user code number and the codes for which files exist on the default drive. The report resembles:

```
Active User: 0
Active Files: 0 9
```

The first line states the active user code. The second lists all user codes for which files exist on the default drive.

Whenever the CCP begins execution it looks for a file $$$.SUB on the A-drive. If it finds the file, it takes its next command from that file rather than from the terminal. The SUBMIT command is a utility whose function is to create the $$$.SUB file in the rather unusual format the CCP requires. SUBMIT, together with the XSUB command, allows any routine series of commands to be initiated with a single command.

The CCP treats lines that begin with a semicolon as remarks. You can use this feature to put remarks and operator instructions in your submit files.

The SUBMIT command in CP/M 2.2 has two bugs. An input line of length zero causes the command to crash; it is impossible to submit a line of zero length. There is no fix available for this problem. It also treats substituted control characters incorrectly. It will reject ^Z with the message Invalid Control Character. It will handle ^z (lowercase) correctly. A patch is available from Digital Research to correct the problem; see Chapter 12 for an example.

SUBMIT {*drivecode*}*filename* { *parameters...* }

The command supplies a filetype of .SUB to make the first operand a complete fileref. That file is read. Wherever in it a dollar sign followed by a decimal digit appears, the two characters are replaced by the *parameter* that corresponds to the digit. The first *parameter* replaces all appearances of $1, the second replaces $2, and so on. The resulting file is written to disk with the name $$$.SUB.

If *drivecode* is given, the input will be read from that drive, but the output is always written to the default drive. When the file *filename*.SUB can't be found, the command reports No SUB File Present and ends. The entire input file must be read before output begins. If there is not enough working storage for this, the command reports Command Buffer Overflow and ends.

Extra *parameters* have no effect. If the file references a parameter that wasn't given, the $*n* signal is replaced by nothing; that is, the characters vanish. The signal $0 is replaced with *filename*. The up-arrow or caret character signals an ASCII control character. For example, ^Z is replaced by the ASCII SUB character produced by control-z.

SYSGEN is discussed at length in Chapter 15; it is used to place the image of the Monitor on the reserved tracks of a disk or diskette so as to make the disk bootable. The command is often modified by the vendor of a system to suit the disk hardware.

SYSGEN is used in two cases. Most often it is used when initializing one or more new diskettes for use. Each new diskette is formatted. SYSGEN is started and told a source drive from which to read a copy of the Monitor. Then the new diskettes are put in the destination drive in turn, and a copy of the Monitor is written on each.

When a new version of CP/M is being prepared, MOVCPM and DDT are used to prepare a copy of the new Monitor in working storage. SYSGEN is started and given no source drive (as the Monitor image is already in storage). The command is used to copy the new Monitor onto one diskette so that it can be tested.

SYSGEN

The command prompts for the letter of a source drive, a drive from which it can read an image of the CP/M Monitor. A null line signals that the Monitor image is already in storage; if given a drive letter, the command reads the Monitor into storage from the reserved tracks of that disk.

The command then repeatedly asks for the letter of a destination drive, a drive onto which it should write the Monitor. A null line signals end of job; a warm start is done. When given a drive letter, the command writes the Monitor image onto the reserved tracks of the disk in that drive.

The TYPE command is most often used to take a quick look at any printable file. A printable file is one that contains only ASCII characters. Files such as .COM files contain data that is not printable. These can be displayed with TYPE but the output will be peculiar because the terminal will respond to the unprintable characters in unpredictable ways.

TYPE can also be used to copy a file to the printer. Enter the command, but before pressing return, enter a control-p. That enables console copy; the lines displayed by TYPE will also be written to the printer.

TYPE *fileref*

The file *fileref* is read from disk and written to the console.

Fileref must be explicit. If it is ambiguous, or if the file cannot be found, the command responds with *fileref*? and ends.

The command STAT USR: will display the active user code and a list of all user codes for which files exist on the default disk.

To copy files from one user code to another, use PIP with the G option. PIP will read a file created under some other user code and make a copy under the active code. Before you can use it, a copy of PIP must exist under the active user code. For instance, in the sequence:

```
user 9
pip file9=file0[g0]
```

the response to pip will probably be PIP? because no copy of PIP has been made under user code 9. The SAVE command must be used to make one:

user 0	go where PIP is
ddt pip.com	load it into working storage
-g0	return to CCP
user 9	enter user code 9
save 30 pip.com	make a copy of PIP

Now a copy of PIP has been made with user code 9 active. It can be used to read other files and make copies under user code 9.

USER *code*

The number specified as *code* is made the active user code. The only files that can be processed are those that were created when that code was active.

The value of *code* must lie between zero and 15 inclusive. If it does not, the command responds with "*code*?" and ends.

XSUB greatly increases the SUBMIT command's usefulness. Commands that require console input can be submitted for unattended execution. Without XSUB such commands require that the operator remain at the terminal to respond to them.

XSUB's potential is stunted by the fact that it can only respond to a request for a full line of input. Many programs request their input a character at a time; these requests are still directed to the console. Only experiment will reveal which form of input a program uses.

Three useful programs can run under XSUB: ED, DDT, and PIP. An ED session can be automated except for bulk input with the I subcommand. A submit file can do a complicated file alteration; the target file can be chosen through a SUBMIT parameter. DDT can run from a script of subcommands delivered through XSUB.

A sequence of PIP transfers can be automated. PIP's use is impaired by a bug in the SUBMIT command of CP/M 2.2 that makes it unable to handle a null line. The null line that tells PIP to end can't be submitted.

A final consideration for some programs: XSUB makes the apparent size of storage smaller than normal, and disables the warm-start mechanism. A few programs may not be able to run in the reduced space. If a program accidentally damages the Monitor, the damage won't be repaired by a warm start when the command ends.

XSUB

The XSUB program alters the system so that when a program issues a Console Input Line service request (BDOS service 10), the request will be satisfied with the next line from the file A:$$$.SUB, rather than with a line from the console. Until that file is exhausted the message XSUB Active is displayed at each warm start. When the submit file has been drained, the system returns to normal.

If XSUB is already active when the XSUB command is given, it reports the fact and does nothing.

ASCII, HEX

The ASCII Code in Hex and Decimal

Use this chart to convert between ASCII characters and their representations in binary, decimal, and hexadecimal. For example, the character "Z" has a decimal value of 90, a binary representation of 01011010, and the name of the character that results from pressing control-z is SUB.

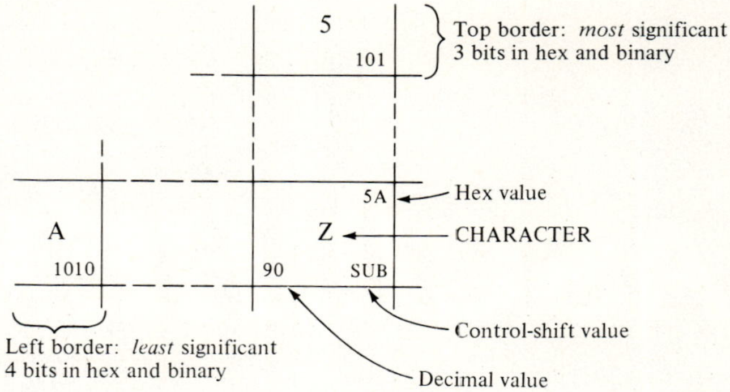

	ϕ 000	1 001	2 010	3 011	4 100	5 101	6 110	7 111
ϕ 0000	00 NUL 0	10 DLE 16 P	20 Space 32	30 ϕ 48	40 @ 64	50 P 80 DLE	60 ` 96	70 p 112
1 0001	01 SOH 1 A	11 DC1 17 Q	21 ! 33	31 1 49	41 A 65 SOH	51 Q 81 DC1	61 a 97	71 q 113
2 0010	02 STX 2 B	12 DC2 18 R	22 " 34	32 2 50	42 B 66 STX	52 R 82 DC2	62 b 98	72 r 114
3 0011	03 ETX 3 C	13 DC3 19 S	23 # 35	33 3 51	43 C 67 ETX	53 S 83 DC3	63 c 99	73 s 115
4 0100	04 EOT 4 D	14 DC4 20 T	24 $ 36	34 4 52	44 D 68 EOT	54 T 84 DC4	64 d 100	74 t 116
5 0101	05 ENQ 5 E	15 NAK 21 U	25 % 37	35 5 53	45 E 69 ENQ	55 U 85 NAK	65 e 101	75 u 117
6 0110	06 ACK 6 F	16 SYN 22 V	26 & 38	36 6 54	46 F 70 ACK	56 V 86 SYN	66 f 102	76 v 118
7 0111	07 BEL 7 G	17 ETB 23 W	27 ' 39	37 7 55	47 G 71 BEL	57 W 87 ETB	67 g 103	77 w 119
8 1000	08 BS 8 H	18 CAN 24 X	28 (40	38 8 56	48 H 72 BS	58 X 88 CAN	68 h 104	78 x 120
9 1001	09 HT 9 I	19 EM 25 Y	29) 41	39 9 57	49 I 73 HT	59 Y 89 EM	69 i 105	79 y 121
A 1010	0A LF 10 J	1A SUB 26 Z	2A * 42	3A : 58	4A J 74 LF	5A Z 90 SUB	6A j 106	7A z 122
B 1011	0B VT 11 K	1B ESC 27 [	2B + 43	3B ; 59	4B K 75 VT	5B [91 ESC	6B k 107	7B { 123
C 1100	0C FF 12 L	1C FS 28 \	2C , 44	3C < 60	4C L 76 FF	5C \ 92 FS	6C l 108	7C | 124
D 1101	0D CR 13 M	1D GS 29]	2D – 45	3D = 61	4D M 77 CR	5D] 93 GS	6D m 109	7D } 125
E 1110	0E SO 14 N	1E RS 30 ^	2E . 46	3E > 62	4E N 78 SO	5E ∧ 94 RS	6E n 110	7E ~ 126
F 1111	0F SI 15 O	1F US 31 _	2F / 47	3F ? 63	4F O 79 SI	5F _ 95 US	6F o 111	7F DEL 127

Table of ASCII Control Characters

Character Name	Value as Dec.	Hex.	Control Shift	Meaning and Use
NUL	0	00	(none)	Null—fills time between data blocks; has no information content. Blank paper tape reads as a series of nulls.
SOH	1	01	A	Start of heading—opens address, format, or other nontext section of a message.
STX	2	02	B	Start of text—starts a text section of a message; ends a heading if one is in progress.
ETX	3	03	C	End of text—ends a section of text in a message. SOH, STX, or EOT may follow.
EOT	4	04	D	End of transmission—ends a complete transmission of one or more texts and associated headings.
ENQ	5	04	E	Enquiry—requests a remote device to send its status or its identification or both.
ACK	6	05	F	Acknowledge—an affirmative response from a receiver to a sender.
BEL	7	07	G	Bell—sounds an audible alarm.
BS	8	08	H	Backspace—moves print head or cursor left one position.
HT	9	09	I	Horizontal tab—moves print head or cursor right to the next defined tab stop (CP/M tab stops are at every eighth column: 9, 17, 25...).
LF	10	0A	J	Linefeed—moves print head or cursor down one line (note 1).
VT	11	0B	K	Vertical tab—moves print head down to the next defined vertical tab stop (note 1).
FF	12	0C	L	Formfeed—moves print head to the defined top line of the next page (note 1).
CR	13	0D	M	Carriage return—moves print head or cursor to the left margin (note 2).
SO	14	0E	N	Shift out—sets alternate font of graphic characters (21h to 7Eh) until SI is seen.

Character Name	Value as Dec.	Hex.	Control Shift	Meaning and Use
SI	15	0F	O	Shift in—returns to standard graphic font. SO and SI are the logical choices to control a graphics mode, but are rarely used.
DLE	16	10	P	Data link escape—marks start of one or more characters to be interpreted as special transmission control characters.
DC1	17	11	Q	Device control 1 (formerly XON)—starts a unit of a remote device. Some printers emit DC1 when they are ready to receive data.
DC2	18	12	R	Device control 2—starts a unit of a remote device.
DC3	19	13	S	Device control 3 (formerly XOFF)—stops a unit of a remote device. Some printers emit DC3 when their buffers are nearly full.
DC4	20	14	T	Device control 4—stops a unit of a remote device.
NAK	21	15	U	Negative acknowledge—a negative response from a receiver to a sender.
SYN	22	16	V	Synchronous idle—fills time on an idle line to maintain synchrony of sender and receiver.
ETB	23	17	W	End transmitted block—marks end of a block of sent data (but not the end of a message, which may span blocks).
CAN	24	18	X	Cancel—causes the transmitted block to be disregarded by the receiver. Logical choice to mark a deleted record.
EM	25	19	Y	End of medium—marks the end of active data on a tape or other medium. Not used in CP/M.
SUB	26	1A	Z	Substitute—replaces a character known to have been garbled in transmission. Used by CP/M to mark logical end of file.
ESC	27	1B	[	Escape—marks the start of a sequence of characters to be interpreted in some special way by the receiving device.
FS	28	1C	\	File separator—see note 3.
GS	29	1D	]	Group separator—see note 3.
RS	30	1E	^	Record separator—see note 3.

Character Name	Value as Dec.	Hex.	Control Shift	Meaning and Use
US	31	1F	—	Unit separator—see note 3.
SP	32	20	(none)	Space—moves print head or cursor one position to the right.
DEL	127	7F	(none)	Delete (formerly rubout)—to be disregarded by the receiver. On paper tape a character may be erased by punching all its holes, resulting in DEL.

Note 1. Normally the print head moves only vertically. When agreed by the sending and receiving parties, the print head may also be moved to the left margin during this action.

Note 2. LF may imply a CR action, serving as a New Line (NL) character, but CR should not imply a LF action. A sender using CR, LF to end lines works properly with a receiver that returns the carrier on LF, but not with one that moves the carrier down the page on CR.

Note 3: FS, GS, RS, and US are optional data delimiters. The standard does not specify their use, except that they form a hierarchy with FS the most inclusive and US the most specific. Note that the four are adjacent to the space, which may be treated as a fifth separator.

Hexadecimal-Decimal Chart

This chart documents the decimal, hexadecimal, binary, and character representations that can be encoded in a single 8-bit byte. Use it to convert between decimal and hexadecimal as, for example, use of the SAVE command requires you to do. If the end address of a program, as reported by DDT, were 25A2h, you need to SAVE the equivalent of 25h pages. The chart shows that 25h is 37 decimal.

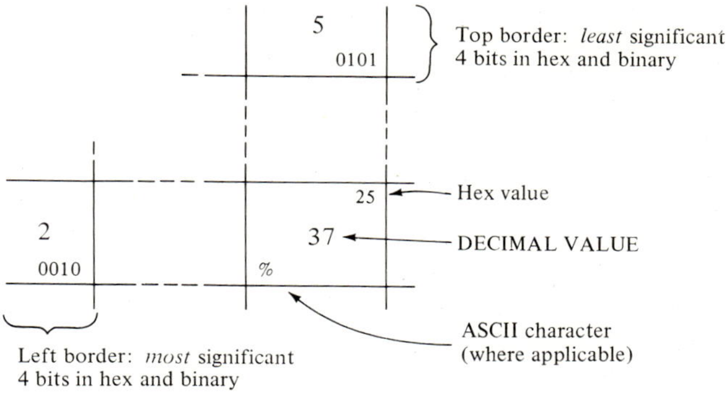

	0 0000	1 0001	2 0010	3 0011	4 0100	5 0101	6 0110	7 0111
0 0000	00 Ø NUL	01 1 SOH	02 2 STX	03 3 ETX	04 4 EOT	05 5 ENQ	06 6 ACK	07 7 BEL
1 0001	10 16 DLE	11 17 DC1(XON)	12 18 DC2	13 19 DC3 (XOF)	14 20 DC4	15 21 NAK	16 22 SYN	17 23 ETB
2 0010	20 32 SPACE	21 33 !	22 34 "	23 35 #	24 36 $	25 37 %	26 38 &	27 39 '
3 0011	30 48 0	31 49 1	32 50 2	33 51 3	34 52 4	35 53 5	36 54 6	37 55 7
4 0100	40 64 @	41 65 A	42 66 B	43 67 C	44 68 D	45 69 E	46 70 F	47 71 G
5 0101	50 80 P	51 81 Q	52 82 R	53 83 S	54 84 T	55 85 U	56 86 V	57 87 W
6 0110	60 96 `	61 97 a	62 98 b	63 99 c	64 100 d	65 101 e	66 102 f	67 103 g
7 0111	70 112 p	71 113 q	72 114 r	73 115 s	74 116 t	75 117 u	76 118 v	77 119 w
8 1000	80 128	81 129	82 130	83 131	84 132	85 133	86 134	87 135
9 1001	90 144	91 145	92 146	93 147	94 148	95 149	96 150	97 151
A 1010	A0 16Ø	A1 161	A2 162	A3 163	A4 164	A5 165	A6 166	A7 167
B 1011	B0 176	B1 177	B2 178	B3 179	B4 180	B5 181	B6 182	B7 183
C 1100	C0 192	C1 193	C2 194	C3 195	C4 196	C5 197	C6 198	C7 199
D 1101	D0 208	D1 209	D2 210	D3 211	D4 212	D5 213	D6 214	D7 215
E 1110	E0 224	E1 225	E2 226	E3 227	E4 228	E5 229	E6 230	E7 231
F 1111	F0 240	F1 241	F2 242	F3 243	F4 244	F5 245	F6 246	F7 247

8 1000	9 1001	A 1010	B 1011	C 1100	D 1101	E 1110	F 1111
08 8 BS	09 9 HT	0A 10 LF	0B 11 VT	0C 12 FF	0D 13 CR	0E 14 SO	0F 15 SI
18 24 CAN	19 25 EM	1A 26 SUB	1B 27 ESC	1C 28 FS	1D 29 GS	1E 30 RS	1F 31 US
28 40 (	29 41)	2A 42 *	2B 43 +	2C 44 ,	2D 45 -	2E 46 .	2F 47 /
38 56 8	39 57 9	3A 58 :	3B 59 ;	3C 60 <	3D 61 =	3E 62 >	3F 63 ?
48 72 H	49 73 I	4A 74 J	4B 75 K	4C 76 L	4D 77 M	4E 78 N	4F 79 O
58 88 X	59 89 Y	5A 90 Z	5B 91 [	5C 92 \	5D 93]	5E 94 ^	5F 95 _
68 104 h	69 105 i	6A 106 j	6B 107 k	6C 108 l	6D 109 m	6E 110 n	6F 111 o
78 120 x	79 121 y	7A 122 z	7B 123 {	7C 124 |	7D 125 }	7E 126 ~	7F 127 DEL
88 136	89 137	8A 138	8B 139	8C 140	8D 141	8E 142	8F 143
98 152	99 153	9A 154	9B 155	9C 156	9D 157	9E 158	9F 159
A8 168	A9 169	AA 170	AB 171	AC 172	AD 173	AE 174	AF 175
B8 184	B9 185	BA 186	BB 187	BC 188	BD 189	BE 190	BF 191
C8 200	C9 201	CA 202	CB 203	CC 204	CD 205	CE 206	CF 207
D8 216	D9 217	DA 218	DB 219	DC 220	DD 221	DE 222	DF 223
E8 232	E9 233	EA 234	EB 235	EC 236	ED 237	EE 238	EF 239
F8 248	F9 249	FA 250	FB 251	FC 252	FD 253	FE 254	FF 255

	Hexadecimal Digit most ⟵	significant	⟶ least	
0	0	0	0	0
1	4,096	256	16	1
2	8,192	512	32	2
3	12,288	768	48	3
4	16,384	1,024	64	4
5	20,240	1,280	80	5
6	24,576	1,536	96	6
7	28,672	1,792	112	7
8	32,768	2,048	128	8
9	36,864	2,304	144	9
A	40,960	2,560	160	10
B	45,056	2,816	176	11
C	49,152	3,072	192	12
D	53,248	3,328	208	13
E	57,344	3,584	224	14
F	61,440	3,840	240	15

16-Bit Hexadecimal-Decimal Conversion (for positive and unsigned values)

Use this chart to convert between decimal and 16-bit hexadecimal numbers when the numbers are positive or are not signed (use the chart on page ?? for signed, negative numbers).

To convert hex to decimal, sum the numbers corresponding to each digit. For example, given 7BDEh:

(1st digit) 7 =		28,672
(2nd digit) B =		2,816
(3rd digit) D =		208
(4th digit) E =	+	14
(result)		31,710

To convert decimal to hex, subtract the largest possible number for each hex digit. Given 11,480:

	11,480	
–	8,192	= 2 (1st digit)
	3,288	
–	3,072	= C (2nd digit)
	216	
–	208	= D (3rd digit)
	8	= 8 (4th digit)

	Hexadecimal Digit most ←	significant	→ least	
0		3,840	240	16
1		3,584	224	15
2		3,328	208	14
3		3,072	192	13
4		2,816	176	12
5		2,560	160	11
6		2,304	144	10
7		2,048	128	9
8	28,672	1,792	112	8
9	24,576	1,536	96	7
A	20,480	1,280	80	6
B	16,384	1,024	64	5
C	12,288	768	48	4
D	8,192	512	32	3
E	4,096	256	16	2
F	0	0	0	1

16-Bit Hexadecimal-Decimal Conversion (for signed, negative values)

Use this chart to convert between decimal and hexadecimal numbers when the numbers are negative. The most significant hex digit of such a number is 8 or greater. Use the chart on page ?? for positive or unsigned numbers.

To convert hex to decimal, sum the numbers shown for each corresponding digit. For example, in order to PEEK location B13Ah the BASIC programmer must convert it:

```
(1st digit) B =    16,384
(2nd digit) 1 =     3,584
(3rd digit) 3 =       192
(4th digit) A = +       6
                ---------
                   20,166   — use PEEK(-20166)
```

To convert decimal to hex, subtract the largest possible number for each digit.

Given -14,283:

```
   14,283
 – 12,288   = C (1st digit)
 --------
    1,995
 –  1,792   = 8 (2nd digit)
 --------
      203
 –    192   = 3 (3rd digit)
 --------
       11   = 5 (4th digit)
```

8080, Z80

8080/8085 Instruction Set—Functional Tableau

This chart displays the instruction set of the Intel 8080/8085 CPU in functional groups. The fixed parts of the instructions are shown in uppercase; the parts that may vary are shown as lowercase abbreviations. For example, the key shows that the abbreviation "bd" may stand for either B or D. Therefore the instruction shown as STAX bd may be coded as STAX B or as STAX D.

Use the chart as a memory aid to recall the use or syntax of instructions. The following chart displays the Z80 instruction set in the same format, with similar instructions at similar locations on the page. Flip between the charts to compare the two instruction sets.

ARITHMETIC INSTRUCTIONS				CONTROL TRANSFER	
8-bit Data			16-bit Data	Unconditional	Conditional
accum : reg	accum : imm.	accum : storage		PCHL	
DAA				JMP addr	Jcnd addr
CMA				CALL addr	Ccnd addr
				RET	Rcnd
INR reg			INX rp	RST s	
DCR reg			DCX rp		
ADD reg	ADI xx		DAD rp		
ADC reg	ACI xx				
SUB reg	SUI xx			**BIT MANIPULATION**	
SBB reg	SBI xx				
ANA reg	ANI xx				
ORA reg	ORI xx				
XRA reg	XRI xx				
CMP reg	CPI xx				

ROTATION	SHIFTS	MACHINE CONTROL
RLA RAR RLC RRC	NOP DI STC	EI IN xx OUT xx CMC RIM SIM

DATA MOVEMENT INSTRUCTIONS

8-bit Data			16-bit Data		
reg : reg	reg → stor	stor → reg	reg : reg	reg → stor	stor → reg
MOV reg,reg	STAX bd STA addr	MVI reg,xx LDAX bd LDA addr	SPHL XCHG	SHLD addr XTHL PUSH ph	LXI rp,xxxx LHLD addr POP ph

Key:

bd : B,D	reg : A,B,C,D,E,H,L,M	cnd : Z,NZ,C,NC,PO,PE,M,P
rp : B,D,H,SP	addr : address constant	xxxx : 16-bit constant
ph : PSW,B,D,H	xx : 8-bit constant	s : 3-bit constant

Z80 Instruction Set—Functional Tableau

This chart displays the instruction set of the Zilog Z80 CPU in functional groups. The fixed parts of the instructions are shown in uppercase; the parts that may vary are shown as lowercase abbreviations. For example, the key shows that the abbreviation "hx" may stand for any of HL, IX, or IY. Therefore the instruction shown as LD SP,hx may be coded as LD SP,HL, or as LD SP,IX, or as LD SP,IY.

Use the chart as a memory aid to recall the use or syntax of instructions. The previous chart displays the 8080/8085 instruction set in the same format, with similar instructions at similar locations on the page. Flip between the charts to compare the two instruction sets.

The following chart shows the syntax for the unique Zilog instructions for the macros distributed with the Digital Research MAC assembler.

ARITHMETIC INSTRUCTIONS

8-bit Data						16-bit Data	
accum : reg		accum : imm.		accum : storage			
DAA							
CPL							
NEG							
INC	reg					INC	rp
DEC	reg					DEC	rp
ADD	reg	ADD	xx	ADD	(xr+d)	ADD	hx,bp
ADC	reg	ADC	xx	ADC	(xr+d)	ADC	HL,bp
SUB	reg	SUB	xx	SUB	(xr+d)		
SBC	reg	SBC	xx	SBC	(xr+d)	SBC	HL,bp
AND	reg	AND	xx	AND	(xr+d)		
OR	reg	OR	xx	OR	(xr+d)		
XOR	reg	XOR	xx	XOR	(xr+d)		
CP	reg	CP	xx	CP	(xr+d)		

CONTROL TRANSFER

Unconditional		Conditional	
JP	(hx)		
JR	xx	JR	cz,xx
JP	addr	JP	cnd,addr
CALL	addr	CALL	cnd,addr
RET		cnd	
RST	s		
RETI			
RETN		DJNZ	xx

BIT MANIPULATION

BIT	s,reg	BIT	s,(xr+d)
SET	s,reg	SET	s,(xr+d)
RES	s,reg	RES	s,(xr+d)

ROTATION	SHIFTS	MACHINE CONTROL
RLA RL reg RL	(xr+d) SLA reg SLA (xr+d)	NOP
RRA RR reg RR	(xr+d) SRA reg SRA (xr+d)	DI EI IN A,(xx) OUT (xx),A
RLCA RLC reg RLC	(xr+d)	SCF CCF IN reg,(C) OUT (C),reg
RRCA RRC reg RRC	(xr+d) SRL reg SRL (xr+d)	EXX EX AF,AF'
RLD		IM 0/1/2
RRD		LD A,I LD A,I
		LD A,R LD R,A

DATA MOVEMENT INSTRUCTIONS

8-bit Data			16-bit Data		
reg : reg	reg → stor	stor → reg	reg : reg	reg → stor	stor → reg
LD reg,reg		LD reg,xx	LD SP,hx		LD rp,xxxx
	LD (bd),A	LD A,(bd)			
	LD (addr),A	LD A,(addr)		LD (addr),rp	LD rp,(addr)
			EX DE,HL	EX (SP),hx	
				PUSH px	POP px
	LD (xr+d),A	LD A,(xr+d)			

Key:

bd : BC,DE	xr : IX,IY	reg : A,B,C,D,E,H.L,(HL)	cnd : Z,NZ,C,NC,PO,PE,M,P
bp : BC,DE,HL,SP	hx : IX,IY,HL	addr,xxxx : 16-bit constant	cz : Z,NZ,C,NC
rp : BC,DE,HL,SP,IX,IY	px : AF,BC,DE,HL,IX,IY	xx : 8-bit constant	s : 3-bit constant

Z80 Assembler Syntax—Cross-Reference

This chart shows the assembler syntax of the instructions that are unique to the Z80 for three different assemblers. The first column shows the standard Zilog syntax. The second column shows the "TDL mnemonics" used in some non-Zilog assemblers. The third column shows the syntax of the macros contained in the file Z80.LIB, distributed with Digital Research's MAC assembler product.

Use the chart when a Z80 instruction is needed in a program to be assembled with MAC. Proceed as follows:

1. Find the instruction wanted in Z80 Instruction Set Functional Tableau, page ??.
2. Flip back one page to the 8080/8085 Instruction Set Functional Tableau. If there is an 8080 instruction at the same location on that page, code that instruction.
3. Look the instruction up in this chart (the chart is organized in the same groups and in about the same order). If the instruction does not appear, then the macro (and the TDL mnemonic) has the same syntax as the standard Zilog instruction; code the Zilog instruction.
4. Code the macro from the third column of this chart.

Arithmetic Instructions, 8-bit

Zilog		TDL		Z80.LIB	
DEC	(xr+d)	DCR	d(xr)	DCRx	d
INC	(xr+d)	INR	d(xr)	INRx	d
ADD	(xr+d)	ADD	d(xr)	ADDx	d
ADC	(xr+d)	ADC	d(xr)	ADCx	d
SUB	(xr+d)	SUB	d(xr)	SUBx	d
SBC	(xr+d)	SBB	d(xr)	SBCx	d
AND	(xr+d)	ANA	d(xr)	ANDx	d
OR	(xr+d)	ORA	d(xr)	ORx	d
XOR	(xr+d)	XRA	d(xr)	XORx	d
CP	(xr+d)	CMP	d(xr)	CMPx	d

Arithmetic Instructions, 16-bit

Zilog		TDL		Z80.LIB	
INC	xr	INX	xr	INXxr	
DEC	xr	DCX	xr	DCXxr	
ADC	HL,bp	DADC	bp	DADC	bp
SBC	HL,bp	DSBC	bp	DSBC	bp
ADD	xr,bp	DADx	bp	DADx	bp

Control Transfer Instructions

JP	(hx)	PCHx		PCHx	
JR	xx	JMPR	xx	JR	xx
JR	cz,xx	JRcz	xx	JRcz	xx

Bit Manipulation Instructions

SET	s,reg	SET	s,reg	SETB	s,reg
BIT	s,(xr+d)	BIT	s,d(xr)	BITx	s,d
RES	s,(xr+d)	RES	s,d(xr)	RESx	s,d
SET	s,(xr+d)	SET	s,d(xr)	SETx	s,d

Rotation and Shift Instructions

RL	reg	RALR	reg	RALR	reg
RL	(xr+d)	RALR	d(xr)	RALx	d
RR	reg	RARR	reg	RARR	reg
RR	(xr+d)	RARR	d(xr)	RARx	d
RLC	reg	RLCR	reg	RLCR	reg
RLC	(xr+d)	RLCR	d(xr)	RLCx	d
RRC	reg	RRCR	reg	RRCR	reg
RRC	(xr+d)	RRCR	d(xr)	RRCx	d
SLA	reg	SLAR	reg	SLAR	reg
SLA	(xr+d)	SLAR	d(xr)	SLAx	d
SRA	reg	SRAR	reg	SRAR	reg
SRA	(xr+d)	SRAR	d(xr)	SRAx	d
SRL	reg	SRLR	reg	SRLR	reg
SRL	(xr+d)	SRLR	d(xr)	SRLx	d

Machine Control Instructions

IN	reg,(C)	INP	reg	INP	reg
OUT	(C),reg	OUTP	reg	OUTP	reg
LD	A,I	LDAI		LDAI	
LD	I,A	LDIA		STAI	
LD	A,R	LDAR		LDAR	
LD	R,A	LDRA		STAR	

Data Movement Instructions, 8-bit

LD	reg,(xr+d)	MOV	reg,d(xr)	LDx	reg,d
LD	(xr+d),reg	MOV	d(xr),reg	STx	reg,d
LD	(xr+d),xx	MVI	d(xr),xx	MVIx	xx,d

Data Movement Instructions, 16-bit

LD	SP,hx	SPhx		SPhx	
LD	xr,xxxx	LXI	xr,xxxx	LXIx	xxxx
LD	(addr),rp	SrpD	addr	SrpD	addr
LD	rp,(addr)	LrpD	addr	LrpD	addr
EX	(SP),hx	XThx		XThx	
PUSH	xr	PUSH	xr	PUSHxr	
POP	xr	POP	xr	POPxr	

Indirect Comparison

CPI	CCI	CCI
CPD	CCD	CCD
CPIR	CCIR	CCIR
CPDR	CCDR	CCDR

ASM, MAC

Most often the parameter letters are omitted entirely, causing all files to be located on the default drive. The assembly of a large file can be speeded by proper use of the parameters.

When the program is expected to have errors, a fast syntax check can be had by suppressing both output files. Errors are reported at the console as usual but the assembly runs faster when no output files are written.

Most of the assembler's time is spent writing the listing file or waiting for the drive to seek between files. Suppressing the listing file will shorten assembly time.

Diskette hardware is usually faster at switching between drives than at seeking on one drive. Putting the input and output files on different drives will often speed a long assembly. Hard disk drives seek very quickly. If you have one, place the output files, or all the files, on it.

A large listing may fill the output disk causing the assembler to abort with the message OUTPUT FILE WRITE ERROR. In this case direct the listing to the console and use control-p to get a paper copy of the file. This allows a complete assembly, but execution is slowed because the assembler is limited by the speed of the printer.

ASM {*drivecode*}*filename*{*.shp*}

The file named *filename*.ASM is assembled. Assembly errors are reported to the console. A file representing the object program may be produced as *filename*.HEX. A file containing the listing may be produced as *filename*.PRN.

If the optional *drivecode* is given, that drive is made the default drive for all files. The parameter letters may specify other drives.

The optional parameter letters *shp* occupy the position of a filetype, but they specify the drives used for the three files. Parameter letter *s* specifies the drive (one of A...P) to be searched for *filename*.ASM.

Parameter letter *h* determines the drive (one of A...P) where *filename*.HEX will be written. If *h* = Z, the object file is suppressed.

Parameter letter *p* controls the destination of the listing. When *p* is one of A...P, a listing file is written to that drive. If *p* = X, the listing is written to the console; *p*=Z suppresses it.

ASM Error Messages

D: The operand is too large to store in the defined space.

E: An operand is required. None can be found, or the operand expression cannot be interpreted.

L: This label is a duplicate of that on another statement, or no label is allowed on this type of statement.

N: This operation is not available in the ASM assembler.

O: Either a character string is too long, or the operand expression is too complex to be evaluated.

P: Label or expression has a different value on the second assembly pass than on the first. May be attributable to duplicate labels or reference to a label before it is defined. Fix all other errors first; P errors often go away with them.

R: The register operand is not correct for the operation, as in DAD A.

S: A required statement field can't be identified, as when the label is omitted from an EQU. May result from the use of double rather than single quotes on a character constant.

U: A label in the operand expression hasn't been defined prior to this statement (an EQU, IF, SET, or ORG), and it must be.

V: The value of the operand expression is wrong for the type of operation, as in MVI A,300.

CANNOT CLOSE FILES: An output file can't be closed, probably because the diskette in that drive was changed and so made R/O.

NO DIRECTORY SPACE: An output file can't be created because that disk's directory is full.

NO SOURCE FILE PRESENT: The filename was omitted from the command line, or filename.ASM is not on that disk.

OUTPUT FILE WRITE ERROR: There is either no more data space or no more directory space for the output file.

SOURCE FILE NAME ERROR: The filename contained an asterisk or question marks. It must be explicit.

SOURCE FILE READ ERROR: This error probably can't occur; the assembler would be terminated with "BDOS Error on x:" instead.

SYMBOL TABLE OVERFLOW: There are more labels defined in the program than the assembler has room to store.

Statement Formation in ASM

1. A statement contains these fields:

sequence label operation operand ;comment

sequence: Any number of decimal digits and spaces. The field is treated as spaces; it is not checked for numeric format or correct statement order.

label: Any number of letters and digits, the first a letter.

Lowercase letters are treated as uppercase.

The first 16 characters are used; others are ignored.

Dollar signs may be interspersed in the label; they are ignored and not counted.

Op codes, directives, and operators (e.g., SHL) are reserved; use of one as a label causes an error.

A colon at the end of a label is treated as a space.

operation: An instruction operation code or a directive.

Op codes and directives are reserved words; they are recognized wherever they appear in the line, even in the first character of the line.

operand: An assembler expression (see the next chart).

;comment: Any characters except exclamation mark. A comment is treated as spaces.

2. All fields are optional and may be omitted, except that most *operations* require an *operand*.

3. More than one statement may appear in an input line. Statements are separated by exclamation marks.

4. Any number of spaces may be used before, between, and after fields.

5. An *operation* can begin in the left margin. When a label is present, a space or colon must separate it from the *operation*. A space must separate *operation* and *operand*.

Elements of ASM Expressions

1. *Numeric constants* represent unsigned 16-bit integers. Dollar signs may be interspersed among the digits; they are ignored.

binary digits and B:	0110B	1010$1100$1110B
octal digits O or Q:	6Q	5316Q
decimal digits, optional D:	6	2766D
hexadecimal digits and H:	6H	0ACEH

2. *Character constants* usually represent their hexadecimal ASCII values as unsigned 16-bit integers. See the DB and DW directives for their different treatment of characters.

   A single character A is equivalent to 41H.
   Two characters AB are equivalent to 4142H.
   Multiple characters MESSAGE are allowed in DB only.

3. *Labels* represent the unsigned 16-bit integer value given them at the point at which they are defined. This is usually the address of the operation the label precedes. EQU, ORG, and SET give their labels the value of their operands.

4. *Operation code names* represent their binary value with zero bits in any register fields.

5. The ten *register names* represent these values:

A = 7	B = 0	C = 1	D = 2	E = 3
H = 4	L = 5	M = 6	SP = 6	PSW = 6

6. The special name $ represents the address of the next byte to be assembled (the location counter).

7. The result of any compound expression is an unsigned 16-bit integer. Use parentheses to force the order of evaluation wanted. In this display *x* and *y* stand for any of the elements above, or any compound expression in parentheses:

+*y*	identity (= *y* alone)	NOT *y*	ones' complement
-*y*	twos' complement	*x* AND *y*	logical and
x+*y*	unsigned sum	*x* OR *y*	inclusive or
x-*y*	unsigned difference	*x* XOR *y*	exclusive or
*x***y*	unsigned product	*x* SHL *y*	*x* shift left *y* bits
x/*y*	integer division	*x* SHR *y*	*x* shift right *y* bits
x MOD *y*	remainder of *x*/*y*		

Here are examples of complete statements using expressions:
MVI A,MOV OR ((A SHL 3) OR B): put a "MOV A,B" opcode in A
ORG ($+00FFH) AND 0FF00H: move to next page boundary.

Most often the parameters are omitted entirely, causing all files to be located on the default drive. The assembly of a large file can be speeded by proper use of the parameters.

When the program is expected to have errors, a fast syntax check can be had by suppressing all output files (HZ PZ –S). Errors are reported at the console as usual but the assembly runs faster when no output files are written.

Except when there are many macros to expand, most of the assembler's time is spent writing the listing file or waiting for the drive to seek between files. Suppressing the listing file (PZ) will shorten assembly time. If the SID debugging tool is not to be used immediately after the assembly, suppress the symbol table as well (PZ –S). Should you later want to use SID, produce a symbol table quickly by writing only that file (PZ HZ).

Diskette hardware is usually faster at switching between drives than at seeking on one drive. Putting the input and output files on different drives will often speed a long assembly. Hard disk drives seek very quickly. If you have one, place the output files, or all the files, on it.

A large listing may fill the output disk causing the assembler to abort with the message OUTPUT FILE WRITE ERROR. In this case direct the listing to the printer (PP or PP +S) to get a paper copy of the file. This allows a complete assembly, but execution is slowed because the assembler is limited by the speed of the printer.

MAC {*drivecode*}*filename* { $ *parameters* }

The file named *filename*.ASM is assembled. Assembly errors are reported to the console. A file representing the object program may be produced as *filename*.HEX. A file containing the listing may be produced as *filename*.PRN. A symbol table file may be produced as *filename*.SYM.

If the optional *drivecode* is given, that drive is made the default drive for all files, unless a parameter specifies otherwise.

The optional *parameters* control a number of features (a complete table of parameter values appears following this topic). The disposition of the four files is controlled by parameters. The parameter A*d* (where *d* is a drive letter) specifies the drive to be searched for *filename*.ASM. The parameter L*d* specifies the drive to be searched for macro libraries.

The parameter H*d* determines the drive (*d* one of A...P) where *filename*.HEX will be written. HZ suppresses the object file.

The parameter P*d* controls the destination of the listing. When *d* is one of A...O, a listing file is written to that drive. Drive P: cannot be specified; PP causes the listing to be written to the LST: device. PX sends the listing to the console; PZ suppresses it.

The parameter S*d* controls the destination of the symbol table, where *d* has the same meanings as for the P*d* parameter. The symbol table may be suppressed with either SZ or –S. Specifying +S sends the symbol table after the listing to whatever that file's destination may be.

MAC Parameters

Command Parameters, Used Following $ *in the* MAC *command:*

A*d*	Search for the source file on drive *d*.
H*d*	Write the .HEX file on drive *d* (with RMAC, use R rather than H to control the .REL file).
HZ	Suppress the .HEX file.
L*d*	Search for all .LIB files on drive *d*.
+L	List the contents of .LIB files as they are read.
–L	Don't list the contents of .LIB files.
+M	List all macro lines as they are substituted (normally, only those that produce object code are listed).
–M	List no lines produced from macro substitution (includes the bodies of IRP, IRPC, and REPT).
*M	List only the object code (hex values in the left column of the listing) produced from macro substitution.
P*d*	Write the listing as a .PRN file on drive *d*.
PP	Write the listing to the logical list device.
PX	Write the listing to the logical console device.
PZ	Suppress the listing entirely.
+Q	Include local symbols (names beginning ??) in the symbol table.
-Q	Don't include local symbols in the symbol table (default).
+R	Add 100h to the operands of all ORG statements; assists in the construction of a .PRL file under MP/M. This function is not available in RMAC where R controls the .REL file.
S*d*	Write the symbol table as a .SYM file on drive *d*.
+S	Write the symbol table following the listing file, whatever its destination may be.
–S	Suppress the symbol table display.

Source File Controls, Inserted as Lines Within the Source Program:

$–PRINT	Stop producing a listing (this line is not printed).
$+PRINT	Start producing a listing (this line is printed).
$+MACRO	Start listing lines produced by macros.
$–MACRO	List no lines produced by macros.
$*MACRO	List only object code produced by a macro.

MAC Error Messages

B: A balanced pair of statements doesn't match; there's an extra ELSE, ENDM, or ENDIF, or one out of place.

C: The statement allows multiple expressions and one expression isn't properly delimited from the next.

D: The operand is too large to store in the defined space.

E: An operand is required. None can be found, or the operand expression cannot be interpreted.

I: An invalid character (not printable, not HT, CR, or LF) appears in this line.

L: This label is a duplicate of that on another statement, or no label is allowed on this type of statement.

M: Macro expansion is out of room; a macro is probably calling itself without limit.

N: This operation is not available in the MAC assembler.

O: Either a character string is too long, or the operand expression is too complex to be evaluated. Within a macro too many substitutions are called for, or 10,000 local labels have been generated.

P: Label or expression has a different value on the second assembly pass than on the first. May be due to duplicate labels or use of a label before it is defined. Correct other errors first; that often makes P errors go away.

R: The register operand is not correct for the operation, as in DAD A.

S: A required statement field can't be identified, as when the label is omitted from an EQU. May result from the use of double rather than single quotes on a character constant

U: A label in the operand expression hasn't been defined prior to this statement, and it must be.

V: The value of the operand expression is wrong for the type of operation, as in MVI A,300.

CANNOT CLOSE FILES: An output file can't be closed, probably because the diskette in that drive was changed and so made R/O.

INVALID PARAMETER: One of the parameter letters in the command line is not known or has the wrong argument.

NO DIRECTORY SPACE: An output file can't be created because that disk's directory is full.

NO SOURCE FILE PRESENT: The filename was omitted from the command line, or there is no *filename*.ASM on that disk.

OUTPUT FILE WRITE ERROR: There is either no more data space or no more directory space for the output file.

SOURCE FILE NAME ERROR: The filename contained an asterisk or question marks. It must be explicit.

SOURCE FILE READ ERROR: This error probably can't occur; the assembler would be terminated with "BDOS Error on x:" instead.

SYMBOL TABLE OVERFLOW: There are more labels defined in the program than the assembler has room to store.

UNBALANCED MACRO LIBRARY: In a macro library a macro definition isn't properly closed with ENDM.

Statement Formation in MAC

1. A statement contains these fields:

sequence *label* *operation* *operand* *;comment*

sequence: Any number of decimal digits and spaces. The field is treated as spaces; it is not checked for numeric format or correct sequence.

label: any number of letters and digits, the first a letter.

Lowercase letters are treated as uppercase.

? and @ are treated as letters in labels. Labels beginning ?? are not listed in the symbol file.

The first 16 characters are used; others are ignored.

Dollar signs in the label are ignored and not counted.

A colon at the end of a label is treated as a space.

Op codes, directives, and operators (e.g., LOW) are reserved; they may not appear as labels.

operation: An instruction operation code or a directive.

operand: An assembler expression (see the next chart).

;comment: Any characters except exclamation mark. A comment is treated as spaces. In a macro a comment headed by ;; is neither stored nor listed.

2. All fields are optional and may be omitted, except that most *operations* require an *operand*.

3. More than one statement may appear in an input line. Statements are separated by exclamation marks.

4. Any number of spaces may be used before, between, and after fields.

5. An *operation* can begin in the left margin. When a label is present, a space or colon must separate it from the *operation*. A space must separate *operation* and *operand*.

Elements of MAC Expressions

1. *Numeric constants* represent unsigned 16-bit integers. Dollar signs may be interspersed among the digits; they are ignored.

binary digits and B:	0110B	1010$1100$1110B
octal digits O or Q:	6Q	5316Q
decimal digits, optional D:	6	2766D
hexadecimal digits and H:	6H	0ACEH

2. *Character constants* usually represent their hexadecimal ASCII values as unsigned 16-bit integers. See the DB and DW directives for their different treatment of characters.

   A single character A is equivalent to 41H.
   Two characters AB are equivalent to 4142H.
   Multiple characters MESSAGE are allowed in DB only.

3. *Labels* represent the unsigned 16-bit integer value given them at the point they appear. This is usually the address of the operation the label precedes. EQU, ORG, and SET give their labels the value of their operands.

4. *Operation code names* represent their binary value with zero bits in any register fields.

5. The ten *register names* represent these values:

A = 7	B = 0	C = 1	D = 2	E = 3
H = 4	L = 5	M = 6	SP = 6	PSW = 6

6. The special name $ represents the address of the next byte to be assembled (the location counter).

7. The result of any compound expression is a 16-bit integer. Use parentheses to force the order of evaluation wanted. In this display *x* and *y* stand for any of the elements above, or any compound expression in parentheses:

+ *y*	identity (= *y* alone)	NOT *y*	ones' complement
− *y*	twos' complement	*x* AND *y*	logical and
x + *y*	unsigned sum	*x* OR *y*	inclusive or
x − *y*	unsigned difference	*x* XOR *y*	exclusive or
x * *y*	unsigned product	*x* SHL *y*	*x* shift left *y* bits
x / *y*	integer division	*x* SHR *y*	*x* shift right *y* bits
x MOD *y*	remainder of *x*/*y*	LOW *y*	same as *y* AND 00FFh
HIGH *y*	same as *y* SHR 8		

The relationals return FFFFh for true, 0000h for false:

x LT *y*	*x* EQ *y*	*x* GE *y*
x LE *y*	*x* NE *y*	*x* GT *y*

NUL returns FFFFh (true) if the rest of the line is blank.

Summary of Macro Substitution in MAC

The Macro Call

A macro is defined with a MACRO directive, which provides a *name* and template of *arguments* for the macro:

```
label       MACRO  {name,...}
AMACRO      MACRO  NAME1,NAME2,NAME3,NAME4
```

The lines following, up to an ENDM directive, compose the macro *body*. These lines are stored for later use.

A macro *call* occurs when, in the source, the macro name is found, delimited by spaces. The rest of that statement is part of the macro call; other statements on that line are discarded.

The assembler finds all *tokens* after the macro label. A token is:

A *list*: any sequence of characters enclosed in <angle brackets>

An *expression*: any sequence of characters between % and a comma

A *string*: any sequence of nonspaces up to a comma.

Tokens are assigned one-to-one to the argument names, according to their delimiters:

Lists: The outer set of angle brackets is dropped; the sequence of characters within is assigned to the matching argument,

Expressions: The characters are evaluated as an expression; the resulting 16-bit unsigned number is converted to decimal; the decimal characters are assigned to matching argument.

Strings: The characters (forced to uppercase) are assigned to the name.

For example, given these two statements,

```
address equ 0200H
        amacro %address shr 8,mvi,<token3,<this too>>,token4
```

NAME1 receives the characters: 32 (evaluated expression)
NAME2 receives the characters: MVI
NAME3 receives the characters: TOKEN3,<THIS TOO>
NAME4 receives the characters: TOKEN4

Extra tokens are discarded. Omitted tokens become null strings.

An S error is reported if a space appears in a string token.

A U or P error is reported if a label used in an expression has not been defined prior to the macro call.

An E error is reported if an expression is badly formed.

The Macro Body

After assigning tokens to names, the assembler processes the lines of the macro body as if they were part of the source program.

Wherever in a body line it finds an argument name delimited by spaces or other special characters, the assembler substitutes the token assigned to that name. Given the previous macro call,

name4 name2 a,name1+1 becomes TOKEN4 MVI a,32+1

As an argument of another macro:

mac2 name3 becomes mac2 TOKEN3,<THIS TOO>

Where an argument is not clearly set off by special characters,substitution can be forced by prefixing it with &:

xyzname4 is not changed, the "name4" argument is not seen.
xyz&name4 becomes xyzTOKEN4

Where an argument runs up to other letters its end must be marked with &:

name4xyz is not changed, the "name4" argument is not seen.
name4&xyz becomes TOKEN4xyz

If an argument name is to be recognized inside a character constant,the & must be used and the name must be coded in uppercase:

db 'name2.' is not changed, the & is required.
db '&name2' is not changed, "name2" doesn't equal "NAME2"
db '&NAME2' becomes db 'MVI'

Assembler

Topical Summary of Assembler Directives

Directive	Assembler	Page	Function
	Data Definition		
DB *operands...*	all	421	Assemble 8-bit constants
DW *operands...*	all	425	Assemble 16-bit constants
DS *operand*	all	423	Reserve space in program
EQU *operand*	all	429	Give name to value (permanent)
SET *operand*	all	443	Give name to value (temporary)
ORG *operand*	all	439	Set location counter
DSEG	RMAC	423	Move to data segment
	Conditional Assembly		
IF *operand*	all	433	Skip input if operand=0
ELSE	MAC	425	Alternate part of IF group
ENDIF	all	427	Close of IF group
	Substitution and Macro Processing		
MACLIB *filename*	MAC	437	Include library file
MACRO *arguments...*	MAC	437	Open macro definition
IRP *dummy,<tokens>*	MAC	433	Repeat text over items
IRPC *dummy,token*	MAC	435	Repeat text over letters
REPT *operand*	MAC	443	Repeat text operand times
EXITM	MAC	431	Stop macro or repeat group
ENDM	MAC	429	Close macro or repeat body
SET *operand*	MAC	443	Give name to value (temporary)
LOCAL *names...*	MAC	435	Declare local label-names
	Program Structure		
DS *operand*	all	423	Reserve space in program
ORG *operand*	all	439	Set location counter
ASEG	RMAC	419	Move to absolute segment
CSEG	RMAC	421	Move to relocatable code
DSEG	RMAC	423	Move to data segment
COMMON */name/*	RMAC	419	Move to a common segment
END *{operand}*	all	427	End source program

Directive	Assembler	Page	Function
	Program Linkage		
NAME *'program'*	RMAC	439	Set name of object code
EXTRN *labels...*	RMAC	431	Declare foreign labels
PUBLIC *labels...*	RMAC	441	Declare entry labels
ASEG	RMAC	419	Move to absolute segment
COMMON */name/*	RMAC	419	Move to a common segment
	Listing Control		
PAGE *{operand}*	MAC	441	Eject; set page height
TITLE *'title-line'*	MAC	445	Enable titling, set line

A relocatable program may have an absolute segment. ASEG is used to force the LINK command to place that code at its assembled origin in storage. The main use for the absolute segment is to establish addresses fixed by the operating system, for instance:

```
        aseg
        org     0   ;   set abs. location counter
boot    equ     $   ;   warmstart jump at abs. 000,h
        org     5
bdos    equ     $   ;   bdos jump at abs. 0005h
        cseg        ;   relocatable code begins
```

Then a call to BDOS in the relocatable segment will be assembled with an absolute target address of 0005h.

Absolute segments containing object code must be linked with care. If two routines assemble through the same absolute addresses, the code of one will overlay that of the other when they are linked.

A common segment is a portion of storage that, at execution time, will be used in common by several separately assembled routines. Each routine contains its own definition of the common segment. The assembler notes the size of the area and passes that information in the object file. The LINK command allocates space for common segments following the code segments, and supplies the absolute addresses needed to reference it.

Common segments can be a fruitful source of bugs. To ensure that all routines use the same definition of common space, put the defining statements (DS, EQU, and labeled ORG statements) in a macro library.

The initialization of a common segment must be handled carefully. Object code assembled in a common segment is placed in the object file; the LINK command places that code in the common area. If two routines both assemble initial values for a common segment, the initial data from the second one linked will overlay that from the first one linked.

ASEG (RMAC)

{ *label* } ASEG

The assembler begins to place object code in the absolute segment of the program. Until a CSEG, DSEG, or COMMON directive is seen, all assembly addresses are absolute addresses that cannot be changed when the program is linked.

The optional label receives the absolute address of the next byte in the absolute segment.

COMMON (RMAC)

COMMON */name/*

The assembler begins to place object code in blank common or the named common segment. Until the next ASEG, CSEG, or DSEG directive is seen all assembly addresses will be relocatable, to be established when the LINK command locates this common segment.

Each named common segment is distinct, and has its own location counter. Each will occupy a distinct area of storage at execution time.

Most or all of the instructions and constants of a relocatable program will be placed in the code segment. The address of the relocatable segment is established by the LINK command. The relocatable segment of the first module linked will be placed at the start of the Transient Program Area; any other code segments will follow it.

A label equated to a relocatable address is called, reasonably, a relocatable label. Such labels may be used in expressions in only these ways:

relocatable label + constant
relocatable label – constant
relocatable label +/– relocatable label

The last form, adding or subtracting two relocatable labels, is only allowed when the two labels are defined in the same segment. These restrictions are needed because only in these cases can the assembler know the result of the operation. The result of any other arithmetic or Boolean operation on a relocatable label cannot be known until the program has been linked.

The most frequent use of DB is to assemble character constants for messages and the like:

```
makemsg   db     'Can''t create output file!','$'
```

The directive will accept an expression in any operand:

```
comsize   db     ((program$end-0100h)+127) shr 7
```

If program$end is the label on the END directive, that statement will assemble a 1-byte count of the number of records (128-byte units) in the program's .COM file. (That expression, however, is not a relocatable one, and will cause an error if used with RMAC.)

DB can be used at any point in the program, even within executable code:

```
lxi       d,to
lxi       h,from
db        0edh,0b0h ; Z80 LDIR instruction
```

CSEG (RMAC)

{ *label* } CSEG

The assembler begins to place object code in the code, or relocatable, segment of the program. Until an ASEG, DSEG, or COMMON directive is seen all addresses used will be relocatable, to be established when the LINK command locates the code segment.

The optional label receives the relative address of the next byte in the code segment.

DB (ASM, MAC, RMAC)

{ *label* } DB *operand*{,*operand*...}

The values of the operands are assembled as 1-byte values in consecutive locations.

Each operand must evaluate to an 8-bit value; if more than 8 bits are needed to contain it, the assembler reports a D error.

An operand that is only a character constant may contain as many as 64 characters. Each character is treated as a separate operand.

The optional label receives the address of the first byte assembled.

DS is most often used to set aside buffer space within the program:

```
buflen    equ  128
buffer    ds   buflen
```

The contents of the reserved space at execution time can't be predicted. Quite likely they will consist of whatever garbage was in storage at those addresses at the time the LOAD or LINK command built the .COM file. The space can be given a known value by loading the program under DDT and using its Fill subcommand to initialize the space.

Programs that will be converted to page relocatable form (.PRL, .SPR) under MP/M should never end with a DS directive. The DS directive produces no output in the .HEX file. MP/M's GENMOD command assumes that the storage requirement of a program is its length through the last byte defined by a .HEX record. Insert a DB 0 at the end of the program to force generation of a .HEX record at the true end address.

The buffers and variables of a relocatable program either may be placed in its code segment with its instructions or isolated in its data segment. It is a good practice to put all modifiable fields in the data segment. The address of the data segment is established by the LINK command. The data segments of all modules linked are placed at the end of the linked program following the code and common segments.

A label equated to a relocatable address is called, reasonably, a relocatable label. Such labels may be used in expressions in only these ways:

relocatable label + constant
relocatable label – constant
relocatable label +/– relocatable label

The last form, adding or subtracting two relocatable labels, is only allowed when the two labels are defined in the same segment. These restrictions are needed because only in these cases can the assembler know the result of the operation. The result of any other arithmetic or Boolean operation on a relocatable label cannot be known until the program has been linked.

DS (ASM, MAC, RMAC)

{ *label* } DS *operand*

The value of the operand is added to the location counter, causing the assembler to skip over part of the program space. The contents of the addresses skipped over are not defined.

The optional label receives the address of the first byte skipped.

DSEG (RMAC)

{ *label* } DSEG

The assembler begins placing object code in the data segment of the program. Until the next ASEG, CSEG, or COMMON directive is seen, all assembly addresses will be relocatable, to be established when the LINK command locates the data segment.

The optional label receives the relative address of the next byte to be assembled in the data segment.

DW is most often used to assemble address constants and 16-bit numeric values:

```
buffstart   dw   buffer
buffend     dw   buffer+bufflen
bytemask    dw   -256
```

It is also convenient for initializing storage, since it requires half the number of operands of DB:

```
ff          equ  -1
bitmap      dw   ff,ff,ff,ff
```

The last example assembles 8 bytes of FFh.

ELSE is used in an IF … ELSE … ENDIF group to select an alternate section of input text for assembly based on some condition. See the IF directive.

{ *label* } DW *operand*{,*operand*... }

The values of the operands are assembled as two-byte values in consecutive locations. Normally each value is stored with its least significant 8 bits first and its most significant 8 bits second, according to the Intel convention for word values.

Signed numbers are extended on the left to 16 bits with their sign bit value. Unsigned values are extended on the left to 16 bits with 0 bits.

Operands that are character constants may have no more than two characters. A two-character constant is treated differently from other operands. The first character given is stored in the first byte of the word, and the second in the second.

The optional label receives the address of the first byte assembled.

{ *label* } ELSE

The true scope of the enclosing IF directive is ended. If the assembler is skipping input text because the IF was false, it begins processing text when ELSE is seen. If the assembler was processing text because the IF was true, it skips text from the ELSE to the matching ENDIF.

The optional label (whose use is not recommended) will be defined and given the address of the next byte assembled, but only if the assembler was processing input text following a true IF. Otherwise it will be ignored.

If there is no matching IF directive, the assembler reports a B error.

The entry address has little use under CP/M. If the .HEX file is loaded under DDT, the debugger will set the initial program counter contents from the entry address. However, commands loaded into the transient program area are always entered at 0100h. It is conventional to code END 0100H to document this fact.

The value of the optional label may be used elsewhere in the program to compute the size of the program. See the DB directive for an example of such a computation.

Elaborate programs sometimes use the address of the end of the program as the base for dynamically established buffer or table space. This is a CP/M technique that can only be used under MP/M by a program that runs as a .COM file in an absolute TPA. The technique should be avoided in relocatable and page relocatable programs under MP/M.

ENDIF terminates its IF ... ENDIF or IF ... ELSE ... ENDIF group. See the IF directive.

The ENDM directive of MAC and RMAC terminates all open IFs, so ENDIF may be omitted preceding an ENDM directive.

END (ASM, MAC, RMAC)

{ *label* } END { *operand* }

The assembler stops reading the input file; following statements will be ignored. If given, the value of the operand will be passed in the .HEX file as the entry point address of the program.

The optional label receives the value of the location counter (the address of the next byte that would have been assembled).

ENDIF (ASM, MAC, RMAC)

{ *label* } ENDIF

The scope of the innermost IF directive is ended. If no IF directive is active, ASM ignores the statement; MAC and RMAC report a B error.

The optional label (whose use is not recommended) receives the address of the next byte to be assembled, but only if the assembler is processing input when it finds the ENDIF. If the assembler is skipping input, the label is ignored and is not defined.

See the MACRO, IRP, IRPC, and REPT directives for examples of the use of ENDM.

The use of a single directive to delimit the bodies begun with four such various directives might appear at first to be inconsistent. However, the statements bounded by IRP, IRPC, or REPT are in fact macro definitions exactly as is a group of statements headed by MACRO. The assembler handles all such groups in the same way. The repeating groups differ in that their definitions are temporary and can be expanded only at the point where they are coded.

The EQU directive is used to give meaningful names to values and so make the program more understandable and easier to modify. There are a number of ways to apply EQU toward these goals:

```
numrecs     equ    16
buffsize    equ    numrecs*128
buffer      ds     buffsize
bufflast    equ    buffer+buffsize-1
```

A single EQU defines the size of a file buffer in standard records (the units most relevant to a buffer). The remaining statements define the buffer itself, but all depend on numrecs. Changing only its definition changes everything about the buffer.

```
false       equ    0
true        equ    not false
printer$support equ true
do$formfeed  equ  term$ADM3 or printer$support
```

False and true are conventional names for use with names that will be used in IF directives. As the last statement shows, Boolean conditions can be given meaningful names in EQUs at the top of the program, simplifying later IFs.

{ *label* } ENDM

The body of the current MACRO, IRP, IRPC, or REPT directive is closed. All IF directives begun within that body and not yet ended are also closed. If there is no open MACRO or repeating structure, the assembler reports a B error.

Where ENDM closes a macro definition, macro expansion stops. Where it closes a repeating structure the assembler either returns to the top of the body or continues, depending on the repetition control.

The optional label (whose use is not recommended) receives the value of the next byte to be assembled. If the label is processed more than once in a repeating structure, the assembler reports a P error.

label EQU *operand*

The operand is evaluated and its value is assigned to the label.

Any labels that appear in the operand expression must have been defined prior to this point in the program. If any have not, a U or P error is reported.

If the statement label is omitted, the assembler reports an S error.

EXITM is used to end macro expansion early. In the case of a macro definition it might be used in place of a level of IF nesting, to simplify the macro:

```
if nul &parameter
   exitm
```

It might be used in an error check, as here where a deliberate assembly error is used to deliver a message:

```
if 255 lt &number
   equ 'number cannot exceed 255'
   exitm
```

Repeating structures are also macros, and EXITM can be used to terminate repetition early. Here it is applied to prevent assembling characters beyond the eighth in a filename:

```
length set 8
          irpc f,afile
              db   '&F' ; filename letter
    length set  length–1
              if  length lt 0
                  exitm ; ignore extra letters
              endif
          endm
```

EXTRN identifies the addresses used in this program that will be provided in other assemblies. External labels may be used in expressions in only certain ways:

external label + constant
external label – constant

This restriction is necessary because the assembler is allowed to pass a fixed offset value for any use of an external label, but it cannot know the value of the label at assembly time.

External labels may be used as operands in any segment. For example, an external address could be assembled into an absolute segment instruction or initialized into a common segment with DW.

{ *label* } EXITM

The assembler stops expanding the current macro definition and continues assembly with the statement following the macro call.

EXITM may be used to stop the processing of an IRP, IRPC, or REPT body. When EXITM is found in one of those structures, the assembler continues processing with the statement following the ENDM that ends the structure.

If no MACRO or repeating structure is active, the assembler reports a B error.

The optional label (whose use is not recommended) receives the address of the next byte to be assembled.

EXTRN *label*{,*label*...}

Each *label* given is identified as being defined external to this assembly. The assembler records the labels and their points of use in the object file. Other programs, assembled separately, will supply meanings for the names through their use of the PUBLIC directive; the LINK program will copy their final addresses into the program.

External labels may be as long as desired, but only their first six characters are recorded in the object file.

The IF directive is used to control the contents of the program on the basis of some condition. The condition is usually expressed as a Boolean combination of labels that have earlier been equated to true (nonzero) and false (zero) values.

A U diagnostic signals that a label in the operand is not defined anywhere in the program. The undefined label is treated as if it had a value of zero. A P diagnostic signals a label that is defined true following the IF, causing the IF to assemble differently on the assembler's second pass.

With ASM the IF can be used only to skip or not skip parts of the program:

```
if printer$support
    ... printer output code ...
endif
```

With MAC the IF ... ELSE ... ENDIF combination can be used to choose between alternates:

```
msg1   if     not expert$mode
            db    'Enter date as MM/DD/YY:'
        else
            db    'M/D/Y:'
        endif
```

Note the use of indentation to make the logic of conditional assembly clearer. With MAC the operator NUL is often used in IF expressions. See the REPT and IRP directives for examples.

IRP is used to automate the assembly of sequences that are repetitive in shape but varied in content. In this example IRP is used to construct a branch table like the BIOS entry table. A null item signals an unused entry to the table:

```
jumptab   irp   target,<sub1,<>,sub3,sub4>
                if     nul &target
                   ret  !  nop  !  nop
                else
                   jmp   target
                endif
             endm
```

In MAC version 2.0 if the list is empty (given as <>) the body is not processed at all. This is incompatible with the Intel assembler, which processes the body once, replacing the dummy name with a null value. MAC version 2.0 does peculiar things when a null item is given as two adjacent commas, as in <one,,three>. A null item given as an empty list as in <one,<>,three> is processed correctly. These problems may not exist in RMAC or in later versions of MAC.

IF (ASM, MAC, RMAC)

{ *label* } IF *operand*

The operand is evaluated. If the result is false (zero), the assembler skips input text until it finds an ENDIF or ELSE directive. If the result is true (not zero), the assembler continues processing input. If it then finds an ELSE directive, it begins skipping input until an ENDIF is seen.

The ASM assembler does not recognize ELSE.

Labels in the operand expression must be defined prior to the IF. If any are not, the assembler reports a U or P error.

The optional label receives the address of the next byte to be assembled.

IRP (MAC, RMAC)

{ *label* } IRP *dummy,<item,item...>*

IRP takes two operands. The first is *dummy*, a name containing no interspersed dollar signs. The second is a list of *items*. The list is enclosed in angle brackets < and >. The elements of the list are simply strings of characters, any characters at all. Each *item* is separated from the next by a comma. If an item contains spaces or special characters, it should be enclosed in angle brackets itself.

The assembler processes the body of statements between IRP and a matching ENDM directive once for each item in the list. On each pass over the body all occurrences of the name *dummy* are replaced by the current *item*.

IRPC is used to automate the assembly of repetitious declarations. Within macros it is often used to count the length of character strings. Here IRPC and REPT are used to assemble a filename in an FCB, padding the name with blanks to eight characters:

```
fcb:    db    0   ; drivecode
length  set   8
        irpc  f,afile
              db '&F' ; filename character
  length      set length-1
        endm
        rept length
              db ' ' ; padding character
        endm
```

Because IRPC always makes one pass over the body of statements it will not give a reliable count of the length of a string that might be null. The IF NUL directive can be used to avoid this problem.

LOCAL provides the programmer with a supply of labels, each guaranteed unique and not in use in the main program. A common use of LOCAL is to provide a name for a constant and a branch target at its end:

```
msg    macro  text
       local  string,over
       lxi    d,string
       mvi    c,9
       call   bdos
       jmp    over
string db    '&TEXT','$'
over   endm
```

Each time the macro msg is called, the assembler will generate new labels to be substituted for string and over. If the macro is called a dozen times, 24 different labels will be produced.

Normally the assembler does not list labels commencing with ?? in the symbol table. If these labels are needed (for instance, if they are to be used as breakpoints under SID), specify the assembler parameter +Q.

{ *label* } IRPC *dummy,item*

IRPC takes two operands. The first, *dummy*, is a name with no interspersed dollar signs. The second, *item*, is any sequence of characters at all, terminated by a space, tab, or comment. If *item* contains delimiters, it should be enclosed in angle brackets (<*item*>).

The assembler processes the body of statements between IRPC and a matching ENDM once for each character in *item*. On each pass all occurrences of *dummy* are replaced by the current character from *item*.

If item is null (given as <> or as two adjacent apostrophes), the assembler makes one pass, replacing *dummy* with the null string.

The optional label receives the address of the first byte generated.

LOCAL *name*{,*name*...}

LOCAL may be used only within the body of a macro definition (including bodies defined by REPT, IRP, and IRPC). It accepts any number of operands *name* each of which is a name with no interspersed dollar signs.

During expansion of the macro the assembler replaces any occurrence of a *name* with a generated label unique to that name. The labels have the form ??*nnnn* where the four decimal digits *nnnn* begin at 0001 and advance with each *name* in each LOCAL statement processed.

As the assembler reads the contents of the macro library it discards comment-only lines. Macro definitions are stored. SET and EQU directives are performed.

Normally only the SET and EQU lines are written in the listing. Specify the +L assembly parameter to have all lines displayed.

A macro may contain another macro definition; on this hinges some programming tricks. The ability is mainly used to solve the first-time problem: to make a macro assemble one way the first time it is called, and another way all the other times. Define the macro in its first-time form but embed a redefinition of the same macro within it. The embedded definition replaces the original one when the macro is called the first time.

The assembler will recognize a macro call in the label or operand field of a statement as easily as in the normal operation field. If a macro attempts to generate a label that is the same as its own name, that is,

```
cosub   macro  ; assemble a subroutine
cosub   equu     $ ; entry to subroutine
```

the assembler will see the generated label as a call to the macro that generated it. After a very long time the nested macro expansions will fill storage and the assembler will either abort or report an M error.

MACLIB (MAC, RMAC)

{ *label* } MACLIB *filename*

The contents of the file named *filename*.LIB replace the MACLIB statement; the assembler processes them as if they had been part of the original program.

The assembler looks for *filename*.LIB on the default drive unless the L*d* parameter has been used to specify a different drive.

If a statement in the macro library changes the location counter (that is, if it is an ORG, DB, DS, DW, or an instruction statement), a P error will occur. The library should contain only SET and EQU directives, MACRO ... ENDM groups, and comments.

MACRO (MAC, RMAC)

label MACRO *name*{,*name*...}

The body of statements between the MACRO directive and the matching ENDM is stored as a macro definition under the name *label* (which may not have interspersed dollar signs). If no matching ENDM can be found, the assembler reports a B error.

The macro body may comprise any sequence of assembler statements, including IF, IRP, IRPC, and REPT structures. Macro definitions may be nested within the current macro's body. Such nested definitions are not processed at the time the enclosing macro is stored. They will be recognized and stored when the enclosing macro is invoked.

When the word *label* appears in the program text, the assembler replaces it with the body of the macro. Operands following *label* in the source are matched to the *name*s. Wherever a *name*, delimited by spaces, commas, or ampersands, appears in the body of the definition, it is replaced by the matching operand from the macro call. See the Summary of Macro Substitution in MAC earlier in this section.

The name of the object program is recorded with the program in object file. The name is noted in a library created by the LIB command, and can be given as a LINK parameter to cause the program to be included at link time.

ORG is used at the beginning of a program to set the program's assembled origin. CP/M programs conventionally begin with statements like this:

```
tpa     equ  0100h
start   org  tpa
```

Within a macro it is convenient to assemble a default or fill value and then ORG backward to overlay the fill with data, as in this method of assembling an FCB with optional filename:

```
fcbfn  db   '        '   ; filename — blanks
fcbft  db   '   '        ; filetype — blanks
         if not nul filename
            org fcbfn
            db  '&FILENAME'  ; filename — blank padded
            org fcb+36
         endif
```

That technique should be avoided in MP/M where the GENMOD command may not be able to handle overlapping load addresses. See the IRPC directive for an different example of padding a filename with blanks.

The R parameter of MAC causes 0100h to be subtracted from the operand of all ORGs. The resulting .HEX file, concatenated with a normal one, forms the input to GENMOD to create a page relocatable program.

NAME
(RMAC)

NAME *'name'*

The assembler notes *name* in the object file as the name of this program.
The *name* given will be truncated to six characters, as are all external symbols.
If no NAME directive appears in a program, the filename of the source file is used.

ORG
(ASM, MAC,
RMAC)

{ *label* } ORG *operand*

The assembler's location counter is set to the value of the operand, causing subsequent bytes to be assembled at a different address.

The location counter may be given any 16-bit value, including one that causes the assembled code to overlap addresses already used.

The optional label receives the value of the operand (the address of the next byte to be assembled).

The first form is used to force a page-eject in order to make the listing more readable. Blocks of declarations, important subroutines, and important phases of processing stand out when they are preceded by PAGE directives.

Titling aside, a PAGE adds only 1 byte (an ASCII FF character) to the size of the listing file. When the listing is typed at the console, the FF may be displayed as a space or it may cause the screen to be cleared, depending on the type of terminal.

The assembler's line counter is initially set to 56. The two lines written at the top of each page when titling is in effect are not counted toward the limit. When planning the listing, it is best to specify two less than the actual capacity of the paper so that titling can be added later.

PUBLIC is used to identify the parts of the program that are available to other linked routines: entry points to public subroutines and the names of constants that may be referenced from other programs.

The assembler records each name, with the address to which it refers, in the object file. The LINK command notes the names. Where another program specified one of the names in an EXTRN directive, LINK supplies the actual address defined in this program.

{ *label* } PAGE
{ *label* } PAGE *operand*

In the first form of the directive the assembler writes a formfeed to the listing file. The formfeed follows the line containing the PAGE, which thus appears as the last line on its page. If the TITLE directive has been used, the assembler writes the title and a blank line as well.

In the second form the assembler sets the value of the operand as the limit of the number of lines on a page of listing. If the operand evaluates to zero, automatic pagination is disabled; the only pagination done will be in response to the PAGE directive in its first form.

When the operand is not zero, it takes effect at once. If there are already that many lines or more on the current page, the PAGE directive itself will start on a new page.

The optional label in both cases receives the address of the next byte to be assembled.

PUBLIC *label*{,*label*... }

Each *label* given is identified as being public. The assembler records the names and addresses of the labels in the object file. Other programs, assembled separately, may refer to those labels; the LINK command will supply their addresses to the other programs.

Public labels must have address values, whether absolute or relocatable. They may not be equated to a constant or an offset, or defined by an EXTRN directive.

Public labels may be as long as desired, but only their first six characters are recorded in the object file.

The purpose of REPT is to automate the assembly of repetitive constants or code sequences. This group assembles 16 word constants, each a different power of two:

```
powerof2   set    1
           rept  16
                dw   powerof2
    powerof2    set  powerof2 shl 1
           endm
```

This example constructs a table of ASCII characters in which control characters appear as nulls (00h). The listing is turned off to suppress the bulky output.

```
table   org    ($+127) and 0ff80h
$-print
        rept   128
    asciival  set   (low $) and 7fh
              if     (asciival lt 20h) or (asciival eq 7fh)
                    db     00h  ;  control char
              else
                    db     asciival  ;  printable char
              endif
        endm
$+print
```

In MAC version 2, if the operand evaluates to zero the REPT body is not processed at all, an incompatibility with the Intel assembler, which always processes the body at least once regardless. This may not be true of RMAC or of later versions of MAC.

SET, like EQU, associates a name with a value. Unlike EQU, a name defined with SET may be redefined later to have another value. This ability finds little use in ASM. In MAC the SET statement is frequently used within macros as a way of assigning values to macro temporary variables and control variables for macro loops. See the REPT and IRPC directives for examples.

REPT (MAC, RMAC)

{ *label* } REPT *operand*

The assembler processes the body of statements between the REPT and a matching ENDM directive some number of times, generating code repetitively. The number of repetitions is set by the value of the operand.

The operand is evaluated only once, when the REPT is first scanned. Labels in the operand expression must be defined prior to the REPT statement; if any have not, the assembler reports a U or P error.

The optional label receives the address of the first byte of code generated.

SET (ASM, MAC, RMAC)

label SET *operand*

The value of the operand is assigned to the label. The label's value may subsequently be changed by another SET statement.

All labels used in the operand must be defined prior to the SET; if any are not, the assembler reports a U or P error. If the label appears as the label of another type of statement, the assembler reports a P error.

The TITLE directive does two things. It enables titling of the listing, and it sets the descriptive constant to appear in the title. Once titling has been enabled it cannot be shut off again.

Titling causes the assembler to write two more lines to each page than are called for by the line counter controlled by the PAGE directive. The blank line after the title line is produced by a single extra ASCII linefeed; it is not a complete line of spaces.

It would be nice to be able to change the title constant partway through an assembly, but the TITLE directive does not allow this. The title constant is saved during the assembler's first pass and used during its second pass. The last TITLE statement seen determines the title constant for the entire listing.

{ *label* } TITLE '*title constant*'

Titling of the listing is enabled. Following each page eject of the listing file the assembler will write a title line and a blank line to the listing. The title line identifies the assembler and its version, gives the page number, and includes the title constant.

The optional label receives the address of the next byte to be assembled.

BDOS

Topical Summary of Selected BDOS Services

Req#	cpm-2	mpm-1	cpm-86	mpm-2	Page	Service Performed	error key	Argument
						System Information and Control		
7	x	-	x	-	463	Get current IOBYTE	-	none
8	x	-	x	-	465	Set IOBYTE	-	E = IOBYTE
12	x	x	x	x	469	Get system identification	-	none
31	x	x	x	x	491	Get disk parameters	-	none
32	x	x	x	x	493	Get/ set user code	-	E = flag/code
45	-	-	-	x	507	Set BDOS error mode	-	E = flag
50	-	-	x	-	511	Call BIOS entry	-	DX→parameters
104	-	-	-	x	525	Set date and time	-	DE→date,time
105	-	-	-	x	527	Get date and time	-	DE→date,time
106	-	-	-	x	527	Set default password	-	DE→password
						Program Control		
0	x	x	x	x	457	Terminate program	-	(86: DL = flag)
47	-	-	-	x	509	Chain to command	-	buffer=command
59	-	-	x	-	521	Load program	f	DX→FCB
						Console Input and Output		
1	x	x	x	x	457	Console input byte	-	none
2	x	x	x	x	459	Console output byte	-	E = byte
9	x	x	x	x	465	Console output string	-	DE→string
10	x	x	x	x	467	Console input line	-	DE→buffer
11	x	x	x	x	467	Console status check	c	none

Req#	cpm-2	mpm-1	cpm-86	mpm-2	Page	Service Performed	error key	Argument
						Other Serial Input and Output		
3	x	-	x	-	459	Reader input byte	-	none
4	x	-	x	-	461	Punch output byte	-	E = byte
5	x	x	x	x	461	List output byte	-	E = byte
7	x	-	x	-	463	Get current IOBYTE	-	none
8	x	-	x	-	465	Set IOBYTE	-	E = IOBYTE
						File Manipulation and Control		
15	x	x	x	x	471	Open existing file	d	DE→FCB
16	x	x	x	x	473	Close output file	d	DE→FCB
17	x	x	x	x	475	Search for first file	d	DE→FCB
18	x	x	x	x	477	Search for next file	d	DE→FCB
19	x	x	x	x	477	Delete file	d	DE→FCB
22	x	x	x	x	483	Make new file	d	DE→FCB
23	x	x	x	x	483	Rename file	d	DE→FCB
30	x	x	x	x	491	Set file attributes	d	DE→FCB
32	x	x	x	x	493	Get/set user code	m	E = flag/code
41	-	-	-	x	503	Test and write record	i	DE→FCB
42	-	-	-	x	505	Lock record	i	DE→FCB
43	-	-	-	x	505	Unlock record	i	DE→FCB
44	-	-	-	x	507	Set record count	-	E = count
101	-	-	-	x	523	Get directory data	-	E = drive
102	-	-	-	x	523	Read XFCB	d	DE→FCB
103	-	-	-	x	525	Write XFCB	d	DE→FCB
						File Input and Output		
20	x	x	x	x	479	Sequential read	r	DE→FCB
21	x	x	x	x	481	Sequential write	w	DE→FCB
33	x	x	x	x	493	Direct access read	i	DE→FCB
34	x	x	x	x	495	Direct access write	i	DE→FCB
40	x	x	x	x	501	Direct write, zero fill	i	DE→FCB
35	x	x	x	x	495	Get file end address	f	DE→FCB
36	x	x	x	x	497	Get direct address	f	DE→FCB
44	-	-	-	x	507	Set record count	-	E = count
45	-	-	-	x	507	Set BDOS error mode	-	E = flag
26	x	x	x	x	487	Set file buffer address	-	DE→buffer
51	-	-	x	-	513	Set file buffer seg. base	-	DX = base adr.
52	-	-	x	-	513	Get file buffer address	-	none

Req#	cpm-2	mpm-1	cpm-86	mpm-2	Page	Service Performed	error key	Argument
						Directory Operations		
17	x	x	x	x	475	Search for first file	d	DE→FCB
18	x	x	x	x	477	Search for next file	d	DE→FCB
19	x	x	x	x	477	Delete file	d	DE→FCB
22	x	x	x	x	483	Make new file	d	DE→FCB
23	x	x	x	x	483	Rename file	d	DE→FCB
30	x	x	x	x	491	Set file attributes	d	DE→FCB
100	-	-	-	x	521	Set directory label	d	DE→FCB
101	-	-	-	x	523	Get directory data	-	E = drive
102	-	-	-	x	523	Read XFCB	d	DE→FCB
103	-	-	-	x	525	Write XFCB	d	DE→FCB
						Disk System Information and Control		
13	x	x	x	x	469	Reset all drives	m	none
14	x	x	x	x	471	Select default drive	-	E = drive
24	x	x	x	x	485	Get active drive map	-	none
25	x	x	x	x	485	Get default drive number	-	none
27	x	x	x	x	487	Get allocation vector	-	none
28	x	x	x	x	489	Protect drive	-	none
29	x	x	x	x	489	Get read-only drive map	-	none
31	x	x	x	x	491	Get disk parameters	-	none
32	x	x	x	x	493	Get/ set user code	-	E = flag/code
37	x	x	x	x	497	Reset drive	m	DE = drive map
38	-	x	-	x	499	Access drive	-	DE = drive map
39	-	x	-	x	499	Free drive	-	DE = drive map
46	-	-	-	x	509	Get disk free space	f	E = drive
48	-	-	-	x	511	Flush disk buffers	f	none
100	-	-	-	x	521	Set directory label	d	DE→FCB
101	-	-	-	x	523	Get directory data	-	E = drive
102	-	-	-	x	523	Read XFCB	d	DE→FCB

Numeric Index of BDOS Services

Req#	cpm-2	mpm-1	cpm-86	mpm-2	Page	Service Performed	error key	Argument
0	x	x	x	x	457	Terminate program	-	(86: DL = flag)
1	x	x	x	x	457	Console input byte	-	none
2	x	x	x	x	459	Console output byte	-	E = byte
3	x	-	x	-	459	Reader input byte	-	none
4	x	-	x	-	461	Punch output byte	-	E = byte
5	x	x	x	x	461	List output byte	-	E = byte
7	x	-	x	-	463	Get current IOBYTE	-	none
8	x	-	x	-	465	Set IOBYTE	-	E = IOBYTE
9	x	x	x	x	465	Console output string	-	DE→string
10	x	x	x	x	467	Console input line	-	DE→buffer
11	x	x	x	x	467	Console status check	c	none
12	x	x	x	x	469	Get system identification	-	none
13	x	x	x	x	469	Reset all drives	m	none
14	x	x	x	x	471	Select default drive	f	E = drive
15	x	x	x	x	471	Open existing file	d	DE→FCB
16	x	x	x	x	473	Close output file	d	DE→FCB
17	x	x	x	x	475	Search for first file	d	DE→FCB
18	x	x	x	x	477	Search for next file	d	DE→FCB
19	x	x	x	x	477	Delete file	d	DE→FCB
20	x	x	x	x	479	Sequential read	r	DE→FCB
21	x	x	x	x	481	Sequential write	w	DE→FCB
22	x	x	x	x	483	Make new file	d	DE→FCB
23	x	x	x	x	483	Rename file	d	DE→FCB
24	x	x	x	x	485	Get active drive map	-	none
25	x	x	x	x	485	Get default drive number	-	none
26	x	x	x	x	487	Set file buffer address	-	DE→buffer
27	x	x	x	x	487	Get allocation vector	-	none
28	x	x	x	x	489	Protect drive	-	none
29	x	x	x	x	489	Get read-only drive map	-	none
30	x	x	x	x	491	Set file attributes	d	DE→FCB
31	x	x	x	x	491	Get disk parameters	-	none
32	x	x	x	x	493	Get/ set user code	-	E = flag/code
33	x	x	x	x	493	Direct access read	i	DE→FCB

Req#	cpm-2	mpm-1	cpm-86	mpm-2	Page	Service Performed	error key	Argument
34	x	x	x	x	495	Direct access write	i	DE→FCB
35	x	x	x	x	495	Get file end address	f	DE→FCB
36	x	x	x	x	497	Get direct address	f	DE→FCB
37	x	x	x	x	497	Reset drive	m	DE = drive map
38	-	x	-	x	499	Access drive	f	DE = drive map
39	-	x	-	x	499	Free drive	m	DE = drive map
40	x	x	x	x	501	Direct write, zero fill	i	DE→FCB
41	-	-	-	x	503	Test and write record	i	DE→FCB
42	-	-	-	x	505	Lock record	i	DE→FCB
43	-	-	-	x	505	Unlock record	i	DE→FCB
44	-	-	-	x	507	Set record count	—	E = count
45	-	-	-	x	507	Set BDOS error mode	-	E = flag
46	-	-	-	x	509	Get disk free space	f	E = drive
47	-	-	-	x	509	Chain to command	-	buffer=command
48	-	-	-	x	511	Flush disk buffers	f	none
50	-	-	x	-	511	Call BIOS entry	-	DX→parameters
51	-	-	x	-	513	Set file buffer seg. base	-	DX = base adr.
52	-	-	x	-	513	Get file buffer address	-	none
53	-	-	x	-	515	Max. relocatable storage	f	DX→MCB
54	-	-	x	-	515	Max. absolute storage	f	DX→MCB
55	-	-	x	-	517	Relocatable storage	f	DX→MCB
56	-	-	x	-	517	Absolute storage	f	DX→MCB
57	-	-	x	-	519	Release allocated storage	f	DX→MCB
58	-	-	x	-	519	Release all storage	-	DX→MCB
59	-	-	x	-	521	Load program	f	DX→FCB
100	-	-	-	x	521	Set directory label	d	DE→FCB
101	-	-	-	x	523	Get directory data	-	E = drive
102	-	-	-	x	523	Read XFCB	d	DE→FCB
103	-	-	-	x	525	Write XFCB	f	DE→FCB
104	-	-	-	x	525	Set date and time	-	DE→date,time
105	-	-	-	x	527	Get date and time	-	DE→date,time
106	-	-	-	x	527	Set default password	-	DE→password

Summary of BDOS Error Codes

The error code groups shown here are keyed to the indices on the previous pages. To find the errors returned by a given service, look it up in the Numerical Index of BDOS Services, then look here under its error key. A code marked with "*" occurs in MP/M 2 only.

Key	Code	Meaning
c	A = 00h	No data available.
	A nonzero	A byte is ready.
f	A = 00h	Success.
	*A = FFh	Failure (returned only in MP/M 2; an extended code is returned in register H).
d	A = 00h	Success (directory code 0)
	A = 01h	Success (directory code 1)
	A = 02h	Success (directory code 2)
	A = 03h	Success (directory code 3)
	A = FFh	File not found or error (MP/M 2: an extended code may be returned in register H.)
i	A = 00h	Success.
	*A = FFh	Physical error, register H contains extended code.
	A = 01h	Attempt to read unallocated record.
	A = 02h	Disk full, no space for a new allocation block.
	A = 03h	Cannot find current FCB to update it.
	A = 04h	Attempt to read in unallocated extent.
	A = 05h	Directory full, no space for new extent entry.
	A = 06h	Direct address larger than allowed.
	*A = 07h	Record mismatch in Test and Write (41).
	*A = 08h	Requested record is locked.
	*A = 09h	FCB was found invalid on a prior service.
	*A = 0Ah	FCB never opened, or corrupted (checksum error).
	*A = 0Bh	Unlocked file's FCB out of step with directory.
	*A = 0Ch	Too many locked records for one process.
	*A = 0Dh	Given File ID is not in list of unlocked files.
	*A = 0Eh	Too many locked records in the system.
m		In CP/M no code is returned. In MP/M, A = 00h signals success, A = FFh signals failure.

Key	Code	Meaning
r	A = 00h	Success.
	A = FFh	End of file (MP/M 2: see register H).
	*A = 08h	Requested record is locked.
	*A = 09h	FCB found invalid on previous service.
	*A = 0Ah	FCB hasn't been opened, or is corrupted.
w	A = 00h	Success.
	A = 01h	No directory space for new extent.
	A = 02h	Disk full, no data space for a new allocation block.
	*A = 08h	Requested record is locked.
	*A = 09h	FCB found invalid on previous service.
	*A = 0Ah	FCB hasn't been opened, or is corrupted.
	*A = FFh	Physical error, see register H.

In MP/M 2 register H contains return code information. If multiple records are in use and not all records can be moved, the most significant 4 bits of register H contain a count of records successfully transferred.

When enabled by Set BDOS Error Mode (45), errors that would have cancelled the program are returned by setting A = FFh and setting an extended code in the low 4 bits of register H as follows:

H = 00h	A = FFh means "end of file" or "file not found."
H = 01h	Permanent disk read or write error.
H = 02h	Attempt to write to a read-only drive.
H = 03h	Attempt to write to a read-only file.
H = 04h	Attempt to select an invalid drive-letter.
H = 05h	File open by another process in locked or read-only mode.
H = 06h	FCB can't be validated during a Close (16).
H = 07h	Password error.
H = 08h	File named in Make (22) or Rename (23) already exists.
H = 09h	Fileref in FCB is ambiguous; an explicit name is required.
H = 0Ah	This process has its limit of open files.
H = 0Bh	The BDOS has recorded its maximum of locked, open files.

In both CP/M and MP/M service 0 duplicates the results of a JMP 00h.

Output files that are not closed will have incomplete allocation data.

In CP/M the disk in drive A must be bootable or a disk error or system hang will follow. This is not true of CP/M-86 or MP/M, which do not reload the system.

In CP/M-86 service 0 is the only way for a program to terminate; there is no jump vector at location 00h in the data segment. CP/M-86 takes a byte operand in the DL register: 00h requests a complete termination as for CP/M and MP/M; 01h merely ends the program, leaving the program image and its memory allocation intact. The latter option is for programs that will be driven by events (I/O or software interrupts) rather than executing sequentially. After initializing itself under the guise of a command, the event-driven program can return control to the CCP, its subsequent execution being triggered by interrupts.

Related requests: none.

The use of direct cursor addressing can invalidate the BDOS's knowledge of the cursor position, causing it to return the wrong number of spaces when a tab character is received.

When a line of input is needed, it is better for a number of reasons to use Console Input Line (10).

Related requests: Direct Console I/O (6), Get Console Line (10), Console Status (11).

Terminate Program

Register	High	Low
A:		
BC:		00h
DE:		
HL:		

The calling program is aborted and control returns to the command level of the system.

Under CP/M a warm start is done to refresh the CCP and BDOS code. The disk system is reset; that is, read-only disks are made read–write and directory check information is discarded.

Under MP/M all resources—storage segments, reserved drives, locked files and records, queues, and mutual exclusions—owned by the calling process are released. The disk system is not reset nor is the Monitor reloaded.

Console Input Byte

Register	High	Low
A:		
BC:		01h
DE:		
HL:		

A byte from the current console device is returned in register A. The byte is echoed to the terminal. If no byte is ready at the time the call is made, the calling program is suspended until a byte becomes available.

The BDOS does not act on control characters received through service 1. Control-c, control-s, control-p are passed through to the program. If a tab character is received, the BDOS notes the number of spaces represented based on its knowledge of the cursor position. It echoes that many spaces (not a tab) to the console. The tab is returned to the program, however.

When controlling a special console device for which bit 7 is significant, use BDOS service 6.

The use of direct cursor addressing may invalidate the BDOS's knowledge of the cursor position, causing it to expand tabs incorrectly. Write tabs only when it is sure that only normal characters have been sent since the last CR.

MP/M: When writing a line, Console Output String (9) is more efficient than using this service in a loop.

Related requests: Direct Console I/O (6), Console String (9).

The RDR: logical device represents a source of ASCII input. It can be assigned to different physical devices depending on the BIOS's support of the IOBYTE.

MP/M: All serial devices are called consoles. A single process has access to only one serial device, which is its logical console. If a command is to drive a second serial input device in addition to the user terminal, the command must attach a second process, giving it the auxiliary input device as its "console." The two processes can then communicate through a queue.

Related request: Punch output (4).

Console Output Byte

A:		
BC:		02h
DE:		byte
HL:		

Bit 7 of the byte in register E (DL in CP/M-86) is set to zero and the resulting byte is sent to the current console device.

If the BDOS has seen a control-s, it waits for another character to be typed before completing the output and returning; the calling program is suspended during this time. If the console-copy flag is set, the byte is copied to the current list device.

If the byte is a tab (09h), the BDOS writes some number of spaces instead, based on its knowledge of the position of the cursor.

Reader Input (CP/M only)

A:		
BC:		03h
DE:		
HL:		

The next byte from the device currently assigned to RDR: is returned in register A. All 8 bits are returned. The program is suspended until a byte is ready.

MP/M: The service request is honored, but it returns input from the current console for the process rather than from a reader.

The PUN: logical device represents a receiver of ASCII data. It may be assigned to different physical devices, depending on the BIOS's support of the IOBYTE.

MP/M: All serial devices are called consoles. A single process has access to only one serial device, which is its logical console. If a command is to drive a second serial output device in addition to the user terminal, the command must attach a second process, giving it the auxiliary output device as its console. The two processes can then communicate through a queue.

Related request: Reader Input (3).

If the BIOS supports printer handshaking, the suspension time may be long. If the printer has a large buffer, the program may wait for many seconds while the printer catches up. If the printer reports not-ready when out of paper or ribbon, the program can be suspended indefinitely. These things usually cause no problem. However, a program attempting to monitor two devices at once may wish to poll the printer through the BIOS LISTST function before requesting this service.

MP/M 1: If two processes use this service at once, their output will be merged at the printer, producing garbage. Use the MXList mutual exclusion queue to get exclusive control of the printer before requesting list output.

MP/M 2: An Attack List Function is performed if the calling process doesn't already own the list device; this prevents contention but may suspend the program.

Related requests: none.

BDOS 4

Punch Output (CP/M only)

Register	High	Low
A:		
BC:		04h
DE:		byte
HL:		

The byte in register E (DL for CP/M-86) is sent to the device currently assigned to PUN:. The program will be suspended until the device is ready to accept the byte.

MP/M: The service request is honored, but the byte is sent to the current console device for the process, not to a punch.

BDOS 5

List Output Byte

Register	High	Low
A:		
BC:		05h
DE:		byte
HL:		

The byte in register E (DL for CP/M-86) is sent to the device currently assigned to LST:. The program is suspended until the device is ready to accept the byte.

Most programs have no need to avoid the BDOS's control of console output. There are programs—full-screen editors and simulation games come to mind—that depend on a very close interaction between keyboard and screen; the program uses the keys as control inputs rather than as character inputs and the screen as a dynamic status display rather than as an echo of the input. Such programs have traditionally used BIOS functions for I/O in order to circumvent the BDOS. Service 6 should now be used instead; to continue calling the BIOS is to risk incompatibility with later versions of the system.

Related requests: Console Input Byte (1), Console Output Byte (2), Console Input Line (10), Console Output String (9), Console Status (11).

Under CP/M the current value of the IOBYTE can be found in low storage at location 03h. That is not true of CP/M-86; this service request is the only way of examining the IOBYTE in that system.

The initial value of the IOBYTE is set during a cold start by code in the BIOS. See Chapter 15 for a discussion of altering this setting.

MP/M: I/O assignments and the IOBYTE are not supported. This function returns FFh, a legal but highly unlikely value.

Related request: Set IOBYTE (8).

BDOS 6

Direct Console I/O

A:		
BC:		06h
DE:		*flag*
HL:		

This request reads or writes the current console device, bypassing all the control-character checks. One of three operations is done depending on *flag*, the value in register E (DL for CP/M-86).

If *flag* is FFh, the console is sampled. If a byte is available, the byte is returned in register A; if no byte is ready, 00h is returned instead. The input character is not echoed to the screen; that is up to the calling program.

MP/M: If *flag* is FEh, the console is sampled and a flag is returned as for service 11.

Otherwise, *flag* is sent to the current console as output. Tabs are not expanded. The console copy (control-p) and halt output (control-s) flags are ignored.

BDOS 7

Get IOBYTE (CP/M only)

A:		
BC:		07h
DE:		
HL:		

The current value of the CP/M IOBYTE is returned in register A. The four fields of the byte have these meanings:

(bit number)	7 6	5 4	3 2	1 0
IOBYTE:	list	punch	reader	console

bit value =	00	01	10	11
console	TTY:	CRT:	BAT:	UC1:
reader	TTY:	PTR:	UR1:	UR2:
punch	TTY:	PTP:	UP1:	UP2:
list	TTY:	CRT:	LPT:	UL1:

The IOBYTE is not reset during a warm start; it is only changed by this request, the STAT command, or by a cold start. Your BIOS may ignore the IOBYTE, or may not support some values.

The IOBYTE is kept in location 03h; older programs may manipulate it directly. *CP/M-86*: The IOBYTE is kept within the BDOS; this call must be used to alter it.

MP/M: The request has no effect; I/O assignment and the IOBYTE are not supported.

Related request: Get IOBYTE (7).

When controlling a special console device for which bit 7 is significant, use service 6.

The use of direct cursor addressing may invalidate the BDOS's knowledge of the cursor position, causing it to expand tabs incorrectly. Avoid tabs unless you are sure that only normal characters have been sent since the last CR.

MP/M: This request is more efficient than a sequence of byte requests, because fewer dispatch sequences are needed.

Related requests: Direct Console I/O (6), Console Output Byte (2).

BDOS 8

Set IOBYTE (CP/M only)

Register	High	Low
A:		
BC:		08h
DE:		IOBYTE
HL:		

bit number:	7 6	5 4	3 2	1 0
IOBYTE:	list	punch	reader	console

The value in the E register (DL for CP/M-86) is set as the current IOBYTE. It begins to control output direction immediately. The meanings of the bit fields are

bit value =	00	01	10	11
console	TTY:	CRT:	BAT:	UC1:
reader	TTY:	PTR:	UR1:	UR2:
punch	TTY:	PTP:	UP1:	UP2:
list	TTY:	CRT:	LPT:	UL1:

BDOS 9

Console Output String

Register	High	Low
A:		
BC:		09h
DE:	↑ string	
HL:		

string:	. . . any text at all ending with . . .	$

The string of ASCII text is written to the current console. The dollar sign (ASCII character 24h, may be another currency symbol outside the U.S.) that terminates the string is not written. Bit 7 of each byte is set to 0 before transmission to the BIOS.

If the BDOS has seen a control-s, it waits for another character to be typed before completing the output and returning; the calling program is suspended during this time. If the console-copy flag is set, the string is also sent to the current list device.

If a tab (09h) appears in the string, the BDOS writes some number of spaces instead, based on its knowledge of the position of the cursor.

Service 10 is to be preferred over other console input requests. It allows the typist to correct errors in a familiar way; this increases user confidence. It is the only input method that can receive input from a submit file via XSUB. Under MP/M it is more efficient than 1-byte requests because fewer dispatch sequences are done.

The cursor returns to its original position on a control-x; this is convenient when a prompt is written before the service is requested. Use of direct cursor addressing can invalidate the BDOS's knowledge of the cursor position.

Input ends with a linefeed, carriage return, or a full buffer; the program can't tell which occurred. Control-p, control-s, and edit characters are not returned; if DESPOOL is active, control-d is swallowed as well.

Related requests: Console Input Byte (1), Console Status (11).

This service has two uses. The most common use is to check for an abort request from the user during a long spell of otherwise silent processing. PIP uses this technique: if the user has pressed a key, it assumes that the user wants to end the current data transfer. This may be too abrupt; the user might be asked if an abort is really wanted.

The second use occurs when a program is managing both the console and another serial device. By polling the console with service 11 it can avoid being suspended should input not be ready. *MP/M*: Polling the console is not recommended; any kind of polling loop degrades the system. Attach a separate process for each device and let each wait for input.

Related requests: Console Input Byte (1), Console Input Line (10), Direct Console I/O (6).

Console Input Line

Register	High	Low
A:		
BC:		0Ah
DE:	↑ buffer	
HL:		

buffer:	*max*	*cnt*	returned data . . .

The BDOS notes the current cursor position as it knows it, then reads characters from the console device until a CR or LF is received, or until *max* characters have been received. The typist may employ all the input editing control characters; the BDOS returns the input line as it finally appears on the screen. Control-r, -u, and -x return the cursor only to the original cursor position. Control-c as the first input byte terminates the program.

The number of bytes received is returned in *cnt*. The terminating byte (CR or LF) is neither returned nor counted. If a tab is received, the BDOS echoes some number of blanks according to its knowledge of the cursor position; the tab byte is returned in the buffer, however.

Console Status Check

Register	High	Low
A:		
BC:		0Bh
DE:		
HL:		

The current console device is polled. If a byte is ready for input, a nonzero value is returned in register A, or else 00h is returned.

The system identification serves two purposes. A program written for CP/M that uses services not available in MP/M can ensure that it is really running under CP/M by checking the contents of register H.

A program written for a certain level of CP/M can ensure that it is not running in an earlier level that lacks the services it needs. For instance, a program that uses the Direct Access file services might contain:

```
MVI     C,12
CALL    BDOS
MOV     A,L
CPI     22H
JC      OLD$VERSION
```

Note that the comparison should not be for equality as CP/M 3.0 will presumably support everything that CP/M 2.2 supports.

Related requests: none.

This request is used to allow the operator to change the diskette on a drive. Without a reset, when the BDOS next accesses the directory of the changed diskette it will detect the change (by comparison with the check vector for the drive) and mark the drive read-only.

The request should be used with care as it removes read-only status from all drives, including those that aren't changed and those where it was set by user command. See Reset Drive (37) for a more specific request, and one more likely to succeed under MP/M.

Related requests: Reset Drive (37), Protect Drive (28), Get Read-Only Vector (29).

BDOS 12

Get System Identification

A:		
BC:		0Ch
DE:		
HL:		

HL:	system	version

A value that identifies the system and version is returned in the HL register pair (BX for CP/M-86).

The system value is 00h for CP/M, and 01h for MP/M.

The version value is the two-digit version number of the system in BCD (e.g., 22h for CP/M version 2.2 and the first release of CP/M-86 and 30h for MP/M 2).

BDOS 13

Reset All Drives

A:		
BC:		0Dh
DE:		
HL:		

The BDOS resets its knowledge of the state of all disks. Read-only disks are set to read–write. Allocation and directory check information is discarded. As each disk is selected a new allocation vector and a new check vector will be built, and R/W disk status will be set.

MP/M 1: If any process has a file open, the reset will not be done and FFh will be returned in register A.

MP/M 2: If a different process has an open file on a drive that is read-only or has removable media, the reset will not be done and FFh will be returned.

Services that take an FCB as their parameter operate on a disk drive according to the drivecode byte of the FCB. If that byte is 00h, those services operate on the default drive.

The current default drive number can be obtained with service 25. (In ordinary CP/M the default drive number can be found in low-storage location 04h. This is not true of MP/M or CP/M-86.)

When a program ends with a warm start the drive that is the default remains the default drive; its letter will appear in the CCP or CLI prompt seen by the user.

Related request: Get Current Drive (25).

The *ex* and *s2* bytes should be set to 00h before the service to ensure opening the first extent of the file. The old direct access technique of opening other extents is not reliable in present systems; use the direct access services instead. The current record number *cr* should be set to 00h after opening a file for sequential access, otherwise the first read will not return the first record.

Once an FCB has been opened don't move it elsewhere in storage. If the file is remote, accessed through CP/NET, moving the FCB will cause subsequent file operations to fail.

MP/M 1: The drive is reserved and cannot be reset until the process ends or issues Free Drive (39). *MP/M 2*: Only removable drives are reserved. File ID is used in services 41-43.

MP/M 2: Use Get Directory Data (101) to see if passwords are enforced. Use Read XFCB (102) to see if this file has one.

Related requests: Close File (16), Make File (22), Set File Buffer Address (26), Read XFCB (102), Set Password (106).

Select Drive

A:		
BC:		0Eh
DE:		drive
HL:		

Register E (DL for CP/M-86) contains a number in the range 0...15, signifying a disk drive A...P respectively. If that drive is not the current default drive, it is made the default drive. If it has not been selected since the last warm start or disk reset, its directory is scanned and used to build allocation and check vectors.

Open Existing File

A:		
BC:		0Fh
DE:	↑fcb	
HL:		

	0	1 . . . 8	9 . . . B	C	D	E	F
fcb:	*dr*	*filename . . .*	*filetype*	*ex*		*s2*	
	cr	*id*					

The drivecode, if not zero, is used to select a drive. The directory is scanned for the first match to the fileref and extent number. The fileref may contain question marks. A matching directory entry is copied into the FCB and register A is returned as 0, 1, 2, or 3. If no match is found, FFh is returned.

CP/M: Only files created under the active user code can be found.

MP/M 1: Files created under user code 0 are equally accessible.

MP/M 2: Set bit f5' if the file is to be unlocked (if other processes may open it for output). Then a File ID is returned in bytes 21h and 22h of the FCB. A password may be given in bytes 0...7 of the current file buffer. Set bit f6' to say the file is to be read-only. In that case, if the search of the active user code fails, the BDOS will also search among user code 0 files that have the SYS attribute.

The purpose of the service is to update the directory entry for the last-altered extent of an output file (extents prior to the last are updated automatically as they are created). A file used only for input need not be closed since its data map has not been changed.

MP/M 1: Closing the file does not release the drive.

MP/M 2: A permanent close (f5'=0) of the last open file on a drive releases the drive.

MP/M 2: The BDOS checks that the FCB has been opened correctly; if not, the close is not done and FFh is returned. Use temporary close (f5'=1) as a checkpoint prior to console input that might cancel the command.

Related request: Open File (15).

Close Output File

A:		
BC:		10h
DE:	↑fcb	
HL:		

	0	1 . . . 8	9 . . . B	C	D	E	F
fcb:	*dr*	*filename . . .*	*filetype*	*ex*	*s1*	*s2*	*rc*
	. . . data map . . .						

The drive code, if not zero, is used to select a drive. The directory is scanned for the first match to the fileref and extent number under the active user code. The fileref may contain question marks.

MP/M 1: Files under user code 0 are equally accessible.

If the search succeeds, the record count and data map from the FCB are copied into the directory entry and 0, 1, 2, or 3 is returned in register A. If the search fails, FFh is returned.

MP/M 2: Set bit f5' to say the close is not permanent; the directory is updated but the file remains locked if it was so. Otherwise the file is unlocked and locked records are released.

Normally a record holding four directory entries is set in the file buffer. If the default drive is remote (reached via CP/NET), then only the matching entry will appear in the buffer; the other three positions will be garbage.

See Chapter 14 for a number of example programs that use Search First and Search Next (18).

When there are question marks in all fields from *dr* through *ex*, the first directory entry that has ever been used will be returned (*MP/M 2*: this may be the Directory Label or an XFCB). An unused entry has E5h in its first byte. Entries that have never been used are not returned.

Related request: Search For Next File (18).

Search for First File

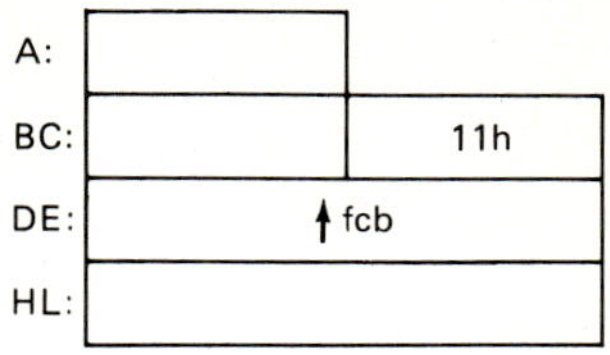

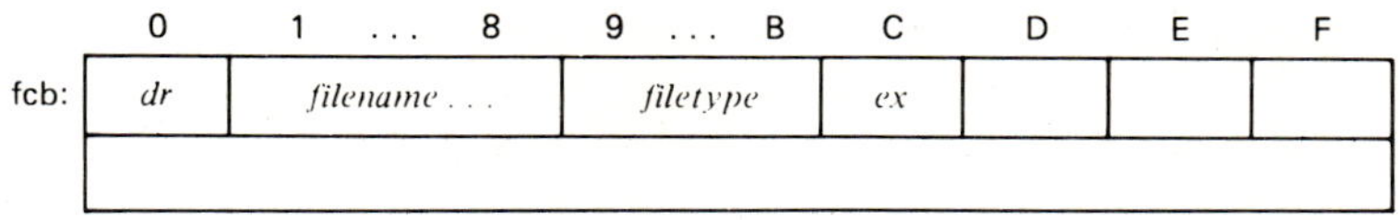

The directory of the default drive is scanned for an entry that matches the fileref and extent number in the FCB, which may contain question marks. If a match is found, the directory entry is placed at some offset in the current file buffer, and register A is set to the position of the entry in the buffer (0, 1, 2, or 3 corresponding to an offset of 0, 32, 64, or 96 bytes). If no match is found, register A is set to FFh.

If *ex* is 00h, only the first extent for a file can be matched. If *ex* contains a question mark, the first entry found will be returned.

Normally *dr* is ignored and only files with the current user code are matched. If *dr* contains a question mark, all directory entries of any user code, and entries of any type including those not in use, are compared.

Normally a record holding four directory entries is set in the file buffer. If the default drive is remote (reached via CP/NET), then only the matching entry will appear in the buffer; the other three entries are garbage.

See Chapter 14 for a number of example programs that use Search First and Search Next (18).

When there are question marks in all fields from *dr* through *ex*, all directory entries that have ever been used will be returned (*MP/M 2*: this may include the Directory Label and XFCBs). An unused entry has E5h in its first byte. Entries that have never been used are not returned.

No other file operation should be done between two Search requests because the BDOS may lose its position in the directory. In some versions of the system this request can be used following Close File to find the next file after the one closed. The technique is not recommended.

Related request: Search for First File (17).

When replacing a file, it is best to write the new version, close it, delete the old one, and rename the new one. By convention files with names beginning with $, and files with the type of .$$$, are scratch files and may be deleted without warning.

MP/M 1: A file deleted by one process might have been in use by another; this is especially true of files under user code 0.

MP/M 2: A file opened unlocked by another process can be deleted, but the service will fail if any matching file is open read-only or locked by another process. Use Get Directory Data (101) to find out if passwords are enforced. Use Read XFCB (102) to see if this file has one.

Related requests: Set File Buffer Address (26), Set Password (106).

Search for Next File

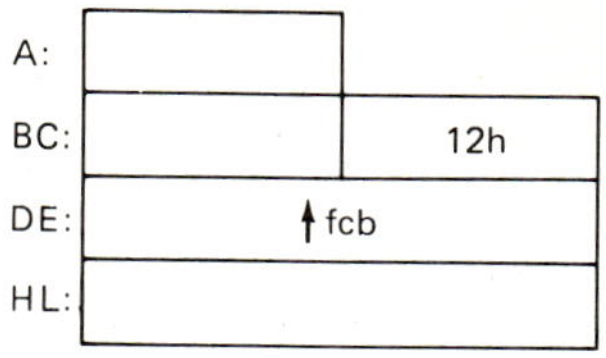

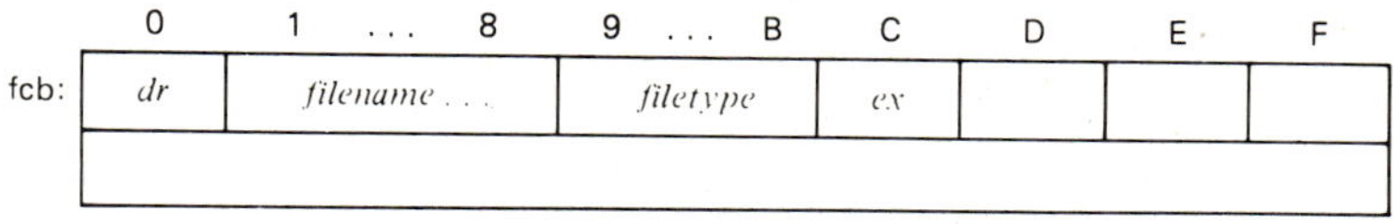

The directory of the default drive is scanned for an entry that matches the fileref and extent number in the FCB, which may contain question marks. The search starts with the entry following the one returned by the last Search (17 or 18). If a match is found, the directory entry is placed at some offset in the current file buffer, and register A is set to the position of the entry in the buffer (0, 1, 2, or 3 corresponding to an offset of 0, 32, 64, or 96 bytes). If no match is found, register A is set to FFh.

If the extent number is 00h, only the first extent entry for a file can be matched. If it contains a question mark, the first extent entry found will be returned.

Normally *dr* is ignored, and only files with the current user code are matched. If *dr* contains a question mark, all directory entries of any user code, and entries of any type including those not in use, are compared.

Delete File

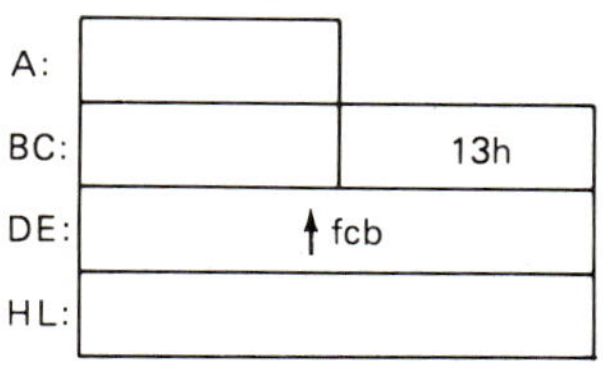

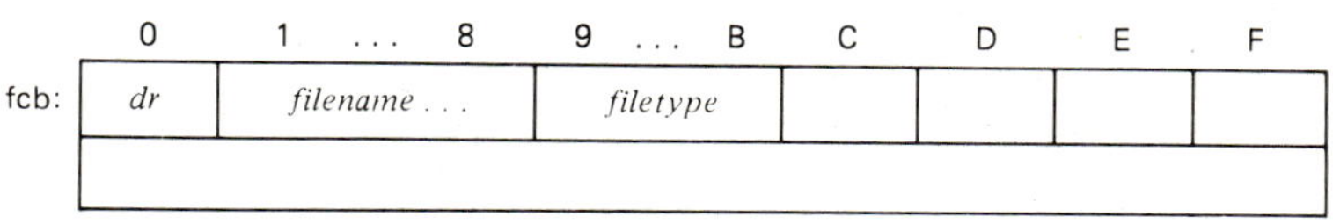

The drivecode, if not zero, is used to select a drive. The directory is scanned for all entries that match the given fileref (which may contain question marks). Only files created with the active user code are considered.

MP/M 1: Files under user code 0 are compared as well.

All matching entries are deleted, and the space they control is made available for other files.

MP/M 2: Set bit f5' to say that only XFCBs are to be deleted; the files themselves will remain. A password check may be made; a password may be given in the current file buffer.

The BDOS doesn't check to see if the FCB has been opened. An attempt to read from an unopened FCB will produce unpredictable results. *MP/M 2*: If the FCB hasn't been opened, 0Ah is returned and no read is done.

Normally *cr* is set to 00h when the file is opened and altered thereafter only by the BDOS. A limited form of direct access can be done by setting *cr* in the calling program. The present direct access services are more convenient and reliable.

The test for end of file assumes that all extents except the last one are full. A file built with direct access may contain unallocated areas that will cause end of file to be reported early.

A file built with direct access may contain unwritten records that can be read with this request. Such records may contain either garbage or binary zeros, depending on the type of direct access write request used to build the file.

Related requests: Open File (15), Set File Buffer Address (26), Set Record Count (44).

Sequential Read

Register	High	Low
A:		
BC:		14h
DE:	↑fcb	
HL:		

	0	1 ... 8	9 ... B	C	D	E	F
fcb:	*dr*	*filename . . .*	*filetype*	*ex*		*s2*	*rc*
	. . . data map . . .						
	cr						

The drivecode, if not zero, is used to select a drive. The 128-byte record at position *cr* of the extent described by the FCB is read and placed in the current file buffer. The *cr* field is incremented. If it then equals *rc*, the entire extent has been read; the directory entry describing the next extent of the file is copied into the FCB and *cr* is set to 00h. If there is no further extent, the data map is set to zero.

MP/M 2: This process may be repeated up to 15 times depending on the current record count; see Set Record Count (44).

When the read is successful, register A is returned as 00h. End of file occurs when the data map position corresponding to *cr* is zero. When it occurs, register A returns FFh.

MP/M 2: On any error, register H contains the count of records read; see Summary of Error Codes.

It is possible to write to an unopened FCB but the extent can't be closed successfully. *MP/M 2*: If the FCB hasn't been opened, error code 0Ah is returned, and no write is done.

Normally *cr* is set to 00h when the file is opened and altered thereafter only by the BDOS. A limited form of direct access can be done by setting *cr* in the calling program. The present direct access services are more convenient and reliable.

MP/M 1: There is nothing to keep two processes from writing to the same file at once.

MP/M 2: Unless the file was opened unlocked, only one process may have it open for output at a time.

Related requests: Make File (22), Close File (16), Set File Buffer Address (26), Set Record Count (44).

Sequential Write

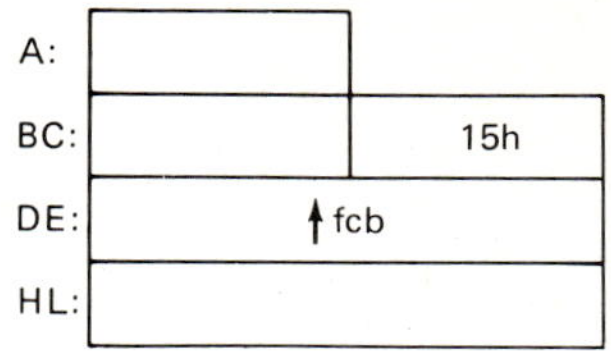

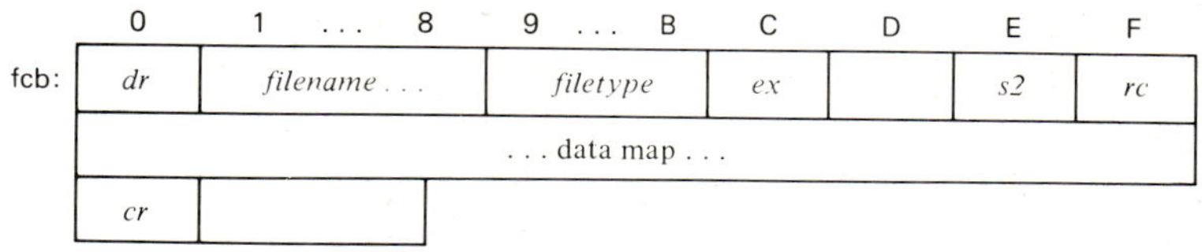

The drivecode, if not zero, is used to select a drive. If no block has been allocated to record *cr* of this extent, one is obtained and entered in the data map. The 128-byte record in the current file buffer is written to position *cr* of the extent, and *cr* and *rc* are incremented. If the extent is then full, the FCB is copied into the matching directory entry, a new entry is made for the next extent, and *rc*, *cr*, and the data map are set to zero.

MP/M 2: This process may be repeated up to 15 times depending on the record count; see Set Record Count (44).

When the write is successful, register A returns 00h. If no directory entry or no allocation block can be obtained when needed, a nonzero value is returned in register A. *MP/M 2*: If the FCB was opened read-only, a nonzero value is returned. On any error, register H contains the count of records written; see Summary of Error Codes.

Normally the extent number is zero, causing the first extent of the file to be created. Later extents are created by the BDOS as writing proceeds. It is possible to make entries for other extents, but this is not recommended.

If the fileref contains lowercase, unprintable, or special characters, a program will be able to access it but the user won't be able to name it in a command. It is possible to create duplicate filerefs; it is up to you to avoid this. *MP/M 2*: The BDOS returns FFh if a duplicate fileref exists under the active user code.

MP/M 1: This request causes the selected drive to be reserved; it can't be reset until this process ends or issues Free Drive (39).

MP/M 2: The drive will be released when all files on it are closed. Use Get Directory Data (101) to see if XFCBs are being created when files are made.

Related request: Sequential Write (21).

If the new fileref contains lowercase, unprintable, or special characters, a program will be able to access it but the user won't be able to name it in a command. It is possible to create duplicate filerefs; it is up to you to avoid this. *MP/M 2*: The BDOS returns FFh if a duplicate fileref exists under the active user code.

MP/M 1: There is no way to keep one process from renaming a file that is in use by another process.

MP/M 2: FFh is returned if the file is in use by another process, unless that process opened the file unlocked. Use Get Directory Data (101) to see if passwords are enforced. Use Read XFCB (102) to see if this file has one.

Related requests: none.

Make New File

A:		
BC:		16h
DE:	↑fcb	
HL:		

	0	1 ... 8	9 ... B	C	D	E	F
fcb:	*dr*	*filename . . .*	*filetype*	*ex*			
		id					

The drivecode, if not zero, is used to select a drive. A directory entry is created for the given fileref and extent number. The new entry shows that no space has been allocated to this extent. If no directory entries are available, FFh is returned in register A; otherwise register A contains 0, 1, 2, or 3, indicating success.

MP/M 2: Set bit f5' if the file is to be opened unlocked; other processes will be able to modify the file while it is open. Set bit f6' if the file is to have a password. Supply the password in bytes 0...7, and the password application flag in byte 8, of the current file buffer.

Rename File

A:		
BC:		17h
DE:	↑fcb	
HL:		

	0	1 ... 8	9 ... B	C	D	E	F
fcb:	*dr*	*filename . . .*	*filetype*				
	00h	*newname . . .*	*newtype*				

The drivecode, if not zero, is used to select a drive. The directory is scanned and all entries for the explicit fileref in bytes 01h...0Bh of the FCB are changed to that in bytes 11h...1Bh. If no such directory entry is found, FFh is returned in register A; else register A is returned with 0, 1, 2, or 3 *MP/M 2*: A password check may be performed. The password can be supplied in bytes 0...7 of the current file buffer.

The drives indicated in the map are active, but some of them may be read-only. The allocation vector and check vector information for read-only drives is undependable, as the diskette in a read-only drive may not be the one that was mounted when the information was built. Use Get Read-Only Map (29) to find out which active drives are read-only.

The bit map returned by this function has the same format as that returned by Get Read-Only Map (29) and input to Reset Drive (37), Access Drive (38), and Free Drive (39).

Related requests: Reset Disk System (13), Get Read-Only Vector (29).

This service allows a program to find out the default drive preferred by the user (the one current at the time the program is entered).

Under CP/M, the default drive number can be found in location 04h of working storage. This is not true of CP/M-86 or of MP/M.

Related request: Select Drive (14).

Get Active Drive Map

Register	High	Low
A:		
BC:		18 h
DE:		
HL:		

A bit map of the drives that are currently active is returned in the HL register pair (BX for CP/M-86). The bits of the map stand for drives as follows:

bit numbers:	7	6	5	4	3	2	1	0	7	6	5	4	3	2	1	0
HL:	P	O	N	M	L	K	J	I	H	G	F	E	D	C	B	A

Each drive indicated by a 1–bit has been selected since the last warm start or Reset Disk System (13) service. These drives have active allocation and check vector information.

Get Default Drive Number

Register	High	Low
A:		
BC:		19h
DE:		
HL:		

A number in the range 0...15 is returned in register A, signifying that the current default drive is A...P respectively.

When a CP/M program is first entered, the file buffer address is set to 0080h. Under CP/M and MP/M there is no service request to discover the present value of the buffer address.

CP/M-86: This request sets the file buffer offset within a segment. Use service 51 to change the file buffer segment base. Use service 52 to retrieve the buffer segment base and offset.

MP/M 2: The file buffer address is taken as the address of a password for those requests that use one (15, 19, 23, 30, 100, 103). Depending on the record count (44) the file buffer may be from 1 to 16 128-byte records long for sequential I/O, and from 2 to 32 records long for Test and Write (41).

Related requests: Set Record Count (44), Set File Buffer Segment Base (51), Get File Buffer Address (52).

See Chapter 14 for an example of a program that displays the allocation vector.

Use the Select Drive (14) service to select the drive whose allocation vector you want. Use Get Disk Parameters (31) to find out the number of allocation blocks, and hence of bits in the map.

Use Get Read-Only Map (29) to find out if the drive is read-only; if so, the allocation vector may not be valid. It reflects the allocation status of the diskette that was loaded when the drive was selected; a different diskette may be in it now.

Related requests: Select Drive (14), Get Read-Only Map (29), Get Disk Parameters (31).

Set File Buffer Address

A:		
BC:		1Ah
DE:	↑ file buffer	
HL:		

The address in register DE (DX for CP/M-86) is established as the address of the file buffer for reading and writing files and for searching the directory.

Get Allocation Vector

A:		
BC:		1Bh
DE:		
HL:		

The address of the allocation vector for the default drive is returned in the HL register pair (BX and ES for CP/M-86). The allocation vector is a bit map with as many bits as there are allocation blocks on the drive. A 1-bit means that the corresponding block is in use; a 0-bit means that it is free.

Use Get Read-Only Map (29) to find out which drives currently have read-only status; use Reset Drive (37) to reset that status. Use Select Drive (14) to select the drive that this service will act upon.

Related requests: Select Drive (14), Get Read-Only Map (29), Reset Disk System (13), Reset Drive (37).

Drives are marked read-only either by user command, by use of Protect Drive (28), or by the BDOS when it detects the fact that the diskette on the drive is not the same as when the drive was activated.

The check vector and allocation vector for a read-only drive describe the disk or diskette that was mounted when the drive was selected. If a different volume is now mounted, the information is invalid.

The bit map returned by this function has the same format as that returned by Get Active Drive Map (29) and input to Reset Drive (37), Access Drive (38), and Free Drive (39).

Related requests: Reset Disk System (13), Protect Drive (28), Reset Drive (39).

BDOS 28

Protect Drive

Register	High	Low
A:		
BC:		1Ch
DE:		
HL:		

The default drive is set to read-only status. It will keep this status until it is reset or until a warm start.

BDOS 29

Get Read-Only Map

Register	High	Low
A:		
BC:		1Dh
DE:		
HL:		

A bit map of the drives that are currently marked read-only is returned in the HL register pair (BX for CP/M-86). The bits of the map stand for drives as follows:

bit numbers:	7	6	5	4	3	2	1	0	7	6	5	4	3	2	1	0
HL:	P	O	N	M	L	K	J	I	H	G	F	E	D	C	B	A

Each drive indicated by a 1-bit has been selected and then set to read-only status since the last warm start, Reset Disk System (13), or Reset Drive (39) service. The BDOS holds allocation and check vector information for these drives dating from the time of their selection, but it may not be valid.

Each file has 11 attribute bits, one in each byte of the filename and filetype, named f1' through f8' and t1' through t3' respectively.

Bit t1' is the file R/O attribute; t2' is the SYS attribute. Bit t3' is the Archive attribute, cleared to zero when an extent is altered in any way. Bits f5' through f8' are reserved for future system use. Bits f1' through f4' are available for the use of application programs.

To change only certain bits use Search First and Search Next (17 and 18) to obtain a copy of the first directory entry for the file. The entry returned has all of the attribute bits at their present values. Alter the bits of interest, zero the drivecode, and use the entry itself as the FCB in this request.

MP/M 2: Use Get Directory Label Flag (101) to find out if passwords are enforced; use Read XFCB (102) to find out if this file has a password.

Related requests: Search (17, 18), Rename File (23), Write XFCB (103).

Use Select Drive (14) to select the drive whose DPB you want to inspect. There is a map of the DPB in the CP/M Maps section. The DPB and its uses are described in Chapter 14.

Access to the DPB is necessary to a program that wants to read the disk directory as it contains the number of directory entries and the track offset. The DPB contains the number of allocation blocks, which is required to make sense of the allocation vector. A program that intends to interpret the data map in an FCB, either to do its own space allocation or in order to do nonstandard direct access, must look at the DPB to find out the size of an allocation block and whether data map entries are 1 or 2 bytes in length.

A programmer with a thorough understanding of the DPB and of the BIOS might modify the DPB in order to handle nonstandard diskettes, but this requires extreme care and would be BIOS dependent.

 Related requests: Select Drive (14), Get Allocation Vector (27), BIOS function Seldsk.

Set File Attributes

A:		
BC:		1Eh
DE:	↑fcb	
HL:		

	0	1 ... 8	9 ... B	C	D	E	F
fcb:	*dr*	*filename . . .*	*filetype*				

The drivecode, if not zero, is used to select a drive. The directory is scanned for all entries that match the given fileref (which must be explicit). The attribute bits (the most significant bits of bytes 01h...0Bh) from the FCB are copied in each matching directory entry, replacing the attribute bits in the directory.

MP/M 2: A password check may be performed. A password may be supplied in bytes 0...7 of the current file buffer.

Get Disk Parameters

A:		
BC:		1Fh
DE:		
HL:		

The BDOS returns the address of the active Disk Parameter Block (DPB) in the HL register pair (BX and ES for CP/M-86). The DPB describes the active drive and contains all the information used by the BDOS to control space allocation.

Only files created under the active user code may be accessed. Only those files can be found by the Search First and Search Next requests (17 and 18), except for one special case of input to those requests.

MP/M 1: Files created under user code 0 are also accessible for all purposes.

MP/M 2: A file created under user code 0 can be accessed (for input only) under these conditions: (1) the file is opened read-only; (2) it can't be found under the active user code; (3) it has the SYS attribute.

This request does not alter the state of the disk system. Therefore a program may alternate user codes in order to read alternately from files created under different codes.

Related requests: none.

When some, but not all, records of an allocation block have been written with Direct Write (34), any record of the block—including those not written—can be read. Avoid the problem by initializing all records of a file, or build the file with Direct Write with Zero Fill (40) so the condition can be detected.

CP/M 2, MP/M 1: The maximum file size is 8 MB; the maximum record address is 65535 (0FFFFh). If the third (most significant) address byte is nonzero, error code 06h is returned.

MP/M 2: The maximum file size is 32 MB; the maximum record address is 262143 (3FFFFh). If the third address byte exceeds 03h, error code 06h is returned.

Related requests: Set File Buffer Address (26), Direct Write (34, 40).

BDOS 32

Get or Set User Code

Register	High	Low
A:		
BC:		20h
DE:		FFh/code
HL:		

This request may either interrogate the active user code or change it. If register E (DL for CP/M-86) contains FFh, then the active code is returned in register A. If it contains another value, then the least significant 4 bits of the value become the new active user code.

BDOS 33

Direct Access Read

Register	High	Low
A:		
BC:		21h
DE:	↑ fcb	
HL:		

	0	1 . . . 8	9 . . . B	C	D	E	F
fcb:	*dr*	*filename . . .*	*filetype*	*ex*	*s1*	*s2*	
	. . . data map . . .						
	cr	*address*					

The drivecode, if not zero, is used to select a drive. The record address and the allocation block size determine an extent number, a data map index, and a record index. If the FCB does not reflect the wanted extent, that extent entry is found and copied to the FCB (if the data map of the FCB has been changed, this extent entry is updated first).

The data map is indexed to find the wanted allocation block number; that and the record index give the disk address. The wanted record is then read to the current file buffer, *cr* is set to the position of the record in the extent, and 00h is returned in register A. Errors are reported by nonzero values of register A. Codes 01h and 04h signal nonexistent data; see the Summary of Error Codes for serious errors.

It is possible to create files with unwritten records or unallocated blocks or extents. Some unwritten records can be read with apparent success by either Sequential Read (20) or Direct Read (33). Sequential reading will stop with apparent end of file at the first unallocated block or extent. The first problem can be handled by Direct Write with Zero Fill (40); all can be avoided by writing all records.

CP/M 2, *MP/M 1*: The maximum file size is 8 MB; the maximum record address is 65535 (FFFFh). If the third (most significant) address byte is nonzero, error code 06h is returned.

MP/M 2: The maximum file size is 32 MB; the maximum record address is 262143 (3FFFFh). If the third address byte exceeds 03h, error code 06h is returned.

Related requests: Set File Buffer Address (26), Direct Read (33), Direct Write with Zero Fill (40), Get File End Address (35).

The address returned reflects the last existing record. It may not represent the actual size of the file, since files created with direct access can contain "holes," or unallocated space.

This service can be used to append data sequentially at the end of a file: open the file, get its end address, decrement the address, use Direct Read (33) to read the last record. The FCB is then prepared for sequential writing; the next write will replace the last record.

CP/M 2, *MP/M 1*: If the third byte of the address is nonzero, the file contains a record at the maximum address of 00FFFFh.

MP/M 2: If the third byte of the address is 04h, the file contains a record at the maximum address of 03FFFFh.

Related requests: Direct Write (34), Get Direct Address (36).

Direct Access Write

A:		
BC:		22h
DE:	↑fcb	
HL:		

	0	1 . . . 8	9 . . . B	C	D	E	F
fcb:	*dr*	*filename . . .*	*filetype*	*ex*	*s1*	*s2*	*rc*
	. . . data map . . .						
	cr	*address*					

The drivecode, if not zero, is used to select a drive. The record address and the allocation block size determine an extent number, a data map index, and a record index. If the FCB does not reflect the wanted extent, that extent entry is found and copied to the FCB. If the data map of the FCB has been changed, this extent entry is updated first. If the new extent doesn't exist, one is created (showing no space allocation) and copied to the FCB.

The data map is indexed to find the wanted allocation block number. A block is allocated if necessary. The block number and record index give the disk address. The record is written from the current file buffer, *cr* is set to its position in the extent, and 00h is returned in register A.

Errors are reported as nonzero values in register A; see Summary of Error Codes. Code 02h signals no room for data, and code 05h signals no room in the directory.

Get File End Address

A:		
BC:		23h
DE:	↑fcb	
HL:		

	0	1 . . . 9	A . . . B	C	D	E	F
fcb:	*dr*	*filename . . .*	*filetype*				
		address					

The drivecode, if not zero, is used to select a drive. The directory is scanned to find the highest numbered extent of the named file. The direct address of the file's last record, plus one, is set in the direct address field of the FCB.

If the data records in a file are all of the same size, the standard record address at which each data record begins can be calculated. When that is not the case, the only convenient way of finding a record directly is through an index that relates some key value of each record to the record's address. By reading a file sequentially, and noting the record address and a key value for each record, you can build an index for a file that was created sequentially.

Related request: Get File End Address (35).

This service allows the program to reset a drive when the user is to change the diskette mounted in it. If the drive is not reset before such a change, the BDOS will spot the fact that the diskette has been changed and will mark the drive read-only.

The service is similar to, but safer than, Reset All Drives (13). Only the drives the program needs are reset; other drives—which might have been made read-only by the user—are left alone.

The drive map input to this service is identical to that returned by Get Active Drive Map (24) and Get Read-Only Map (29).

Related request: Reset Disk System (13).

Get Direct Address

Register	High	Low
A:		
BC:		24h
DE:	↑fcb	
HL:		

	0	1 ... 9	A ... B	C	D	E	F
fcb:				*ex*	*s1*	*s2*	*rc*
	... data map ...						
	cr	*address*					

The extent number and current record number of the FCB are used to calculate the direct address of the last record that was returned by Read Sequential (20). The address is placed in the direct address field of the FCB.

Reset Drive (MP/M only)

Register	High	Low
A:		
BC:		25h
DE:	drive map	
HL:		

bit numbers:	7	6	5	4	3	2	1	0	7	6	5	4	3	2	1	0
drive map:	P	O	N	M	L	K	J	I	H	G	F	E	D	C	B	A

The drives specified by 1-bits in the drive map in the DE register are reset. Each such drive is marked read-write, and the BDOS discards its allocation and check vector information for that drive. New allocation and check information will be built when a drive is next selected.

MP/M 1: If any process has a file open on a selected drive, nothing is done; FFh is returned in register A.

MP/M 2: If a selected drive has removable media or is set read-only, and if another process has a file open on that drive, nothing is done and FFh is returned.

Drives are reserved automatically when an Open File (15) or Make File (22) service request is issued. If a program intends to access a drive in some nonstandard way, without opening a file on it, it should use this request to prevent the drive's being reset during its work.

The only way to free a drive reserved by this request is for the program to terminate, or to issue the Free Drive (39) request.

The bit map input to this request has the same format as that returned by Get Active Drive Map (24) and Get Read-Only Map (29) and input to Free Drive (39).

Related requests: Get Active Drive Map (24), Free Drive (39).

This service allows the program to give up the drives it might have reserved by issuing Open File (15), Make File (22), or Access Drive (38) service requests. The only other way to free the drives reserved by a process is for the process to terminate.

The bit map input to this request has the same format as that returned by Get Active Drive Map (24) and input to Reset Drive (37) and Access Drive (38).

Related requests: Get Active Drive Map (24), Access Drive (38).

BDOS 38

Access Drive (MP/M only)

A:		
BC:		26h
DE:	drive map	
HL:		

bit numbers:	7	6	5	4	3	2	1	0	7	6	5	4	3	2	1	0
DE:	P	O	N	M	L	K	J	I	H	G	F	E	D	C	B	A

The drive map in the DE register is used to reserve drives to this process. Where the input map has a 1, the corresponding drive is reserved by this process. That drive cannot be reset until this process (and any other process that has reserved it) frees it or terminates.

BDOS 39

Free Drive (MP/M only)

A:		
BC:		27h
DE:	drive map	
HL:		

bit numbers:	7	6	5	4	3	2	1	0	7	6	5	4	3	2	1	0
DE:	P	O	N	M	L	K	J	I	H	G	F	E	D	C	B	A

The drive map in the DE register is used to release drives reserved by this process. Where a bit in the map is a 1, and if the corresponding drive has been reserved by this process, the drive is released.

MP/M 2: If this process has an open file on a released drive, the BDOS forgets it; the file is considered to be not open and any further use of its FCB will return an error code.

When Direct Access Write (34) is used to build a file, unwritten records within an allocation block contain unpredictable garbage. This request fills the unwritten records of each new block with binary zeros.

It remains possible to create a file with "holes" (unallocated blocks or extents). Sequential reading will stop with apparent end of file at the first unallocated block or extent. A direct read to an unallocated area returns a nonzero code in register A.

Related Requests: Set File Buffer Address (26), Direct Write (34).

Direct Access Write with Zero Fill

Register	High	Low
A:		
BC:		28h
DE:	↑fcb	
HL:		

	0	1 . . . 9	A . . . B	C	D	E	F
fcb:	*dr*	*filename . . .*	*filetype*	*ex*	*s1*	*s2*	
	. . . data map . . .						
	cr	*address*					

The drivecode, if not zero, is used to select a drive. The record address and the allocation block size determine an extent number, a data map index, and a record index. If the FCB does not reflect the wanted extent, that extent entry is found and copied to the FCB. If the data map of the FCB has been changed, this extent entry is updated first; if the new extent doesn't exist, one is created (showing no space allocation) and copied to the FCB.

The data map is indexed to find the wanted allocation block number. If necessary, a block is allocated and all records in it filled with binary zeros. Then the record in the current file buffer is written to disk, *cr* is set to its position in the extent, and 00h is returned in register A.

Errors are returned as nonzero values in register A; see Summary of Error Codes. Code 02h signals no data space, and code 05h no directory space.

This service allows several simultaneous processes to update the same file without loss of data. Each process must open the file unlocked, then proceed thus:

1. Read the desired records,
2. Build updated records following in storage,
3. Test and write all the records,
4. If error code 7 occurs, repeat from step 1.

Error code 7 occurs only if, during step 2, another process updated the same records. When such conflicts are infrequent, this service is more efficient than Lock and Unlock Record (42 and 43).

The service is subject to most of the error codes that can result from Direct Read (33) and Direct Write (34); see Summary of Error Codes.

Related requests: Direct Read (33), Direct Write (34), Lock Record (42), Unlock Record (43).

Test and Write Record (MP/M 2)

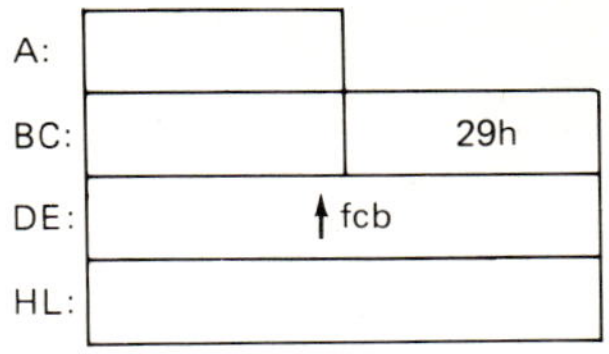

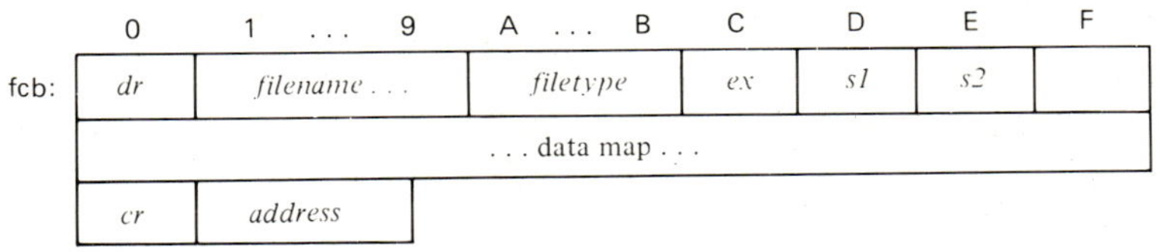

The BDOS performs a direct read, as for service 33, into a private buffer. It compares the record with that in the current file buffer. If the records are not equal, the service returns 07h in register A and ends. If they are equal, the BDOS performs a direct write as for service 34, taking the data from a position following the comparison record.

If Set Record Count (44) has been used, up to 16 consecutive records are compared with as many adjacent records in the file buffer. If all comparisons are equal, all tested records are updated from adjacent records following the comparison records.

No other process is allowed to access the file while the service is underway. Errors other than unequal compare are reported as for services 33 and 34; see Summary of Error Codes.

This service allows several simultaneous processes to operate on the same file without loss of data. Each must open the file unlocked, then proceed thus:

1. Decide what records are needed.
2. Lock them.
3. Read, alter, and write the records.
4. Unlock them.

Test and Write Record (41) is more efficient when conflicts are infrequent. This service is dangerous: if step 3 takes too long (if it includes a wait for terminal I/O, for instance), or if a bug prevents step 4 from being done, the other processes could be hung up indefinitely.

The service is subject to most of the errors that can occur with Direct Read (33); see Summary of Error Codes.

Related requests: Test and Write Record (41), Unlock Record (43).

See Lock Record (42) for the use of this service. It is not necessary to unlock the identical set of records that were locked by service 42; more or fewer records can be unlocked, although doing so has obvious possibilities for program error.

The service is subject to most of the error codes that can occur in Direct Read (33); see Summary of Error Codes.

Related requests: Test and Write Record (41), Lock Record (42).

Lock Record (MP/M 2)

Register	High	Low
A:		
BC:		2Ah
DE:	↑fcb	
HL:		

	0	1 ... 9	A ... B	C	D	E	F
fcb:	*dr*	*filename . . .*	*filetype*	*ex*	*s1*	*s2*	
	. . . data map . . .						
		address					

The record address specifies a record to be locked. The File ID returned when the file was opened or made must be given in bytes 0...1 of the current file buffer. If the specified record has not been allocated to the file, or if it exists but has been locked by another process, the service ends with an error code. Otherwise the record is locked; any other process attempting to access it will receive an error code until it is unlocked.

If Set Record Count (44) has been used, up to 16 consecutive records are inspected. If all exist and are unlocked, all are locked.

If the file was opened locked or read-only, the service does nothing and does not validate the File ID.

Unlock Record (MP/M 2)

Register	High	Low
A:		
BC:		2Bh
DE:	↑fcb	
HL:		

	0	1 ... 9	A ... B	C	D	E	F
fcb:	*dr*	*filemane . . .*	*filetype*	*ex*	*s1*	*s2*	
	. . . data map . . .						
		address					

The record address specifies a record to be unlocked. The File ID returned when the file was opened or made must be given in bytes 0...1 of the current file buffer. If the specified record exists and has been locked by this process, it is unlocked.

If Set Record Count (44) has been used, up to 16 consecutive records can be unlocked.

The service ignores records that do not exist, records that are not locked, and records that are locked by another process. If the file was opened locked or read-only, the service does nothing, and does not validate the File ID.

It is common practice to read or write records in blocks to avoid excessive disk activity. This service allows sequential (but not direct) reads and writes to access a block of up to 16 records (2048 bytes) in one service request. The amount of system overhead will be less than that incurred by a programmed loop, since fewer dispatch cycles are needed.

When this service is used with one file but not another, or for locking but not for accessing, there is a clear chance of error. Since the record count will usually change when the file buffer address does, it might be wise to put both services in a single subroutine.

Related request: Set File Buffer Address (26).

With this service a program can intercept a serious error and either correct it or terminate in an orderly way. This is especially important when files are protected by passwords. A password mismatch will cancel the program unless extended error mode is on.

Related requests: none.

Set Record Count (MP/M 2)

Register	High	Low
A:		
BC:		2Ch
DE:		*count*
HL:		

If the count in register E is not in the range of 1...16, FFh is returned in register A. If the count is in range, it is set as a repetition count for the following services:

20 Sequential Read	42 Lock Record
21 Sequential Write	43 Unlock Record
41 Test and Write Record	

These services normally operate on single records. When the count is set higher than 1 they repeat for consecutive records until the total reaches the record count. When a repeated operation is interrupted by end of file or an error, the count of successful iterations is returned in the most significant 4 bits of register H.

Set Error Mode (MP/M 2)

Register	High	Low
A:		
BC:		2Dh
DE:		*flag*
HL:		

If *flag* is FEh or FFh, the BDOS will no longer trap serious disk I/O errors but will return them to the calling program as FFh in register A and a code in the least significant 4 bits of register H. The services affected are

14 Select Disk	41 Test and Write Record
20 Sequential Read	42 Lock Record
21 Sequential Write	43 Unlock Record
33 Direct Read	46 Get Disk Free Space
34 Direct Write	48 Flush Buffers
35 Get File Size	100 Write Directory Label
38 Access Drive	102 Read XFCB
40 Direct Write Zero	103 Write XFCB

If *flag* is FEh, the BDOS will continue to display its usual Bdos Err messages when an error occurs; if *flag* is FFh the BDOS will not display a message when an error occurs.

If *flag* is 00h, the BDOS reverts to normal; a serious error will terminate the program and a Bdos Err message will be displayed to the user.

Prior to MP/M 2 a program could discover this information, but only by referring to the Disk Parameter Block (DPB) and the allocation vector for the drive.

The maximum value that could be returned is 4,194,303 decimal or 3F,FF,FFh: the maximum disk capacity (536,870,912 bytes) divided by 128. The value shows the number of records that could be added to any one file. If the third byte exceeds 03h, then there is room for a file of the maximum size (32 MB).

Related requests: Get Allocation Vector (27), Get Disk Parameters (31).

This service allows a program to end and pass control to a command. "Chain" usually implies changing programs while retaining storage variables and open files. In this case the program terminates completely, controlling only the command that follows it.

Related request: Terminate Program (0).

Get Disk Free Space (MP/M 2)

Register	High	Low
A:		
BC:		2Eh
DE:		drive
HL:		

Register E contains a number in the range 0...15, signifying a drive from A...P respectively. If the drive has not been selected since the disk system was initialized, it is selected. The BDOS counts the free allocation blocks on the drive, multiplies by the number of 128-byte records in a block, and returns the count as a 3-byte binary integer. The number is returned in bytes 0...2 of the current file buffer in the form of a direct file address; that is, byte 0 is the least significant and byte 2 is the most significant.

Chain to Command (MP/M 2)

Register	High	Low
A:		
BC:		2Fh
DE:		
HL:		

file buffer:	*command*	00h

The current file buffer must contain a character string that the system will treat as if it were a command typed by the user. The command will be executed next, even if a submit file is active.

The command string may be from 1 to 100 bytes in length and must be followed by a byte of 00h (which is not counted in the length).

Ordinarily control will not be returned to the program; it will be ended as for service 0. If the process is not attached to its console, control will return.

Some BIOSes manage large storage buffers. A BIOS of proper design will never delay writing changed data for very long. However, the most recent program output may be retained for some time, especially when direct access is being used. This request allows the program to ensure that the data it has written has actually been put on the disk. Its real application is in large MP/M systems, especially those that keep a large disk cache and use fixed-media disks. The service, in combination with the temporary close feature of service 16, allows a long-running program like a CP/NET server to take periodic disk checkpoints, thus assuring file integrity.

Related request: Close Output File (16).

This request provides the only way for a CP/M-86 program to call on a BIOS function. The address of the BIOS entry table is not placed in low storage in CP/M-86; there is no way for a program to discover its address. The BDOS must intervene to set the various segment registers correctly for BIOS execution before the BIOS is entered.

The BDOS does not censor BIOS requests made with this service; all the functions of the BIOS are still available to programs that need them.

Related requests: none.

BDOS 48

Flush Disk Buffers (MP/M 2)

A:		
BC:		30h
DE:		
HL:		

The BDOS calls on the BIOS to write any output disk records it may be holding in internal buffers. If the BIOS buffers large disk sectors, or if it keeps a cache of disk sectors, it will write the data to disk. If the BIOS doesn't buffer data, nothing happens.

BDOS 50

Call BIOS Entry (CP/M-86 only)

AX:	
BX:	
CX:	0032h
DX:	↑ parameters

parameters:	*fnc*	CX value	DX value

The BDOS loads the 16-bit values given in the parameter list into the CX and DX registers and enters the BIOS at the function entry indicated. The 8-bit *fnc* value is an offset into the BIOS entry table, with *fnc* = 0 corresponding to the first (cold start) entry, *fnc* = 3 corresponding to the second (warm start) entry, and so on.

The registers are returned as the BIOS set them.

When a program is initialized, the file buffer segment address is set identical to the data segment address in the program's DS register, and the file buffer offset address is set to 0080h. This conforms to the conventions of CP/M and MP/M, where the default buffer is at 0080h in (the only segment of) working storage.

The Set File Buffer Address (26) request alters only the buffer offset in CP/M-86; that request can be used to place the buffer anywhere in the Data Segment but not elsewhere. This request allows the file buffer to be located in the program's Code, Stack, or Extra Segments.

Related request: Set File Buffer Address (26).

This request can be used to find and save the current file buffer address before setting another, temporary one. There is no comparable request in CP/M or MP/M.

Related requests: Set File Buffer Address (26), Set File Buffer Segment Base (51).

Set File Buffer Segment Base (CP/M-86 only)

BDOS 51

AX:	
BX:	
CX:	0033h
DX:	segment base adr.

The address in the DX register is saved as the segment base for the file record buffer whose offset is set by Set File Buffer Address (26). The address is taken to be a paragraph address, the most significant 16 bits of a 20-bit address.

BDOS 52

Get File Buffer Address (CP/M-86 only)

AX:	
BX:	
CX:	0034h
DX:	

The complete address of the active file buffer is returned. The segment address is returned in the ES register and the offset address in the BX register.

This request acquires a large area of storage that the program will subdivide according to its own rules. Note that a program loaded according to the CP/M-86 rules for the Compact Model can have as many as six storage areas allocated for it when it is loaded.

Use Relocatable Storage (55) when an area of a specific size is needed. Use Absolute Storage (56) or Maximum Absolute Storage when an area at a specific address is required.

Related requests: Relocatable Storage (55), Release Storage (57).

This request acquires a large area of storage at a specific storage address. To do so implies some hardware dependency, as the program must know that the address is defined in this machine. To get an area of a particular size at an absolute address (for example, the area that defines a memory-mapped display), use Absolute Storage (56).

Related requests: Absolute Storage (56), Release Storage (57).

Maximum Relocatable Storage (CP/M-86 only)

AX:	
BX:	
CX:	0035h
DX:	↑ mcb

bytes:	0 1	2 3	4
mcb:	*base*	*length*	*flg*

This request asks the BDOS to provide the largest area of contiguous storage available. The BDOS sets the paragraph address of the storage area in the first 2 bytes of the MCB, and the length (in paragraph, or 16-byte, units) in the second 2 bytes. If no storage areas are available, FFh is returned in the AL register, otherwise 00h is returned.

If there are other storage areas that could be allocated, the flag field is set to 01h. If this is the last area, it is set to 00h.

Maximum Absolute Storage (CP/M-86 only)

AX:	
BX:	
CX:	0036h
DX:	↑ mcb

bytes:	0 1	2 3	4
mcb:	*base*	*length*	*flg*

This request asks the BDOS to provide the largest area of contiguous storage available at a specific storage address. The paragraph address required must be passed in the first 2 bytes of the MCB. The length available (in paragraph, or 16-byte, units) is returned in the length field. If the address requested doesn't exist or falls in an area already allocated to some other use, FFh is returned in the AL register; otherwise 00h is returned.

If there are other storage areas that could be allocated, the flag field is set to 01h. If this is the last area, it is set to 00h.

Use this request to acquire a block of storage of some known size: a file buffer, perhaps, or space for a table or array of known size. Note that a program loaded according to the CP/M-86 rules for the Compact Model can have as many as six storage areas allocated for it when it is loaded.

Use Maximum Relocatable Storage (53) when an area of the largest possible size is needed. Use Absolute Storage (56) or Maximum Absolute Storage when an area at a specific address is required.

Related requests: Maximum Relocatable Storage (53), Release Storage (57).

This request acquires a specific area of storage at a specific storage address: perhaps a section of storage that is mapped by some hardware device such as a memory-mapped display. Using this or the Maximum Absolute Storage request (54) implies a hardware dependency. Use Relocatable Storage (55) when the storage address doesn't matter.

Related requests: Maximum Absolute Storage (56), Release Storage (57).

Relocatable Storage (CP/M-86 only)

BDOS 55

AX:	
BX:	
CX:	0037h
DX:	↑ mcb

bytes:	0	1	2	3	4
mcb:	*base*		*length*		*flg*

This request asks the BDOS to provide an area of contiguous storage of a specified length. The length needed must be passed as a number of paragraph (16-byte) units in the second 2 bytes of the MCB. The BDOS sets the paragraph address of the storage area in the first 2 bytes of the MCB. If no storage area of the size requested is available, FFh is returned in the AL register; otherwise 00h is returned.

If there are other storage areas that could be allocated, the flag field is set to 01h. If this is the last area, it is set to 00h.

Absolute Storage

BDOS 56

AX:	
BX:	
CX:	0038h
DX:	↑ mcb

bytes:	0	1	2	3	4
mcb:	*base*		*length*		*flg*

This request asks the BDOS to provide a certain amount of contiguous storage at a specific storage address. The paragraph address required must be passed in the first 2 bytes of the MCB and the length required (in paragraph, or 16-byte, units) in the second 2 bytes. If the address requested doesn't exist or falls in an area already allocated to some other use, or if the length requested isn't available following it, FFh is returned in the AL register; otherwise 00h is returned.

If there are other storage areas that could be allocated, the flag field is set to 01h. If this is the last area, it is set to 00h.

The storage released must have been obtained by one of the allocation requests (53–56). Storage allocated as part of the program load should not be released.

When a single area is released, the area may be identical to an area obtained with an allocation request, or may be the low end (*base* = allocated address) or high end (*base* + *length* = allocation end) of an allocation. The middle part of an allocation may not be released alone.

A released area is available for later allocation.

Related requests: Maximum Relocatable Storage (53), Relocatable Storage (55), Maximum Absolute Storage (54), Absolute Storage (56).

This request is meant for the use of the CCP; it is included here only for the sake of completeness. It is impossible to predict what would happen if a command program issued this request, but it wouldn't be anything good.

Related requests: none.

Release Storage (CP/M-86 only)

BDOS 57

AX:	
BX:	
CX:	0039
DX:	↑ mcb

bytes:	0 1	2 3	4
mcb:	*base*	*length*	*flg*

The storage area whose paragraph base address is given in the MCB is released for other uses.

If *flg* = FFh, then all storage allocated by preceding requests is released. In this case the *base* and *length* values are ignored.

If *flg* = 00h, the area described by *base* and *length* is released. This area must be a complete area as allocated by a previous request, or must be adjacent to one end of such an area.

Release All Storage (CP/M-86 only)

BDOS 58

AX:	
BX:	
CX:	003Ah
DX:	

All storage areas in the machine (except the space occupied by the BDOS, BIOS, and CCP) are released.

After loading a program you can examine the first bytes of its data segment (via the base address in register BX) to discover which program model (8080, Small, or Compact) it uses and the addresses of its various storage segments.

In order to call the loaded program you must find its entry point. The base address of the program's code segment appears at offset 0001h in its data segment. If the program was built on the 8080 model, the byte at 0003h in its data segment will be nonzero. In that case the program's code segment and data segment are identical, and the program should be entered at offset 0100h. Programs built on the other models should be entered at the beginning of their code segments.

The default FCB in the new program's base page has not been initialized, nor has the default file buffer address set for it. If the program will expect these things to have been done, the loading program must do them before calling it.

Related requests: none.

The name and type fields serve only as user identification; they can be displayed with the SHOW command but a program can read them only with the Search requests (17, 18).

The *flg* settings are very important for file processing. If bit 7 is 0, passwords can be supplied for files but will never be checked; if it is 1, then a password may be required whenever a file is opened, deleted, renamed, or has its attributes changed.

If bit 4 is 1, then an XFCB will be created whenever a file is made. That consumes an extra directory entry for every new file.

A return code of FFh will usually indicate that the directory is full and so a label could not be created. If extended error mode has been set (service 45), FFh in register A will be accompanied by a code in register H.

Related request: Get Directory Data (101).

Load Program (CP/M-86 only)

AX:	
BX:	
CX:	003Bh
DX:	↑fcb

Register DX specifies the offset of a file control block in the data segment. The FCB, which must have been opened, names a file of type .CMD. The BDOS loads the program, allocating segments of storage as required. Register AL contains 00h if the load is successful, and register BX contains the segment base of the loaded program's data segment.

If the file cannot be read, or doesn't contain a valid header record, the load is not done and FFh is returned in register AL.

Write Directory Label (MP/M 2)

A:		
BC:		64h
DE:	↑fcb	
HL:		

	0	1 . . . 9	A . . . B	C	D	E	F
fcb:	*dr*	*filename . . .*	*filetype*	*flg*			

The drivecode, if not zero, is used to select a drive. The Directory Label of that disk is created or updated. The filename and filetype fields provide user identification for the disk. The bits of *flg* establish the handling of passwords and XFCBs:

Bit 7 = 1: Enforce file password protection.
Bit 6 = 1: Timestamp an XFCB when its file is opened.
Bit 5 = 1: Timestamp an XFCB when its file is closed.
Bit 4 = 1: Create an XFCB during Make File (22).
Bit 0 = 1: Assign a (new) password to the Directory Label.

If the current label has a password it is checked. The password may be given in bytes 0...7 of the current file buffer, or previously through Set Password (106). If *flg* bit 0 is set, the new password must be in bytes 8..15 of the file buffer.

If the directory label is created or updated successfully, 0, 1, 2, or 3 is returned in register A, otherwise FFh is returned.

Check bit 7 to find out if a password may be required when a file is opened, deleted, renamed, or has its attributes changed. If so, you can check the file's XFCB to see if the file has a password.

Check Bit 0 to see if a label entry exists at all. If one does, then service 100 may require a password.

If extended error codes have been set on (service 45), register A is returned as FFh when a physical error occurs.

Related request: Write Directory Label (100).

The timestamps may not be accurate. Timestamping is controlled by the Directory Label. Depending on the setting of bits in the label the BDOS may update only open times, only close times, neither, or both.

Password enforcement is also controlled by the Directory Label. If it specifies password checking, then this file's password will be checked on the operations indicated by *flg*. It is possible for all three *flg* bits to be 0; in that case the file may have a password but it will not be checked.

Related requests: Read Directory Data (101), Write XFCB (103).

BDOS 101

Get Directory Data (MP/M 2)

A:		
BC:		65h
DE:		drive
HL:		

Register E contains a number from 0...15, signifying drive A...P respectively. If the drive has not been selected since the disk system was initialized, it is selected. If the directory contains no label entry, 00h is returned in register A. Otherwise the Directory Label flag byte is returned:

Bit 7 = 1: Passwords are checked for files that have them.
Bit 6 = 1: An XFCB is timestamped when its file is opened.
Bit 5 = 1: An XFCB is timestamped when its file is closed.
Bit 4 = 1: An XFCB is created whenever a file is made.
Bit 0 = 1: A Directory Label exists on the drive.

BDOS 102

Read XFCB (MP/M 2)

A:		
BC:		66h
DE:	↑fcb	
HL:		

	0	1 ... 8	9 ... B	C	D	E	F
fcb:	*dr*	*filename ...*	*filetype*	*flg*			
			open timestamp		close timestamp		

The drivecode, if not zero, is used to select a drive. The BDOS searches for the given fileref (which must be explicit). If it is not found, or if the file has no XFCB, FFh is returned in register A. If a matching XFCB is found, its fields are returned in the given FCB. The open timestamp in bytes 18h...1Bh marks the last time the file was opened in any mode; the close timestamp in 1Ch...1Fh marks the time the file was last closed after output. The *flg* field controls password enforcement for this file. Passwords are checked on these operations:

Bit 7 = 1: Read-only open, plus...
Bit 6 = 1: Locked and unlocked opens, plus...
Bit 5 = 1: Delete, rename, and attribute change.

Only one of *flg* bits 7, 6, and 5 should be set. If none of them are set but bit 0 is 1, the file will be given a new password but it will be disabled. The new password can be enabled at a later time by updating the XFCB again.

Related requests: Read XFCB (102), Read Directory Data (101).

The system maintains the time and date mainly for use in timestamping XFCBs. The current time can be obtained with Get Date and Time (105).

Related request: Get Date and Time (105).

Write XFCB (MP/M 2)

BDOS 103

A:		
BC:		67h
DE:	↑fcb	
HL:		

	0	1 ... 9	A ... B	C	D	E	F
fcb:	*dr*	*filename . . .*	*filetype*	*flg*			

The drivecode, if not zero, is used to select a drive. The BDOS searches for the given fileref (which must be explicit). If there is no Directory Label, or if the file does not exist, or if there is no directory space to create an XFCB, FFh is returned in register A.

If an XFCB exists and calls for password checking, the password is checked against the one in bytes 0...7 of the current file buffer. If no XFCB exists, the BDOS creates one. Then bits 7, 6, and 5 of *flg* are copied to the XFCB; they control password application:

Bit 7 = 1: Check on read-only open, plus...
Bit 6 = 1: Check on any open, plus...
Bit 5 = 1: Check on delete, rename, and set attribute

If *flg* bit 0 is 1, then a new password is taken from bytes 8...15 of the current file buffer.

Set Date and Time (MP/M 2)

BDOS 104

A:		
BC:		68h
DE:	↑data	
HL:		

bytes:	0 1	2	3
data:	*date*	*hh*	*mm*

The system's clock and calendar are set. The *date* value is a 16-bit integer, a count of days since 1 January, 1978; that is, *date* would have been 0001h during that day, turning to 0002h at 00:00:00 hours, 2 January, 1978.

The *hh* and *mm* bytes represent the hour and minute, respectively, in Binary Coded Decimal (BCD).

Note that the sign bit of *date* will be 0 until 2066 A.D. Therefore a date prior to 1978 may safely be constructed by subtraction, with dates back to 1880 being represented by negative numbers.

Related request: Set Date and Time (104).

If the password string is shorter than 8 bytes, it should be left-justified in the field and padded with blanks.

If the user has set a default password, it will be replaced.

Related requests: none.

BDOS 105

Get Date and Time (MP/M 2)

Register	High	Low
A:		
BC:		69h
DE:	↑ data	
HL:		

bytes:	0 1	2	3
data:	*date*	*hh*	*mm*

The system's clock and calendar values are returned in a 4-byte field in storage. The *hh* and *mm* values represent the current hour and minute in Binary Coded Decimal (BCD).

The *date* value is a 16-bit binary integer that is a count of days since 1 January, 1978. That is, *date* would have been 0001h on that date, 0002h the next, and so on.

BDOS 106

Set Password (MP/M 2)

Register	High	Low
A:		
BC:		6Ah
DE:	↑ password	
HL:		

bytes:	0 1 2 . . . 7
password:	characters . . .

Register DE addresses an 8-byte character string that can be used as a password in subsequent file services. The string is set as the default password. Each time a file service requires a password check the BDOS will test the 8 bytes at the then-current file buffer address. If that test fails, it will try the default password before reporting a password error.

The default password remains in force until another one is specified or until a cold start is done.

NDOS

Topical Summary of CP/NET NDOS Services

Req. No.	Page	Service Performed	Argument
64	533	Login to a master system	DE→login msg
65	533	Logout from a master system	E = master id
66	535	Send message	DE→message
67	535	Receive message	DE→buffer
68	537	Get network status byte	E = master id
69	537	Get configuration table	none

If a login request fails, it might be that the master processor rejected it, or that the master couldn't be contacted or didn't respond. Use Get Network Status (68) to find out if a send or receive error occurred.

It is not clear what will happen if two login requests are issued in succession to the same master. The second request might be rejected, or it might be accepted and ignored.

If this processor is connected to more than one master, or if the program wants to log in through the local master to a processor in some higher layer of the network, the master id must be given explicitly.

Related request: Logout from Network (65).

If a logout request fails, it may be that the master processor didn't recognize the source processor id. This could occur if this processor had never successfully logged in to that master, or if the master had crashed and been restarted since the login took place. Use Get Network Status (68) to find out if a transmission error took place.

Related request: Login to Network (64).

Login to Network

Register	High	Low
A:		
BC:		40h
DE:	↑ log-in msg	
HL:		

	0	1 2 7
log-in msg:	*id*	password . . .

The message addressed by the DE register pair is transmitted to the master processor indicated by *id*. If the master is active, can accept a login, and finds the password correct, this processor is logged in as a slave processor. It may then use the master for I/O.

A value of 00h is returned in register A if the login is accepted by the master processor. FFh is returned if the login is not successful.

An *id* of 00h specifies the only master processor to which this processor is directly connected.

Logout from Network

Register	High	Low
A:		
BC:		41h
DE:		*id*
HL:		

A logout message is sent to the master processor indicated by *id*. If that processor can be contacted, and recognizes the source processor id, it will free any resources it holds for this processor.

A value of 00h is returned in register A if the logout succeeds. If not, FFh is returned.

A processor id of 00h specifies the only master to which this processor is directly connected.

The great bulk of network messages relate to redirected I/O; these are produced by the NDOS as a result of I/O service requests. This request allows a program to send a message for some other reason.

One use of this request is to send a message to a processor elsewhere in the network. The message will have the Send Message on Network format. After sending such a message, execute a Receive Message request (67) to get the master processor's return code.

To receive a message from a processor elsewhere in the network, use this request to send a Receive Message from Network format to the master processor, then use Receive Message (67) to get the message.

Related request: Receive Message (67).

Don't confuse this service request with the CP/NET message format of the same name. The service causes this processor to receive a transmission from the master processor to which it is directly connected.

When a network message is sent (Send Message on Network format, transmitted to the master with a Send Message (66) request), this service should be requested immediately afterward. The message that is received will be the master processor's response, indicating whether it was able to handle the network message.

In order to receive a message from another processor elsewhere in the network, transmit a Receive Message from Network format to the master processor (using a Send Message (66) request), then issue this request. The resulting message, if it contains *siz* greater than 1, is from the network.

Related request: Send Message (66).

NDOS 66

Send Message

Register	High	Low
A:		
BC:		42h
DE:	↑ message	
HL:		

	0	1	2	3	4	5 . . .
message:	*fmt*	*did*	*sid*	*fnc*	*siz*	contents . . .

The CP/NET message addressed by the DE register pair is transmitted on the network. The calling program is suspended until the entire message has been transmitted. The message must contain a complete message header. Any type and format of CP/NET message may be sent in this way.

NDOS 67

Receive Message

Register	High	Low
A:		
BC:		43h
DE:	↑ buffer	
HL:		

	0	1	2	3	4	5 . . .
buffer:	*fmt*	*did*	*sid*	*fnc*	*siz*	results. . .

The next message from the master processor will be placed, exactly as received, in the buffer. The calling program is suspended until a message is received. No length check can be made; the program must provide a buffer large enough to contain the message.

This request can be used to distinguish between a logical and a physical error; that is, between a message that was rejected by the master processor and one that couldn't be sent.

The request returns the status byte kept by the SNIOS in this system. Don't confuse it with the Get Network Status message format. A message in that format would be sent to a master system using Send Message (66). The master's response, obtained with Receive Message (67), would contain the master's status byte, with a different bit layout.

Related requests: none.

Examine the configuration table to find out if I/O for a particular disk drive or logical device is travelling over the network. Network disk I/O is likely to be slower than local disk I/O. This is not usually important, but a few programs may depend on disk speed. For instance, a program that reads from a device prone to overrun (such as a streaming tape drive) might not work when its output was to a remote disk file.

Get Network Status

Register	High	Low
A:		
BC:		44h
DE:		*id*
HL:		

This processor's status relative to the master whose id is in register E is returned in register A. The format of the network status byte is

bit numbers:	7	6	5	4	3	2	1	0
				log			*rcv*	*snd*

where *log* indicates that this processor has logged in to the master, *rcv* indicates that a receive error has occurred, and *snd* indicates a send error. The two error bits are reset when the request is made, hence they reflect errors only since the last request.

Get Configuration Table

Register	High	Low
A:		
BC:		45h
DE:		
HL:		

The address of this processor's network configuration table is returned in the HL register pair. The configuration table layout is shown in the CP/M Maps section. The table defines which logical devices are having their I/O redirected to the network.

BIOS

Topical Summary of BIOS Entry Points

Entry No.	Page	Service Performed	Argument	Valid Systems -80	-86	MP/M
		System Information and Control				
0	543	Initialize (warm boot)	none	X	X	X
1	543	Console status	none	X	X	X
14	551	List status	none	X	X	X
11	549	Set file buffer address	BC→buffer	X	X	X
16	553	Set file buffer segment base	CX = segment	-	X	-
17	553	Return region table	none	-	X	-
18	555	Return current IOBYTE	none	-	X	-
19	555	Set new IOBYTE	CL = IOBYTE	-	X	-
		Serial Input and Output				
2	543	Console input	none	X	X	X
3	545	Console output	C = byte	X	X	X
1	543	Console status	none	X	X	X
4	545	List output	C = byte	X	X	X
14	551	List status	none	X	X	X
5	545	Punch output	C = byte	X	X	-
6	547	Reader input	none	X	X	-
		Disk Drive Operations				
7	547	Home drive (set track 0)	none	X	X	X
8	547	Select drive	C = drive	X	X	X
9	549	Set track	BC = track	X	X	X
15	553	Translate record number	BC = record	X	X	X
10	549	Set record number	BC = record	X	X	X
12	551	Read record to buffer	none	X	X	X
13	551	Write record from buffer	C = type code	X	X	X
11	549	Set file buffer address	BC→buffer	X	X	X
16	553	Set file buffer segment base	CX = segment	-	X	-

Under CP/M and MP/M this function entry is directly addressed by the jump instruction at location 00h. The address in that instruction may be used as the base address of the BIOS entry table. Under CP/M-86 the BIOS is called by way of BDOS service 50; there is no jump instruction in low storage.

In all systems BDOS service request 0, Terminate Program, has the same effect as BIOS function 0. It is traditional for CP/M programs to end with a "jump to boot," (JMP 0). The BIOS entry is difficult to get to under CP/M-86. For best compatibility with all versions of the system, use the BDOS service request.

This function duplicates that of BDOS service request 11.

The value returned in register A is specified to be either FFh or 00h. The Z flag will usually reflect the value in the register, but this depends on the code of the BIOS and should not be relied on.

Under MP/M the number of the console assigned to the process can be obtained with Get Console Number, XDOS service request 153.

This function duplicates that of BDOS service 6 for input. It can be used in place of BDOS service 1, but it bypasses all monitor functions. If CP/NET is present, the NDOS is bypassed; console I/O cannot be redirected to a network location. If DESPOOL is active, it cannot get control to test the printer status. The BDOS will not be able to echo the input byte to the terminal screen (or to the printer, if control-p has been pressed).

Under MP/M the number of the console assigned to the process can be obtained with Get Console Number, XDOS service request 153. Under MP/M the most significant bit of the first byte of the process name in the Process Descriptor should be set to 1 when this BIOS call is to be used.

WBOOT

BIOS 00

The calling program is terminated and the system is initialized.

Under CP/M 1 and 2 the code of the CCP and BDOS is refreshed from the reserved tracks of the A-drive disk and low storage is initialized. The CCP selects the A-drive. If a file $$$.SUB exists, the next command is taken from it; else the user is prompted for a command.

Under MP/M this function simply performs BDOS service request 0, Terminate Program. All resources owned by the calling program are freed, the storage it occupied is made available, and control of the terminal is returned to the CLI.

CONST

BIOS 01

The status of the console device is sampled. A nonzero value is returned in register A if a character is ready for input, otherwise 00h is returned.

Under MP/M register D must contain the number of the console device to be tested.

CONIN

BIOS 02

The next character is read from the console device. The calling program is suspended until a character is available. The parity bit (bit 7) of the character is set to zero, and the resulting byte is returned in the A register.

In MP/M the number of the console device must be passed in register D.

This function duplicates that of BDOS service 6 for output. It can be used in place of BDOS service 2, but all monitor functions are bypassed. If CP/NET is present, the NDOS is bypassed; console output cannot be redirected to a network location. Console output will not be duplicated at the printer if control-p has been pressed.

Under MP/M the number of the console assigned to the process can be obtained with Get Console Number, XDOS service request 153.

This function duplicates that of BDOS service request 5 except that if CP/NET is present, the NDOS is bypassed; list output cannot be directed to a network location.

Under MP/M the MXlist mutual exclusion queue should be obtained before writing to the list device.

This function duplicates that of BDOS service request 4.

CONOUT

BIOS 03

The character in register C (CL for CP/M-86) is sent to the console device. The BIOS assumes that the parity bit (bit 7) has been set to zero. The calling program is suspended until the character has been transmitted.

Under MP/M, register D must contain the console number for the operation.

LIST

BIOS 04

The character in register C (CL for CP/M-86) is transmitted to the logical list device. The BIOS assumes that the parity bit (bit 7) has been set to zero. The calling program is suspended until the character has been sent.

PUNCH

BIOS 05

The character in register C (CL for CP/M-86) is sent to the logical punch device. The BIOS assumes that the parity bit (bit 7) of the character has been set to zero. The calling program is suspended until the character has been sent.

This BIOS entry performs no function under MP/M; it consists of a return instruction only.

This function duplicates that of BDOS service request 3.

This function is effectively the same as a call on SETTRK (9) with a track number of zero.

The main reason for calling this BIOS function from a command program is to obtain the address of the Disk Parameter Header. The DPH contains the address of the skew translation table for the selected drive, which is needed as an input to the SECTRAN function (15).

The BDOS keeps track of the drive it thinks it has selected. It is not wise to call the BIOS to select a drive without first calling on the BDOS (via service 14) to select the same drive. If this is not done, the BDOS will be out of step; false disk error messages, or worse failures, may occur.

Some CP/M and all MP/M BIOSes use register E bit 0 to determine if a diskette may have been changed. If they receive a 0-bit, indicating that this is the first select since the disk system was reset, they may sense the media for density and sector size. If they receive a 1-bit, they may assume that the disk cannot have been changed and so still has the same format.

The best sequence of operations to cope with all these considerations is (1) call BDOS service 13 if you want the BIOS to sense the media, (2) call BDOS service 14 to select the drive, and (3) call the BIOS to get the DPH address.

BIOS 06

READER

The next character from the logical reader device is returned in register A (AL for CP/M-86). The calling program is suspended until the character is ready. The parity bit (bit 7) will be set to zero.

Under MP/M this BIOS entry has no function; it consists of a return instruction only.

BIOS 07

HOME DISK

The read-write head of the disk last selected by the SELDSK (8) function will be moved to track zero (the outermost track). Whether the head is moved immediately depends on the drive hardware and the code of the BIOS; disk motion is usually deferred until a READ or WRITE call occurs.

If the head is moved immediately, the program may or may not be suspended until it reaches track zero. In some systems (especially MP/M) the BIOS disk code may initiate the operation and return, relying on a hardware interrupt to signal that the motion is complete.

BIOS 08

SELDSK

The disk drive specified by the drive number in register C (CL for CP/M-86) is selected for further operations. The drive number must be in the range of 0...15, signifying drives A...P respectively.

Under MP/M and some CP/M systems, the least significant bit of register E (DL in CP/M-86) is a signal to the BIOS: 0 says that this is the first time the disk has been selected; 1 says that it was selected previously since it was reset.

The address of the Disk Parameter Header for the selected drive is returned in the HL register pair (BX and ES for CP/M-86). If the drive number is not valid for this system, or if an I/O error occurs while selecting the drive, 0000h is returned to indicate the error.

Information in the Disk Parameter Block (DPB) can be used to calculate the first and last track numbers of a drive while avoiding hardware dependencies. The address of the DPB can be obtained through BDOS service 31. See Chapter 14 for a discussion of its use.

The track number passed in BC is a physical track number. A request for track zero is a request for the outermost track on the physical drive. The first track containing data is the track whose number appears as the track offset value in the DPB. The disk directory appears in the first logical records of that track. If the track offset is zero, or larger than 3, the drive is likely to be a logical drive, part of a hard disk.

If the drive is a double-sided diskette or a hard disk with multiple heads, the BIOS will translate the track number into a cylinder number and a side (or head) number.

When the disk involved actually uses 128-byte sectors, the record number is also a physical sector number. On other disks the BIOS determines the relation between the record number and the sector that contains it. The calling program need not be aware of the size of a physical sector, only of the number of standard records per track. The maximum record number can be found in the Disk Parameter Block (DPB), obtainable through BDOS service request 31.

The record number passed is a physical record number stating the position of the record on the track. If skew translation is used on the selected disk, the number given must be the one returned from a SECTRAN (entry 15) call.

Under CP/M-86 this function sets the segment offset of the file buffer; the segment base address is set with function 16.

The BDOS keeps track of the buffer it thinks it has selected. The BDOS selects either the buffer named in the most recent service 26 or, during drive selection and directory scan operations, its own directory buffer. To avoid conflict with the BDOS use BDOS service requests to select the drive and the initial buffer address. Then request no file services from the BDOS until your BIOS work is complete.

SETTRK

BIOS 09

The track number given in the BC register pair (CX for CP/M-86) is established as the track for the next operation on the drive that has been selected by SELDSK (8).

Whether or not head motion is initiated at this time depends on the disk hardware and the code of the BIOS; the seek may be deferred until it is required.

SETSEC

BIOS 10

The standard record number in the BC register (CX for CP/M-86) is established as the record to be read or written in the next call for disk I/O. The record number is in the range of 1 through the maximum number of standard records on a track. It should be the result of skew translation by the SECTRAN entry.

Whether or not any disk operation is started at this time depends on the disk hardware and the code of the BIOS. Sector selection may be deferred until the READ or WRITE call occurs or, if the BIOS is buffering physical sectors, may not be needed at all.

SETDMA

BIOS 11

The address in the BC register pair (CX for CP/M-86) is set as the file buffer address for the READ and WRITE calls that will follow.

Under CP/M the BIOS will usually defer all disk operations until a READ or WRITE call occurs. Only then does it seek the desired track, search for the necessary sector, and perform the I/O. If the BIOS buffers physical sectors, it may not need to do any disk I/O at all.

Under CP/M the BIOS will usually defer all disk activity until a READ or WRITE call occurs. Then it will seek to the track, select the sector, and perform the I/O. If the BIOS buffers physical sectors, no disk activity may be needed.

It is essential to pass the sector buffering parameter under CP/M 2 and later systems. There is no way to tell whether or not the BIOS supports sector buffering. If it does, and if a parameter of 02h is passed by accident, the write may cause the destruction of all the records in the allocation block except for the one being written.

Don't place too much trust in the indication returned by this function. The BIOS need not support it (although most do). If it does not, it should always return 00h.

When the BIOS does support the function, the returned value indicates whether or not a program that calls for list output will be delayed. If the result is nonzero, a call for list output should return very quickly. If 00h is returned, the program may be suspended for some time before the output completes.

Calling LISTST is not a defense against printer overrun. If the printer isn't configured for handshaking, LISTST will only report the condition of the UART transmit buffer. The transmission rate might still be too high for the printer to handle.

READ

BIOS 12

The standard record selected by preceding SELDSK, SETTRK, and SETSEC calls is read and placed in the buffer selected by the last SETDMA call. The calling program is suspended until the record has been read.

If the read is successful 00h is returned in register A; if an error occurs, a nonzero value is returned. The BIOS will retry an error several times. The number of retries, and the technique used, depends on the hardware and on the code of the BIOS.

WRITE

BIOS 13

The standard record in the buffer selected by the last SETDMA call is written to the location selected by the preceding SELDSK, SETTRK, and SETSEC calls.

Register C (CL for CP/M-86) should contain an indication of the type of data being written. This indicator directs the sector buffering algorithm of the BIOS, if one exists:

00h = Normal write: preread if necessary, defer write if convenient.
01h = Directory write: preread if necessary, do not defer writing.
02h = First write to this allocation block: no preread needed, write may be deferred.

LISTST

BIOS 14

The list logical device is polled. If it is ready to accept a character, a nonzero value is returned in register A. If it is not ready for a character, 00h is returned.

Skew translation is not required on all drives. Use the SELDSK (8) function to obtain the Disk Parameter Header. Its first word contains the table address to be passed in DE, or 0000h if translation is not required. Do not call SECTRAN at all in the latter case.

Do not assume that the address in the DPH points to a simple table of permuted record numbers, one for each record on a track. All you can be sure of is that it points to parameters needed by the SECTRAN function. These may not be a table at all but a few numbers input to a greatest common divisor algorithm.

The segment base need only be set when it changes. The SETDMA entry (11) may be called several times to set different buffers within the same segment.

The BDOS keeps track of the base and offset it last set as the file buffer. If you use this call from a command program, the BDOS is put out of step with the BIOS. Use BDOS service 52 to get the present value of the buffer segment base before changing it, then restore it afterward.

The MRT contains a physical description of the system's storage layout. The BDOS keeps more elaborate information on the storage allocations it has made. The MRT can be used to find the actual layout of storage, perhaps to find if a particular address exists before requesting it in an Absolute Storage service request.

BIOS 15

SECTRAN

The record number in the BC register pair is translated using the skew table addressed by the DE register pair (CX and DX, respectively, for CP/M-86). The translated record number is returned in the HL register pair (BX).

BIOS 16

SETDMAB

(CP/M-86 only) The address in the CX register is set as the segment base of the file buffer for subsequent reads and writes.

BIOS 17

GETSEGT

(CP/M-86 only) The BIOS returns the address of the Memory Region Table (MRT) in the BX register:

MRT:	*cnt*	base 1	length 1	base 2	length 2 . . .

Each of the *cnt* entries of the MRT describes an area of contiguous storage in the system. The storage reserved to 8086 interrupt vectors and the storage occupied by the CCP, BDOS, and BIOS are excluded. A system that has but one area of storage would have only a single entry in its MRT.

This function duplicates that of BDOS service request 7. In CP/M-86 the BIOS holds the IOBYTE in private storage, because there is no reliable low-storage location in which to keep it.

This function duplicates that of BDOS service request 8. In CP/M-86 the BIOS holds the IOBYTE in private storage, because there is no reliable low-storage location in which to keep it.

BIOS 18

GETIOB

(CP/M-86 only) The BIOS returns the present setting of the IOBYTE in register AL.

BIOS 19

SETIOB

(CP/M-86 only) The byte in the CL register is set as the current IOBYTE.

Maps

CP/M-80 Storage Map

Storage is divided into three areas. Low storage extends from 00h to FFh; Monitor storage extends downward by approximately 9200 bytes, depending on the size of the BIOS. The area between is the Transient Program Area.

Name	Contents
BIOS	The system's builder (the vendor or hobbyist) supplies this code to drive I/O devices under control of the BDOS. Its standard size is 600h bytes, but many builders must expand it to E00h, especially if disk sector buffering is included.
BDOS	This code operates the file system in response to service requests from the CCP or command programs. Its size is E00h bytes in version 2.
CCP	The Console Command Processor is loaded on a warm start and may be overlaid by a command program. It gets a command from the console or a submit file and processes it. The CCP executes DIR, REN, ERA, TYPE, and SAVE itself, and loads the .COM files that represent other commands. Its size is 800h bytes in version 2.
TPA	The size of the TPA depends on the size of storage and the size of the BIOS: Storage size: 64K 48K 32K Standard TPA: E300h (56K) A300h (40K) 6300h (24K) Typical TPA: DB00h (54K) 9B00h (38K) 5B00h (22K)

Low storage is described on the following map.

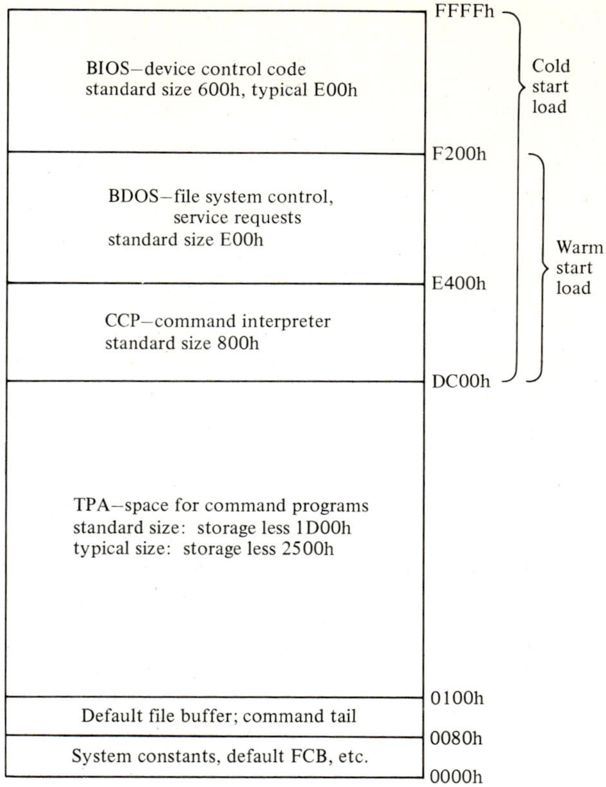

FFFFh
BIOS—device control code
standard size 600h, typical E00h
Cold
start
load
F200h
BDOS—file system control,
service requests
standard size E00h
Warm
start
load
E400h
CCP—command interpreter
standard size 800h
DC00h
TPA—space for command programs
standard size: storage less 1D00h
typical size: storage less 2500h
0100h
Default file buffer; command tail
0080h
System constants, default FCB, etc.
0000h

Low Storage Map

Storage from 00h to FFh is an interface area, used for communication between CCP, BIOS, BDOS, and command programs. Low storage is initialized by the BIOS during a warm or cold start, and maintained by the CCP.

Offset	Contents
00h	JMP operation code; vector to the BIOS for a warm start. Should a RST 0 occur, a warm start will follow.
01h–02h	Address of the warm start entry to the BIOS.
03h	The current IOBYTE, defining serial device assignments.
04h	Default drive and active user code: Bits 7–4 contain the active user code, Bits 3–0 contain the default drive (0 = A, 1 = B, etc.)
05h	JMP operation code; vector used to call the BDOS for a service request.
06–07h	Address of the BDOS service request entry point. Used as the address of the end of storage; subtract 806h to avoid overlaying the CCP.
08h–37h	RST jump vectors, reserved for I/O interrupts.
38h–3Fh	RST 7 jump vector, reserved for use by debugging tools such as DDT and SID.
40h–4Fh	BIOS work area (typically disk operation variables).
50h–5Bh	Reserved by CP/M (*MP/M 2*: the lengths and addresses of the passwords from the first two command operands are set up here.)
5Ch–7Fh	Default File Control Block (FCB); set up by CCP to: 5Ch first operand drivecode or 00h 5Dh–64h first operand filename or spaces 65h–67h first operand filetype or spaces 6Ch second operand drivecode or 00h 6Dh–74h second operand filename or spaces 75h–77h second operand filetype or spaces
80h–FFh	Default file buffer, set up by CCP to: 80h length of command tail 81h–FFh command tail

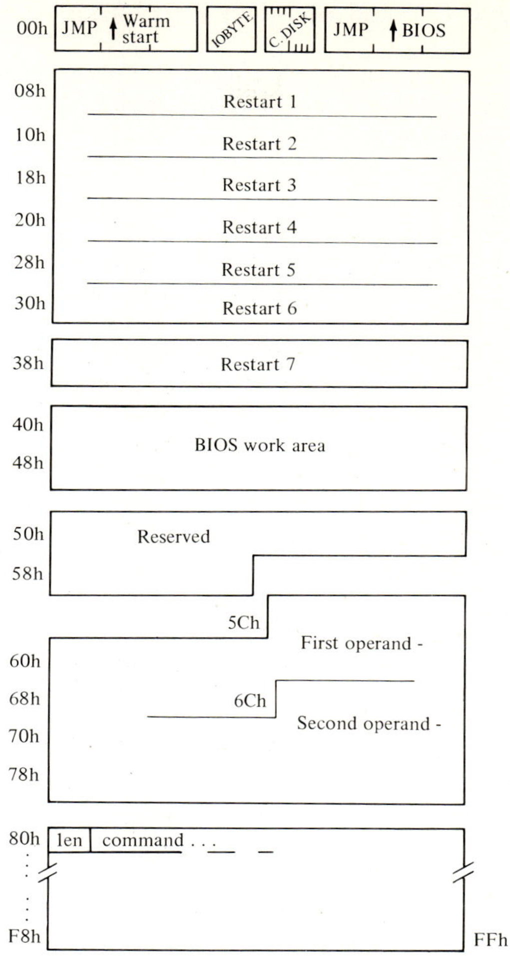

00h
JMP
Warm start
IOBYTE
C. DISK
JMP
BIOS
08h
Restart 1
10h
Restart 2
18h
Restart 3
20h
Restart 4
28h
Restart 5
30h
Restart 6
38h
Restart 7
40h
48h
BIOS work area
50h
58h
Reserved
5Ch
First operand -
60h
68h
6Ch
Second operand -
70h
78h
80h
len
command . . .
F8h
FFh

File Control Block (FCB) and Directory Entry Map

The FCB is built by a program and passed with many service requests. The Directory Entry, which differs only in its first byte, is maintained on disk by the BDOS.

Offset	Name	Contents
00h	dr	FCB: drive number for I/O 00h = use current default drive 01h = drive A, 02h = drive B, etc.
	a/u	Directory: activity/user code 0*x*h = extent entry, file created by user *x* 1*x*h = XFCB for file created by user *x* 20h = directory label entry E5h = inactive entry
01h–08h		Filename in ASCII, left justified and padded with spaces; attributes coded in bit 7 of each byte.
09h–0Bh		Filetype in ASCII, left justified and padded with spaces; attributes coded in bit 7 of each byte.
0Ch	ex	Extent number for extents 0–31 (00h–1Fh).
0Dh	s1	BDOS flags (*MP/M 2*: FCB checksum).
0Eh	s2	Extent number for extents over 31.
0Fh	rc	Count of 128-byte records controlled by this extent.
10h–1Fh		Data map (list of allocation block numbers).
20h	cr	(FCB only) Current record of extent, from 00h up to one less than "rc".
21h–23h		(FCB only) Direct address, from 0 to 65535 (000000h to 00FFFFh). In MP/M 2, from 000000 to 03FFFF.

File Control Block, Directory Entry

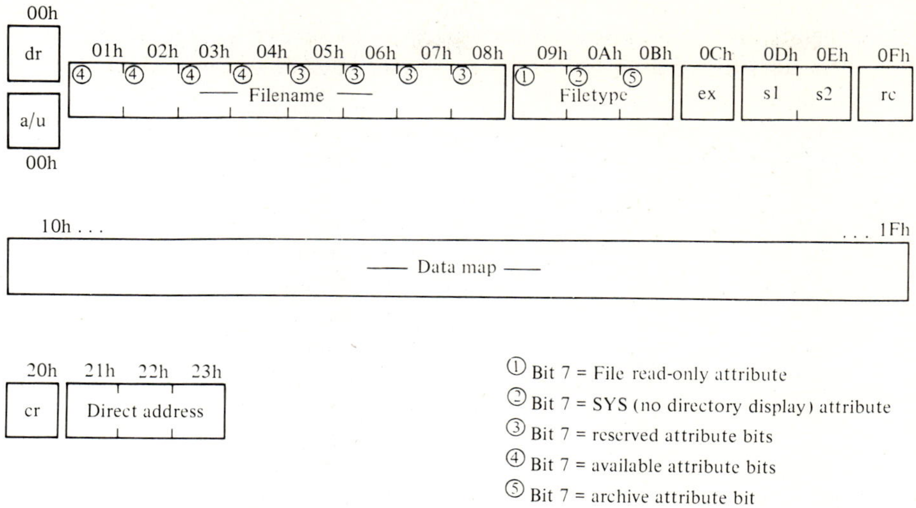

Directory Label Map

The Directory Label exists only on disks written by MP/M 2. It is created and updated by Write Directory Label, service request 100. The label provides identification for a disk, and controls the enforcement of file passwords. There can be only one Directory Label on a disk.

Offset	Contents
00h	20h signals that this is the Directory Label.
01h–08h	Disk name in ASCII, left justified and padded with spaces.
09h–0Bh	Disk type (or any identification) in ASCII, left justified and padded with spaces.
0Ch	Flag which determines password enforcement: Bit 7 = 1: Enforce password checks on files that have XFCBs Bit 6 = 1: Timestamp an XFCB when its file is opened. Bit 5 = 1: Timestamp an XFCB when its file is closed. Bit 4 = 1: Create an XFCB whenever a file is created (Make File, 22).
0Dh–0Fh	Reserved, undefined.
10h–17h	Encrypted password for the Directory Label.
18h–1Bh	Timestamp of label creation. Format is that of system time of day: date: 16-bit integer, days since 1/1/78 hh: hours in BCD mm: minutes in BCD
1Ch-1Fh	Time stamp of the last update of the label. Format as above.

Directory Label

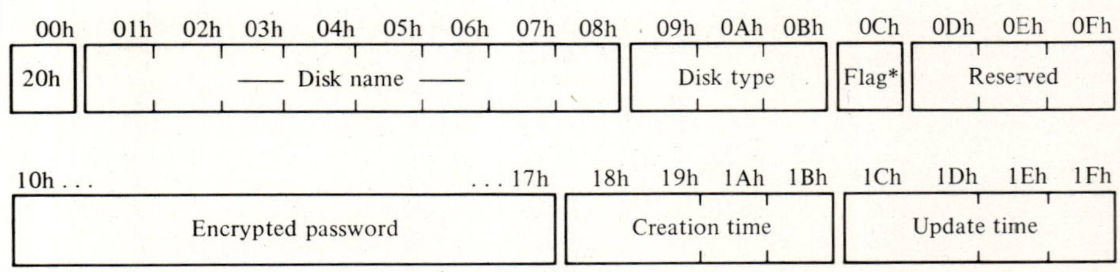

*Flag:

Bit 7 = 1: enforce password checks on files with XFCBs
Bit 6 = 1: perform access (open) time-stamping on XFCBs
Bit 5 = 1: perform update (close) time-stamping on XFCBs
Bit 4 = 1: create an XFCB whenever a file is created

Extended File Control Block (XFCB) Map

The XFCB exists only on disks written by MP/M 2. It may be built automatically by the BDOS when a file is created, or explicitely by a program. The XFCB determines contains the password for its file, and determines when it will be checked.

Offset	Contents
00h	1*x*h, where *x* is the user code under which the file was created.
01h–08h	Filename in ASCII, left justified and padded with spaces.
09h–0Bh	Filetype in ASCII, left justified and padded with spaces.
0Ch	Flag that determines password enforcement: Bit 7C = 1: Check on a read-only open and... Bit 6 = 1: Check on normal open and... Bit 5 = 1: Check on directory change. Each bit implies all the bits after it; only one bit needs to be set.
0Dh–0Fh	Reserved, undefined.
10h–17h	Encrypted password.
18h–1Bh	Time stamp of XFCB creation or the last open of the file. Format is that of system time: date: 16-bit integer, days since 1/1/78 hh: hours in BCD mm: minutes in BCD
1Ch–1Fh	Time stamp of the last close of the file. Format as above.

Extended File Control Block

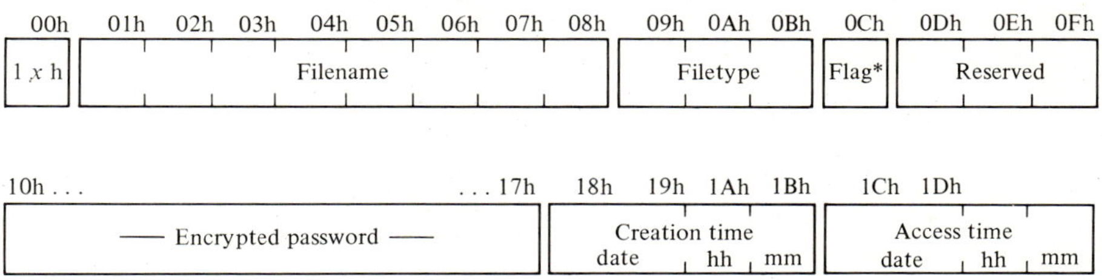

*Flag:

Bit 7 = 1: password check on read-only open, plus . . .
Bit 6 = 1: password check on normal open, plus . . .
Bit 5 = 1: password check on delete, rename, write XFCB
Bits 4 . .0: reserved

Disk Parameter Header (DPH) Map

The address of the DPH is obtained by calling the SELDSK entry of the BIOS, which returns its address in the HL register pair.

Offset	Name	Contents
00h	XLT	Address of parameters used for skew translation. Pass the address when calling the SECTRAN entry to the BIOS, unless it is 0000h meaning that the drive does not use sector skew.
08h	DIRBUF	Address of a 128-byte buffer, located in the BIOS, used for directory I/O by the BDOS. Only one buffer is provided; all DPH blocks address it.
0Ah	DPB	Address of the Disk Parameter Block (DPB) that describes this drive and the disk mounted in it. There will be a single DPB for each disk type in the system.
0Ch	CSV	Address of an area where the BDOS builds a directory check vector when it logs in the disk on this drive. The size of the area is given in the DPB, and may be zero, in which case this field is ignored.
0Eh	ALV	Address of an area where the BDOS builds an allocation vector when it logs in the disk on this drive. The size of the area is determined from the disk capacity, which appears in the DPB.

Disk Parameter Header (DPH)

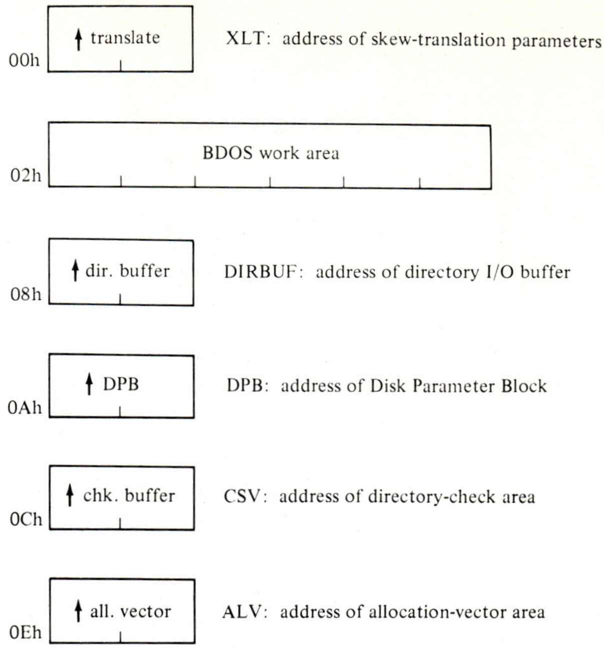

Disk Parameter Block (DPB) Map

The address of the DPB is obtained with BDOS service request 31, Get Disk Parameters. The table is located in the BIOS.

Offset	Name	Contents
00h	SPT	"Sectors" (128-byte records) per track.
02h	BSH	Number of times a record number should be shifted right to yield its allocation block number (or the base-2 log of the number of records in a block). Get the size of an allocation block by doubling 128 BSH times.
03h	BLM	Mask which, if ANDed with a record number, yields its index within an allocation block (or BSH minus 1).
04h	EXM	Number of times a logical extent number should be shifted right to yield a physical extent (directory entry) number (the base-2 log of logical extents per entry).
05h	DSM	Highest allocation block number (count of blocks is one greater). Get disk capacity in records by shifting DSM+1 left BSH times.
07h	DRM	Highest directory entry number (count of entries is one greater). Shift right twice for number of records in the directory; shift BSH times for number of blocks.
09h	ALn	Initial value for the first 2 bytes of the allocation vector, with a leading 1-bit for each directory block.
0Bh	CKS	Number of bytes in the directory check area. Either (DRM+1)/4, 1 byte per directory record, or 0000h to signify no checking of a fixed disk. *MP/M 2*: Most significant bit is set to 1 to show that this drive's disk is fixed, not removable.
0Dh	OFF	Count of reserved tracks, usually 2 or 3 for diskettes, but may be large when a rigid disk is partitioned into logical drives.

Disk Parameter Block (DPB)

Offset	Field	Description
00h	SPT	number of records/track
02h	BSH	block shift factor
03h	BLM	block mask
04h	EXM	extent mask
05h	DSM	drive capacity
07h	DRM	directory size
08h	ALØ, AL1	initial allocation vector
0Bh	CKS	check area size
0Dh	OFF	reserved tracks

CP/NET Configuration Table Map

The address of the configuration table is obtained with NDOS service request 68, Get Configuration Table Address. The table is part of the body of the Slave Network I/O System, loaded below the BDOS by the CPNETLDR command.

Offset	Contents
00h	Network status byte as kept by SNIOS: Bit 4 = 1 if system is logged in to any master, Bit 1 = 1 if a receive error has occurred, Bit 0 = 1 if a send error has occurred.
01h	Slave's (local system's) network identification number.
02h–25h	Device redirection fields: 02h, 04h, ... 20h describe drives A, B, ... P respectively. 22h describes CON:, 24h describes LST:. In each 2-byte field: Byte 0, Bit 7 = 1 if device is accessed via network; Bits 3–0 = number of the remote drive or console; Byte 1 contains the id of the master handling I/O.
26h	List buffer index, names the next free byte in the buffer at offset 2Dh.
27h	Header of a List Output format message: FMT = 00h (all header fields 1 byte) DID = master-id from 25h SID = slave-id from 01h FNC = 05h (List Output) SIZ = length of data less one (from 26h) dev = master console number (from 24h)
2Dh	List buffer, where output bytes are collected.

CP/NET Configuration Table

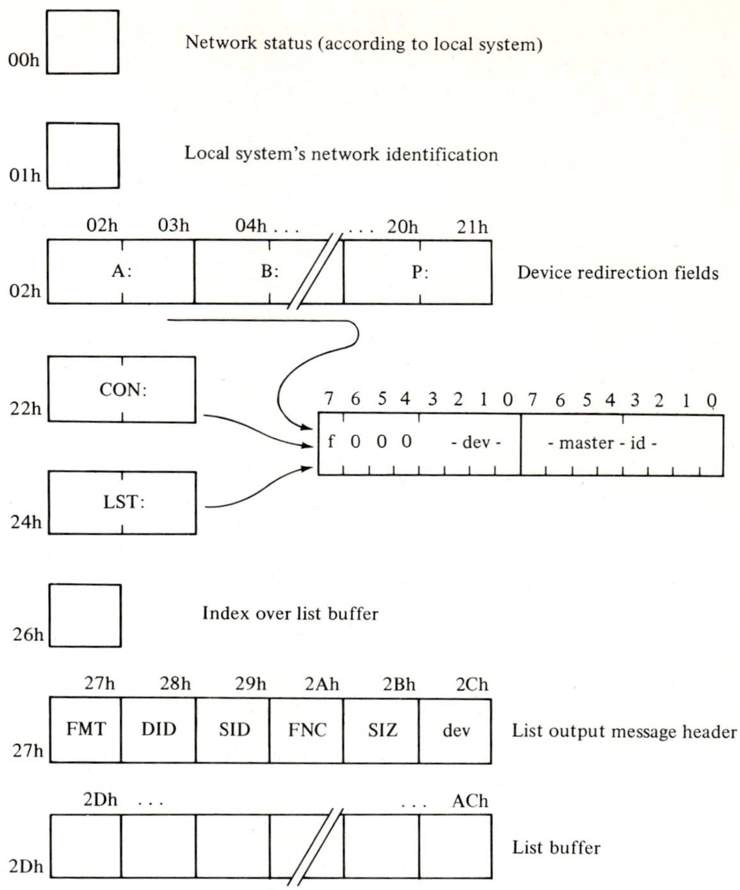